The Messiah of Brooklyn:
Understanding
Lubavitch Hasidism
Past and Present

The Messiah of Brooklyn:
Understanding Lubavitch Hasidism Past and Present

M. Avrum Ehrlich

KTAV Publishing House, Inc.
Jersey City, New Jersey

Library of Congress Cataloging-in-Publication Data

Ehrlich, Avrum M.
  The Messiah of Brooklyn : understanding Lubavitch Hasidism past and present / Avrum
M. Ehrlich.
     p. cm.
  Includes bibliographical references and index.
  ISBN 0-88125-836-9
  1. Habad. 2. Hasidism--History. 3. Schneersohn, Menaòhem Mendel, 1902- 4.
Zaddikim. 5. Messiah--Judaism. I. Title.
BM198.54.E373 2004
296.8'3322--dc22
                            2004014552

Published by
KTAV Publishing House, Inc.
930 Newark Avenue
Jersey City, NJ 07306
Email: orders@ktav.com
www.ktav.com
(201) 963-9524
Fax (201) 963-0102

Contents

Acknowledgments

This work began more than ten years ago at the University of Sydney and only reached maturity years later at Clare Hall, Cambridge University. Thus it is natural that many forces helped to form this book. Some people read parts of the manuscript and offered advice, scrutiny, or balance, others made editorial and grammatical corrections, still others were partners in discussion on all sorts of subjects which, as things do, were filtered into one's own specific interests. To these people, both those mentioned and those unmentioned, to the institutions that facilitated ephemeral endeavor and allowed me free exchange of scholarship, intellectual fraternity, and access to provocative ideas, I am deeply indebted.

I spoke at some length on the subject with Lord Immanuel Jakobovits and Sir Isaiah Berlin (who himself was a member of the extended Schneerson family) among others who have since, sadly, passed away. I hope that their insights on the subject, which I found extremely thought-provoking, are loyally reflected herein. Many thanks go to Rabbi Shaul Shimon Deutsch of the Lioznei Habad community for his suggestions, Dr Allana Cooper, Baruch Thaler, Andrei Ruvel, and Monique Barda for reading earlier incarnations of this work and offering their erudite comments. Credit is also due to Raquel Hasofer, who made important comments about the book, particularly concerning the role of women in the Habad movement. I am grateful to Bernie Scharfstein and company at KTAV for their faith in this work and their expedience in its publishing.

Special thanks are due my editor, Matthew Charet. As a scholar of new religious movements, he lent this study his unique perspective, which may prove to be this work's most relevant context. His hard labour and dedication are much appreciated, and indeed the adage that "behind every philosopher is an editor" takes on extra significance.

Deep thanks go to my family, without whom my scholarly endeavors would not be possible. My parents and my brothers (and sisters) have, in an almost Levitical exchange, offered abundant material support for me over the years. Perhaps it is their recognition that nothing short of ideas sustains the world, and without the ephemeral, a family or indeed a civilisation may, God forbid, become fallow. Perhaps it is their own desire to ensure that in this age of conformism, at least a few might be permitted to thrash about in un-navigated territory and ponder those things most dare not consider, and that it is in this sanctuary that life becomes most interesting. It is to them that this book is dedicated.

MAE

Preface

This work was started during the final year of the late Habad Rebbe's life, while I was completing my doctoral dissertation on issues of leadership and succession in the historical Habad movement. My initial aim was to understand the strategies Rabbi Menachem Mendel Schneerson had employed in building a powerful international religious movement within the framework of Orthodox Judaism. On Schneerson's death in 1994, the question of succession was a subject that I could not ignore, although it fell somewhat outside the scope of my doctoral research. At that time, and despite having no empirical evidence to identify a future course for the movement, I began to explore a number of theoretical models for succession in contemporary Habad, using models found both throughout the history of the movement and in other social, political, and religious contexts. It is these models and the successional issues that surround them that form the basis of the present work.

On the advice of Professor Menachem Friedman, a sociologist of ultra-Orthodoxy and a mentor, I decided to postpone my examination of succession for a time, not only to gain perspective after completing my doctoral research of many years, but to let the issue of succession begin to settle into observable patterns. This was good advice, as it provided me with an opportunity to check the hypothetical models I had been developing against the reality of a movement in severe existential dilemma caused in large part, I believe, by its messianic ideology.

Ten years have passed since Rabbi Schneerson's death, and there is still no sign of a clear succession to his leadership of Habad. Many interesting phenomenon are occurring within the movement, however, which are outgrowths of the movement's ideology and structure, and lend support to some of the successional models I have formulated. The delay in completing this study has, if anything, simply reinforced my opinion of Habad as a movement with complex successional problems, such that even a decade after the issue became vital to the continuation of Habad, there still remains no clear succession.

The delay has also given me the opportunity to contextualize the movement both in time and in comparison with other religious movements that I have since observed. Although the present work provides a comprehensive examination of the modern Habad movement, its Rebbe-cum–aspiring mashiach (messiah), and the nature of messianism and succession after intense messianic expectation, it is equally a study of general religious behavior and leadership. Many of the successional issues raised here have been found in many other religious movements, both historical and current, most obviously including early Christianity, Shi'a Islam, and the Sabbatean movement within Judaism.

Quite apart from the issue of succession, the growth and development of the Habad movement throughout the latter half of the twentieth century invites comparison with the emergence and dissemination of other new religious movements. Habad shares not only sociological but ideological and methodological concerns with such religious movements as the Church of Scientology, the Unification Church, and the International Society for Krishna Consciousness. Habad, like Scientology, relied on the establishment of missions throughout the world to spread the teachings of its leader, and features a voluminous canon of religious writings and commentaries. Messianic expectation within Habad invites comparison with the messianic theology of Reverend Moon's Unification Church, which relies on a similar ideological tension to heighten the feeling of the imminence of the redemption, and the sense of living in the final days before the revelation of the mashiach. The emergence of a new religious trend within a long-standing, traditional, and conservative religion invites comparison with the Hare Krishna movement. The adoption of a distinctive mode of dress, diet, and culture at variance with the mainstream is another factor that explains the attraction of many to both of these movements. The successional issue within Hare Krishna also raises parallels with the post-Schneerson Habad movement, which I will leave to others to explore.

The comparison of a respected Hasidic dynasty with so-called cults is not intended to be insulting or confrontational to traditional Judaism or to Habad's many followers, but rather suggests the possibility of identifying patterns by which religious ideas are disseminated in the context of the modern world. The intention of the present work is to identify the governing dynamics of leadership and discipleship, the nature of religious movements, and the way that ideas are employed in the management of society. I believe that this can best be done by limiting the study to the evolution of a single movement, and so have limited my attentions to Habad in the middle to late twentieth century. This has not been done with the purpose of limiting the scope of the study, and it is to be hoped that by presenting the emergence of ideology and action in one movement, the mechanisms whereby similar trends emerge in other groups will be made more explicit. The lessons to be drawn from the Habad movement may therefore be universally applied to movements with similar ideological paradigms.

In this connection, brief mention must also be made of the emerging similarities between Habad and Christianity. While outside the scope of this work, the messianic strivings surrounding Schneerson are fascinating, no less because they provide us with a live model by which classic Jewish messianic movements have emerged. They also demonstrate how Jewish theology and culture provide a fertile ground for the emergence of resurrectionist doctrine and messianism, as is to be found in originally Jewish splinter movements such as Christianity and Sabbateanism. While it is clear that every situation is different, some of the same agents are at work within contemporary Habad as were evident in the appearance of Christianity in the first century and Sabbateanism in the sixteenth century, and with other messianic movements throughout Jewish history.

Habad messianism may therefore be viewed by students of sociology, religion, and mysticism as a perfect opportunity to understand the past from observing the present. The emerging situation within Habad should prove intriguing to followers of other messianic religions such as Christianity, if only for the similarities between the doctrines that have developed since Schneerson's death and the emergence of Christology. These points of similarity become particularly acute in connection with a small group of Habad mystics, located mainly in Safed, who argue in a polemical way that Schneerson was a divine incarnation, and may be worshipped and bowed to.[1] The ecumenical possibilities between Judaism and Christianity provided by the current situation might also prove interesting to relations between these two traditions.

The source material produced by this Habad fringe in support of its ideology has been carefully selected from the Bible, Talmud, Midrash, Kabbalah, and works of Jewish thinkers. Because these sources are accepted by traditional Jewish scholarship, this group may challenge the Jewish theological and hermeneutical opposition to Christian doctrine.[2] In trying to prove Schneerson's messianic status despite the event of his passing, they argue that the mashiach must suffer as part of his role, may die before the complete revelation of his messianic status, and can resurrect from the dead to complete his mission. That the zaddik, or righteous person, is perfect, flawless, and at one with the Divine is already a commonly accepted truth in Hasidism, but these new messianists within Habad take the idea to an extreme position, all supported by a careful reading of classic rabbinic sources. A popular Habad work, *Al ha-Zaddikim*, brings together much of the source material in relation to the new messianism, sources that permit kneeling before a zaddik, praying to him, and making requests and supplications of him. According to these sources, bowing to a man devoid of ego and annulled to the will of God (as the zaddik is believed to be) is no different from bowing before God himself.

These ideas have become an almost indistinguishable part of the Habad messianists' latter-day theology. With the increasing influence of messianists in the movement, however, this material is often studied in mainstream Habad yeshivot, and through them may infiltrate into mainstream Jewish thinking via the community presence of Habad emissaries in congregations throughout the world. One of the most pernicious aspects of this ideology is that it is supported by a reading of classically recognized rabbinic sources, and thus a comparison of the ideology with Christianity simply does not occur to the average yeshiva student, Habad rabbi, or emissary. Habad messianists see no likeness between themselves and "that heresy," Christianity, despite the obvious connections that can be drawn by an outside observer, and thus they preach the ideology as though it were an accepted part of Jewish theology.

Two major reactions to Habad's new messianism seem to have developed over the last decade from outside the community. One, opposed to the messianist ideology, has been spearheaded by an Orthodox rabbi and academic, Dr. David Berger, who is at the forefront of calls for the Jewish community to take drastic action against what he sees as an extreme form of heresy that goes against millennia of Jewish theology and tradition. Berger advocates, among other things, the excommunication of Habad adherents who advocate any form of messianist ideology, and the removal of community leaders who espouse it from their pulpits. He even calls into question the kashrut status of food prepared under Habad supervision, effectively removing Habad from the Jewish world.

Another reaction, this time in support of the messianist ideology in Habad, comes from movements such as Jews for Jesus and their offshoots, generally known as "messianic Jews." They have argued for some time that belief in the resurrection of the messiah is acceptable in Jewish tradition, as illustrated and documented by one of the strongest and most prominent Jewish groups, Habad, which have been helpful in gathering all of the talmudic sources in support of messianist and resurrectionist ideology.

The members of Jews for Jesus argue that belief in Jesus as the long-awaited Jewish messiah is not in conflict with Jewish thought, nor is his death and resurrection, long cited by Jews as a disqualification for acceptance of Christian teachings and theology.[3] Their active evangelizing of other Jews on this premise has been bolstered by the emergence of a messianist ideology in Habad, and they argue that if Habad can missionize to Jews about a Jewish messiah named Schneerson, they can evangelize about a Jewish messiah named Jesus. As far as their ideology is concerned, the theology is the same; only the identification of the messianic figure is different.

Another important factor in the dissemination of messianist ideology in the general Jewish world is the conjunction of terminology. As the community of Hebrew-speaking Christians in Israel grows and fuses, the cultural differences with Hebrew-speaking Jewish groups may contract. Large numbers of Russian and Ethiopian Orthodox Christians immigrating to Israel are beginning to pray in Hebrew; long-term representatives of Christian denominations in the Holy Land use Hebrew in debate and to define religious concepts in discussion with Israelis; local Arab Christians speak Hebrew on the street; and messianic Jews who move to Israel, primarily from the United States, together with Israeli converts to Christianity use Hebrew as an evangelical device to illustrate Christianity's origins in Judaism. The growing use of Hebrew terms in Christian worship and theology, especially in Israel, has led to an interesting phenomenon; whereby Christian messianic language is almost identical to Habad's use of the same terms. As language and culture unite in Israel, it will be interesting to observe how these two diametrically opposing groups come to view one another, and perhaps identify elements of commonality.[4] Only time will allow us to explore this further, but it promises to be an interesting area for future analysis.

I feel it necessary to assure any concerned reader that the comparison of Habad with Christianity and new religious movements is not intended to taint Habad as a "cult," but to show the effects of practical and ideological structures shared by other groups. Simply because one can identify a process, give it a name, and be able to explain it, such examination or categorization does not necessarily detract from its holiness and religious significance. Elements of the Habad movement can indeed be understood by the social scientist. Its adherents share many traits in common with other modern religious groups, both mainstream and marginal, but it is acknowledged not only here but throughout this work that Habad has nonetheless served a very important and positive function in Jewish culture, and indeed in world society.

---

[1] See David Berger's most recent work, *The Rebbe, the Messiah, and the Scandal of Orthodox Indifference.* The groups refers to Schneerson as "our master, our teacher, and OUR CREATOR."

[2] See Raquel Hasofer, "Messiah from the Living—Messiah from the Dead."

[3] See Juliene G. Lipson, *Jews for Jesus*, esp. pp. 61–80.

[4] See Avrum Ehrlich, "Arab Christian Views on Judaism and the State of Israel."

Introduction

The Habad movement is one of the most influential subcultures of Orthodox Judaism. Since at least the 1980s, and arguably since 1950, many of its followers have maintained that their last leader, Rabbi Menachem Mendel Schneerson, known as "The Rebbe", would reveal himself as the mashiach (messiah) and bring on the messianic redemption. Habad programs, social goals, and outreach efforts were focused, designed, and undertaken primarily in order to bring about this messianic goal, which had become the central focus of the movement, and its prime motivational ideology. While he was alive, Schneerson seemed to encourage the messianic fervor that grew around him, but his death, on June 12, 1994,[1] created a dilemma for the movement and raised many questions, ranging from the ideological basis underlying the movement to issues surrounding the leadership succession. Nearly a decade after the death of the Rebbe, the Habad movement is still divided in its understanding of the significance of his death. The divisions pertain less to the question of how to replace the deceased leader than to issues of control and ideology. A variety of solutions to the long-term continuation of Habad seem to be emerging, as we shall see.

The present work seeks to locate the successional and leadership problems confronting the movement in the leadership of the last Rebbe. It describes how Rabbi Menachem Mendel Schneerson (1902–1994), the seventh Rebbe of the Habad-Lubavitch movement, consolidated his authority over the movement during his forty-five years in office. It also distinguishes between the act of assuming power and the very different skills required to maintain and expand influence. This work examines the basis for Schneerson's assumption of leadership and the techniques he developed to consolidate his control over the movement, expanding it from a collection of dispirited refugees after the Second World War to arguably the most influential group in the modern Jewish world.

After an examination of the history and development of Hasidism generally and of Habad in particular, this work turns to a detailed study of Schneerson's career and leadership tactics. We will focus primarily on the mechanisms by which he consolidated his authority over the movement, from the time of his assumption of office until the time he died. His administrative techniques, his encouragement of independence among his emissaries across the globe, and the ideology behind Habad outreach will all be discussed for their contribution to the dilemma of succession.

The examination of the present state of the Habad movement will naturally involve an examination of its internal politics, social groupings, and ideological factions, and one purpose of this work is to locate these elements in their historical and developmental contexts. The analysis of how natural these groupings are, and how much they were the result of a conscious process on the part of Schneerson and his consolidation of leadership, is one of the primary tasks of this book. One basic assumption is that many of the crises of the contemporary movement are the result of either Schneerson's leadership technique (decentralization of authority, financial independence of communities) or his ideological ambiguity (especially concerning the concept of the messianic redemption). The effect these elements had on the movement as it evolved will also form part of the examination. The emergence of curious sociological patterns, religious crises, and the evolution of a local dynasty into a universal religion are elements of this, and provide a subject of fascination not only for students of Judaism, but also for scholars in the fields of politics, sociology, and religion.

The examination of the Habad movement is important for several reasons. As the influence of Habad on contemporary Judaism has been significant, the importance of recording a history and an analysis of its development, especially in the latter half of the twentieth century, cannot be understated. The challenges presented by the movement to conventional understandings of Judaism, Orthodoxy, outreach, conversion, and many other aspects of contemporary religious life in the United States and around the world make it an important part of the modern religious scene. The development of opposition to the movement, especially as a consequence of its growing and increasingly vocal messianist faction, has led to what might become one of the most significant challenges to Judaism since the messianic stirrings surrounding Sabbetai Zevi. Part biography, part social history, and part theological examination, the present work could perhaps be seen as an almost Josephian attempt to record the fascinating beginnings of what might prove to be a new sectarian breakaway from Judaism, on par with the origins of Christianity.

Difficulties with the Proposed Study

Much of this work, and most particularly those sections that deal with models of succession and the possibilities for the continuation of the movement since the death of Schneerson, is the result of speculation and supposition on my part, and as such some details are not given to empirical validation. The speculative elements of this work nevertheless serve an important function in attempting to set the dilemma of succession against other models found in the history of Habad, against the ideological and organizational development of the movement, and in context with other cults of personality. Although the conclusions reached are hypothetical, they attempt to provide an informed evaluation of the difficulties faced by the post-Schneerson Habad movement, and seek to at least open some possibilities for their resolution.

A number of significant and varied difficulties were confronted during the course of this study. The problems include, but are not limited to, expositional difficulties that affect the way readers interpret the movement; accessing material and information; and the general difficulty of predictive attempts, especially of a movement that is still fluid and developing, changing even as the study is being carried out. An explanation of the effects of each of these difficulties, and how I have attempted to overcome them, is in order to enable the reader to gain an appreciation of the fundamental limitations of this work.

Expositional Difficulties

The Habad movement today comprises a cross-section of people from different countries, cultural influences, and individual theological dispositions. From this melting-pot of influences, there appear to have emerged some distinct groupings within the movement, each with elements of commonality and with a different effect on the question of succession. Schneerson's ability to amalgamate these elements of the movement under a single ideology was one of his marks of genius, and demonstrates perhaps more than anything else the skill with which he led the movement. In his absence, however, these groupings, along ethnic, educational, economic, and ideological grounds, appear to be reasserting themselves. The most significant division is the ideological one between the messianists (those who assert that Schneerson is the long-awaited mashiach) and the non-messianist factions, although other divisions are emerging, especially along cultural lines. Habad in Israel, for example, appears to be developing along different lines from the movement as found in the rest of the world. How these factions may affect the question of succession will be examined throughout this work.

Because there is much confusion within Habad as to how the movement should interpret the absence of its leader, it is still too early to define or predict the ideological and behavioral direction in which these various factions will develop, given enough time and independence. In its later chapters, this work presents some possible scenarios of future organization and leadership within the Habad movement. This is not intended to hamper the internal dynamics of the movement and its search for self-definition, but represents an attempt to provide a conceptual framework in which the succession might best be viewed. The suggestions offered are by no means definitive, or mutually exclusive, but serve to offer a number of solutions for the resolution of the continuation of the Habad movement. The hope is that this work will be treated as a seminal contribution, and not a definitive statement, as to the direction the Habad movement might take in future.

The extrapolation of possibilities for the future of the movement, through the use of various leadership models and a description of possible scenarios, might appear to indicate that there is a way to divine the outcome of the present crisis in the Habad movement. This, however, is not necessarily the view of the author. While unlikely, it is certainly possible that the contemporary movement and its goals have neither precedent nor peer in the history of Habad. It is also possible that the study of past models of Habad leadership, as appears in my previous work and in the introductory sections of this one, will offer no insight into the future direction of the movement. The author does not claim to provide the only, or even the best, method by which to understand the movement. It might confidently be asserted, however, that the current work elucidates the basic ideological, historical, and social principles at work within the movement, and that by examining them, some indication of the future direction of Habad might be divined.

There is a fundamental difficulty inherent in the nature of this study: the difficulty of validating, in an academic sense, the ideological basis for many of the assertions presented by the movement and its leadership. For example, the assertion by most Habad adherents, including Schneerson himself, that the Habad movement is spear-heading the messianic redemption—a unique historical event leading to an unprece-dented cosmological change in the very nature of the universe—cannot be disproved as a hypothetical possibility. The assertion must be taken at face value, and examined for its effects, rather than as a statement of actuality. While it is impossible to argue with the assertion as an expression of reality that by its very nature cannot be quali-fied by academic deliberation, its effects can nevertheless be measured. The ideolog-ical effect of the idea on the followers of the movement, its practical realization as a tool for driving outreach, the theological implications of living at the dawn of the messianic era, and the social unification it provided for the movement to rally behind Schneerson, the messianic candidate, can all be examined for their influence on the development of Habad. This technique is frequently employed in the current work.

The expositional structure of this work, while in many ways somewhat limiting, is a standard and useful way of describing social movements. Despite its acknowledged limitations, it is the most descriptive and informative way of contributing to the aca-demic comprehension of the Habad movement and the dynamics of leadership and succession in post-Schneerson Habad. The work therefore employs elements of nar-rative and biography, as well as social and historical commentary, to elucidate the themes found in the development of the movement.

Accessing Material and Information

One of the fundamental difficulties involved with any academic study of Habad lies in the movement's censorship of information. Some editing and intentional deletion of unpleasant information, especially in published sources, has been carried out deliberately, and it is to be hoped that the reconstruction or rediscovery of original sources may undo some of this censorship.[2] However, it appears that much of the cen-sorship within Habad is unconscious. There are, for example, natural processes with-in charismatic social movements that allow for the idealization of the leader. Any information that might appear to contradict the received image of the leader is automatically dismissed as either erroneous or misguided, and is certainly not to be given credence. When dealing with a political leader, as Schneerson undoubtedly was, this self-censorship becomes more important, especially in the presentation of the leader as a figurehead. This becomes especially evident when public image is important to the movement, for fundraising purposes, for example, or those with political stakes. Both of these influences are certainly to be found in the presentation of the public persona of the last Rebbe of Habad, as we shall see.

Another source of censorship, albeit possibly not a conscious one, is carried out in the process of transcribing and editing Schneerson's orally transmitted talks. His long and frequently interrupted talks (some of which continued for hours, interspersed with singing) were edited into a more readable format, and were often not loyal to the original talk. While the sense might often remain the same, the necessary editing process often meant that subtleties of nuance were lost, and there was room for the interpretation of the editor to influence the presentation of the text. This type of censorship is understandably difficult to detect, much less correct, and so must be a factor in determining the reliability of sources.

An additional obstacle to be overcome in accessing information about Habad comes from the fact that many of the movement's publications confuse quality of scholarship with quantity. Works produced by enthusiastic Hasidim often pay little attention to editing or organization of sources presented, and this makes the task of finding useful information difficult in the extreme. Even collections of newspaper articles selected and published by the movement share this trait: many articles are unsourced, the referencing is frequently unclear, and origins are difficult to determine, even as the texts themselves demonstrate the intended point. Some of the translations from non-English sources also leave something to be desired, and confuse those without access to the original texts, which are often obscure and difficult to locate.

The plethora of ideologies and factions within the movement has to be kept constantly in mind, too, when determining the validity of sources. Selective editing to support certain ideologies is commonplace in the movement, so the background of each text must be examined before use to determine what possible biases are contained therein. An additional problem with sources and ideology is that most published studies of the Habad movement and its ideology, with only a few exceptions, have been carried out by Habad Hasidim themselves or by the movement's sympathizers, which often makes for biased scholarship. One reason for this is the linguistic barrier confronting many scholars in accessing the Hebrew, Yiddish, and Russian source material, the challenges presented by which few outside the movement have thus far been able to overcome. Understanding of the technical religious and kabbalistic terminology employed in the movement has also proven to be an obstacle for sociologists, historians, and other scholars who do not possess the necessary theological tools to provide more than a superficial examination of the movement from the perspective of their own discipline. From what has been seen in the academy thus far, those who have the necessary theological background to examine the movement are more likely to be members of Habad or else sympathetic to it, and so do not provide the critical analysis necessary to a proper understanding of the movement.

One of the most difficult obstacles in any study of Habad is the wariness of members about parting with information deemed esoteric and reserved only for those within the movement. Information about Habad practices and beliefs, especially since the death of Schneerson, is increasingly being kept from others, primarily, it seems, as a result of the marginalization of the messianist elements of the movement. The insider-outsider attitude has taken on ideological proportions within the movement, and Schneerson's own teachings have been used to warn Hasidim of the need to restrict certain information from public consumption. The difficulty in accessing information about the theological differences in the post-Schneerson Habad movement is therefore not just an obstacle to our study, but is perhaps indicative of deeper currents within the movement than appear to exist when glimpsed from the surface. One cannot help but wonder what is being kept secret, and more importantly, why. The motivation seems to be a desire to avoid conflict and opposition within the movement, although some marginal elements are becoming increasingly vocal, as we shall see.

A Complex Issue

The study of the Habad movement requires a familiarity with a range of disciplines and subdisciplines. Talmudics, philosophy, theology, mysticism, history, sociology, politics, and a range of contemporary issues must, of necessity, form components of this study, due not only to the complexity of the subject, but also to the nature of the movement. Habad combines theology with activism, ideology with administration, history with mythologization, and deep textual scholarship with a vibrant oral culture.

Moreover, the multifunctional capacity of the Habad Rebbe makes the skills necessary to approach a study of his life and impact broad and difficult to define. Schneerson, like the Rebbes before him, acted as leader, manager, administrator, scholar, halakhic authority, ideological and spiritual guide, and final authority on every issue and every aspect of the Hasidic lifestyle. His followers regarded him as virtually infallible, his every pronouncement an act of prophecy and divine decree, not to be questioned. Because of this, his theological and ideological background needs to be understood from a variety of perspectives. Schneerson was regarded as an authority on everything, from psychological and spiritual affairs to business and finance, from politics to social activism, advertising and publishing. As such, the task of analyzing his leadership tactics and the process whereby he consolidated his authority over Habad must examine his impact from a variety of positions in order fully to encompass every aspect of his personality and technique. Many followers of

Habad would argue that the nature of a Rebbe is not given to human understanding, so any analysis of him based on the assumption of his humanity is bound to fall far short of the complexity of his office. It is, to these believers, a matter of defining the way the divine spirit settles into the perfect human leader, to make him the mashiach of the generation, come to lead his followers, and indeed all Jews, out of exile and into the messianic era. Despite this, it is nevertheless possible to examine Schneerson's personality, not least for the effect he had on people, and thereby to determine the most evident features of his leadership technique and the causes of his rise to prominence. This will be one of the primary tasks of the study.

Additionally, this work seeks to study the development of one of the most significant social movements in the contemporary Jewish world, if not in the religious world generally. As social movements grow slowly and often pick up their characteristics over a long time, assessing them as we might assess an individual is inappropriate. The Habad movement has developed a fixed identity over the centuries since its origins, and both its ideology and its social mechanisms have changed and developed significantly beyond those found in the movement's origins. While certain trends of practical or ideological continuity can be identified in its history, one cannot deny that the movement as inherited by Schneerson was very different from, and faced with different challenges than, the movement led by Shneur Zalman, the founder of the Habad school. Further, the movement as it currently stands has been greatly affected by the forty-five years of Schneerson's leadership, which will have an effect on the question of succession now that he is dead.

One other difficulty that Habad poses for the scholar attempting to examine it is the fact that the movement is still very much alive, and is perhaps more active since the death of Schneerson than it ever was while he was alive. If this were a study of an historical movement that had already become stagnant or even disappeared, such as the messianic phenomena surrounding Sabbetai Zevi, it might be possible to more emphatically present a complete picture of the mechanisms by which the movement evolved, and to discuss the causes of its failure. The Habad movement is quite probably still in its youth, for it has shown no sign yet of disintegrating as a movement, and thus it would be inappropriate to speak of the movement as if it were no longer living and growing. More time will certainly be needed to understand the full implications of the death of Schneerson for the future of the movement, but it is possible to at least suggest some possible futures. These are based on the social mechanisms found in the history of Habad, and in the ideology and administration of Schneerson. The predictive elements of this work are preliminary only, and suggestive of possibilities; they are not a definitive statement of what will happen in the movement over the coming decades. In many ways the most significant occurrences in Habad's history to date are occurring as we write, and it will be interesting to see how the movement develops from this point.

The difficulty of predicting the course of a still-developing social movement, especially one as dynamic as Habad, is complicated by the endless list of variables and alternative courses available to it. The abundance of information that would have to be integrated into such a project so as to lend it true predictive ability is still beyond the realm of social scientific research. The present work seeks out and identifies obvious patterns of behavior and authority in the history of the movement and uses them to explore the implications of possible scenarios for the future course of Habad. It is also necessary, of course, to discover the leadership philosophy of Schneerson and incorporate the effect this has had on the ideology and organization of Habad.

Any predictive attempt made here is further complicated by the assertion in Habad that there is no precedent for the leadership of Schneerson in the development of the movement, or for that matter in the entire course of Jewish history. The idealization of Schneerson has evoked an ideological resistance to any form of conventional succession. His idealized status and the sense of finality inherent especially in the last days of his leadership (he was the mashiach, and therefore did not need a successor) has lessened the utility of history for the movement. As Habad history does not readily provide ideological fuel for the messianic hopes of the present-day movement, it is becoming less relevant to the propagators of messianist ideology in the post-Schneerson era. They can more readily draw justification for their beliefs from other sources in the vast archives of Jewish history and thought, including Midrash and Kabbalah. The continual breaking of patterns and expectations by Habad initiates and major proponents of the messianic drive makes any predictive attempt more like an exercise in educated guessing.

Messianism and Succession

What emerges from this study is the fact that Schneerson, through the forty-five years of his leadership, succeeded in building a powerful and influential (and in many ways surprisingly modern) Jewish movement, with hundreds of thousands of sympathizers worldwide and an outreach-missionary apparatus reaching most Jewish communities across the globe. One of the foremost elements in his success was the strong belief system he imparted to his followers. This was not only a spiritual comfort to the Habad community but a unifying influence on the disparate elements of which it was composed, and a strong motivational impetus for community activism and cohesion. Messianic fervor became the most important ideological factor in the movements dedication to outreach, and conversely success in attaining the outreach goals set by Schneerson further strengthened his messianic prestige.

The messianic fervor in Habad grew with the movement's success, along with the dignified appearance and aura of authority that Schneerson developed as he grew older. One of the factors examined in this work is the influence that the personality of Schneerson had on the success of the Habad movement, especially with the development of a strong cult of personality around the aging leader. How the messianism he encouraged affected the movement while he was alive, and how it has transformed the question of succession after his death, will also be of central importance. While messianic ideas were present in the movement from its origins, Schneerson appears to have more fervently endorsed messianic enthusiasm as he grew into the role of Rebbe. By the late 1980s, messianic ideology had become a central component of mainstream Habad dogma, and it reached new heights of enthusiasm after Schneerson suffered a paralyzing stroke in 1992. From this time, a vocal and enthusiastic faction began to rise to prominence, and in some respects to dominate the movement, and the beginnings of the current ideological division appeared.

While there are some Habad leaders who resisted or tried to moderate the more extreme expressions of this messianic fervor (there was even an official coronation ceremony to declare Schneerson the mashiach, arranged in 1992 by a group portrayed as "fringe" by the official Habad spokesperson) few could deny the power or attraction of the messianist ideology. What is interesting is the fact that this fringe element eventually succeeded in capturing the hearts of the Hasidim, and has become the most vocal part of the community, while the more moderate elements in the movement are barely tolerated. But the struggle between the camps means that the balance of power can change and change again. The messianic idealization of Schneerson was facilitated by his incapacity from 1992 onwards, for he was unable to oppose the process because of his inability to communicate due to a stroke. Despite physical signs of severe deterioration, his followers still believed him to be completely lucid and aware of his environment, and communication with him was still attempted by his aides, who began to gain more power and influence than they had previously exercised.

Schneerson's death some two years after his initial stroke ended the mode of "rule through aides," and the reality of the Rebbe's death became more apparent as the burial proceedings were carried out. For many Hasidim, the death of the supposed mashiach should have signaled the end of any idea that Schneerson was the mashiach. Instead, it caused a split in the movement, or at least exacerbated an existing division, and provoked debate as to how to interpret the physical "disappearance" of Schneerson.

There were several different initial reactions to Schneerson's death. Some Habad Hasidim accepted that Schneerson had died, and were confused and upset by the realization that their messianic expectations had failed. Because they accepted the fact of his death, they mourned according to the prescribed rituals and laws set down in Jewish law, but were concerned about the future of the movement now that it was without a leader. Various explanations emerged from this camp for the failure of the messianic expectation, but most significantly, these Hasidim recognized that Schneerson, because of his death, could no longer be regarded as the mashiach. They deliberated the question of whether he had failed in his mission, and was therefore not able to assume the messianic mantle, or their own unworthiness had caused the failure of the revelation.

Others refused to believe that Schneerson had died. They claimed that his death and burial were illusions and therefore not to be believed, citing religious sources to defend their ideas. Many of these messianists did not attend the Rebbe's funeral or observe any of the customary rituals that mark a death in Judaism; many are still convinced that Schneerson has simply gone into "hiding" and will emerge as the mashiach at some future point.

Linked with this faction are those Hasidim who interpreted Schneerson's death as the final, or at least an important, stage of the redemption. Members of this faction, albeit initially not a large group, sang, drank, and danced at Schneerson's funeral procession, expecting that the Rebbe would rise soon from the dead to assume his messianic status. At first they predicted that this would occur immediately, but when Schneerson remained dead, they modified their position, stating that he would reappear in a few hours, then after one day, after seven days, one month, and one year. Nearly a decade after the event, some allow for one generation of twenty-five years to pass, and others declare that a period of forty years will have to pass before they disavow their belief in Schneerson's resurrection. These initial reactions have changed somewhat from their original expression at Schneerson's death, but may signal the emergence of a sub-branch of Judaism with elements akin to Christianity. These Hasidim have caused the most ideological difficulty within the movement since the death of Schneerson, not only because of the theological tensions inherent in the idea of a resurrected mashiach (traditionally rejected by Judaism) but also because of their refusal to consider the question of succession. Schneerson is still in command of Habad, and will soon return in physical form, so what need has the movement for a successor?

Since any discussion of Schneerson's impending death was effectively taboo in Habad circles before the event, there was surprisingly little serious deliberation, political posturing, or preparation, and certainly no contingency plans, for action to be taken in case of the passing of the Rebbe. The one leader who dared to raise the issue of funeral plans before the death of Schneerson was silenced, and thus no action was taken to prepare the movement for a transfer of power. One result of this is the factionalism that has threatened to split the movement as each group attempts to divine the will of the deceased Schneerson and implement what it considers to have been his desires for the future leadership of the movement. The factions are slowly beginning to articulate their intentions (or rather, what they interpret as Schneerson's intentions) for the future of the movement, and it will be one of the purposes of this work to explore the basis for these competing ideologies. We will see which, if any, are emerging as possible guidelines for the organization of the Habad movement in the twenty-first century.

---

[1] In the Hebrew calendar, 3 Tammuz 5754.

[2] See, as an example, the scholarly efforts of Shaul S. Deutsch in *Larger Than Life*. The two volumes of this work, rejected by Habad as unreliable, reconstruct the life of Yosef Yitzhak Schneerson, the former Rebbe of Habad, and, especially, the early career of Menachem Mendel Schneerson.

Part One
History

Chapter 1
Historical Context

To contextualize the manner in which Menachem Schneerson consolidated his power over the Habad movement during his reign as Rebbe, and to understand the nature of the crisis of leadership in the Habad movement since the death of this powerful figure, it is necessary to examine the origins of Hasidism and the historical emergence of Habad and the concept of zaddik (saint). This will be the purpose of the next two chapters.

The Beginnings of Hasidism

The Hasidic revolution during the eighteenth century saw the emergence of a style of prophetic/mystical Jewish leadership that had previously been dormant, although latent, in the tradition. The new leadership model was considered marginal, undesirable, and even dangerous by the traditional leaders of the community, the so-called mitnagdim,[1] who were themselves undergoing an internal crisis caused by the challenges to traditional Judaism offered by the Enlightenment, the rise of Hasidism, and general sociopolitical changes in Eastern Europe.[2] Leadership models were beginning to change and the mystic, the miracle-worker, and the saint attracted stronger followings, particularly in Eastern Europe.[3]

Traditionally, the mitnagdic religious hierarchy of East European Jewry ordered itself by the standards of scholarship, wealth, and family relationships. In this scheme, piety and fervor were complementary traits in a person, but were not the requisite for eminence, eligibility for marriage, or leadership in the community. The hallmark of honor, prestige, and envy, by tradition, was the pursuit of scholarship, through success at which an individual could win renown, a wealthy wife (and thus a handsome dowry), and positions of honor and standing.[4] As scholarship was generally more accessible to the wealthy and excluded the impoverished masses, the latter were not often represented in honorable positions or in leadership circles. Although there were instances of nonscholarly, charismatic leadership, these were considered aberrations, dangerous, or simply exceptions to the rule.[5] The purely charismatic leader did not usually play a dominant and consistent role in the community; moreover, there was no method for this type of leadership to perpetuate itself over more than one generation, so its irregular appearance was often short-lived.

3

This trend began to change in the eighteenth century, with the beginnings of what came to be known as Hasidism.[6] Throughout this period, charismatic personalities began to attract a larger number of followers, including some from the disillusioned scholarly classes, as friction between the traditional intelligentsia and the unschooled masses brought on deep-seated support for change in the religious leadership.[7] What emerged was a phenomenon that has been compared to the attraction of the masses to various false mashiachs and mystics throughout the ages.

While the precise reasons for the emergence of Hasidism are much debated in the academy, messianic/charismatic figures such as Sabbetai Zevi (1626–1676)[8] and Jacob Frank (1726–1791),[9] and other cultic personalities who preceded the rise of Hasidism, are often associated with the stirrings in this direction. The factors that gave rise to the Hasidic identity are not clear, but it is generally believed that Hasidism incorporated trends found in Sabbatianism, Frankism, and a general antinomianism found in the European Judaism of the time.[10]

Where Hasidism differed from these earlier cults of personality, some of which were extremely long-lived and influential, was in its ability to stabilize popular sentiment into an institutionalized social dynamic that could not be halted by the mainstream hierarchy of mitnagdim. This may have been due in part, as Etkes suggests, to the fact that the early Hasidim often mingled with the upper echelons of society,[11] a view supported by the social status of the traditional founder of Hasidism, the Ba'al Shem Tov. He was both a healer (and thus of high social status)[12] and a mystic (and thereby a Hasidic teacher) who attracted many middle-class people to his night-time study sessions. He enjoyed the community's patronage until his death, at which time his privileges were passed to his son,[13] thereby helping to establish an essential process of leadership succession in Hasidism that ensured its continuity, a factor absent in the earlier charismatic movements.[14] According to Dubnow, the Ba'al Shem Tov's son was considered incapable of leadership, so the Hasidim found a new leader in the person of the Maggid of Mezritch, but the precedent of genealogical descent was established at least in principle.[15]

The Ba'al Shem Tov

Rabbi Israel Ba'al Shem Tov ("Master of the Good Name," 1698–1760) is traditionally seen as the founder of the Hasidic movement. Until recently, little was known about him from primary sources—indeed, some speculated that his existence was entirely legendary—but there were many stories about his exploits, personality, and teachings.[16] While the historical details surrounding the life of the Ba'al Shem Tov are important to the emergence of the Hasidic movement, it must be acknowledged that to his followers, such knowledge is of secondary importance. The stories of his life in the minds of his followers, although possibly (or probably) completely fictitious, have precedence, because they are the basis of Hasidic custom, theology, and tradition.[17] This factor, more than any other, indicates the critical importance of popular perceptions in the establishment of leadership credibility, rather than any claim to independent truth as a basis of authority. Legends of the Hasidic masters are thus often exaggerated, a factor that must be kept in mind in the context of Schneerson's leadership of the Habad movement; the romantic mood and vision inspired by the stories of the Hasidic Rebbes is often much more important than historical actuality.[18]

In this context, the presentation of the Ba'al Shem Tov in Hasidism is important; as the founder of the tradition, he sets the standard against which later leaders are measured, and his characteristics are exemplary for any Rebbe in the Hasidic tradition. The Ba'al Shem Tov has been characterized primarily on the basis of his ability to work miracles and perform wonders.[19] To the world at large, he presented an image of apparent simplicity that, according to tradition, disguised a true genius. While famous for his emotional style of worship and simplistic presentation of complex theological principles, in contrast to the scholarly approach offered by the traditional mitnagdic Judaism of his era, later Hasidic tradition describes him as a brilliant scholar and talmudist.[20] The ability for profound meditation, insight, prophecy, and awareness of the presence of God in every living thing was attributed to him, a quality shared in the public perception of other Hasidic leaders since, including Schneerson. This was also to be an important factor in the emergence of the idea of the leader as a zaddik (saint), to be examined in the next chapter. According to tradition, the Ba'al Shem Tov was often to be found in private study of intricate talmudic tractates and rabbinic scholarship, thus providing a connection between the charismatic and communal traditions of worship that he implemented, and the longer-held respect for scholarship and learning. This connection would later be exploited by Habad, as we shall see.

Recently found Polish municipal documents shed a more sobering light on the real personality of the Ba'al Shem Tov as a member of his community. As a registered doctor, he served as a healer and teacher to his community, with a tendency toward mysticism, but little of the aura of mystical reverence that was later to surround his name appears to have been present at the outset. It seems most likely that the Ba'al Shem Tov was used by later Hasidic figures and charismatic leaders as a repository for their own imaginative projections and aspirations.[21] Whether these later personalities had known the Ba'al Shem Tov personally, or had a brief but significant encounter with a nondescript Lithuanian villager whom they later magnified into the personality of the Ba'al Shem Tov, is impossible to say. However, they and later Hasidic masters have all, unanimously, attributed their teachings and practices to the Ba'al Shem Tov.[22]

The Maggid of Mezritch

The Ba'al Shem Tov had many disciples, including both his offspring and Yakov Yosef of Polonya, his alleged scribe, but it was the charismatic preacher Rabbi Dov Ber, also known as the Maggid of Mezritch (d. 1772), who became the most dominant Hasidic master after the Ba'al Shem Tov. The Maggid is generally regarded as the Ba'al Shem Tov's primary disciple and confidant, and was responsible for the education of the largest class of future Hasidic Rebbes. Hasidism as we know it emerged from the teachings and vision of this man, perhaps more than from any other, including the Ba'al Shem Tov. The Maggid was seen as a supreme mystic, saint, and scholar who, by virtue of his reputed discipleship with the Ba'al Shem Tov, became a legitimate interpreter of the new teachings of Hasidism.[23] He was instrumental in carrying out the Ba'al Shem Tov's teachings, and executing the mission entrusted to him by his teacher to disseminate the esoteric secrets of the Torah to the Jewish masses.[24] The success of this mission was seen as vital for the future messianic redemption.[25]

Because of his dual status as both a learned rabbinic scholar, versed in classic Jewish argumentation and interpretation, and a mystic, able to elucidate the esoteric meaning *behind* the traditional interpretations, the Maggid attracted a wide range of people.[26] All levels of Jewish society were drawn to his court, from rabbinical scholars of eminence and learning to illiterates drawn by the mystical and charismatic elements of his teaching. Many hundreds of students were taught by him, and he instructed them in mysticism and divine service. He also cultivated a more intimate group of around thirty disciples, who became, after the Maggid's death, the first generation of Hasidic Rebbes. These men are traditionally considered the second generation of Hasidism.

The work and teachings of the Maggid of Mezritch were instrumental in the eventual reintegration of Hasidism into mainstream Judaism. There was much suspicion of the popular new movement in the established authority structure, and indeed some Hasidic writings and behavior indicate a variance from traditional behavior and halakhic commitment.[27] Under different circumstances, Hasidism could have split irrevocably from Judaism, but even so, its reintegration into the traditional mainstream took time. The success of the integrative trend may be attributed in the main to strong rabbinic and scholarly interest in the movement, fostered from the time of the Maggid of Mezritch, who was renowned for the depth of his scholarship. Despite opposition from traditional authorities, many scholars defected from the mitnagdic camp to Hasidism and were among the students of the Maggid who became Rebbes of later Hasidic dynasties.[28] The emergence of strong scholarly and rabbinic figures in the movement during its formation counter-balanced its antinomian tendencies and possibly halted the movement's defection from Judaism. The Habad movement was to play a large part in this reconciliation, from the time of its foundation under Rabbi Shneur Zalman of Liadi (1745–1812).[29]

After the Maggid

After the death of the Maggid of Mezritch, many of his disciples returned to their respective places of origin and began to attract followers through a defined program inspired by the Maggid.[30] Most of the Maggid's disciples came from Poland or Ukraine, but there were a few from Russia; two, Rabbi Menahem Mendel of Vitebsk (1730–1788) and Rabbi Shneur Zalman of Liadi, were among this group of Russian leaders. The former, one of the senior disciples of the Maggid, left Russia with a large number of disciples, believing that Hasidism would not be permitted to succeed there; the latter became the founder of the Habad movement. They too returned to their homeland to disseminate the new Hasidic teachings to the large Jewish community in Russia. Many of the students of the Maggid of Mezritch were innovative men with their own personal charisma, ideas, and aspirations. They injected these qualities into the new movement with vigor.

The Hasidic movement, led by a number of charismatic individuals, became more or less a workshop for the frustrated and the gifted who had found themselves handicapped in the traditional community of mitnagdim, and desired to participate in the general spiritual renaissance offered by Hasidism.[31] Their reverence for the Maggid had united them under his guidance. On his death, they were liberated from discipleship, and with their master's reputation preceding them, they managed to attract curiosity and interest among the masses, and the more successful among them were able to build a following. In time, the status of Rebbe within the Hasidic context became dependent on proving one's connection with the Ba'al Shem Tov and the Maggid. The deference given to the Ba'al Shem Tov and the Maggid by their followers was a central uniting factor of the new movement.

An unspoken tradition or pattern was emerging whereby, in order to be accepted as a Rebbe, one had to give proof of having been a disciple of the Maggid, and through him of the Ba'al Shem Tov.[32] This was called *hitkashrut* ("connection"), and in certain cases the link to the master was no doubt fabricated as a means of securing authority and influence, although this is impossible to prove. Despite this, however, a tangible system of authority transferral between generations was in the process of formation, although it was not initially without problems. Within a generation, arguments over successional authority became widespread, and led to the development of nepotistic and patriarchal dynasties of Hasidic leadership, which became the norm, replacing leadership based on personal accomplishments and *hitkashrut* with the movement's founders. Arguments raged between the biological children and the disciples of the various Rebbes over the rights of succession within the movement and the integrity of the movement's principles.

Leadership theory reached a crisis point; there were many difficult questions to resolve. When a Rebbe had many sons, which would succeed him? Was a gifted disciple preferable to a less able son? Could a son-in-law be an acceptable, or even preferable, successor? Could the Rebbe's brother take the mantle away from the Rebbe's son? These questions did not have clear-cut answers in Jewish tradition, so each dynasty sought its own solution. The Habad movement, too, has struggled with these issues throughout its development, not only in the early period of establishment, but throughout its history, to the current succession dilemma.

The Emergence of the Habad Movement

What came to be called the Habad movement was founded by Rabbi Shneur Zalman of Liadi, a pragmatic kabbalist and halakhist who combined the traditional demands of scholarship and intellectualism with Hasidic simplicity and faith.[33] By his commitment to traditional scholarship, and especially to its reconciliation with the devotion and emotional spirituality of Hasidism, the movement founded by Shneur Zalman was instrumental in the preservation of Hasidism within mainstream Judaism. It allowed for some of the mystically inclined Hasidim to reacquaint themselves with traditional scholarship and the significance of strict halakhic observance and behavior, concerning which other Hasidic schools were sometimes less exacting. Shneur Zalman also provided the opportunity for traditionalists and scholars to access the Hasidic mood and its spiritual integrity without betraying their traditional scholarly allegiances.

The reconciliation of these two worlds is reflected in the name given to the school of Shneur Zalman: *HaBaD* is a Hebrew acronym for *Hokhmah* ("Wisdom"), *Binah* ("Understanding") and *Da'at* ("Knowledge"), which are the first three *sefirot* (degrees of divine emanation) in the kabbalistic system. The name reflects a new interpretive system that integrated intellectualism and scholarship with the values of spirituality, faith, and simplicity. Other forms of Hasidism, (those that emerged in Ukraine and Hungary, for example), emphasized other *sefirot* in their practices which caused them to differ from Habad,[34] especially in the relationship between the Hasid and his teacher.

The Habad movement was unique specifically because of its leadership by Shneur Zalman, who held that a Rebbe was not a miracle-worker, as other schools of Hasidism believed, but a guide.[35] The Habad movement grew based on the principle of *yehidut*, personal guidance given by the Rebbe to Hasidim seeking enlightenment. Because of this, each Habad Rebbe in the succession maintained a unique leadership style, often quite different from that of previous Rebbes.

After the death of Shneur Zalman, the Habad movement underwent a number of successional difficulties and divisions over approximately six generations of leadership.[36] The movement split into several dynastic groups with their respective Rebbes living in such towns as Lubavitch, Liadi, and Kapost. There were no doctrinal differences between most of these groups, but they had different leaders. Over time, the Lubavitch dynasty and its tradition of leadership became the most distinct and influential Habad subgroup, and today it is considered by Habad Hasidim to be the true Habad dynasty. Indeed, the terms "Habad" and "Lubavitch" are frequently used interchangeably both within the movement and without.[37]

The leadership of the Habad movement generally followed the pattern of father-son succession, although there were exceptions. The precise details of these power transfers are not relevant here: suffice it to say that there was a continuous line of authority from the Ba'al Shem Tov into the modern period, and that the succession of leadership was sometimes controversial and open to challenge. The controversy surrounding the succession on the death of Rabbi Yosef Yitzhak Schneerson, the sixth Rebbe of Habad, and the point from which the body of this study will commence, was not a new issue in the movement. Over the course of six generations of leadership, the Habad movement had cemented a reputation within the broader Jewish tradition for combining Hasidut, scholarship, and strict adherence to halakhah. Most importantly for the succession of Menachem Mendel Schneerson, Habad had also, from the time of its foundation, amalgamated the administrative and spiritual functions of the movement under one figure: that of the Rebbe. Schneerson was to excel at all of these facets of Habad, and used them not only to consolidate his authority over the movement, but to expand the activities of Habad to embrace the world community.

[1] Literally, "the opposed," a name given to those who opposed the Hasidic trend. See Gershom Scholem's "Demuto ha-historit shel R.Yisrael Ba'al Shem Tov," *The Messianic Idea in Judaism*, and *Sabbatai Sevi*. See also Simon Dubnow, *History of Hasidism*; I. Etkes "Hasidism as a Movement"; and S. Ettinger, "Ha-Hanhagah ha-Hasidit be-Izuvah."

[2] See Menachem Friedman, "Habad as Messianic Fundamentalism," p. 330. In describing the background to the rise of Habad, he describes how the advent of Hasidism shattered the traditional community from a sociological point of view. Loyalties began to develop around Hasidic dynasties, thereby weakening the traditional *kehillah kedoshah* ("holy community"). See also Laura A. Klapman, "Sectarian Strategies for Stability and Solidarity," p. 124. She argues that the disintegration of the *kahal* shortly before the 1795 partition of Poland left a communal leadership vacuum to be filled by the founders of Hasidism.

[3] See Benzion Dinur, "The Origins of Hasidism and Its Social and Messianic Foundations," pp. 102–114.

[4] For an examination of the social strata and leadership of pre-Hasidic Eastern Europe, see Simon Dubnow, *History of the Jews in Russia and Poland*, and Ch. Abramsky, "The Crisis of Authority within European Jewry in the Eighteenth Century."

[5] See Avrum M. Ehrlich, *Leadership in the HaBaD Movement*, p. 22.

[6] See Court Protocols, *Agudas Hasidei Habadof United States* against *Barry S. Gourary and Hanna Gourary* (hereinafter cited as "Protocols"): Louis Jacobs testimony, p. 495–496. Jacobs describes the changes in the leadership with the advent of Hasidism: "Rabbi is the name given to [a] traditional rabbi whose function is to give decisions in Jewish law. . . . with the rise of Chasidism you had a new type of leader. His function was no longer to decide Jewish law unless he was a rabbi and some of them were rabbis. But his function was a new one, although Chasidim would say that it is old. . . . from the historical point of view it was a new idea ... a guru, a sort of guide, to this spiritual life."

[7] See Dinur, "Beginning of Hasidism."

[8] Sabbetai Sevi was perhaps the most important messianic figure in Judaism after Jesus of Nazareth. He led one of the most popular and influential messianic movements in Jewish history, but eventually converted to Islam and effectively faded from view. See Scholem, *Sabbatai Sevi*, for an exhaustive account of his life and impact. See also Harris Lenowitz, *The Jewish Messiahs*, pp. 149–165.

[9] Frank was a follower of the Sabbatean movement after the death of Sabbetai Sevi. He did

not believe in halakhic Torah, but in what he called the Torah of emanation, which included indulging in sexual practices forbidden by the Torah. He and his movement converted first to Islam, then to Catholicism, and finally to Russian Orthodox Christianity. See Lenowitz, *Jewish Messiahs*, pp. 167–197, for more information.

[10] See Gershom Scholem, "The Neutralization of the Messianic Element in Early Hasidism."

[11] See Israel Etkes, "Hasidism as a Movement"; see also M. Rosman, *Founder of Hasidism*, p. 151.

[12] Rosman, *Founder of Hasidism*, pp. 126, 134–135.

[13] See M. J. Rosman, "Miedzyboz and Rabbi Israel Baal Shem Tov."

[14] See Joseph Dan, "The Contemporary Hasidic Zaddik.

[15] See Simon Dubnow, "The Maggid of Miedzyrezecz, His Associates, and the Center in Volhynia," p. 59.

[16] The character of the Ba'al Shem Tov is much debated. There are numerous versions of his life story, covering a range of levels of devotion from his presentation as a great mystic and scholar to theories that his existence is entirely fictitious. Some say he was a kindergarten (heder) teacher; others that he was a shochet (ritual slaughterer). For examples of popular and devotional stories, see Yanki Tauber, *Once Upon a Chassid*, p. 127; Y. Y. Klapholz, *Tales of the Baal Shem Tov*, and Elie Wiesel, *Souls on Fire* and *Somewhere a Master.* There have also been a number of historical and academic studies of the Ba'al Shem Tov: see especially the works of Rosman, and Simon Dubnow, "The Beginnings."

[17] As Elie Wiesel relates in the name of his grandfather, "There will, of course, always be someone to tell you that a certain tale cannot, could not, be objectively true. That is of no importance; an objective Hasid is not a Hasid." See Wiesel, *Souls on Fire*, p. 18.

[18] See Yosef Yitzhak Schneerson, *Iggerot Kodesh*, vol. 5, pp. 327–328, on the significance of stories in Hasidism; Menachem Mendel Schneerson, *Likkutei Sichot*, vol. 10, p 160, on the significance of stories in communicating ideas that otherwise would be uncommunicable.

[19] See Wiesel, *Souls on Fire*, pp. 15–41.

[20] See Yosef Yitzhak Schneerson, *Sefer ha-Zikhronot;* Nissan Mindel, *Lubavitcher Rabbi's Memoirs.*

[21] See Wiesel, *Souls on Fire*, pp. 15–41.

[22] See Schneerson, *Sefer ha-Zikhronot.*

[23] See G. Scholem, *Major Trends in Jewish Mysticism*, pp. 334–350.

[24] See Dubnow, *History of Hasidism*, p. 62. The mission of the Ba'al Shem Tov was recorded in a letter published in R. Yakov Yosef Ha-Kohen of Pollonoye, *Ben Porat Yosef.*

[25] See R. Yakov Yosef Ha-Kohen, *Ben Porat Yosef*, reproduced in A. Kahane, *Book of the Hasidim*, pp. 76–77. See also Loewenthal, *Communicating the Infinite*, p. 13. He cites *Ben Porat Yosef*'s version of the Ba'al Shem Tov's dream, "I asked the Messiah: 'When will you come?' He answered me: 'Through this you will know—when your teachings are publicized and revealed in the world, and your fountains will be spread to the outside.' " This idea has been interpreted by Habad Hasidism as indicating the necessity of outreach activities as a precursor to the messianic redemption. See Chapter 15 below for more on outreach in modern Habad.

[26] Dubnow, " Maggid of Miedzyrezecz," esp. pp. 62–65.

[27] See Dinur, "Origins of Hasidism," p. 165; Scholem, *Major Trends*, p. 336.

[28] Dubnow, " Maggid of Miedzyrezecz," pp. 64–66.

[29] Nissan Mindel, *Rabbi Schneur Zalman of Liadi*, vol. 1, pp. 189, 218.

[30] See Dubnow, *History of Hasidism,* and Martin Buber, *The Tales of the Hasidim*, for stories of how Eastern Europe was divided between the disciples of the Maggid in preparation for the Hasidic expansion.

[31] Scholem, *Major Trends*, p. 335.

[32] Dan, " Contemporary Hasidic Zaddik," p. 203.

[33] For Shneur Zalman's life and works, see M. Teitelbaum, *Ha-Rav Mi-Liadi u-Mifleget Habad* and *Sefer Haken.* See also Mindel, *Rabbi Schneur Zalman.* For a more academic treatment, see Charles Chavel, "Shneur Zalman of Liadi"; Gershom Kranzler, *Rabbi Shneur Zalman of Liadi*; Moshe Hallamish, "The Theoretical System of Rabbi Shneur Zalman of Liady." For a brief and interesting perspective on the evolution of Habad, see Friedman, "Habad as Messianic Fundamentalism," pp. 328–357; and Roman Foxbruner, "*Habad.*"

[34] The sefirot, according to Hasidic doctrine, are *Hokhmah* (Wisdom), *Binah* (Understanding), *Da'at* (Knowledge), *Hesed* (Grace), *Gevurah* (Might), *Tiferet* (Magnificence), *Nezah* (Eternity), *Hod* (Nobility), *Yesod* (Foundation), and *Malkhut* (Kingship). Most other Hasidic groups emphasize the lower sefirot as fundamental to their spiritual service and thus are often known as *HaGaT Hasidim,* i.e., Hasidim of *Hesed, Gevurah,* and *Tiferet.*

[35] See *Tanya,* pt. 4 (*Iggeret ha-Kodesh*), chap. 22. See also Harry M. Rabinowicz, *The World of Hasidism*, p. 186. Other schools of Hasidism (Kotzk, for example) shared this belief with Habad.

[36] For a full account of these leaders and the succession difficulties experienced, see Ehrlich, *Leadership in the HaBaD Movement*, pp. 123–288.

[37] Other schools of Habad Hasidim do exist. For example, the Malakhim are a school of Habad Hasidim that is not connected with the Lubavitch movement. Its members are followers of Avraham the Malakh, a Hasid of Shalom Dov Ber. See Ehrlich, *Leadership in the HaBaD Movement*, pp. 269–271.

Chapter 2
The Ideal of the Zaddik

Whichever way one looks at the early composition of the Hasidic movement, it seems clear that its leadership was the most influential factor in its expansion, proving to be the focus of popular interest and the prime attraction for growing numbers of adherents. Why this was so is due to much more than human attraction to charismatic personalities, although this factor was an important element in the popularizing of Hasidism.

From its origins, Hasidism has devoted much energy to examining the temporal, spiritual, and theological status of its leaders.[1] Efforts by early Hasidic leaders to define the role of the zaddik and Rebbe led to fragmentation among Hasidic groups and affected their relationships with the traditional non-Hasidic authorities, who were concerned about the temporal and spiritual power given the Rebbes by their followers. Understandably, the non-Hasidic authorities also feared that Hasidism would cause renewed messianic tension, as leaders were elevated, practically and theologically, to a status approximating that of the mashiach.[2] This tension would come to a head during the lifetime of Schneerson, who is still regarded by many of his followers as the mashiach. The messianic mystique surrounding Schneerson will be examined in greater detail in a later chapter, but the Hasidic conception of the Rebbe as zaddik was to play a significant role in his emergence as seventh Rebbe of Habad, his consolidation of power, and in the present successional difficulties within the movement. The background to this idea is therefore of significance to us here.

The Concept of the Zaddik

The concept of the zaddik is a popular one in both scholarly and popular Jewish literature.[3] At the time of the emergence of Hasidism, the ideal Jew was one who was a learned scholar of the Torah, but Hasidism did much to change this ideal. As Scholem has observed,

The opinions particular to the exalted individual are less important [in Hasidism] than his character, and mere learning, knowledge of the Torah, no longer occupies the most important place in the scale of religious values. A tale is told of a

12

famous saint who said: "I did not go to the 'Maggid' of Meseritz to learn Torah from him but to watch him tie his boot-laces." . . . The new ideal of the religious leader, the Zaddik, differs from the traditional ideal of rabbinical Judaism, the *Talmid Hakham* or student of the Torah, mainly in that he himself "has become Torah." It is no longer his knowledge but his life which lends a religious value to his personality. He is the living incarnation of the Torah.[4]

The idea of the zaddik was transformed by Hasidism to signify a superior form of humanity, a being who is close to God and sometimes inseparable from Him; in Hasidism, the zaddik's soul is generally perceived to have emerged from the most sublime source within the Godhead.[5] The personality of this newly created paradigm became a primary focus of Hasidic worship,[6] although there was a great deal of debate within Hasidism as to what qualities a zaddik must possess and what his role in the world should be.[7] It appears that each school of Hasidism developed a concept of the zaddik that fit in with its particular leader, and many of the conceptions reflect the personalities of the founders of the dynasties.

As Hasidism evolved, the notion of the zaddik also changed. It is generally agreed among Hasidim that a zaddik possesses certain qualities: he is often said to possess a common soul with his followers, and in fact with all Jews.[8] He is often considered to be the Moses of his generation, that is, a prophet and leader of the Jewish people;[9] and the pillar on which the world stands: according to the Talmud, "the zaddik is the foundation of the world."[10] He is a source of holiness, standing between heaven and earth like an intermediary.[11] He is humble and modest, subjected to the will of God, and careful not to reject the flow of spirituality into his being. But the zaddik is also able to influence God: "He is the chosen one who is refused nothing in heaven or on earth. God is angry? He can make him smile. God is severe? He can induce him to leniency."[12] He suffers for his people and for the will of God, and is considered to have descended into a world where he does not belong by virtue of his superior spiritual status and connection to the Divine. He does this, however, because of his love for the world, and especially because of the care he has for his Hasidim.[13] Due to his connection to God, he also has great insight into the nature of humanity, and is able to read the souls of all. The zaddik is thus in a superior position to dispense advice and counsel, especially regarding spiritual matters.

The foregoing descriptions establish the zaddik as a source of life and spirit, even in an impure world. The Hasid who associates with him, eats from his plate, receives blessings from him or his advice, is connected with a more direct divine path than could be achieved through the regular channels of creation and existence. The act of watching a zaddik tie his shoes, an activity accessible to learned and unlearned alike, therefore takes on immense spiritual significance in Hasidism.

According to Hasidism, the zaddik has forged a spiritual identity so strong that some Hasidic literature almost deifies him, comparing the zaddik to God,[14] stating that God dwells in the body and soul of the zaddik,[15] and that the zaddik incorporates

God into an inseparable union with himself.[16] Literary sources are found that justify, at least to some degree, the worship of the zaddik,[17] primarily by comparing the zaddik to the Temple; just as God dwells in the Temple, so too does He occupy the zaddik. To extend the idea, just as one does not pray to the Temple but to what resides therein, likewise it is not the zaddik that is worshipped, but the Godly presence within him. This idea would come to have immense significance in the life of Menachem Mendel Schneerson, and in the succession debate.

The zaddik is often described as a lonely man, not necessarily by force of ideology but by the weight of his responsibility. His characteristics of solitude and isolation are ironically those that make him the central figure in the community and most sought after for advice. The less he needs the community and instead turns to God, the more the community needs him and attempts to distract him from his holy service.[18]

Social Functions of the Zaddik

The authority of the various zaddikim grew in relation to their personal popularity with the masses. Because of his connectedness to God and a life of righteousness, the zaddik was seen by many as the ideal human being. In time the idea of the zaddik merged with that of the Rebbe, who was responsible primarily for the physical, social, political, and economic well-being of the community, and thus the Rebbe came to be regarded as a zaddik by his followers. This is not to say that all zaddikim are Rebbes,[19] but that a Rebbe, by definition, must always be a zaddik. The role of Rebbe is much better filled by a zaddik than by an ordinary man, because thanks to his advanced spiritual status, the zaddik is considered to be ethically superior to others.[20]

As the dynastic courts of the Hasidic Rebbes began to grow, the zaddik/Rebbes provided their followers with the social support and encouragement they needed to resist the opposition ranged against them not only by political and governmental forces, but by the traditional Jewish authorities.[21] The charismatic and religious power held by the early Hasidic Rebbes caused the institution to come under criticism from opponents. According to Wiesel,

> In the Chasidic movement the Tzadik rapidly became an institution, but though a spiritual model, when exposed to temptation, he was not always able to resist, going as far as to proclaim himself intermediary between his disciples and G-d, presiding over . . . veritable courts and founding dynasties.[22]

Criticism of a more contemporary nature has compared the influence of the Rebbe over his followers to that of a modern cultic guru.[23] Whatever the interpretation, however, the role of the Rebbe has often been simply to unify the community behind a figurehead. A modern account of the dilemma of transfer summarizes this neatly.

When the Kapitshinitzer Rebbe died in 1975, his most probable successor was reluctant to take on the role. He recounts that

> the Amshinover Rebbe, who was sixty-five or seventy years old at the time and a Rebbe of considerable stature in Israel, turned to me and said: "You say you're not a Rebbe? None of us are Rebbes today. None of us are like the rabbeim of old times. I'm not like my father and I imagine you're not like your father. But the role of a Rebbe has changed today. A Rebbe today is just somebody who binds his people together. He has to strive to keep them together and give them spiritual strength. In their being together they will be better people for it. And that's what I do," he told me, "and that is what you can do."[24]

Whether this account reflects a characteristic humility or a desire to laud the achievements and status of previous Rebbes over one's own is immaterial; either way, the social function of the Rebbe as leader of a community and the source of solace and guidance is paramount. Whatever the case, it cannot be said that Schneerson was merely a figurehead of the Habad movement; he took an active role in the functioning of the movement, and aggressively led its outreach and expansion efforts to bring Habad to a wider audience than ever before.

The Idea of the Zaddik in Habad

The Habad movement shares many of the standard ideas about the nature and function of the zaddik discussed above. Nonetheless, throughout its history the movement has developed views on the zaddik that differ from those of the other Hasidic schools. Within the movement, the various schools of Habad have also held different views on this subject. As developments in the history of Habad have played a role in the development of the Rebbe's function, the concept of the zaddik has changed over time, especially during the more recent history of the movement.

Habad conceptions of leadership were often developed by example, that is, not by an *a priori* conception of what a zaddik should do, putting theory into practice, but because the concept evolved based on what the zaddik actually did. The personal example of each generation of leadership set the standard for later Rebbes. Throughout Habad, and Hasidism in general, emulation of the Rebbe's behavior, however uninspired it might have been, became a criterion for the aspiring leader. Examples may be found in the origins of the movement: the theological debates between Shneur Zalman and the mitnagdim created a standard for future Habad leaders, who were subsequently expected to be the representatives of Hasidism to the mitnagdim; his successor and son, Dov Ber, established the precedent of publishing literature, and all subsequent Rebbes have been compelled to continue the tradition in order to live up to their predecessor's standards. This process continued through the succession of Habad Rebbes until Schneerson, who idealized and emulated his predecessor's behavior. In doing so, he created new criteria and precedents that future leaders, if such should emerge, would need to match.[25]

A situation occurred whereby the practices of the Habad Rebbes standardized the theological teachings on the zaddik's nature and function. Hence, the theoretical idealization of the concept of zaddik in Habad has changed since the inception of the movement, and is still changing with the passage of time and the activities of each generation of leadership.[26] While present before his time, this change became quite pronounced during the leadership of Schneerson, who expressed significantly different notions of the Habad Rebbe's status than had his predecessors.[27]

This has become one of the significant features distinguishing Habad from other Hasidic groups. Throughout history, Habad's leadership theory and practice evolved along with the actions of its leaders, often including outreach and community activity of an active nature. By contrast, in the period up to the Second World War, other schools of Hasidism remained secure within their geographical confines, effectively guarded against challenge or threat except from their immediate neighbors.

As these communities had no extensive Diaspora, unlike Habad, they did not need an ideology concerning the nature of the leader to keep them united; their locality provided them with an effective cohesive device.[28] Their conception of the Rebbe had been articulated by their forebears, and the status of the Rebbe would (ideally) remain the same for their descendants without change, adjustment, or embellishment.

The twentieth century, however, with its disruptive history of warfare, persecution, and mass migration of Jews from Eastern Europe to Israel and the United States, necessitated changes in the make-up of the Hasidic community. Developments have also called for an adjustment to new circumstances in Hasidism generally, as movements spread into a geographically diverse Diaspora. The emergence of non-geographical devices to maintain a distinctive Hasidic identity beyond their once territorial scope became a necessity for the survival of many schools, and some have developed these with more success than others.

Habad, however, is far more evolved in these translocal techniques than most other Hasidic groups, because it underwent these changes during its formative years and has had decades to respond to the challenges of distance and ideology. One might speculate that some other Hasidic dynasties will in future also develop new ideologies regarding their Rebbes and follow an as yet undefined pattern of transition, as has happened with the Breslav dynasty. Whether these new paradigms will reflect the Habad experience and ideology remains to be seen; suffice it to say that the Habad model as it exists today is the only Hasidic dynasty whose broad-ranging ideological commitment to its Rebbe has been the determining factor in the movement's cohesiveness over a geographically divisive Diaspora.[29]

The difference between the Habad conception of the zaddik and the general Hasidic conception are subtle, but carry some far-reaching implications. The Hasidic zaddik is often portrayed as descending into a sinful world for the sake of his followers. In his descent he himself is tainted and commits a sin or undergoes imperfection, yet he does this out of sacrifice, for the sake of his love for his Hasidic following.[30] For Shneur Zalman, the first Habad Rebbe, the zaddik could literally do no wrong, and therefore Shneur Zalman was not able to conceptualize his descent into the physical world as sinful. Because of this, another motive for the Habad zaddik to enter the world needed to be revealed, and thus the first Rebbe argued that the descent into the world is part of the zaddik's spiritual journey.[31] He does not sin by the descent, but strengthens himself and becomes a greater zaddik. The zaddik, in this view, needs to descend into the physical world for his own perfection.[32]

The Habad zaddik, in order to perfect himself, must therefore concern himself with the world. He has a unique soul that shares in the life of the community, but remains untouched by the mundane and spiritually damaging aspects of being in the world. As a spiritually pure soul, he is able "to filter the experiences of the modern world so that the Chasidim could understand and keep to their faith."[33] Further, as a person who has attained the highest level of communion with the Divine, his "perceptive eye and proper spirit allows him to interpret the *Torah* to a contemporary situation. . . . the Rebbe's speech is treated as if it was pure *Torah*."[34] This was to be especially important in Schneerson's consolidation of authority over Habad, but the concept is to be found in the origins of the movement.

The Rebbe has fully invested himself into his community; he shares the souls of the community members, and cannot be separated from them.[35] As part of this conception, which is a fundamental one in Habad ideology, the Rebbe actually elevates himself by helping and elevating the community of followers;[36] hence, the emphasis on outreach and community-building found throughout the history of Habad. Further, because the zaddik is the spiritual reflection of the community, joined to them as the head is to the body, his ability to channel their energies will benefit them as much as himself. In fact, in his role as the head of the community, he is more sensitive to the true spiritual condition of his community, and is thus able to most effectively guide it. In turn, as the community grows in strength and stringency of adherence to the practices of Hasidism, the Rebbe is the prime benefactor from its spiritual growth, because he is the conduit through which his community has been enabled to establish a closer relationship with the Divine.

Throughout his life, Shneur Zalman never emphasized the importance of miracles or wonders in the career or effectiveness of a Rebbe or zaddik; instead, he promoted the virtue of hard and disciplined spiritual work. He saw his function, and that of all Rebbes, to be as an instructor to those trying to achieve and maintain a spiritual discipline. He therefore viewed the role of the zaddik in his community as one primarily of personal example and inspiration to his followers. As the channel for spiritual instruction, though, he is indispensable in the lives of his followers: "the Rebbe is a basic necessity for every Hasid who aspires to reach the Habad level of contemplation. This level cannot be achieved without the Rebbe."[37]

Further,

> Because the Rebbe has realized the fullest of human potential and *bitul* [nullification of self],[38] he is capable of instructing the Hasid, who seeks self-nullification and who is committed to an ideal principle of spiritual attainment. The function, therefore, of the Rebbe is to ascertain the Hasid's spiritual purpose and instruct him in the way to achieve his goals.[39]

The source of the authority of the Rebbe throughout Hasidism is thus related directly and powerfully to the needs of his Hasidim, to which we will now turn.

The Rebbe/Hasid Relationship

In this conception, which is found throughout Hasidism, the zaddik is the source of the Hasid's very life; any obstruction by the Hasid of the zaddik's will or activities may result, therefore, in the obstruction of the Hasid's life-force. Thus, if a Hasidic following is in any way doubtful of the leadership guiding it, then the following would cease to be. For the Habad Hasidim, this idea came to be magnified, and during the leadership of Schneerson, the Habad Rebbe came to be considered the definitive and infallible *nasi* ("leader" [of the generation]),[40] with a central role in the sustenance of the world.

The identification of the Hasid with the Rebbe is emphasized in the ideal of subordination to the Rebbe's will. As a spiritual practice, this is termed *bitul* ("nullification of ego"), and is the primary task of every Hasid. According to this idea, the zaddik may not be questioned or doubted after he is elected. Even if his actions seem unbecoming, even unhalakhic, they must be accepted by the Hasidim as something holy which they do not understand.[41]

> His followers owe him blind and unconditional allegiances. . . . he who hesitates, who wavers, cannot be helped. To question the Rebbe is worse than sin; it is absurd, for it destroys the very relationship that binds you to him.[42]

However one describes the relationship, it would appear that so far as the Hasid considers himself a Hasid, his existence is dependent on his Rebbe.[43] Equally, a Rebbe cannot be a Rebbe without the voluntary acceptance of his leadership by the Hasidim.

Shneur Zalman devoted much of his teaching work to the benefit of his Hasidim and their enhanced spiritual commitment to observance. His major work, the *Tanya*, was written for and dedicated to the spiritual service of the common person. Its primary theme revolves around the personality of the *beinoni*, the intermediate. This is a level of spirituality that every person can attain, if only one puts one's mind to it.

The spiritual heights of the *beinoni* were often described by Shneur Zalman as supe-rior to those of the zaddik, despite the latter's holy birth.[44] Indeed, the first Rebbe's role as educator and guide to his students simply indicates the practical manifestation of the centrality of the Hasidim to Habad philosophy, a factor that subsequent gener-ations have only served to enhance. This emphasis on the role of the Hasidim in the health of the movement was maintained by Schneerson, who held that a Hasid is in fact a miniature Rebbe, or even a mashiach, with a crucial role to play in the mes-sianic process.[45]

The relationship that developed between the Hasid and his Rebbe assisted in the process of encouraging people to remain religiously observant even in the face of poverty and persecution, and of the insensitivity of the leadership hierarchy of the time. The Jewish populace found solace in Hasidic notions of simplicity, equality, and love. The zaddik gave people his personal attention and a glimmer of hope, and was believed to perform wondrous actions. Because of the zaddik,

> it was suddenly easy to be a Hasid, to be a Jew. One knew where to go, what to do and say, what blessing to request and how to obtain it. The Rebbe had all the answers. By taking upon himself all the suffering of his followers and of the entire Jewish people he alleviated that suffering. Did he really accomplish mira-cles? yes or no, yes and no, it didn't matter.[46]

Thus, the Rebbe of any Hasidic community formed the focus not only for the com-munity's life and worship, but also for the lives of his individual followers. What the Rebbe advised was to be done, without question, and with implicit faith that he had a greater-than-human insight into the true needs of every Hasid.

The Rebbe/Hasid Financial Relationship

Just as the Hasid was spiritually dependent on the Rebbe, many Rebbes developed an economic dependence on their Hasidim. Some Hasidic masters had professions apart from their position as leader of the community, but most did not. Because it was considered inappropriate for the Rebbe to appear to be a dependent or an employee of his Hasidim, and thus open himself to accusations of selling favors or advice, the financial support given to the Rebbe did not take the form of wages. Instead, the Rebbe was supported by his Hasidim by a voluntary system of gifts and money. Often this financial support was lavish, and there were Hasidic dynasties that took pride in the wealth of their Rebbes. This perhaps reflected the popular desire to behold a king-ly figure of royalty and majesty, power and privilege,[47] an idea which can be traced to talmudic sources.[48]

Some Hasidic groups justified the wealth of their Rebbe not only as a means of spiritual service, but also as a facilitator of divine communication. They believed that as the zaddik has no essence, being greatly advanced in the pursuit of *bitul*, the only way that a Hasid can attach himself to the zaddik is through the zaddik's material existence. According to this, the zaddik becomes more attached to his supporters through the process of amassing material wealth, and is therefore able to nurture them more effectively.[49]

In most cases, though, the Rebbe received gifts and money only in sufficient quantities to allow him to carry out his duties. Thus he was seldom independently wealthy. The Hasid's support for the zaddik was perceived as a way to form a soul bond between the two through a shared physicality.[50] The essence of the zaddik's soul was considered to be too elevated and concentrated on the divine to enable deep connection at this level, so physical support provided sufficient connection between Rebbe and Hasid.

The financial support given the Rebbe is designated differently in the various schools of Hasidism. Habad has two terms for this financial support that go back to Shneur Zalman and the origins of the movement.[51] The first is *ma'amad*,[52] a "voluntary" offering to the Rebbe that is expected of every member of the community. The second is *pidyon nefesh*, or "redemption of the soul," and is more like a personal, voluntary gift to the Rebbe. It demonstrates a more intimate connection to the Rebbe, and is a sign of the Hasid's having a shared destiny with him. It is primarily given when the Hasid requests help from the Rebbe or asks him to pray or intervene on his behalf.

It is generally understood that the *ma'amad* contribution is given by the Hasid with the knowledge that it is for the Rebbe to do with as he pleases, although there is some debate as to what this actually means. While some Habad Rebbes were known to own private property, it was argued that the Rebbe's private and public lives were indistinguishable, as was the life of the Rebbe from the life of the Hasid. All of the Habad Rebbes were therefore known to keep detailed accounts of their expenditures, despite the license to dispose of the *ma'amad* contributions at their discretion. Most of these personal contributions went to pay for public projects for the betterment of the community and the Rebbe's Hasidim.[53]

Just as the zaddik was seen to be sacrificing his very life for the sake of the community, so the Hasid was expected to sacrifice his resources and even livelihood for the Rebbe. There was a conception that all material success achieved by the Hasid was due to the guidance of and spiritual support of the Rebbe, so continued support of the Rebbe in fact ensured the financial well-being of his Hasidim. The idea also developed that the Hasid's soul was purified and redeemed through the offering of financial pledges. A mutual relationship of sacrifice for each other emerges from this Hasid-Rebbe relationship, while the issue of providing the Rebbe with a respectable livelihood is addressed at the same time.

Schneerson was to become the epitome of the zaddik to his followers. A greatly learned and pious man, he was also charismatic and administratively gifted, and was able, not only to ensure the spiritual well-being of his followers through his explanations of Hasidic ideology and practice, but to effectively endow his followers with a grand sense of spiritual mission. This latter was to be one of the most important aspects of Schneerson's rule over Habad, and his consolidation of authority through employment and ideological enthusiasm will be examined later. Suffice it to say that, far from being content to view him solely as an administrator or teacher, Schneerson's followers embraced him as a living zaddik, and indeed many regarded him as one of the greatest men who ever lived. His every action was viewed as a manifestation of his perfection, and his behavior was emulated by Habad Hasidim throughout the time of his rule. Because he was held in such high esteem, the task of replacing him (if a replacement is needed) will be formidable.

[1] See Arthur Green, "The Zaddiq as Axis Mundi in Later Judaism."

[2] Gershom Scholem, *The Messianic Idea in Judaism*, pp. 176–203.

[3] See Martin Buber, *The Origins and Meanings of Hasidism*, *The Tales of the Hasidim*, and *Hasidism and Modern Man*. See also Isaac Bashevis Singer, *The Collected Short Stories of Isaac Bashevis Singer* and *A Day of Pleasure*; Elie Wiesel, *Four Hasidic Masters and Their Struggle Against Melancholy*; Chaim Potok, *The Gift of Asher Lev*, *My Name Is Asher Lev*, and *The Promise*.

[4] Gershom Scholem, *Major Trends in Jewish Mysticism*, p. 344.

[5] See Joseph Dan, "The Contemporary Hasidic Zaddik," pp. 200–201.

[6] See "Protocols": Louis Jacobs testimony, pp. 486–487.

[7] Dan, "Contemporary Hasidic Zaddik," pp. 203–211.

[8] See Avraham B. Pozner, *Al ha-Zaddikim*, which collates references to the zaddik from Kabbalah and Hasidut. See also Benzion Dinur, "The Origins of Hasidism." Dinur agrees with Dubnow that Hasidism grew from poverty and discontent.

[9] See, for examples, R. Benjamin Zalozhtsy, *Torey Zahav*, Parshat Korah 83d–84a, as quoted in Arthur Green, "Typologies of Leadership and the Hasidic Zaddiq."

[10] Talmud Bavli: Hagigah12b.

[11] Samuel H. Dresner, *The Zaddik*.

[12] See "Protocols": Elie Wiesel testimony, p. 2531.

[13] See Dresner, *Zaddik*.

[14] See Rabbi Hillel Halevi of Paritch, *Pelah ha-Rimon:* Parshat Vayare, the "zaddik is like the creator, he is unified in the lower and higher worlds."

[15] See Rabbi Moshe Briah, *Be'er Moshe:* Parshat He'ezinu, in A. B. Pozner, *Al ha-Zaddikim*: "God Himself actually shines on the zaddik of the generation and comes before him. . . . and everywhere he goes, God, so to speak, goes with him."

[16] See Rabbi Dov Ber of Mezritch, *Likkutei Amarim, Magid Devarav le-Yakov*: "the will of God and the will of the zaddik are one."

[17] See Rabbi Levi Yitzhak of Berdichev, *Kedushat Levi:* Parshat Shoftim. He describes how Ya'akov was called God because he was pure. From this he derives that one may bow to a zaddik by virtue of his purity and obedience to God. He further notes that to bow to an angel for its own sake is heresy, whereas to bow to him as a messenger of God is permissible.

[18] See Dresner, *Zaddik*.

[19] The famous example is that of Levi Yitzhak of Berditchev, who was considered by the Hasidic leadership and following to be a zaddik, but did not command a following of his own.

[20] Dan, "Contemporary Hasidic Zaddik," pp. 208–209.

[21] Harry Rabinowicz, *The World of Hasidism*, pp. 91–92.

[22] "Protocols"; Elie Wiesel testimony, p. 2521. He discusses the first generation of Hasidic leadership.

[23] See M. Herbert Danzger, *Returning to Tradition*, pp. 298–305; Jerome R. Mintz, *Hasidic People*, pp. 168–169; 287–288.

[24] See Mintz, *Hasidic People*, p. 81.

[25] One of the problems with the post-Schneerson successional dilemma is caused by the belief that there is nobody who can live up to Schneerson's achievements or aspirations, and therefore nobody can succeed him. See Chapter 18.

[26] The contemporary movement is seeing a change whereby the Rebbe no longer has to be alive to function as the movement's reigning leader.

[27] See Avrum Ehrlich, *Leadership in the HaBaD Movement*, particularly sec. 3.

[28] While it is true that Hasidic groups like the Zanze had a large diaspora in Poland, East and West Galicia, and various parts of Hungary, and the Ruzhin had communities in Ukraine and Galicia, one might argue that Habad's more developed philosophy provided a more cohesive identity for its Hasidim.

[29] One might argue that Hasidic groups like Satmar maintain a broad Hasidic community based on an ideological commitment to anti-Zionism and conservatism which unites them despite distance. While this is true, the unitive issues for most groups do not encompass a range of subjects, but tend to focus on one idea, which tends to be reactionary. These groups also remain relatively static, especially in their relations and interaction with the outside world, and do not approach the growth, popularity, or vibrancy of Habad. See especially Mintz, *Hasidic People*.

[30] See Dresner, *Zaddik*.

[31] *Tanya*, pt. 1, chap. 3.

[32] See Mosehe Hallamish "The Theoretical System of Rabbi Shneur Zalman of Liady," p. 356, n. 51. He explains how the preoccupation of non-Habad (Polish) zaddikim with community issues is for them considered almost sinful, as it detracts from contemplation of Godliness. Despite this, these zaddikim are willing to "sin" in self-sacrifice for the sake of their Hasidim. Shneur Zalman's worldview, however, considers even a light transgression of a rabbinical decree sufficient for one to be branded an evil person (see *Tanya*, pt. 1, chap. 1). Shneur Zalman, therefore, could not tolerate the perception of sin, even as an act of sacrifice by the zaddik. This led him to interpret the zaddik's community service as a holy "mission" that would strengthen the leader's soul and not bring him to sin. The descent into the physical world was in fact a fulfillment of the zaddik's quest for divinity and perfection; his endeavors within the community therefore, far from compromising his holiness, enhance his own spirituality. This perception has been retained by the Rebbes throughout the history of Habad, including Schneerson.

[33] See "Protocols": Louis Jacobs testimony, p. 619.

[34] See "Protocols": Zalman Posner testimony, p. 842.

[35] See Hallamish "Theoretical System of Rabbi Shneur Zalman," p. 356.

[36] Jacob I. Schochet, *Chassidic Dimensions*, vol. 3, p. 93.

[37] See "Protocols": Zalman Posner testimony, p. 497.

[38] The idea of *bitul* is basic to the mystical practice of Habad Hasidism, as it is in other schools of Hasidim. See Rachel Elior, "The Anthropocentric Position in Habad Thought" and "Habad," available in an expanded Hebrew version, "Iyunim be-Machshevet Habad."

[39] See "Protocols": Posner Testimony; p. 797.

[40] Schneerson reportedly said that "the leader of the generation is also the Moshiach of the generation." He also stated that "every Chasid believes with complete faith that the Rebbe of his generation, just like the leader of our generation, is the Moshiach." See Ehrlich, *Leadership in the HaBaD Movement*, pp. 93–95.

[41] See "Protocols": Menachem Friedman testimony, p. 1572, where he describes the differences between a Rebbe and a rabbi. A Rebbe cannot be challenged, because the moment one does this, one ceases to be a Hasid. This is aptly expressed in the Yiddish Hasidic adage "*freg men nicht kleiner kashes*," that is, don't question the zaddik. This attitude is almost the opposite of one's relations with a community rabbi. He is often criticized, and is expected to prove himself, particularly on a halakhic or scholarly level. According to Friedman, these rabbinic models involve two different structural relations; see also "Protocols": Memorandum Decision and Order, pp. 16–17. This describes how the Hasidim tried to conceal apparent lies told by Yosef Yitzhak in relation to his book collection. They quoted biblical sources to justify his lies.

[42] See Eli Wiesel, *Souls on Fire*, p. 22 . Wiesel is describing his own Rebbe, the Lizensker Rebbe, but the conception is found throughout Hasidism.

[43] See "Protocols": Louis Jacobs testimony, p. 497.

[44] See *Tanya*, pt. 1, chap. 1.

[45] See Menachem Mendel Schneerson, *Sichot Kodesh* 5752, p. 168, and *Sichot-Hanahot*.

[46] See Wiesel, *Souls on Fire* p. 209.

[47] Wiesel, for example, has described the wealth of the Ruzhiner dynasty. See "Protocols": Elie Wiesel testimony, p. 2508.

[48] See Talmud Bavli: Nedarim 38a. "The holy one does not permit his presence to rest except upon one who is strong , wealthy, wise and humble and all are derived from Moshe." See also Yosef Karo, *Kesef Mishneh* on Hilkhot Yesodei ha-Torah 7:1. He notes that "where the Talmud talks of strong, it means the words literally, that he should be a man of physical strength, and the same with wealthy—that he should literally have a large amount of money."

[49] See "Protocols": Louis Jacobs testimony, p. 521.

[50] See "Protocols": Arthur Green testimony, p. 2158; see also his discussion of *ma'amad*, pp. 2332–2343.

[51] See S. B. Levine, *Sefer Sifriot Lubavitch*. He discusses the issues concerning the Rebbe's financial support, which enabled Yosef Yitzhak to purchase a large library of valuable books. See also Zemakh Zedek, *Derekh Mizvotekha*: Introduction—*Shoresh Mitzvah ha-Tefillah*.

[52] See "Protocols": Menachem Friedman testimony, p. 1682. He notes that the term *ma'amad* is used only in Habad, although the concept is common to all Hasidim.

[53] See "Protocols": Memorandum Decision and Order, p. 15. This lists the expenditure of Yosef Yitzhak's *ma'amad* money. There were six categories: the *Ha-Kriya Ve-ha-Kedusha* magazine, books, free loans, charity, personal expenses, and salaries and other administrative costs. The relatively loose categories, mixing personal expenditure with corporate, would suggest that he saw little difference between his public and private funds.

Chapter 3
Habad in America

By the time Habad came to the United States, it had already been in existence through six generations of leadership and was probably the most influential school of Hasidism in Europe. The leader who brought the movement to the United States, Rabbi Yosef Yitzhak Schneerson, also known as the *Freirdicker* ("Former") Rebbe, had become renowned throughout Russia for his perseverance in Hasidism despite persecution and opposition. The history and development of the Habad movement has been examined elsewhere;[1] our purpose here is to set the scene for the emergence of the last Habad Rebbe, Rabbi Menachem Mendel Schneerson, by examining some of the significant features of the movement he was to inherit.

After the death of Shneur Zalman, Habad underwent a series of developments that changed its nature and influence on the emergence of a new form of Hasidism. While much of this history is not of relevance here, there were several important developments that brought Habad into the modern world before the headquarters of the movement were physically relocated to the United States in the 1940s. With the Hasidic tradition of later Rebbes continuing the practices of their predecessors, and if possible expanding on them, these developments were to take on immense significance in the translation of Habad from Europe to the United States. They would also assist in the consolidation of the movement as the bastion of the popularization of Hasidism across the world under the leadership of Schneerson.

Shalom Dov Ber, the Fifth Rebbe

The leadership of Shalom Dov Ber, the fifth Habad Rebbe, is important to the development of Habad for a number of reasons. First, his teachings and correspondence represent the emergence of an emphasis on outreach that later Rebbes were to expand upon. Shalom Dov Ber conducted a lengthy correspondence, not only with the geographically fragmented Habad community (many had migrated to the United States and elsewhere), but also with non-Habad Hasidim and members of other Jewish groups who wrote to him for advice.[2] This practice was to emerge as possibly the most significant development in the history of Habad, and in the ability of a Rebbe to support and guide a community that was separated by distance. We will see the effect that this was to have on the spread of the Habad movement, through the lives of Rabbi Yosef Yitzhak (the sixth Rebbe) and especially Rabbi Schneerson.

Most significantly, the correspondence of Shalom Dov Ber represented a divergence from the traditional Hasidic practice of Hasidim traveling to the court of the Rebbe, for it meant that Hasidim could maintain contact with their spiritual guide despite not residing locally. In his correspondence, Shalom Dov Ber wrote prolifically to places in Russia, Europe, and the United States, and he also met with other Jewish and Hasidic leaders, working with them on such issues as Hasidic education, unity, policy, and strategy.[3]

The second area in which Shalom Dov Ber influenced the later development of Habad was through the establishment of a Habad yeshiva, in which students from throughout the Jewish community could learn Talmud and Hasidism. This institution was to provide him with much-needed community leaders drawn from the yeshiva's student body, most of whom were dedicated to Habad ideology and activities.[4] Shalom Dov Ber's yeshiva was one of the first such institutions in Hasidic history, and therefore was important in establishing the Lubavitch sect as the dominant Habad dynasty. Its success as a means of training students and providing a rich source of intelligent and able men to lead the movement would be perpetuated by Shalom Dov Ber's successors, especially Schneerson.

In addition to his wide correspondence, Shalom Dov Ber sent emissaries to remote Jewish communities, such as the Sephardi community in Georgia, to teach and serve as rabbis and leaders. This helped Habad to change from a geographically restricted movement to a universally applied ideology, and was a prefigurement of the outreach efforts of Schneerson during the late twentieth century.

Yosef Yitzhak Schneerson, the Sixth Rebbe

Rabbi Yosef Yitzhak succeeded his father as Rebbe on the latter's death in 1920, although he had been involved in the administration of Habad as his father's assistant since the age of thirteen.[5] He was to lead the movement through some of the most potentially destructive events it had ever faced, including the 1917 Russian Revolution and the Holocaust. He assumed the mantle of Rebbe immediately on the death of his father, and was able to maintain a position of strength from which he consolidated authority over the Hasidim. Active in Jewish politics in Russia before becoming Rebbe, with the encouragement of his father, Yosef Yitzhak emerged during this time as the sole Habad Rebbe, and he developed a reputation and authority as a Jewish leader first in Russia and later throughout the world.

Shortly after Yosef Yitzhak assumed the office of Rebbe, the Communist Party's assumption and consolidation of control over the Russian government in 1921 led to some of the harshest suffering ever faced by Russian Jewry.[6] The Soviet government began the systematic eradication of Jewish religious observance,[7] and by 1924 nearly all of Russia's Jewish leaders had fled to other areas of Eastern Europe, Israel, or the United States. This migration left a leadership vacuum in Russian Judaism that Yosef Yitzhak was able to fill.

A member of the underground Rabbinic Council of Russia, Yosef Yitzhak devoted the first twenty years of his leadership to the survival of Judaism in Russia, despite a concerted and sustained effort by the government to eradicate religious observance of any kind. He was primarily responsible for the maintenance of the now-clandestine Habad yeshiva system, which had ten branches throughout Russia by this time. Yosef Yitzhak had been placed in charge of the yeshiva system by his father when he was eighteen, and had set up an "old-boys" alumni program through which he was able to maintain contact with its graduates. On assuming the role of Rebbe, he was able to draw the next generation of Habad leaders from its ranks, and sent them throughout Russia (and eventually outside Russia) as emissaries of Habad. He was also involved with the ordination of rabbis and the training of *shochatim* (ritual slaughterers) to enable Jewish communities to eat kosher meat, the building of *mikvaot* (ritual baths), and the printing of prayer books (*Siddur Tehillat Hashem*).

Yosef Yitzhak achieved all this while under continual surveillance by agents of the NKVD (People's Commissariat of Internal Affairs), which imprisoned him in May 1927 and sentenced him to death. His arrest attracted a great deal of international attention, and prominent world figures, including the International Red Cross, inter-vened on his behalf.[8] Consequently, his sentenced was dropped, and he was released three weeks after his arrest. The arrest helped elevate Yosef Yitzhak to prominence as a figure of international reputation, a man who had surrendered his freedom for the sake of Jewish survival. After his arrest, he was able to more easily raise funds and attract support for his projects from world Jewish organizations, and was even able to travel abroad, including an extensive visit to New York in 1929.[9]

Throughout the persecution that Jews and Jewish institutions were experiencing under Communist rule, Yosef Yitzhak maintained an anti-emigration policy. He insisted that there were enough Habad followers around the world to build the move-ment there, and that Judaism in Russia was in much greater need of qualified leader-ship than communities elsewhere, especially in the United States. He further insisted that those of his followers who left Russia were tantamount to deserters.[10]

Increasing persecution in the 1920s, including the discovery and closing of two Habad yeshivot and the main rabbinic seminary in Nevel in 1928,[11] began to tell on Yosef Yitzhak's resolution to remain in Russia. Starting in 1930 with a large-scale crackdown on rabbis and educational institutions, religious observance became increasingly difficult. Seeing the fruits of his work in Russia crumbling, and recog-nizing the futility of continuing there, he migrated first to Warsaw and eventually to the United States, arriving in New York on March 19, 1940. Fortunately, he had already established contacts with many migrant Habad and other Jewish leaders in the United States, commencing when he became Rebbe and maintained through his habit of correspondence; indeed, much of the funding for his activities in Russia had come from American Jews. Some of these supporters had assisted in the process of obtaining visas for the Rebbe and his staff, thereby enabling Yosef Yitzhak to enter the country in the first place. Two major sources of support were the Agudat Hasidim Anshei Habad (*ACHACH*, the Union of Hasidim [People of Habad], which had been established in 1924 as a forum for Hasidic unity and support;[12] and the unofficial Agudat Hasidei Habad (AGUCH, the Union of Habad Hasidim), which was not officially established until 1940, but had been operating since the 1930s. The latter organization had assisted Yosef Yitzhak at the time of his arrest, had organized his 1929 visit to the United States, and now provided a means to unite Habad affiliates across America.

AGUCH formed a core of support for Yosef Yitzhak in the United States, but support for the Rebbe was also to be found outside Habad. There were approximately two hundred synagogues and communities around the country, loosely affiliated with Habad, that were the basis of Habad support and activities in the United States before Yosef Yitzhak immigrated. Further, the old-boys network, fostered by Yosef Yitzhak in Russia, was built upon in America, where it became the organization Ahi Temimim, which gave spiritual and material support to Habad immigrants. It did this by providing Habad scholars with employment and a social network, and secured for Habad a mutually supporting and community-oriented infrastructure in the United States, centered around and guided by the Rebbe even before the arrival of Yosef Yitzhak. All of these groups provided funding and support for the Habad Rebbe when he arrived in the United States.[13]

Shortly after his arrival, Yosef Yitzhak set up the new Habad world headquarters and synagogue at 770 Eastern Parkway in Crown Heights, which was at the time a comfortable, upper-middle-class section of Brooklyn. His residence, which came to be known simply as "seven-seventy," was located in the same building as the administrative offices of various organizations under his direction, including the headquarters of AGUCH and a new yeshiva of twenty students. He used the new premises to continue to gather support for Habad, founding the Hasidic journal *Ha-Kriah Ve-ha-Kedusha* and collecting funds for his institutions as well as *ma'amad* for his own support. He also began to gather aides and supporters from overseas and integrate them into the institutions he had established, including the man who was eventually to replace him, Rabbi Menachem Mendel Schneerson, who arrived from Paris on June 23, 1941.

When Yosef Yitzhak escaped from Europe, making his way to New York to settle and consolidate his leadership, he was the sole surviving Habad Rebbe,[14] and he faced some daunting challenges. Before the Second World War, many of the centers of Judaism in Eastern Europe had been disrupted by the Communist Revolution, but the postwar period saw world Jewry struggling to recover from the unprecedented convulsions of the Holocaust and the destruction of one-third of the world's Jews. Many centers of Jewish learning and culture in Eastern Europe had been wiped out, and many of Judaism's leaders and scholars had died, including much of the Habad community in Russia. Ironically, those who had escaped war and persecution were often less committed to religious observance, and had made their way to the United States against the will of the European religious leadership, including Yosef Yitzhak.[15] Effectively, all that remained of Habad after the Communist crackdown and the disruption of the Holocaust were remnant communities in foreign countries: the Habad community in New York was described as a "demoralised band of holocaust survivors, new arrivals in a country they found modern and bewildering."[16]

The challenges of bringing Orthodox Judaism to the United States were great. Many New York Jews from Eastern Europe had shed their outer Jewish appearance, and answered questions about this from newcomers simply with the phrase, "America is different." Later, after he was more settled in America and had begun outreach to the American Jewish community, Yosef Yitzhak established various organizations dedicated to his new slogan and catch-phrase: *"America is nisht anderst"*—"America is no different."[17] To have a beard and dress in Hasidic style in America was to declare oneself a Jew, and to be proud of it. However, it was obvious that America *was* different. Habad was perceived as curious even by Orthodox Jews,[18] let alone the assimilated, and faced challenges that it was slow to surmount.

Despite the necessity of relocation, Yosef Yitzhak reactivated his educational programs, with the intention of retaining and continuing traditional observance and learning. Education was at the center of his efforts to restructure and revive the Habad movement in its new home, the United States, a feature that was to be further emphasized and expanded upon by his successor. As with most of the Hasidic schools that made the transition from Europe to America, Yosef Yitzhak's ambition seems to have been to continue the traditions of observance followed in Europe. These were central to the practice of Judaism, and were necessary to secure the support of the older, more traditional members of the migrant community. The practice of educating the young, who were to form the next generation of Habad, was central to the inculcation of these traditions and values, and in fostering a sense of pride in being Hasidic, especially as the younger members of the community faced external pressure to secularize.

Under the leadership of Yosef Yitzhak, the Habad movement had begun to recover from the difficulties of relocation, but it was still largely in disarray when he died on January 28, 1950. The movement had survived a strong messianic belief that had falsely predicted the impending redemption in 1943,[19] and many followers were left bewildered by ideological and practical failures. Habad had only a sparse presence and influence in many countries, and in the United States a number of institutions had been established, but there seemed to be no way to achieve their lofty goals for Jewish outreach.[20] It was Yosef Yitzhak's son-in-law and successor, Rabbi Menachem Mendel Schneerson, who succeeded him a year after his death in January 1951, who would truly globalize the Habad movement and succeed at outreach beyond anyone's expectations. Furthermore, it was precisely because "America is different" that his entirely new approach to spreading the ideology and practice of Habad was to become so successful.

Location as a Form of Movement-Building

Before moving our discussion to the personality of Menachem Mendel Schneerson and his rise to power, a word is necessary about the importance of location and sacred geography, especially as related to the concept of Rebbe and to the history of Habad. While this subject will be discussed further in relation to Schneerson and his consolidation of the movement, it is important to situate the presence of Habad in America in its new setting. During the decade he spent in the United States, Yosef Yitzhak worked to coordinate and unite a wide but sparse network of contacts, emissaries, Hasidim, affiliates, and sympathizers throughout the world. He maintained contacts with people who had fled from Eastern Europe because of the anti-Semitism of the pogroms and later the hardships of religious life under Communism.[21] Over the past century or so, groups of Hasidim had migrated to Israel, Western Europe, North America, South Africa, Australia, and other places, resulting in a thinly spread scattering of Habad sympathizers around the world. A new headquarters for the movement was needed, however, to unite these geographically disconnected communities, and to serve as a focus for the Habad Diaspora. That location was found in Crown Heights.

One cannot overemphasize the importance of location in Jewish history in providing an ideological base from which the religion was able to survive. The Jewish people emerged originally from the province of Judea, and were dispersed over the centuries to countries and civilizations across the world, where they made their presence felt.[22] Despite this separation from the land of their origins, however, the idea of Eretz Yisrael has for many centuries served as a cultural and ideological focus for the Jewish people, a mechanism for unity and commonality throughout persecution and dislocation.

Various places in the Diaspora have also taken on symbolic significance for segments of the Jewish people. Scholem theorized that the origins of the Sabbatian movement and the spread of Lurianic Kabbalah, which so dominated seventeenth-century Jewish religiosity, were made possible by the ideological focus provided by Safed in Upper Galilee.

From about forty years after the expulsion of the Jews from Spain in 1492, Safed was the ideological and communal center of Judaism, where scholars and mystics congregated from all over the Jewish world to study and exchange ideas.[23] The Safed experience has been described as "the quintessential historical experience of Jewry in exile," and it was here that two of the greatest kabbalists of the sixteenth century, Moses ben Jacob Cordovero and Isaac Luria, formulated and discussed their ideas. From here, the ideas of Lurianic Kabbalah, and especially its conception of exile, "without which Sabbatianism would be unthinkable,"[24] were eventually dispersed to all the Jewish communities on earth via travel to Safed, messengers from Safed, and other forms of communication. Because of this ideological dispersion, the way was paved for the widespread acceptance of Sabbatian messianism when it emerged in the years 1665 and 1666. Rather than remaining a localized phenomenon, the interaction of people in a single locality was able to universalize an idea. Quite possibly the Russian town of Lubavitch, although in a smaller way, performed much the same function for the Habad movement as Safed had for Sabbatianism, by providing a geographical focus for the distribution of an ideology.

Friedman, in his work on Habad's ideological and practical transformation from local particularism to universal mission, describes how historically the town of Lubavitch and its emissaries and yeshiva students, in a manner similar to Safed, acted as a postal service for the surrounding area, focusing community activity on the town and the Rebbe who lived there. This focus was made possible by the large number of people who made pilgrimages to Lubavitch, to visit either the resident Rebbe or the gravesites of the previous Rebbes. This last activity still provides an important focus for the movement, and the location of the grave of Yosef Yitzhak in the United States was to be a major influence on the transition of Habad from Russia to America. It was also to provide an important link between Yosef Yitzhak and his successor, Schneerson.[25]

Historically, the focus on the town of Lubavitch was made possible largely because mail would be left there for collection when associates of Habad visited from their widespread communities, but the fifth Rebbe, Shalom Dov Ber, used this factor to consciously unite the disparate elements of Habad. He was the first Rebbe to utilize modern means of communication for Hasidic purposes, a practice that was to be expanded upon by his successors, Schneerson in particular. Shalom Dov Ber used the postal system to gradually create internal links with adherents that were totally unaffected by territorial barriers, distance, and borders, enabling the movement to expand beyond the limitation of physical proximity to the Rebbe.

The non-territorial cohesion of the movement is described by Friedman as one of the signs of Habad's transition to a non-particularistic, non-local movement. Friedman notes that by utilizing correspondence as a unifying factor, the Habad movement even crossed the ethnic divide between Ashkenazi and Sephardi. Until that time, Hasidism had been an East European, Ashkenazi movement. When Shalom Dov Ber sent emissaries to the old Sephardi community of Georgia he established Habad as an ideological movement, divested of the territorial or ethnic foundations characteristic of other East European Hasidic groups.[26] This was furthered by a continuing correspondence that kept the connection alive.

Over the many years of his leadership, Shalom Dov Ber taught the ideals of the movement, founded a yeshiva, educated the Hasidic elite, and socialized them toward the ideal of outreach and *shlihut* as "the soldiers of King David."[27] The congregating of people from all over Eastern Europe in Lubavitch and their later dispersal throughout the Western world may have served the same effect as was described above. Hence the role of a locality should not be underestimated in the propagation of an idea. Crown Heights may have served a similar role in the modern period, its effects unknown for many years.

Crown Heights

Crown Heights in the 1930s, before Yosef Yitzhak settled there after fleeing Europe, was a respectable upper-class Brooklyn neighborhood. It had a high concentration of Jewish residents, many of whom were religiously observant. In addition, many distinguished Hasidic Rebbes lived there, including the Bostoner Rebbe, the Bobover Rebbe, and the Skoloner Rebbe, all at the center of active, if not flourishing, communities.[28] Other Hasidic groups also had representation in the neighborhood. Initially, the predominantly newly migrated Habad Hasidim could not afford to buy property in the area, but the movement officially entered the neighborhood in 1941 with the purchase of a building at 770 Eastern Parkway. As noted, this building was to serve as the home of Yosef Yitzhak and his wife, as well as a synagogue and administrative center for Habad.

The move to Crown Heights had a direct physical and communal role in uniting the Habad movement in the United States. It was common practice throughout the history of Hasidism in Eastern Europe to travel from one's home to the Rebbe's town for holy days, so as to be in the presence of the zaddik for these special occasions. In a continuation of this tradition, it was customary from the time of settlement in the United States for Habad Hasidim to travel to Crown Heights on the festivals, most particularly on Rosh Ha-Shanah,[29] to be close to Yosef Yitzhak and later to Schneerson. This custom persisted in most Hasidic dynasties over intercontinental distances, and in Habad's case, among other dynasties, it created a cohesive network of Hasidim periodically centralized in a small Brooklyn neighborhood. As Lubavitch had come to serve as a postal town in Russia because of the high rate of visitors moving through, so too did Crown Heights become a place of communication, transaction, and dispersal of Hasidic ideology, unity, messages, materials, and goods to Hasidim returning home from 770.

Yosef Yitzhak's residence in Crown Heights prompted his Hasidim to visit the area regularly. During his lifetime, those Hasidim who could afford the area began to move in permanently, but others visited from surrounding (and cheaper) areas, such as Brownsville, Borough Park, Flatbush, and Williamsburg (all in New York City). Many Hasidim used to walk to Crown Heights on Shabbat and during festivals to be at the Rebbe's gathering, in a continuation of the traditions of Eastern Europe.[30] By the time Yosef Yitzhak passed away in 1950 there was an established community, albeit not a large one, of Habad Hasidim in Crown Heights, surrounded by other Hasidic groups, Rebbes, and prominent elements of American Jewry. The community was reinforced by the existence of the movement's yeshiva with its twenty-odd students. Their presence, although they were in Crown Heights primarily to study, allowed them time to become involved in community affairs. The students were therefore able to contribute to Hasidic life in the neighborhood, and many of them would later be instrumental in Schneerson's election to the office of Rebbe. However, during the lifetime of Yosef Yitzhak the community was small, and the records show that in some months of 1950, for example, it was difficult to gather a minyan in the central headquarters.[31] This would seem to indicate a community that was small and lacked cohesion.

During the last decade of his life, from the time of his arrival in the United States in 1940 to his death in 1950, Yosef Yitzhak succeeded in transplanting much of the traditional observance of Habad to a new homeland. He established an administrative infrastructure for the movement, found sources of funding, settled into an international headquarters at 770 Eastern Parkway, Crown Heights, founded the first Habad yeshiva in America, and commenced outreach to many segments of the American Jewish population. The movement he left at the time of his death was extremely fragile, with high expectations of its role in America and the world, but possessing few of the resources necessary to carry them out. What Habad had was a number of strong, energetic, and determined youth who would become the next generation of leadership of the movement. Among them was Rabbi Menachem Mendel Schneerson.

[1] See Edward Hoffman, *Despite All Odds*; Menachem Friedman, "Habad as Messianic Fundamentalism," pp. 328–357; Avrum Ehrlich, *Leadership in the HaBaD Movement*; Nissan Mindel, *The Philosophy of Chabad* and *Rabbi Schneur Zalman of Liadi*, vol. 1.

[2] Friedman, "Habad as Messianic Fundamentalism," p. 337.

[3] Ibid., pp. 334–337.

[4] See Ehrlich, *Leadership in the HaBaD Movement*, p. 245.

[5] Ibid., p. 247.

[6] Hoffman, *Despite All Odds*, p. 23.

[7] Ibid.; Friedman, "Habad as Messianic Fundamentalism," p. 338.

[8] These included President Calvin Coolidge and government leaders from France, Germany, and Latvia. See Hoffman, *Despite All Odds*, p. 24.

[9] Ehrlich, *Leadership in the HaBaD Movement*, pp. 267–238.

[10] Ibid., p. 265.

[11] Ibid.

[12] Ibid., pp. 272–273.

[13] Ibid., p. 281.

[14] There had previously been other Habad Rebbes in the towns of Kapotz, Reziza, Liozni, and Staroselye. See ibid., pp. 202–203, 217–223.

[15] Friedman, "Habad as Messianic Fundamentalism," p. 340.

[16] See Laurie Goodstein, "Death of Lubavitcher Leader, Rabbi Schneerson, Stuns Followers." *Lubavitch in the News*, compiled by the Lubavitch News Service, is an invaluable collection of newspaper articles that appeared following the death of Schneerson, and contains a great deal of information about the state of Habad at that time.

[17] Friedman, "Habad as Messianic Fundamentalism," p. 340.

[18] Ibid.

[19] See Ehrlich, *Leadership in the HaBaD Movement*, pp. 115–117.

[20] Friedman, "Habad as Messianic Fundamentalism," pp. 340–341.

[21] See ibid., p. 333.

[22] See, for example, Haim Hillel Ben-Sasson, "Diaspora Configuration and Jewish Occupation Patterns at the Beginning of the Middle Ages."

[23] See Solomon Schechter, "Safed in the Sixteenth Century."

[24] Gershom Scholem, *Sabbetai Sevi*, pp. 40–50.

[25] Friedman, "Habad as Messianic Fundamentalism," p. 343.

[26] Ibid., p. 337.

[27] Ibid., pp. 334–337.

[28] See Jerome R. Mintz, *Hasidic People.*

[29] The Jewish New Year.

[30] The Hasidim walked because of the religious prohibition against using other methods of transportation at these times.

[31] A minyan, consisting of ten Jewish adult males, is the minimum number of men essential for some rituals and desirable for all events of communal significance. See diaries of Kahn and Gross.

Chapter 4
Schneerson's Pre-Rebbe Life

The Problem of Sources

One of the greatest difficulties facing any account of the life of Menachem Schneerson before he became the seventh Habad Rebbe is the reverence with which his followers have come to regard him. The tendency of Habad Hasidim to provide their own "historical" accounts of the life of Schneerson and the history of the movement borders on historical revisionism. Despite the fact that the events in the public life of Schneerson occurred in the last forty-five years, and therefore were recorded in print, on television, and by other means, there are significant questions to be asked about the reliability of the movement's sources, especially concerning the early life of the leader. Forgery, outright censorship, selective omission of facts contrary to the desired presentation, and poetic exaggeration have made historical details hard to interpret by the traditions of the academy.[1]

To be fair, this selective presentation of material often appears to be without malicious intent or a premeditated desire to deceive; it comes from a sense of religious enthusiasm and willful blindness to the uncomfortable details of history. The idealization of the zaddik as a figure without fault, who can do no wrong and whose actions are not to be questioned, has also contributed to a lack of objective observation on the part of the faithful, making it difficult for them to record information without distortion.

Reliance on written and oral sources provided by Habad is therefore problematic, but to completely ignore their contribution would be equally undesirable. Stories told about Schneerson's early life—whether true, partly true, exaggerated, or blatantly false—are important contributions to his image, and provide insight into the idealized manner in which he is viewed by his followers. Perceptions of the Rebbe, originally projected by his followers through oral transmission of stories and tales, contain the material that generates his authority and the veneration felt for the zaddik. In this view, the perceptions of a leader by his followers are as important, if not more so, than the true facts of his life, and tell us as much about the community he led as about the leader himself.[2]

The stories and qualities projected onto a willing yet unassuming candidate for Rebbe, as Schneerson undoubtedly was, are indicative of the leadership expectations of the Hasidim. They also indicate to what extent the Hasidic followers would stretch the limits of truth by revising history, among other things, in order to suit their choice of leadership. This is not to say that Schneerson was not a suitable candidate, nor that he lacked the qualities necessary to become Rebbe; rather, the selective presentation of Schneerson's early life history is interesting to see, and the omissions, in particular, tell us much about the idealization of the zaddik in Habad.[3]

Early Life

Menachem Mendel Schneerson was born on April 18, 1902, the eldest of three brothers, all of whom were reported to be of unusual character.[4] Their father, Rabbi Levi Yitzhak Schneerson, held the position of rabbi in the city of Yakatsrinoslava in Ukraine, and was known as a venerable talmudic scholar and mystic. He was a devotee of the Habad philosophy and a direct descendant of the Zemakh Zedek, Rabbi Menachem Mendel of Shachna, the third Habad Rebbe and grandson of the movement's founder, Shneur Zalman, through his eldest son, Baruch Shalom. Levi Yitzhak kept in contact with the rest of the extended Schneerson family, and had been an associate and friend of the fifth Rebbe, Shalom Dov Ber.[5] It is possible that he even had a Rebbe-like status among a small group of followers, as did many of the Schneerson descendants.[6]

Menachem Mendel Schneerson's early education included intense study both in classical talmudic/halakhic works and Hasidic mysticism, as well as secular studies. Schneerson was reputedly involved in the communal affairs of his father's office throughout his upbringing, and his secular education and familiarity with the Russian language made him a useful aide in his father's public administrative work. He is said to have been an interpreter between the Jewish community and the Russian authorities on a number of occasions.[7]

Schneerson completed his secular secondary school matriculation, which was unusual for someone from his milieu, where undertaking secular studies was considered an irrelevance, let alone completing them to the point of matriculation. Throughout this time, at least according to Habad historians, Schneerson maintained a high standard in Jewish studies as well, a view that is difficult to dispute, especially given the depth and complexity of his later knowledge of traditional Jewish learning.

In 1923, Schneerson visited his cousin, the Rebbe Yosef Yitzhak, for the first time, and it is believed that this is when he met the woman who was to become his wife, Yosef Yitzhak's middle daughter, Chaya Mousia. It is uncertain whether a match between the two was contemplated;[8] stories describe the elderly Shalom Dov Ber, father of Yosef Yitzhak, mentioning a proposed match between "the son of Levi Yitzhak" and his grand-daughter,[9] but it is not certain that Menachem Mendel Schneerson was the son mentioned here. At any rate, over a year later Schneerson's mother arranged another meeting between the two, and most likely negotiated the

terms of a match. Deutsch argues that Schneerson's mother and father had condi-
tioned the betrothal of their son on a "high-stakes" dowry. He would, they stipulated,
inherit the dynastic leadership.[10] This agreement has not been definitively proven, but
it is certain that the marriage increased Schneerson's prestige in the court of Yosef
Yitzhak, and increased his chances of succeeding his father-in-law to the leadership
of the movement. For reasons unknown, it was another five years before Schneerson
was able to marry Chaya Mousia, at the Habad yeshiva in Warsaw.

The betrothal to Chaya Mousia allowed Schneerson to enter the distinguished inner
circle of Yosef Yitzhak's personal life and closest students.[11] This could be compared
to an apprenticeship under a master tradesman; he obtained first-hand information
and practical knowledge of the experiences, trials, and tribulations of a Jewish leader.
He received the treatment of a dignitary and distinction that otherwise would not have
been afforded him, and was given the opportunity to study in European universities
and take on executive functions within the movement. His very survival and escape
from war-torn Europe and permission to enter the United States can be attributed to
his status as son-in-law of Yosef Yitzhak. Schneerson himself testified to this:
"Marriage is a general matter with any private person, but with me this was the way
I entered public events. . . . this was the day that my connection with you [Yosef
Yitzhak] was formed."[12]

Schneerson had commenced a degree in marine engineering in 1928 at the
University of Berlin before he married, and soon after the wedding the couple moved
to Berlin, where he was able to resume his studies. Schneerson was also registered in
the Hildesheimer Seminary in Berlin, where he was able to pursue secular studies and
privately continue his study of religion. Yosef Yitzhak paid for Schneerson's education, but there is reason to suspect that he did not approve of Schneerson's decision
to pursue secular studies, as evident from his strong criticism of the synthesis of secular and religious subjects at the Hildesheimer Seminary. This would seem to indicate that, contrary to popular Habad belief, Schneerson *did* oppose the will of his
father-in-law in his decision to undertake secular studies. The fact that Schneerson
was economically supported by his father-in-law throughout the period of his studies
would seem to indicate, at the least, that Yosef Yitzhak trusted in Schneerson's
staunch religious convictions and recognized that these studies could further develop
his potential as a leader of the movement.

At any rate, it appears that Schneerson failed to complete his course of study at the
University of Berlin,[13] and the couple moved to Paris in 1934, where they remained
until the outbreak of war and their escape from Europe in 1941. During Schneerson's
stay in Paris, in addition to attending courses at the Sorbonne until 1938,[14] he carried
out certain duties for Yosef Yitzhak, including editing several issues of *Ha-Tamim*, the
Habad yeshiva publication. It is evident, however, that Schneerson did not lead a typical Hasidic existence in Berlin and Paris, although it appears that he remained steadfast in his religious commitment and piety despite the cultural and intellectual alternatives to which he was exposed. There are rumors suggesting that he did not wear a

skullcap at the university; some say that he wore a toupee. He dressed in modern clothing even at his wedding, wore a stylish hat, and it is not unlikely that he trimmed his beard or otherwise kept it rolled up for a substantial period of time.[15] He was known to like libraries and museums, was an avid reader of newspapers and, like his father-in-law, kept abreast of political events. He no doubt took advantage of his time in Berlin and Paris to pursue these interests.[16] All this remains hearsay, however, and was not ultimately to prove important for his succession to the position of Rebbe.

As noted, Schneerson's upbringing differed remarkably from that of other Hasidic Rebbes. Unlike his predecessors, who had been raised in the closed and very traditional communities of Eastern Europe,[17] Schneerson pursued his religious studies while interacting with the modern world. This gave him a unique perspective from which to launch the most successful outreach program in the history of Habad, if not of Judaism generally.

The charges that Schneerson was excessively influenced by modernity, brought against him later by other Hasidic Rebbes,[18] appear not to have been a major consideration preventing his election to office. While his education was the cause of much contention and suspicion, especially among the older followers of Yosef Yitzhak, it was also considered by many to be the asset that attracted attention to him and proved to his followers his ability to "learn and not be injured."[19] It came to be believed in Habad circles that for the leader of the generation, knowledge of the secular world could only benefit his service of God.[20] Schneerson was to take advantage of new advances in technology to literally spread the teachings of Habad around the world,[21] an act seen by him as a fulfillment of the prophetic vision of the Ba'al Shem Tov.[22] The results he obtained, as we shall see, spoke for themselves.

The United States

Menachem Schneerson and his wife arrived in New York on June 23, 1941, and joined a large immigrant community in New York. Upon his arrival in the United States, Schneerson did not immediately begin to work for his father-in-law; instead, with his background in engineering, he found employment at the New York Navy Yard. Habad sources claim that the work involved matters of national security, but this is unlikely; Deutsch asserts convincingly that Schneerson's lack of American citizenship at the time makes it improbable that he worked in a security-sensitive position. The absence of Schneerson's work-related records at Social Security and the National Archives would seem to support this.

Whatever the case, from 1943 Schneerson was given charge of several aspects of the activities of Habad in America, but kept a low public profile within the movement. His work, until the death of Yosef Yitzhak, was purely executive and administrative, and not generally considered political. Indeed, the organizations he headed were not important to the running of Habad or its major activities at the time. He was appointed head of the Centre [*sic*] for Educational Affairs, having been given official control by Yosef Yitzhak of three fledgling organizations, all aimed at public education and outreach.[23] He became the director of the official educational wing of the movement, called Merkaz Le-Inyanei Chinuch,[24] which was responsible for the establishment of schools (as distinct from yeshivot) and for the movement's education program; and he oversaw the movement's publishing houses, Kehot and Otzar ha-Hasidim–Lubavitch,[25] and its social service arm, Mahane Yisrael.[26]

These organizations, under the ultimate control of Yosef Yitzhak, were in their infancy and entailed neither a large amount of responsibility nor substantial expenditure, especially given the size of the movement at the time. The more important organizations within Habad, including the yeshiva, AGUCH, the main Habad umbrella organization, which predated Yosef Yitzhak's arrival in America, and responsibility for fundraising, were under the management of another of Yosef Yitzhak's sons-in-law, and his most probable successor as Rebbe, Shemaryahu Gourary. Gourary's administrative duties were more significant than Schneerson's, and he was considered to be both able and effective in them, but these facts did little to help him secure the office of Rebbe on the death of Yosef Yitzhak.[27] The "products" of these different types of organizations (Gourary's ideological and practical, Schneerson's physical and quantifiable) no doubt contributed to the perception among followers that Schneerson was the more effective administrator. The results of his efforts were more immediately visible, in the form of publications or statistics, whereas the successes of Gourary were less easy to measure. Whatever the bearing of these factors on the succession, it is certainly true that before the death of Yosef Yitzhak, Schneerson expanded the comparatively minor institutions he administered. These were not only to become the backbone of his rise to power and consolidation of leadership over Habad, but also embodied his vision for the future of the movement.

Scheerson's control of the educational arm of Habad from 1943 to 1950 did not at the time seem to be a source of political strength, but it made him an authority figure among the youth of the movement. He encouraged them to take an active role in its administration and activities, and as they grew older, they became the primary activists in the Habad yeshiva system and the community as a whole. The support these men gave Schneerson was to be instrumental in his appointment as Rebbe, and his influence during the formative years of many of the later leaders of the movement helped to further secure his position.

Schneerson also took on a number of other, more social and spiritual roles during the lifetime of Yosef Yitzhak, which increased his standing in the community. He frequently presided at Hasidic gatherings (known as *Farbrengen*), the center of the community's social and spiritual life; he acted as a sympathizer and confidant, writing many letters of comfort and instruction to Hasidim around the world, telling them how to conduct themselves.[28] He often acted as a conduit between Yosef Yitzhak and his Hasidim; when they did not receive a response to a letter they had written him, they would write Schneerson to find out why, or to seek his assistance. This endeared him to many of his father-in-law's followers, and did not cease with the death of

Yosef Yitzhak. As we shall see, Schneerson's actions after the death of his father-in-law also played a significant part in his eventual selection as the new Rebbe.

When Yosef Yitzhak died, Menachem Mendel Schneerson was one of several men in the best position to take over as Habad Rebbe. As we shall see, his administrative experience, family connections, personality, and absence from the political aspects of the movement under Yosef Yitzhak all contributed to his elevation to the status of Rebbe. Throughout his life, Schneerson emulated the ideological drive of his predecessor in attempting to unify Jews across the globe behind a return to religious observance. Like his father-in-law before him, Schneerson felt that education was the best means by which this could be brought about. He presented himself as perpetuating the mission and goals set for the movement by Yosef Yitzhak, and as we shall see, he attributed any personal success on his part to the inspiration and direct guidance of the deceased Rebbe. The implantation of Habad on American soil had begun under Yosef Yitzhak, but Schneerson would make the movement one of the most vocal and prominent groups on the American religious scene.

---

[1] Censorship and other devices impeding the free flow of information are dominant in many communities that desire harmony and homogeneity and the Habad movement is no exception. The present work makes frequent reference to censorship of information concerning the movement's development, ideology, and leadership. Enthusiastic Hasidim often engage unintentionally in censorship, historical revisionism, and other modes of restricting information. Perhaps they do so in an attempt to find easy solutions to potential conflicts resulting from the cognitive dissonance that might arise from contradictions or apparent blemishes in the movement's history. Examples range from the perpetration of violent acts to the omission of important information in the official literature, particularly concerning conflicts in the movement. A prime example of such an act appears in *Ha-Yom Yom,* trans. by Y. M. Kagan as *From Day to Day.* Its preface on the genealogy of the movement's leaders and their offspring completely omits the other children and grandchild of Yosef Yitzhak as offspring and possible successional candidates because they were embroiled in a fight with the Habad mainstream over Schneerson's succession. It is appropriate to note a conversation with Professor Aviezer Ravitzky (February 1996), who advised that all documents from a community with the above-mentioned disposition, even documents believed to be original and unblemished, must be viewed with suspicion, as if they had in some way been forged or altered to further the dominant view. Such an assumption would lead one to deduce probable events from the conspicuous absence of information that would have otherwise been freely available. This kind of censorship is particularly serious because it also affects free access to Habad's large Hasidic library (see Chapter 16), where the selectivity of information open to the general public is controlled. There have been incidents of forgeries emerging from the library's archives, and one must be wary of this when discussing the movement. Additionally, the fear among some scholars of being blackballed by the growing influence of the Habad community and denied access to literature or archives, or of encountering social tension in the often tight-knit Jewish community, is a deterrent to presenting views that conflict with mainstream Habad beliefs. Often scholars carefully word sentences to avoid open conflict. Hence, careful reading of scholarly

works is also appropriate. In addition, the basic Habad works that discuss the election of Schneerson make remarkably few references to the other contenders. For example, *Yemei Be-Reishis*, Laufer's *Yemei Melech*, and Schneerson's *Ha-Yom Yom* all fail to include in the family tree any mention of the daughters of Yosef Yitzhak, Shemaryahu Gourary, and Barry Gourary. This may have been motivated by a desire to exclude any idea that there were contenders to leadership other than Schneerson.

[2] See Elie Wiesel, *Souls of Fire*, pp. 16–18.

[3] See Shaul S. Deutsch, *Larger Than Life*, vol. 1, pp. 1–2.

[4] Little had been published about these two individuals, due to Habad censorship, until Deutsch's works appeared in 1995 and 1997. See *Larger Than Life*, vol. 2, pp. 125–145. Deutsch describes how Schneerson's brother, Dov Ber, spent his years in an institution for the mentally disabled near his hometown and was eventually murdered by Nazi collaborators. Yisrael Aryeh Leib spent time in Lubavitch circles in Yosef Yitzhak's court but was influenced by Zionist and, later, socialist and Communist ideas. He was considered brilliant and was especially interested in the sciences. According to Zvi Hakarvi, as quoted by Deutsch (*Larger Than Life*, vol. 1, pp. 101–103, and vol. 2, p. 118), he dissented from mainstream socialism and became a Trotskyite. Despite the fact that he abandoned Orthodoxy, he lived with Schneerson for some time in Berlin but eventually was forced to flee Eastern Europe, using the name Mark Gourary. He lived in Israel for a while, failing in a number of attempts at small business. He moved to Liverpool to pursue doctoral studies in mathematics/physics at Liverpool University but died in 1951 before he completed them. His wife died in 1996 in London. He left offspring who presently live in Israel.

[5] See Laufer, *Yemei Melech*, vol. 1, p. 161, n. 2. quoting S. Y. Yitzchaki. There are accounts of communications between Levi Yitzhak and Shalom Dov Ber. Shalom Dov Ber sent congratulations to Levi Yitzhak on Schneerson's birth, and there are also accounts of a visit by Shalom Dov Ber to their home when Schneerson was three years old, possibly to discuss a betrothal. This is not improbable, considering that the Rebbes married young, fourteen having been the average age of marriage for previous Habad Rebbes.

[6] It is not unlikely that Levi Yitzhak had a following of sorts and was to a lesser degree considered a Hasidic Rebbe. Schneerson sometimes described his father as a significant player in the Habad movement and its leader in the Soviet Union after Yosef Yitzhak left. Some say that he counted Levi Yitzhak as one in the line of Habad Rebbes. There are a few references to Levi Yitzhak with the title of "Rebbe"; for example, it is "good that she marries the seed of Rebbe Levi Yitzhak" (see Laufer, *Yemei Melech*, vol. 1, p. 161, n. 2, quoting Shalom Dov Ber). While this term could also indicate the post of rabbi of a town, the argument that Levi Yitzhak saw himself as a kind of Rebbe is not without merit. Also see *Larger Than Life*, vol. 1, pp. 15–48, for a discussion of Schneerson's immediate family history.

[7] See Schneerson, *Likkutei Sichot*, vol. 3, pp. 565–566. Schneerson in later life said of himself that the years he spent assisting his father and enduring the scorn of government officials had given him insight into political intrigue, the art of negotiation and public relations, responsibility, and the mentality of the Russian authorities.

[8] See Avrum Ehrlich, *Leadership in the HaBaD Movement*, p. 297, and n. 9, pp. 305–306, for more details.

[9] A few sources indicate that Shalom Dov Ber initiated contact with "the son of Levi Yitzhak" and influenced Yosef Yitzhak regarding betrothals for his (Yosef Yitzhak's) daughters. See Rivkin, *Ashkavta de-Rebbe*. Shemarhayu Gourary was clearly endorsed as a suitable match

for Chana, Yosef Yitzhak's eldest daughter. Schneerson's marriage is believed to have been similarly endorsed by Shalom Dov Ber. A story confirming this describes how Yosef Yitzhak sent a letter to the gravesite of his father, following Schneerson and Chaya Mousia's wedding, "informing" him that his will had been carried out. See also N. Yochanan, *Yiddishe Heim* (5724), p. 5.

[10] See *Larger Than Life* 1, pp. 161–164.

[11] Ehrlich, *Leadership in the HaBaD Movement*, p. 11.

[12] Ibid., p. 318, n. 1.

[13] See *Larger Than Life*, vol 2, p. 91.

[14] No evidence has been found, however, that Schneerson completed his studies at the Sorbonne. The Sorbonne files only register graduates. An exhaustive search by the author found no mention of Schneerson.

[15] The trimming of one's beard is not acceptable according to contemporary Hasidic standards, based on Leviticus 19:27, "You shall not round off the side-growth on your head, nor destroy the side-growth of your beard." For an outline of laws and customs regarding this, see Moshe Wiener, *Hadros Ponim-Zokon*. However, it may have been more tolerated in Europe. Pictures from the Lubavitch yeshiva in Poland and in the United States in the 1940s show a number of students who were shaved, including prominent Hasidim and Habad activists such as Nissan Mindel, Deutsch, and Menachem Horenshtein. From a study of pictures of Schneerson over the years, it would appear that he too had trimmed his beard, or kept it neatly rolled up, for at least some time, perhaps during the war. Schneerson's critics among opposing Hasidic sects point to his secularism and his trimmed beard as an indication of his unsuitability to be a Rebbe. Although trimming one's beard might appear to be a trivial point, for Habad Hasidim the Rebbe's alleged perfection and his status as a role model make the trimming issue a matter of extreme significance, and therefore they vigorously deny that he did so.

[16] See Laufer, *Yemei Melech*, vol. 1, p. 373. These points bother Hasidic sensibilities and are vigorously denied. For example, a story in Laufer, *Yemei Melech,* recounts that Schneerson was seen reading a newspaper in Paris (an act of un-Hasidic behavior), but Hasidim maintain that he was hiding a kabbalistic work under it.

[17] Menachem Friedman, "Habad as Messianic Fundamentalism," pp. 341–342.

[18] Jerome R. Mintz, *Hasidic People*, pp. 22, 51–59.

[19] Talmud Bavli: Hagigah 14b.

[20] Ehrlich, *Leadership in the HaBaD Movement*, p. 320, n. 13.

[21] Schneerson used technology extensively. When he gave speeches, for example, Habad centers around the world telephoned the Habad headquarters in Crown Heights, New York, and were connected to listen to them live. These were called "hookups." Later, there were live satellite television connections across the world for major events taking place at the headquarters. This was in addition to the use of large billboards and advertisements in newspapers worldwide, including the infamous advertisements in the *New York Times* focusing on Schneerson's announcements regarding the coming of the Messiah. See the *New York Times*, April 11, 1995, p. B5, for an example.

[22] Schneerson's words to this effect have often been quoted. See, for example, "The Fountains Have Been Disseminated," where he is said to have proclaimed, "The time for the dissemination of the fountains [of *Chassidus*] to the far reaches (as well as the spiritual achievements during this time) which commenced on Yud Tes Kislev 192 years ago, has finally reached the 'cut off' period, and been completed at last. Therefore we are ready for the real-

ization of the promise that when the fountain [of *Chassidus*] will be disseminated to the farthest reaches, the Master, King Moshiach, will come."

[23] These organizations essentially existed in name only when handed to Schneerson; he built them into the administrative and organizational forces they were to become during his leadership of Habad.

[24] Center for Educational Issues

[25] *Ha-Yom Yom* was Schneerson's first publication in 1943 in his capacity as head of Kehot and Merkaz.

[26] See *Ha-Yom Yom*, 1943–1996.

[27] See Ehrlich, *Leadership in the HaBaD Movement*, pp. 344–345.

[28] Ibid., pp. 373–375.

Chapter 5
Schneerson's Succession

On January 28, 1950,[1] Rabbi Yosef Yitzhak Schneerson, the sixth Habad Rebbe, died. His death came at a crucial time in the rebuilding of Judaism, and of Hasidism in particular, after the dislocations of the preceding half-century. The events of the Holocaust and the systematic destruction of Judaism under Communist rule in Eastern Europe had brought with them many questions concerning the future of Habad and its policy of expansion and outreach.

In the decade before his death, Yosef Yitzhak had established his control over the American Habad community. When he arrived in America in 1940, he came, like many thousand others, as a refugee, with only a skeletal network of contacts and a fledgling support network to assist him in the process of rebuilding. He arrived in a wheelchair, a physically frail man, but was preceded by a reputation for bravery and feats of courage earned during his fight against the enemies of Judaism in Europe.[2] Coming from the Old World, he had great appeal for American Jews, many of whom desired to feel a sense of continuity with the illustrious East European Hasidic past. Because of his status as Rebbe, his authority was unquestioned in America, and many of the organizations, such as AGUCH, that were to be found in America before his arrival, voluntarily offered him directing control over them.[3] He had used this authority and trust to appoint many of his close aides, especially those who had accompanied him to the United States, to positions of prominence in Habad. This applied also to his relatives, and especially his sons-in-law, Shemaryahu Gourary and Menachem Mendel Schneerson.

The success of Yosef Yitzhak in consolidating Habad worldwide was based largely on his administrative skill, and his talent for appointing men of ability where they might best serve the movement. Unlike many of his learned followers, who had studied in the Habad yeshivot, he was not renowned as a scholar or a teacher, although none denied his knowledge of Hasidism. In America, he did not have a power base of large numbers of loyal Hasidim as he might have had in pre-Communist Russia, and his power base in Eastern Europe had been strongly propped up by overseas charities, especially through financial support from the United States.

Largely by means of correspondence, Yosef Yitzhak was able, in his ten years in America, to unite the scattered Habad communities throughout the world that had come into existence unintentionally as a result of migration to escape oppression, but also intentionally because of the assignment of Habad rabbis and emissaries to communities worldwide. These circumstances gradually led to the establishment of a far-flung Habad Diaspora in Europe and America, with significant communities in Paris, Montreal, New York, and Israel.[4] Communities in London, Australia, South America, South Africa, and North Africa began to consolidate during the decade Yosef Yitzhak spent in America, and Habad Hasidim had also remained in the Soviet Union. All of these Hasidim slowly associated themselves with the reigning Habad Rebbe in New York, and began to look to him for guidance and advice.[5]

As the larger Diaspora communities turned to Yosef Yitzhak for leadership, so too did the smaller communities. They turned to him because they had Hasidic roots, he was the sole surviving Habad Rebbe, and he had a reputation for initiative in rebuilding Judaism and defending it against opposition and oppression. He saw Habad's role in the new, postwar world as one of rehabilitating Hasidism,[6] and to that end he had focused on Jewish education around the United States and in areas where he had already established a foothold. By the time of his death, some of the programs he had established were beginning to bear fruit, while many others were in their planning stages. But the death of the Rebbe temporarily halted this expansionist rehabilitation program. The year 1950–51 was characterized by doubt and questions about the future of the movement. While Yosef Yitzhak had succeeded in establishing his Hasidic authority, it was not certain what would happen to the movement and its leadership after his death.

There had been no apparent political jockeying for succession before Yosef Yitzhak's death, but the state of the movement seemed to indicate a need for continued centralized leadership. A centralized leader could build on the sense of unity, pride, and dedication to Habad fostered by Yosef Yitzhak, and this was crucial to the rehabilitation of the Habad communities, let alone the reconstruction of world Jewry that the movement had established as its goal. Overseas pressures may have a vital influence in prompting the Habad community in the United States to appoint a successor, but who was chosen as the new leader was probably less important to the continuity of Habad than the need for a leader be chosen.

During the period of mourning, Schneerson made himself useful to Habad. He wrote letters of explanation and comfort to many inquirers, who had failed to get a response from Yosef Yitzhak. In addition to offering advice on how the Hasidim could perpetuate the memory and commemorate the life of Yosef Yitzhak, these letters frequently contained instruction of a personal nature: what people should study, how they should pray, the goals they should set for the coming year, and the personal duties they should attend to.[7] Such advice was offered only in Schneerson's capacity as a concerned friend, and not as a spiritual instruction or advice from a Rebbe. Gradually, as letters requesting guidance continued to arrive, and indeed increased in number, his responses often took on a more spiritual nature, offering blessings and advice in religious matters.[8] His letters were so detailed that the recipients frequently felt a more personal level of consideration and connection, increasing their emotional attachment to Schneerson. The level of detail also caused some to speculate about Schneerson's seemingly mystical understanding and apprehension of events of which the recipient was unaware.

He also offered personalized instruction to many, especially the yeshiva students, giving direction on what to study, when, where, and for how long. This gave many of the students a sense of purpose and focus, and accounts of the time recall the charged atmosphere in the study hall, due largely to Schneerson's instruction and presence.[9]

Needless to say, his new role as solace-giver to the movement attracted much personal attention to him from the Habad community, and raised his profile as a caring, concerned leader. Indeed, within a short time, Schneerson had regular visiting hours during which Hasidim could consult him personally for advice, which many came to identify as *yehidut*, the rite of communication reserved between Rebbe and Hasid, despite the fact that he was not a Rebbe. Within eight months, there were so many people requesting Schneerson's time that a secretary was needed to coordinate the visits.[10]

Schneerson was concerned also with the collection and preservation of Yosef Yitzhak's publications, and the collating of writings for print, at a time when the movement felt the greatest need to preserve contact with him. Within a week of the Rebbe's death, Schneerson had printed a collection of Yosef Yitzhak's work, with more in planning.[11] His activities with Kehot, the Habad publishing arm, placed him well for this task, and he developed an intimate familiarity not only with the works of Yosef Yitzhak, but also with the Habad archives. In this way he was able to provide a much-needed service to preserve the customs and history of the movement and the lives of its Rebbes, making him a force for continuity with Habad's history and traditions. He also knew a wealth of stories concerning the Habad Rebbes, and had attended closely to the casual discourses of Yosef Yitzhak,[12] making him more attractive than if he merely had book knowledge of Habad philosophy. His familiarity with Habad customs and trivia, the mannerisms and personal details of the lives of the Rebbes, and songs and cultural traditions of the movement also assisted his rise to prominence.

Most important for many was the speed with which Schneerson initiated actions to cope with the loss of the Rebbe, and to continue the programs and goals he had established. His administrative skill became evident to the community at large at this time; he had been a successful administrator and organizer before, but few had heard of him, securing him a reputation as something of a "quiet achiever." Schneerson was the only person who was really doing anything to ensure the survival and continuity of the movement. He took on a greater role in the general administration of the movement, and delegated responsibility for many of the purely administrative elements of his former posts to others, while overseeing their operations and providing direction personally. This practice was to serve him well throughout his life, and was especially important in the running of Habad during his years of leadership. He was also prepared to leave these greater responsibilities if they prevented him from carrying out the commission given him by his Rebbe,[13] which in the eyes of many demonstrated his commitment to the goals of Yosef Yitzhak.

The dedication of Schneerson to his father-in-law and Rebbe was one of the main reasons for his eventual election to succeed Yosef Yitzhak. During the year after Yosef Yitzhak's death, Schneerson was frequently overcome with extreme emotion in public, even in mid-speech, on occasions that were described as dramatic, tense, and awe-inspiring. This was more so because of his former reticence to be a public figure. The outward expression of grief encouraged many Habad Hasidim to believe that Schneerson not only shared their own grief, but understood their suffering better than anyone. And if he could look ahead and anticipate a future for the movement, so too could Hasidim everywhere.

In everything Schneerson did after the death of Yosef Yitzhak, he was careful to acknowledge the primacy of the Rebbe's instructions and the mission he had laid out for Habad.[14] Advice and directions were given not as personal instruction from Schneerson, but as communication of the will of Yosef Yitzhak. Indeed, Schneerson was extremely reluctant at first to even contemplate succeeding his father-in-law as Rebbe of Habad, and considered that Yosef Yitzhak was still in contact with the movement, and even that he might yet return from the dead.[15] This was made more insistent by the messianic expectations of imminent cosmic redemption fostered during Yosef Yitzhak's lifetime. Schneerson formulated a teaching that the central role in this redemption would be played by Yosef Yitzhak, an idea that would play a major part in the messianism that emerged as one of the motivating factors for Habad throughout Schneerson's leadership. The successful outcomes of the advice given by Schneerson were attributed by him to Yosef Yitzhak, and this was to continue until the time of his own death. Indeed, on his gravestone is inscribed: ". . . here lies Menachem Mendel Schneerson, substitute for Yosef Yitzhak Schneerson."[16] He never came to see himself as living up to the role of Rebbe, and always referred to his own Rebbe as the source of his authority.

By this means, Schneerson was able to retain the alliance and backing of his father-in-law's Hasidim, who might not have given their support to his succession as Rebbe. Rather than becoming a *Rebbe far de kinder*, a "Rebbe for the children"(the next generation of Habad followers), he was accepted by the old generation as a leader of the movement, remaining true to the mission of his own Rebbe throughout his life.[17] In this manner, he was also able to appear as non-innovative, merely perpetuating the movement and its traditions as they had been handed down to him. Support for Schneerson therefore came to be regarded as support for Yosef Yitzhak, and not necessarily for a new Rebbe, for the younger leader was merely carrying out the unfulfilled mission of his own teacher.

Within ten months, Schneerson was attracting larger crowds to Habad headquarters in Crown Heights than had been seen in many years. Although still officially refusing to accept the role of Rebbe, he had changed his dress from the modern style he had favored to a much more traditional long black coat and East European rabbinic garb. He came more frequently to be referred to as *Admur*, an acronym for *Adoneinu Moreinu ve-Rabeinu*, "Our Master, our Teacher, and our Rabbi," a term traditionally used only in reference to Hasidic Rebbes.[18] He continued to answer all questions put to him, and gave religious instruction, some of which was beginning to be published. Throughout the Habad Diaspora, many called on him to accept the position in order to "arrange all matters of Habad institutions and to put them in order."[19] These requests expressed not only a growing discontent at the lack of leadership in the movement, but confidence in Schneerson's ability to put things right and not permit Yosef Yitzhak's work to go to waste. Many activists publicized the suitability and appropriateness of Schneerson's succession, and conducted a private campaign to further his cause throughout the global Habad community. This included the transcription from memory and publication of his discourses,[20] which were sent at the expense of individual Hasidim to Habad communities throughout the world.

Such support paid off, and on January 29, 1951, the day after the first anniversary of his father-in-law's death, Schneerson officially accepted the leadership of the movement and delivered his first Hasidic discourse. He began this address in a manner atypical of a Rebbe, and throughout questioned the validity of his election and his lack of qualifications for the office. He attributed his appointment to the low standards of the generation and the imminence of the messianic era.[21] His apparent humility only served to bolster the support for him, and many came to his defense against such needless self-criticism.

News of Schneerson's appointment was communicated to Habad Hasidim worldwide, and letters informing them of events and encouraging support for the new Rebbe were dispatched to Diaspora communities. The appointment was even advertised and reported in Jewish newspapers in New York.

> [F]or the first time in the "heathen" history of American Jewry, a bona fide hasidic divine donned the "tzaddik" purple in dramatic coronation rites which seemed possible only in the Polish-Ukraine, where hasidism was born. Youthful Menachem Mendel Schneerson, heir apparent to the old-world dynasty of "Habad," humbly took his ecclesiastical vows and, with tears which he tried hard to restrain, agreed to become hasidic oracle to half a million devotees. . . . only the inner circle—the hasidic elite—knew of his inevitable succession.[22]

The succession secure, it now remained for Rabbi Menachem Mendel Schneerson, the seventh Habad Rebbe, to justify the faith shown by the Habad Hasidim, and assume the full power and authority of his post. This he would do through a process of consolidation and outreach over the next forty-five years.

---

[1] In the Hebrew calendar, 10 Shvat 5710.

[2] See *Sefer Ha-Toldos*; Avrum Ehrlich, *Leadership in the HaBaD Movement*, pp. 266–267.

[3] Ibid., p. 278.

[4] Menachem Friedman, "Habad as Messianic Fundamentalism, p. 339; Ehrlich, *Leadership in the HaBaD Movement*, p. 267.

[5] Ehrlich, *Leadership in the HaBaD Movement*, p. 268.

[6] Friedman, "Habad as Messianic Fundamentalism," p. 340.

[7] Ehrlich, *Leadership in the HaBaD Movement*, pp. 373–375.

[8] Ibid., pp. 375–376.

[9] See Kahn diary.

[10] Ehrlich, *Leadership in the HaBaD Movement*, pp. 382–384.

[11] Ibid., p. 384.

[12] Ibid.

[13] See ibid., pp. 370–371, for details.

[14] See Chapter 19 for more detail.

[15] Ehrlich, *Leadership in the HaBaD Movement*, p. 374; Friedman, "Habad as Messianic Fundamentalism," p. 343.

[16] Ehrlich, *Leadership in the HaBaD Movement*, p. 382.

[17] Ibid., pp. 385–386.

[18] Ibid., p. 380.

[19] Mordecai M. Laufer, *Yemei Melech* vol. 3, p. 1210.

[20] Published as *Likkutei Sichot* (26 vols.) (Brooklyn, 1967–88), trans. J. I. Schochet; *Likkutei Sichot* (Brooklyn, 1980–87); and also trans. Jonathan Sacks, *Torah Studies* (London, 1986).

[21] Ehrlich, *Leadership in the HaBaD Movement*, p. 378.

[22] See Yosef. Y. Grynberg, *Yemei Be-Reishis*, p. 400, quoting an article by Charles Raddok in the *Jewish Forum*.

Part Two
Consolidation

Chapter 6
Transitional Consolidation

Authority by Virtue of Office as Rebbe

Menachem Schneerson had been elected as the official successor of Habad Hasidism, but did not immediately inherit all the authority that his predecessor had possessed. His position was constricted by internal squabbles over the leadership,[1] the larger-than-life reputation of his predecessor as a universal Jewish leader, hero and zaddik, and the fact that he was relatively little known within the movement. It was evident, even to his supporters, that he would have to prove himself, despite the demonstrated ability that had led to his election in the first place. However, with his election, Schneerson did inherit many of the paraphernalia of Rebbehood and hence enjoyed authoritative standing that would have been hard to come by except through election. The symbolism, popularity, and attention awarded him as the tangible representation of Habad leadership to the outside world were tools that would help Schneerson to create real and genuine acceptance of his own authority beyond the call of his office. The perception of authority, the ritual of eminence, and the elevation of Schneerson by sheer virtue of his office had a significant contributory effect on the real consolidation of his personal authority.

As incumbent Rebbe, Schneerson had inherited the good reputation that the Habad movement had built in the United States by the merits of his predecessors and particularly by virtue of Yosef Yitzhak's heroic stature and reputation in the world Jewish community. Additionally, he was perceived by the strictures of Habad ideology as the sole mouthpiece and licensee for the interpretation of Habad philosophy, with which he already had an intimate familiarity. He was therefore able, and indeed required, to interpret the traditional teachings of Habad for the new generation of Hasidim. As the Rebbe, he must principally be seen as a paragon of virtue, virtually infallible, a reputation that Schneerson had already begun to develop during the year preceding his election through the assurance and perceptiveness of the advice he gave to those who had asked for it.

As the Habad Rebbe, his work would primarily be administratively oriented; hence, he would have to be informed of everything that happened in the movement, and would need to keep track of developments in projects already commenced during the reign of Yosef Yitzhak. Here his demonstrated administrative abilities and skill at delegation would come to the fore. As Rebbe, he would also have veto authority at all times on projects undertaken by the movement as a whole, and further, would be expected to initiate his own programs to carry out the mission assigned to Habad by Yosef Yitzhak. He was also expected to provide fresh direction and instruction for the entire movement as need arose. In addition to the ideological guidance he was required to give as Rebbe, Schneerson was also legally registered as the controlling authority in many of the movement's institutions, signifying that his control of the movement was, at least potentially, complete.

Of course, the level of his involvement in the day-to-day running of Habad was entirely at his discretion. Were he to opt not to involve himself in menial bureaucratic or administrative affairs, he was certainly free to do so. It was certainly his prerogative as Rebbe to define the composition of his workload (many Hasidic Rebbes before him had served primarily as administrative guides to their students; others provided ideological or theological focus; and many, especially in Habad, fulfilled both functions). Schneerson chose to take a completely "hands-on" approach to the running of Habad. Thus his official and legal authority was soon translated into active authority over its institutions, schools, publishing companies, and outreach efforts of the movement. With the success of these institutions, he would then develop his personal authority beyond that of his inherited office.

The authority inherent in the office of Rebbe is similar in many instances to the monarchical notion of "authority by divine right."[2] History has shown that the authority inherent in the office of monarch is not sufficient to maintain the holder of that office indefinitely, but it is sufficient to maintain authority through a transitional period until the incumbent proves worthy (or unworthy) of the office. During his early years as Rebbe, Schneerson's authority was effectively "on credit." While he had demonstrated the potential to effectively replace his father-in-law as leader of the movement, and indeed had been elected over his brother-in-law Shemaryahu Gourary based on his performance under the guidance of Yosef Yitzhak, Schneerson would have to rely largely on the fame of his predecessors and the movement's past achievements until he could demonstrate his own fitness for office.

The authority inherent in the office of Rebbe also meant that many would turn to Schneerson as the official representative of Habad. All queries, questions, and requests would be addressed by the non-Habad world to the office of the official Rebbe. Hence, members of the Ari-affiliated synagogues,[3] communal rabbis of Habad affiliation, community activists, American and Israeli politicians, reporters, and the merely curious turned to Schneerson as the official head of the movement. This was by virtue of his office, and had no relationship to his personality, individuality, or position in the internal workings of the movement.[4] In this respect, from the moment of his inception, Schneerson commanded a large degree of authority. Were he to be a worthwhile recipient of this authority, he would have a platform to express himself and impress his audience. Recognition of authority from outside the movement would in turn attract further veneration from within the community, for his own following would draw pride from the respect given their Rebbe.

If Schneerson had functioned casually, solely reliant on the prestige of his position, and had not developed the qualities and authority of leadership in his own right, he might still have won the respect of his community, but would have been a leader of mediocre quality and of little standing in the broader society. He might even have grown into the role by the operation of natural forces, a model of leadership common in other Hasidic dynasties, whose leadership is internally solid but relatively unknown outside the confines of the community. Schneerson, however, managed to use his position to advance not only his own prestige, but the image of the Habad movement in the broader community. The people with whom he met and talked were generally impressed by him and came away with a favorable impression, which further added to his prestige.

The public perception of Schneerson was favorable, and he would soon prove himself as a leader in his own right, establishing a real influence and affecting real change in the institutions of Habad. He would reinterpret Habad perceptions and teachings for the modern world, and thereby effect change in the Hasidic approach to outreach. Schneerson's secular education and charisma made him popular with many modernists, who saw the necessity for Habad to reconcile with the modern world and embrace its technology if it was to survive as a living, vital force in the life of the Jewish community. This would further affect the influence and reputation of Habad in the broader Jewish community, beyond the limits of those committed to the movement.

Most important for the successful transfer of authority as Rebbe from Yosef Yitzhak to Schneerson was the fact that people were amenable to Schneerson and his teachings. At least initially, his ability as an individual to bring people to the movement was limited, but as a Hasidic Rebbe, ordained in a continual tradition of generations, he represented the entire Habad movement.

The respect for Schneerson within Habad, evident before the death of his father-in-law, had contributed to his election. It would now no longer remain dormant but could be channelled through the machinery of the movement to not only enhance his reputation but direct attention to Habad. The perception that Schneerson headed an ideological strain within Judaism allowed people to join its ranks, to enlist, to unite with a movement that had transgenerational legitimacy. That the movement was in fact too small to be taken seriously as an influence on the broader Jewish community, let alone on world affairs, was not an issue. The importance of Habad and its mission of universal outreach were perceived by those within the movement, and especially by its new leader, to be real, and were to chart a strong course of action and means of consolidation for the new Rebbe.

The new occupant of the office of Rebbe, although his power and influence were more imaginary than real, was perceived to be the legitimate heir to a long and prestigious tradition. With this appointment to a position of eminence that was largely imaginary (at least outside Habad), Schneerson was able in time to draw more people to recognize the nature of the office, and even to increase its esteem. The continuity that he represented, combined with the charisma of his personality, served as a point of focus for the hopes and expectations of many within the Jewish community. Soul-searching students, those traumatized by the Holocaust, others searching for old-time Hasidic values in the modern world, and a variety of people from all walks of life and social and economic backgrounds were to find their identity in the Habad Rebbe and the movement he headed. In his formal capacity as Rebbe, Schneerson was a more effective leader than he had been before his appointment, but he was to use his gifts to become a more effective leader still.

Hasidic Discourses: Consolidation of Public Life

As part of the process of his ordination as Rebbe, Schneerson delivered a Hasidic discourse, and this was to be one of his primary duties from the time of his election until ill health prevented extensive public speaking in the last years of his life. In his role as Rebbe, Schneerson was entitled and expected to give informal Habad philosophic discourses called *sichot*, and formal expositions of ideology and theology called *ma'amarot*. Like the Rebbes before him, he had the sole right to interpret Hasidic teachings for his followers, and thus was expected to perpetuate the Habad philosophy and extend its interpretation and application to meet modern challenges. This authority of interpretation was a powerful and attractive factor for many Habad adherents, especially those attracted to the movement for philosophical reasons, including many young students. They wanted to hear the legitimate and authoritative interpretation of Hasidism, as given by someone authorized by tradition to do so, and Schneerson's intellect and evident skill at discussing complicated philosophy and theology in an easily understood manner gained him a devoted following. Such adherents, full of youthful idealism and eager to fulfil the Habad Hasidic ideals of outreach and missionary activity, were naturally attracted to the synagogue at central headquarters to hear Schneerson speak.

Over time, Schneerson's Hasidim would focus on him and observe his every movement, in accordance with his role as zaddik and exemplar to his followers.[5] This attention was initially more due to his position of centrality in the rite of the discourse than to any real interest in his mannerisms or speech, but it changed over the course of time as Schneerson developed a personal reputation. Eventually, he was accorded a level of respect traditionally reserved for royalty. When he entered or exited a room, a human corridor would open for him to pass through. He would receive distinguished guests who deferred to him with the highest formality and the greatest respect, making his regular audiences all the more intimidating and awe-inspiring for the average follower. Hasidim preceded an audience with him by ritual immersion and a letter of introduction, in addition to a long wait outside his office, often deep into the night. The paraphernalia of regality taken on with the office of Rebbe served, in essence, to project the image of a truly regal person. The very right to sit in the place of honor and represent the heritage of Habad was useful in the consolidation of Schneerson's assumption of office, and was beneficial for the prestige it conveyed.

However, were it not for Schneerson's ability to maintain the imagery in his one-on-one encounters with people or in his public discourses, this perception of regality and mystique would quite probably have dissipated in time. If Schneerson had had little to say in his Hasidic discourses, and had done nothing to innovate or inspire, then his leadership might not have survived, or at the very least would not have succeeded as it did. Indeed, the opposite is true. His discourses expressed his personality, worldview, and scholarship. By his appointment as Rebbe, Schneerson was given a platform to openly express his innovative ideas and demonstrate his knowledge of Hasidic theology and practice. People were attracted by the charisma so evident from his position on the raised platforms from which he spoke. Through his discussions and discourses, he encouraged the Hasidim to further commit themselves to the mission at hand, explained by Schneerson in connection with his messianic vision and often mystical interpretation of the world scene, politics, and contemporary issues. In this way, he came to be at first appreciated, and later loved, as an individual beyond the authority of his office.

By the end of his life, Schneerson had built a movement from

> little more than one Brooklyn synagogue and several refugee clusters in Europe and Israel. . . . the rebbe transformed Chabad-Lubavitch into an international conglomerate of Jewish activity in 1,500 outposts in 35 countries on six continents, as well as virtually all of the 50 states [of the United States]. . . . [He] was the first Jewish leader to sense the potential of satellite, mass publishing, broadcasting in dozens of languages, and utilizing modern advertising techniques to bring vast public awareness to the chasidic model of Judaism.[6]

His leadership stature was widely considered to be unprecedented, at least in the modern age. He was to have an effect on Israeli politics and Jewish emigration from the Soviet Union, and was the only Ashkenazi leader to vociferously aid the ancient Jewries in Arab countries.

His organization and Hasidim were largely responsible for a Jewish religious and educational revival in the United States and other countries. During his leadership, he was responsible for the ordination and employment of the largest number of rabbinical students in recent Jewish history. He was even to be awarded the prestigious Congressional Gold Medal as an American hero. So great was his success to be, and so elevated his reputation, that many of his followers came to believe that he was the long-awaited *machiach*, an idea that he did little to dispel. How this reputation was earned will form the focus of our attention in the remainder of this section.

---

[1] See Avrum Ehrlich, *Leadership in the HaBaD Movement*, esp. pp. 370–352 and 394–406 for details of the successional rivalry.

[2] This is particularly so with Schneerson. See David Berger, "Is the Rebbe Becoming God?", p. 19.

[3] See Ehrlich, *Leadership in the HaBaD Movement.*, p. 271.

[4] David Ben-Gurion was one of the first Israeli dignitaries to visit in 1954. See Herb Brin, "Through the Night." Thus he may well have set the precedent for other heads of state and Israeli politicians to pay their respects to Schneerson. If Ben-Gurion had not visited Schneerson so early in his reign, his prestige as a figure of international importance might have been considerably less.

[5] See Gary Rosenblatt, "The Sounds of Lubavitch."

[6] Jonathan Mark, "A Kingdom of Faith."

Chapter 7
Consolidation Through Ritual

Schneerson's success in consolidating his movement was largely dependent on his capacity to serve in the traditional role of Rebbe. Aside from the delivery of Hasidic talks, there were many other duties to be fulfilled (ideological, administrative, and social) by the Rebbe in traditional Hasidic culture. One of the means whereby Schneerson consolidated his position as Rebbe of Habad was by his embracing of these traditions, assuming the role of an old-style Hasidic Rebbe despite his modernist leanings. As the movement expanded worldwide, and became numerically too large for him to develop a personal relationship with each of his Hasidim, new techniques of ritual and social consolidation were developed.

In the development of Hasidism, the ability of the Rebbe to act on a one-to-one basis with his Hasidim gradually became more difficult, especially if the Rebbe was popular or charismatic. The success of some Rebbes in attracting Hasidim to their courts meant that more of a burden, in time and energy, was placed on the shoulders of the leader, and various solutions were arrived at. In Habad, Shneur Zalman was faced with this crisis, and devised as an alternative the one-on-one ritual of *yehidut* to commune spiritually with his Hasidim. In order to provide guidance to his followers, who were often scattered geographically and unable to visit his court in person, he composed a spiritual manual called the *Tanya*.[1] This book was widely published and distributed, and was intended to make it unnecessary for the Hasid to visit the Rebbe with queries. As a guide to spirituality, it was effectively a textbook of Hasidism and Habad ideology, enabling the Hasidim to remain in their own localities and not require individual attention, regular visits, or personal instruction by the Rebbe. The effect this had on the expansion of the movement was important, as were the precedents it set for later Rebbes. Habad Hasidism were able to keep in touch with their Rebbe, and their Hasidic identity, even while physically remote from him. Hasidim were thus able to travel and spread the influence of Habad.

Despite the freedom of travel that written works like the *Tanya* allowed, the Habad Hasidim were still focused on the person of the Rebbe. The movement, due to geographic dispersal and the practice of outreach, needed a focus of its own, a source of personal vitality, culture, and lifestyle belonging solely to the members of the community. This communal identity was provided by the Rebbe. Learning from the Rebbe's example, they could better appreciate their Judaism and their reason for being on the earth, as well as understand the nature of their spiritual struggle. Habits and rituals dear to Hasidim made their lifestyle attractive to them and helped them cope with troubles and travails.

This dependence on the Rebbe and Hasidic social and cultural paraphernalia became more important after the destruction of East European Jewry in the early twentieth century. Hasidism might not have survived its transfer to the West without the living vestiges of old Hasidism inherent in the body of the Rebbe and the rituals and rites surrounding him. The survival of Habad in America was largely due to the arrival of Yosef Yitzhak; before that time, the movement was small and dispirited, and it only began to grow with his physical presence. Schneerson, on assuming leadership, recognized the importance of the Rebbe to the lives of the Hasidim, and fostered an environment of which he was the center.

Most of the ritual and practice that make up the fiber of the Hasidic lifestyle emanate from the Rebbe's actions, or at least in some way involve the Rebbe. These acts centralize the Hasidim and create a sense of personal relationship despite the many obstacles of geography and change.[2] The personal connection of the Hasid with the Rebbe goes beyond the Hasid's work in Habad institutions. To have a relationship with the Rebbe, one does not need to be promoted in his institutions but rather must commit one's soul to him, doing as he instructs and communicating with him.[3] Habad Hasidim worldwide have a number of ritualized methods for doing this, as will be explored further on.

Schneerson, in time, performed every function required of him as Rebbe, and despite some initial discomfort, evident in his rejection of the office when it was first offered to him and his reticence about being in the public eye, he eventually became comfortable in his duties. Schneerson himself noted that, although he might often have believed different things than his Hasidim, he nevertheless sought to fulfill their needs, and acted as they expected their Rebbe to act.[4] He conceded to the demands made of him and did what was expected of a traditional Rebbe, down to the last detail. Some elements of the role came to him naturally as a part of his charismatic and personable character, whereas other aspects required a distinct change in character, as was caused by his inclination toward modernity. Throughout his leadership, he was able to subtly change the role of the Habad Rebbe, and even introduced new rituals that became extremely popular.

The *Farbrengen*

Since the beginning of Hasidism in Eastern Europe, the Hasidic gathering has been one of the central occasions in the life of the community.[5] The precise nature of the gathering differed from sect to sect, but most often it would take place on Shabbat, holidays, and special occasions, either in the evening or during the day. Non-Habad sects called this rite a *tish*. Initially, the *tish* would involve the Hasidim gathering in the Rebbe's home around his dinner table, singing with him, listening to his words, and eating the scraps off his plate. The eating of the Rebbe's food (*shirayim*) was highly symbolic, and indicated the Rebbe's function as an intermediary for godly blessing.[6] As the various courts grew numerically, this simple meal became a ceremonious occasion, and often catered for thousands of Hasidim on stands around a large table.

Habad Hasidim called this rite a *Farbrengen* or *hitva'adut*, meaning a gathering or communion.[7] In this rite, the Hasidim would gather around the Rebbe at a table or on stands, where he would deliver either a general talk called a *sichah* or a mystical Hasidic discourse called a *ma'amar*, sometimes lasting many hours, interspersed with the singing of Hasidic songs and consumption of alcohol. When Schneerson chaired these gatherings, often of hundreds of people, he was known to glance around the room and focus his gaze on individuals here and there. This was taken as his extension of "long life and blessing" to the person involved,[8] and was one way in which he maintained individual communication with his Hasidim.

These gatherings and the talks that Schneerson gave were private "pep" rallies for the movement's activists. They provided an opportunity for representatives of the movement from around the world to take a break from their own leadership responsibilities and renew their connection to the Rebbe. Habad Hasidim who in their own localities were respected rabbis, leaders, wealthy personalities, and dignitaries, and were therefore treated with the utmost deference, would arrive at Habad headquarters for a *farbrengen* in equality.

The nature of the *farbrengen* also fostered the feeling of equality and fraternity. The pushing and bustling of masses of people gathered from around the world, squeezed into a small, confined space, and strenuously jostling for a good position to catch a glimpse of Schneerson, served to unite those involved. The gatherings on major festivals would attract even larger crowds, particularly in later years as the movement grew and Schneerson's popularity increased. Over the forty-four years that he chaired these occasions, the Hasidic audience grew continuously, so that the rooms in which the *farbrengen* was held had to be first widened, then extensively renovated to accommodate the crowds. At present, the gatherings are held in a large underground conference room/synagogue/hall that extends under the street fronting the building at 770 Eastern Parkway, where sizable crowds still gather despite Schneerson's passing.

The gatherings allowed the Hasidic movement to come together, particularly for holy days and festivals. The occasion of a *farbrengen* was an opportunity for family reunions, further enhancing the occasion for many Hasidim. The presence of leaders of the international Habad communities allowed networking to occur, as educational congresses and discussions took place, ideas were exchanged, stories of success were recounted, and a competitive spirit was fostered to outdo the efforts of other communities. Business was discussed, weddings were arranged, and other relationships were formed. As a result of the tradition of *farbrengen*, the international community became smaller and more cohesive, with its central focus provided by Habad headquarters and Schneerson. Without these public gatherings, the group dynamics, competitiveness, and Hasidic spirit within the movement would not have been the same. The sense of community and distillation of meaning conveyed by the *farbrengen* and the presence of Schneerson propelled the movement to further consolidation and strength.

The difference between the Habad *farbrengen* and other Hasidic gatherings has traditionally been the Habad focus on scholarship. The Habad philosophy emphasizes scholastic achievement and the development of philosophical insight, especially from its Rebbe. The assembled Habad Hasidim expected original interpretations of the movement's thought from each Rebbe, and Schneerson continued this tradition.[9] His talks and discourses would extend for hours on end, sometimes from Shabbat afternoon to late on Saturday night. He generally talked intermittently throughout the evening, and in between the elements of his discourse traditional songs were sung by the Hasidim with the encouragement of Schneerson. During the singing, Schneerson would lift his hands, clap, swing his arms, or bang his hands on the table, provoking renewed enthusiasm among the assembled crowds. Often a song would be sung and repeated in mantra-like fashion for hours, interspersed with segments of talk from Schneerson. The effect of this communal singing and discourse on a mass of people packed like sardines for several hours was often euphoric, and left a deep impression on those who were there.

The subjects discussed in these discourses were varied not only on each occasion, but throughout individual discourses, from deep mystical insights and biblical/rabbinic interpretation to topical matters such as world politics. Schneerson regularly included suggestions for future activities (taken as instruction by his eager Hasidim) and enthusiastic demands that they be carried out in fulfillment of particular "missions."[10] He would insist on improvements to the movement's operations, and in the same discourse encourage his Hasidim to develop their own piety. He would offer scathing criticism of political events, particularly in the State of Israel but also worldwide. Although the talks were given in a scholarly format, the content was evidently intended to evoke activity and enthusiasm for the movement's goals of outreach.

The tradition of focusing on the physical person of the Rebbe continued in the movement, and Hasidim would watch Schneerson closely, picking up every detail of his actions and mannerisms. Through this close observation, the talks given by Schneerson became more than just words to be listened to; the event became a holy communion with a godly intermediary and zaddik. They would notice Schneerson's emphasis and gestures when speaking—a raised voice, a cry, a pause, a nod of the head or sweep of the hand—and interpreted the deeper meaning and significance of these mannerisms. Hasidim also noted who he looked at while speaking, and observed many other details of a seemingly superfluous nature. These became important and even necessary details for the Hasid, communicating a deeper meaning than was conveyed by the words alone. Hasidim would later reconstruct and analyze every movement during these discourses, and the speeches themselves were memorized for later transcription.[11]

Quite apart from the mystique surrounding him as Rebbe, Schneerson's personality provided the onlookers with sufficient material to keep them wondering and intrigued at the significance of his mannerisms. If Schneerson had been any less brilliant a scholar, or had been deficient in halakhic observance, or had been perceived in any way as impious, his at-times marginal behavior might have worked against him.[12] As it stood, his personality was such that he was perceived to have saintly qualities. His peculiarities, his enthusiastic demands and mannerisms of speech became matters of remark, interest, and excitement for those who gathered around him. His personality and its effects on his manner of discourse became a mark of his sainthood, not an indication of deviation from the expected behavior of a Rebbe and zaddik.[13] Thus the *farbrengen* assisted Schneerson's consolidation of authority within the movement, not only inspiring his followers to action, but giving them a sense of unity, a focus for spirituality, and a source of endless speculation.

Yehidut

Yehidut is the term applied to the time that a Hasid spends "at one with" his Rebbe in personal spiritual guidance. When involved in *yehidut*, the souls of the Rebbe and the Hasid were believed to be bonded,[14] and so the occasion represented a unique opportunity for the Hasid to have contact with a truly godly being. The practice had been a priority in Habad even since its foundation by Shneur Zalman. At the time of its establishment, Habad emphasized the role of the Rebbe as a guide, and not as a miracle-worker, this latter being more prominent in other schools of Hasidism,[15] and as developed later under Schneerson's leadership.

Even before he was elected to office, Schneerson had commenced the practice of *yehidut* with the followers of Yosef Yitzhak, in this way beginning to assert his personality on the people who would later accept his leadership. Throughout his time as Rebbe, Schneerson generally accepted audiences for *yehidut* on Sunday, Monday, and Thursday nights, often continuing until the early hours of the following morning. He saw Hasidim, dignitaries, and general visitors, and an informal conversation took place where questions might be asked by either side.

In time, being able to access the Rebbe for *yehidut* became harder because of the crowds the occasion attracted; soon after he assumed leadership, bookings were required to meet Schneerson, and there were long waiting periods. Over time, the personal exposure in *yehidut* was offered more seldom, and to ever-larger groups; later, access was restricted to dignitaries, on the excuse of ailing health. Although this may seem to be a reasonable motive for restricting personal access to Schneerson, there were practical reasons for restricting his exposure to the public. As he advanced in years, the image of the Rebbe as indestructible would have suffered if Schneerson's fallibility, ailing physical health, and loss of mental sharpness were noted by more than a few people. By making his presence rare and decreasing accessibility to him, his image within Habad would be enhanced, he would be more treasured, and larger than life, without having to justify this reputation.

While it may seem uncharitable, this position is reinforced by the fact that Schneerson continued with a vigorous and demanding timetable long after the reduction of opportunities for *yehidut*. He stood in public for hours on end handing out dollars and cakes, speaking, and singing. He did not seem to lack energy or vigor until his strokes toward the end of his life.

The *yehidut* encounters also had something of a public relations function for Schneerson and the movement. Not only did he see Hasidim, but the occasion was expanded to include non-Hasidim and even non-Jews, who came to pay their respects, request assistance, or ask advice. Many who came to see Schneerson were prepared in advance to be profoundly impressed by the encounter. The reputation of the Rebbe and word-of-mouth accounts of other meetings were often conveyed to those requesting audiences. The long wait to see the Rebbe served to increase the sense of anticipation, and many people crowded the Rebbe's antechamber in the middle of the night waiting for audiences. Schneerson himself, while acting as secretary for Yosef Yitzhak, made dignitaries wait unnecessarily for their audiences with the Rebbe. He justified this by explaining that the wait would heighten their anticipation of the encounter and serve to enhance Yosef Yitzhak's image.[16] Often the weather outside was cold and quiet, and in winter covered with snow. The ambience of a late-night encounter with a grand mystic is conducive to a heightened sense of spiritual awareness, especially when the encounter takes place in surroundings designed to inspire awe.[17]

On finally entering to see Schneerson, visitors have described themselves as astonished at the sight of his grand appearance, long flowing beard, bright blue eyes, and fixed stare. He has often been described as friendly and convivial.[18] Many meetings were short, with a single question asked, a brief piece of advice given, a comment made, or a blessing bestowed. On other occasions, particularly if dignitaries or people with a high public profile were involved, he would ask them some general questions after which a thoughtful philosophical discussion would follow. Schneerson often demonstrated familiarity with a range of issues, including science, medicine, philosophy, politics, economics, and languages. This would often delight and impress visitors, who described him as a mystic whom they could respect as a modern man.[19] Schneerson used such occasions to ask his guests about their Jewish commitment, and frequently urged them to strengthen their connection to Judaism. His technique was to try to get his questioner to agree to a tangible obligation to stronger Jewish commitment, while maintaining the familiarity and warmth of the occasion. The technique worked for some, and many visitors have described how their preconceived perceptions and stereotypes of Schneerson and Hasidism were changed for the better by the *yehidut* encounter.

Exiting from the encounter was also a moving process for many. As guests left Schneerson's room and returned to the antechamber full of people, the contrast between the serenity of the Rebbe's room and the bustle of the waiting crowds was profound. The interest shown by onlookers and Hasidim who crowded around exiting guests in order to hear descriptions of the *yehidut* encounter brought the visitor back to earth. Many have told how they marveled at Schneerson's capacity not only to meet with so many people, but also to satisfy their expectations. Of course, stories of dissatisfaction were not perpetuated within the movement, so there is some obvious bias in the accounts of universal wonder at Schneerson's profundity. Many who returned for a subsequent visit, however, were delighted by the fact that Schneerson would often remember them, and sometimes he even maintained personal contact with individuals after the encounter. Because they knew the demands on his time, underscored by the crowds and the wait to see him, many visitors were grateful for even the few minutes he was able to give them. The fact that Schneerson would see them at all was often enough to create a feeling of personal attachment. If a miraculous event in the lives of a Hasid could be attributed to the meeting, as was often the case,[20] then Schneerson's stature was even further enhanced.

Letters from Schneerson

Even before *yehidut* with Schneerson was stopped, people were encouraged to communicate with the Rebbe by letter. This was in part due to the difficulty of obtaining an audience with him, but was also an effective and economical means whereby the international communities could keep in touch with their leader without the necessity and expense of traveling to Crown Heights. Schneerson attempted to answer all the letters that were sent him, but if a reply was not forthcoming, it was understood that he had at least read the letter at the grave of Yosef Yitzhak. He continued this practice until his first stroke, which occurred, oddly enough, at the gravesite as he was reading letters.

Habad Rebbes have traditionally written letters of advice, encouragement, blessing, teaching, and instruction to their followers.[21] In this way, the physical distance from the Rebbe was felt less than if there were no communication. The need to find a substitute for personal contact with the Rebbe became important as Hasidic groups grew and decentralized, and so letters and written teachings began to replace, or at least augment, the direct and personal relationship of Rebbe and Hasid. Shneur Zalman's teachings were often originally written in the form of letters to his students, Yosef Yitzhak conducted a wide correspondence, and Schneerson followed in his footsteps.

To the Hasid, the receipt of a return letter was in many ways more auspicious, and certainly more momentous, than receiving a verbal answer or message. A letter addressed to an individual appealed to the recipient as a more personal gesture, especially when the writer of the letter was the Rebbe, a person perceived as holy. That such a man should give his very precious time to consider the petty problems of an individual was regarded as a compliment of the greatest order. Indeed, many letters were framed and displayed by the recipients in a prominent position in their home or workplace, to reinforce this sense of connection to the Rebbe. In a sense, and quite apart from the wisdom of their contents, the letters became a type of relic, providing a physical connection with a geographically distant figurehead. Receipt of a letter strengthened the sense of belonging to a community and being held as a valuable member of the movement whose contribution was especially appreciated.

Due to the volume of mail received by Schneerson, people often waited for many weeks, or even months, before receiving a reply to their letters, and some no doubt gave up hope that they would ever receive one. The receipt of a reply after waiting so long surely increased the thrill of being remembered, but had other interesting consequences. Because of the delay, the question asked in the original letter was often resolved by the time the answer came. Often, the absence of a speedy reply was interpreted by the requester as an omen, with the benefit of foreknowledge always being given to Schneerson. If matters resolved themselves in favor of the letter-writer, Schneerson would be credited with the success, and was said to have not replied because he knew that a reply would be unnecessary. On the other hand, if matters did not favor the writer, Schneerson had not replied because he did not wish to be the bearer of bad tidings. In either case, or even if, as often occurred, Schneerson sent his blessing and nothing more, the very act of so many people communicating with Schneerson served to strengthen his stature within the movement.

According to postal officials, Schneerson received more letters than any other individual in New York,[22] and throughout his life he wrote over 300,000 letters, many of which were subsequently recorded in the many volumes of his *Collected Letters*. The letters contained a strong spiritual content, instructive to his Hasidim and also filled with encouragement of their endeavors. From the earliest days of his leadership, he felt completely comfortable about instructing people on educational or organizational approaches to their communal work. He was, after all, the educational director of the movement, a responsibility assigned him by Yosef Yitzhak. Yet when it came to giving personal direction, blessings, and advice on spiritual issues, which is considered to be the trademark of a traditional Hasidic Rebbe, he had hesitations. It took him some time to become comfortable with the chores expected of him in his new role; even to the end of his life, he considered himself merely the conduit between the Hasidim and the movement's true leader, Yosef Yitzhak, at whose gravesite he read the letters he received, and who guided his responses.

The writing of letters to Schneerson increased, and replies were treated with more prestige, as Schneerson reduced the hours he devoted to *yehidut*. As noted, the writing of letters was one of the only avenues for communication with Schneerson, especially within the international Habad community. In time, Schneerson dealt with every aspect of the Hasid's life in his letters. Permission to marry, health problems, business and spiritual issues, and administrative details for the running of the movement were all asked of and responded to by him. Schneerson encouraged communications from his followers, despite the burden of reading and replying to them, as his only real means of communicating with and directing the movement.

Schneerson was often seen carrying large envelopes around Crown Heights, believed by onlookers to contain some of the many letters he received. These envelopes would frequently accompany him on his regular visits to the grave of his predecessor, whose direction he sought before offering guidance. Schneerson saw himself as an intermediary; requests for direction would be made to him but answered by Yosef Yitzhak.[23] The awaited answers from Schneerson thus had an expectation of divine guidance, an impression that was bolstered by the accuracy of his insights and the suitability of his advice.

"Dollars"

Another ritual of leadership significance and of great interest was initiated by Schneerson as Rebbe: the public distribution of money. Initially, the practice involved the distribution of coins to visiting Habad children as a reward for good conduct, but the practice evolved into a ritual of immense significance. In its final form, adults and children, Hasidim and visitors, people with disabilities, pregnant women, concerned parents, scholars and returning emissaries, and inquisitive passers-by would visit 770 to have a moment with the Rebbe. From 1986, every Sunday, and throughout the year on special occasions, crowds in the hundreds, and even thousands, would line up outside 770 house to meet him and spend some time, however brief, in his presence. Schneerson would bless each person in turn, sometimes answer a brief question or make a comment, and maintain eye contact while handing the visitor a one-dollar bill. On many of these occasions, as much as $6,000 was distributed, indicating the size of the crowds that came to see him. Over the course of Schneerson's leadership, millions of dollars were distributed, one bill at a time.[24]

The distribution of money in this fashion has been explained in a several ways, and had an effect on the consolidation of Schneerson's authority over Habad. Apart from allowing the Hasid to spend a personal moment with his Rebbe, it also helped Schneerson to keep in touch with his following. He was able to capture the feelings of the people, which he could not achieve in the isolation of his room. Until the distribution of dollars was adopted, his main connections with his followers occurred through his assistants, in brief *yehidut* encounters with the select few who were able to get an audience, and with the largely impersonal mass of people who came to hear him speak. The ritual of "dollars" gave him wider exposure to the people, in a format where little was expected of him beyond his physical presence. The distribution of money thus resisted any attempts to keep him away from his following, and kept the Hasidim in touch with their leader.

The ritual had some important social functions. It provided children with a focus in the community, gave them something to do, and fostered a greater connection to the Rebbe. It attracted visitors to the neighborhood who might otherwise be too shy to attend a personal audience or write a letter to Schneerson, but who nevertheless liked to see him. The occasion also made it possible for people who did not spend Shabbat in the neighborhood to see Schneerson and perhaps exchange a word or two. The handing out of dollars often created something of a carnival atmosphere. Many Habad-centered stores were open for business, taking advantage of the crowds to sell books, photographs, souvenirs, and food. Since many people who received a dollar wished to keep it as a memento of the encounter and a connection to Schneerson, there was an industry in laminating and mounting the dollar bills for display purposes. For the local community, the development of the dollar ritual generated an industry.

There were some highly symbolic and even mystical reasons for Schneerson's choice of ritual. As it originally developed, the distribution of money to the children of Habad served a charitable cause, but the principle expanded with the ritual. Schneerson was obligated, like other Jews, to distribute charity, but he chose to do so in a strategic manner. The dollars were distributed as charity, and were also given with the idea that the recipients would be encouraged to give charity in turn, and thus fulfil a mitzvah, or commandment, that hopefully would lead to further observance and a turn to the religious life.[25]

Not only did the ritual encourage generosity and charity among the assembled visitors, but it also, more practically, directly generated more charity money for the movement. As noted, every dollar handed out was usually kept by the receiver as a memento of the encounter, and other money would be given in charity in place of the original note. Such donations were often made immediately, or within a very short time afterward, so more often than not the money was returned to Habad charitable institutions in the Crown Heights neighborhood. Many donors felt compelled by the example of Schneerson to give more than just the dollar they had received from him, and gave considerable sums to Habad charities or institutions. Thus, in practical terms, the money distributed by Schneerson as part of the ritual was not only immediately returned but grew manifold.

Giving charity plays an important part in Jewish religious observance, and especially in Habad has become a means of imparting spiritual growth, as outlined in Shneur Zalman's *Tanya*.[26] The mystical and spiritual benefit derived from acts of charity is twofold: first, it fulfills the biblical obligation to give charity; and second, it extends real charitable assistance to others. In giving money as charity, the individual is able to overcome the connection to the material world, moving beyond the use of money as a tool for self-preservation and power for the sake of others. Giving money away is a means to lessen one's attachment to physical existence and cleave more strongly to the spiritual. Money can provide sustenance, pleasure, and tangible goods, but is also a means of filling spiritually empty lives. The energy that might have been channeled in harmful ways by the unwise use of money is harnessed through the charitable act for the service of good. In Habad ideology, charity has two positive outcomes: the act of doing good deeds itself, and the detraction from vitalizing the evil material element. By this process, a unique spiritual state may be achieved, which elevates the individual beyond the material self. In this manner, the zaddik, by using his material energy for the service of the spiritual, in this case through the distribution of dollars for charitable purposes, is able to more fully achieve spiritual greatness.[27]

It has been suggested that Schneerson's obsession with handing out dollars was, in fact, a mystical process he was undergoing to purify himself in a form of catharsis. According to this suggestion, the distribution was consciously intended to develop Schneerson's spiritual strength in the fashion outlined in the *Tanya*. By carrying out such purification, the messianic redemption would be hastened, a view supported by the fact that distribution of dollars commenced in Schneerson's later years, when his messianic drive was at its peak. If this understanding of his motivation is accurate, then the handing out of dollars was Schneerson's attempt to divest himself of wealth, and physically render himself an empty vessel ready to be filled with divine guidance. If so, then his Hasidim were his tools in achieving this spiritual stature.

The dollar ritual also reflected the Habad notion of the zaddik working within the world and through the world for the redemption of humanity. Money, one of the most powerful expressions found in the material world, could be a tool to hasten the redemption if its power was harnessed correctly. The symbolism was also continued in the choice of currency: the American one-dollar bill bore the motto "In God We Trust." Schneerson's admiration of America as the new home of Habad may therefore have played a role in the adoption of the ritual.

Other Rituals

Along with the major rituals described above, *yehidut* and the distribution of dollars, Schneerson participated in many smaller and more traditional rituals on different occasions during the year. The blowing of the shofar on Rosh Ha-Shanah, the Lag Ba-Omer parades, the priestly blessing before Yom Kippur, the handing out of cake before Rosh Ha-Shanah,; dancing with the Torah scroll on Simchat Torah, and other rituals all were a source of special excitement in the community when Schneerson participated in them. In this way he was able to fulfill the traditional role of a Rebbe as a preserver of tradition, and his participation made an emotional connection between the ritual and him that was significant in the lives of his Hasidim.

Schneerson's public exposure through these rituals, and his willingness to perform the traditional functions of a Rebbe, allowed the mythical imagery and imagination of his Hasidim to transform him into an ancient sage and miracle-worker. As his leadership of Habad continued, stories of miraculous occurrences, especially in relation to the advice he offered, began to spread.[28] His predictions were believed to be prophetic, and his blessings were naturally seen to have borne fruit. One reason for this is that the advice offered by Schneerson was often sensible and had positive results. Through providing practical advice, he was able to instruct individuals on ways they could contribute to the building of the movement. In addition to giving his follower spiritual directedness and an attractive ideology, Schneerson's advice enabled him to direct their activities in accordance with the needs of the movement, and this was his priority. By providing sensible direction, Schneerson succeeded both in improving the lives of his followers and in achieving his goals for Habad.

There was an additional benefit accompanying the giving of advice and the performance of ritual. Schneerson's controlled participation in the lives of his followers gave impetus to the tendency for myths and stories to develop around him, especially regarding his status as a prophet and miracle-worker. While Hasidim have a predisposition to idealize the figure of their Rebbe, they need a starting point, and the personality of Schneerson and his charismatic effect on his followers required only a little encouragement to develop into a self-perpetuating, unifying mythology. Schneerson's willingness to play the role of Rebbe allowed for his Hasidim to play their role and sew a fabric of fantasy and myth around him that was to form an important part of the Habad Hasidic lifestyle. These myths, an important element in his consolidation of authority, were to play an even more central part in the development of messianic ideology in Schneerson's later life, all of which has an impact on the question of succession in the movement after the Rebbe's death.

Participation in rituals contributed to the fabric of Habad Hasidic life and the feeling that Schneerson indeed was truly a Hasidic Rebbe in the classical sense. After a time, he transcended the title, becoming not just *a* Rebbe but *the* Rebbe, and the role was elevated to one of unprecedented eminence. The esteem and reverence with which he was regarded by the end of his life add to the complicated issues surrounding the question of succession.

---

[1] Nissan Mindel, *Rabbi Schneur Zalman of Liadi*, vol. 1. See also Harry M. Rabinowicz, *The World of Hasidism*.

[2] Hasidism had not survived outside of Eastern Europe. Even in Israel it was not a robust social movement. When it was transplanted to America after the Second World War, the only thing that could ensure the Hasidic identity was a renewed dedication to the movement's epicenter, that is, to the Rebbe.

[3] Samuel H. Dresner, *The Zaddik*, pp. 128–132.

[4] See Herbert Weiner, *9½ Mystics*. Schneerson is quoted as acknowledging that much of what he did was for the sake of the Hasidim and not a genuine concern or belief of his own.

[5] See Jerome R. Mintz, *Hasidic People*, pp. 275–280.

[6] See ibid., pp. 137, 277; Jerome R. Mintz, *Legends of the Hasidim*, pp. 96–97.

[7] See Mintz, *Hasidic People*, pp. 48–50, for an examination and description of this rite.

[8] See Gary Rosenblatt, "The Sounds of Lubavitch."

[9] Yosef Yitzhak's talks had great popular appeal but lacked deep mystical insight. Schneerson combined Yosef Yitzhak's approach with the older tradition of expounding mystical ideas, concepts, and Hasidic thought. In this way, he satisfied eager Hasidic scholars without compromising his respect for Yosef Yitzhak's style.

[10] These "missions" or campaigns were enacted on a regular basis, and were designed to bring households gradually into full observance of Jewish law. Some campaigns were educational, including a demand that every Jewish household should contain at least the basic Jewish books (a Bible, siddur, and Book of Psalms) to assist in the education of the family. Jewish education for children was also encouraged in another campaign, as was the training of children in the performance of mitzvot (commandments). Giving charity (tzedakah) was the focus of

one campaign, and Shabbat candle-lighting for women and girls was another. Other missions were practical, and encouraged elements of observance, such as the use of a mezuzah (a small scroll attached to the doorposts of every home) and the maintenance of family purity; and a fund was established to help families make their homes kosher. See Mintz, *Hasidic People*, pp. 44–47 for details.

[11] See Simon Jacobson, *Toward a Meaningful Life*, pp. xii–xiii. They could not be electronically recorded or written down at the time because such discourses were frequently given on Shabbat or holy days, when recording and writing were prohibited.

[12] Examples include his modernism, his use of the latest technology, and his contact with the nonreligious, and even the non-Jewish, world.

[13] These personality traits eventually led many in the movement to announce that Schneerson was the potential mashiach. An advertisement in the *Washington Jewish Week*, October 5, 1995, declared that "Schneerson . . . has in the course of the past forty-five years, completely changed the face of world Jewry and spread a message of goodness and morality to the entire world. The Rebbe's lineage from the royal house of David, his unique scholarship, leadership, care for every individual, and even after what transpired to the Rebbe MH"M on Gimmel Tammuz [the day Schneerson died] match the descriptions from Jewish law and tradition."

[14] See Lawrence Schiffman, "Rebbe's Legacy of Hope Transcends His Death."

[15] See the essays in Dan Cohn-Sherbok, ed., *Divine Intervention and Miracles in Jewish Theology*, especially Joseph Dan, "The Contemporary Hasidic Zaddik."

[16] See Mordecai Laufer, *Yemei Melech*, vol. 3.

[17] See Harvey Swados, "He Could Melt a Blizzard."

[18] See *Lubavitch in the News*.

[19] See, for example, Herbert Weiner, "Farewell, My Rebbe"; Jeanette Kupfermann, "How I Nearly Succumbed to the Charm of the Rebbe"; Marc Wilson, "The Rebbe's Counsel."

[20] Eliyahu Tauger and Malka Tauger, *To Know and to Care*.

[21] Menachem Mendel of Vitebsk claimed that he was able to lead the Russian flock from Israel primarily through correspondence by means of letters and emissaries. Shneur Zalman's works were often adapted from letters that he wrote to Habad and other Jewish communities, and to individual Hasidim.

[22] Jonathan Mark, "A Kingdom of Faith."

[23] See Avrum Ehrlich, *Leadership in the HaBaD Movement*, pp. 385–387.

[24] See Mark, " Kingdom of Faith"; idem, "The Last Dance." Mass distribution of money commenced in 1986.

[25] The same idea of mitzvah multiplication was a significant reason for the outreach work carried out by Habad. This is especially evident in the use of "mitzvah tanks" to visit areas with significant Jewish populations and encourage the nonobservant to keep at least one commandment, thereby turning their minds to the religious life.

[26] *Tanya*, pt. 4, chap. 12.

[27] See ibid., pt. 1, chap. 32.

[28] See Tauger and Tauger, *To Know and to Care*.

Chapter 8
Leadership Qualities

Schneerson's Style

Even before he assumed the leadership of Habad, Menachem Schneerson was known as something of a radical and freethinker. He was university-educated, familiar with secular subjects, and a modernist, and many of these factors contributed to his leadership style.

Many stories are told in the movement that demonstrate aspects of Schneerson's personality, and it might prove instructive to examine several of them. One particularly intriguing one is as follows: On Rosh Ha-Shanah of 1955, on his way to carry out a religious ritual beside a lake in the Brooklyn Botanical Gardens, Schneerson, accompanied by a large group of followers, came across a fence with a locked gate. Schneerson, who at the time was over fifty years old, proceeded to climb the fence and continued on to perform the ritual. Later that day, he gave a speech about one of the former Habad Rebbes and his persistence at overcoming all obstacles.[1] Such actions by Schneerson presented the image of a dynamic, determined person to whom ordinary rules did not apply, but who was going to carry out his religious obligations despite any obstruction.

Schneerson's public willingness to accept different strands within Judaism was also refreshing, although his private opinions, especially in later years, demonstrate less tolerance for views divergent from his own. In 1980, for example, Schneerson wrote a letter to the Zionist Federation of South Africa emphasizing the need for pluralism and tolerance in respect to Ashkenazi, Sephardi, and other legitimate Jewish traditions. He stated that "experience has shown that whenever a uniform educational system has been imposed on a multi-faceted community, it has inevitably proved disastrous."[2] This view helped in the depiction of Schneerson as a genuine pluralist who recognized and appreciated the divergent strands within Judaism and saw a place for them all.

Further indication of Schneerson's pluralism and leadership style is found in the testimony of Rabbi Jonathan Sacks, now Chief Rabbi of the United Kingdom and not officially connected with Habad, in whose career Schneerson took an interest. The Rebbe admired the United Synagogue and Jews' College in England, and urged Sacks to become involved in the leadership of these organization.[3] Bemoaning the shortage of English rabbis and encouraging the training of an increased number of qualified religious personnel, Schneerson directed Sacks to play an active role in the British rabbinate. He not only encouraged Sacks to take on the challenge, which would benefit Judaism if met, but even offered him detailed instruction on how best to teach new students. An exceptional leader himself, Schneerson helped others to develop qualities of leadership and in this manner to achieve much more than they might have alone. His interest in the lives of others is further demonstrated by his encouraging Sacks to change his doctoral dissertation to one with Jewish content and asking to read it on completion.[4] When Schneerson was later shown this work, he made detailed corrections and suggestions, once again demonstrating how much time he would give to helping others and to cultivating trained, knowledgeable leaders for the general Jewish community, and not solely for Habad. Schneerson continued to show an interest in Sacks's life and career until the time of his death.

This personal contact frequently took the form of positive religious instruction to the Hasidim, and Schneerson often followed up his advice with personally initiated requests to be kept abreast of progress. This delighted his Hasidim, and also many visitors to the movement. In an emotional obituary, Herbert Weiner, a Reform rabbi and author, describes how Schneerson kept in contact with him after their first encounter, using positive encouragement to deepen Weiner's halakhic observance. Schneerson sent him a gift on Rosh Ha-Shanah, along with instructions as to further religious and spiritual commitment. Despite their ideological differences, Weiner said, he was unable to control his emotions of warmth and love for Schneerson, and always stood up publicly in his Reform synagogue to expound Schneerson's teachings. Weiner's attachment to Schneerson derived from the personal attention given him over the years by the Rebbe, and the positive and encouraging nature of the communications he received. There was no animosity, division, or remonstrances to return to traditional observance, but rather reinforcement and deepening commitment to the elements of commonality shared by the two. Weiner further noted that "no event of consequence occurred in my professional or private life without notice from you."[5]

This positivity was also expressed in other forms. Schneerson encouraged his followers with positive persuasion. He insisted that people are essentially good and connected innately to God, and so he adopted a positive approach to most issues. This is perhaps most simply illustrated by his insistence that a hospital, called *beit holim*, "house of the sick," in Hebrew, should instead be referred to as *beit refu'ah*, "house of cure." Likewise, a cemetery was to be referred to as a *beit hayim*, "house of the living." By emphasizing a positive ideology and the elements of commonality shared by all Jews, Schneerson turned the thoughts of his followers to good deeds, and managed to develop influence and trust with other, potentially opposing, schools of Judaism.

Peculiarities of Personality

The Hasidim were intrigued by Menachem Schneerson's personality, and throughout the era of his leadership he maintained the mystique that so fascinated them. Visitors pondered the paradoxes of his personality. His doctrinal views were strictly Orthodox, yet he was, at least publicly, very open regarding technology, women's activities, and dialogue with the secular world. Within the traditionalist world of Hasidism, he was viewed as a modernist and presented something of a challenge to traditional ways. To the outside world, however, his traditional garb and religious outlook, and the relatively insular and idealistic community he inspired, all seemed to impede a dialogue with modernity. His combination of fundamentalism and dogmatism with rationalism was something of an anomaly. Many who had audiences with him claimed that he did not conduct himself in accordance with the stereotype of a sage. He was audacious at times and persistent, and was known for doing the unusual yet being very serious. He was a university scholar, admired by academics who respected his training and felt an affinity with him,[6] and yet he discouraged others in the movement from attending university. He was philosophically anti-Zionist, yet took an active interest in the welfare of the Jewish populace in Israel. He was never known to take a vacation or indeed to leave New York, except for a visit to the Catskills Mountains in 1957, when he reputedly visited a Habad youth camp, yet he led an international movement with emissaries across the globe. He claimed that he communicated with the deceased, and insisted that Yosef Yitzhak was still alive and guiding the movement. His stubborn insistence that this communication was real confused and fascinated people, as did his insistence that Yosef Yitzhak was the mashiach and would return to lead the redemption.[7] He was known for his mystical bent, and for his focus on setting unrealistic goals for the movement, then enthusing his followers into actually achieving them. In short, his character was an enigma, and as such contributed to the depiction of Schneerson as belonging to "another world."

Personal Contact

A major component of Schneerson's leadership style was the maintenance of personal contact, not only with his followers, but also with a wide cross-section of the general community. Contact was maintained by means of letters, personal *yehidut*, *farbrengen*s, distribution of dollars, and instruction through others.

From the beginning of his involvement in the Habad movement, and even before he became Rebbe, Schneerson was known to write to dignitaries, politicians, and rabbis to open discussion on a range of subjects, and the practice continued throughout his life. As has been mentioned, Schneerson wrote and received literally hundreds of thousands of letters.[8] This correspondence enabled him to establish a familiarity, which would otherwise have been impossible, with many people of diverse interests and backgrounds. As he increased in prominence and importance to world Jewry, those who had received correspondence from him came to treasure the intimate contact the letters represented.

Schneerson did not limit his correspondence to dignitaries. He wrote to a variety of people on a wide range of issues: interpretation of halakhah, the performance of ritual, business or general advice, and guidance. The practice of letter-writing was a way to keep in contact with Schneerson, and many who received a letter in reply to a query felt themselves to be intimately connected with a "holy man." Sympathy for the movement he led was increased, and useful contacts for Habad were made at a remote distance, all of which contributed to the success of the movement worldwide.

In addition to this voluminous correspondence, Schneerson met with many people in *yehidut*. As described above, this consolidated his connection with the Habad community, and established acquaintances with a vast array of people. Israeli and world politicians, academics, writers, artists, and business leaders all visited and had personal contact with Schneerson, and at least in the early years, anybody who desired an interview was able to obtain one.[9] Because of the circumstances of these meetings, coupled with the charismatic personality of Schneerson, many emerged from the *yehidut* encounter with a very favorable opinion of the Habad leader. Over the years, many of them published accounts of their meetings with him in the media, increasing both Schneerson's personal stature and that of the movement he led. In this way, personal contact helped Schneerson develop strong alliances and friendships with people of importance, as well as with the public and his own Hasidim. It also put him into closer contact with world issues, the business community, academia, and other sectors of importance to the future of the movement.

The *farbrengen* too was an occasion for personal contact, although on a briefer and more communal scale. Because of the crowds present at a *farbrengen*, the most personal contact one could expect was to be gazed at by Schneerson during the course of the gathering. Such a look was believed to penetrate the soul, and was accompanied by blessings and wishes for long life.[10] While such contact was brief, the recipients considered it to be profound. The impression of Schneerson obtained at these public appearances was generally very positive, and many visitors from outside the community have described the experience favorably.

The distribution of dollar bills on Sundays occasioned a brief encounter between the uninitiated and Schneerson, and allowed him to maintain contact with the public. Although a symbolic act of great significance to the Hasidim, many people from outside the community treasured the notes they received, and kept them as mementos of the meeting. This ritual provided an opportunity to meet Schneerson with no obligation to talk, so that those who did not wish to speak with him or to write to him were able to satisfy their curiosity from up close. The curiosity of the many visitors made the ritual itself something of a curiosity; it was viewed as a family activity and a place to take the children on the weekend. Whatever the motivation of the visitors, the ritual was notably successful in spreading the contact between Schneerson and the public, and in attracting positive attention to Habad.

Consolidation Through Charisma

Schneerson has been described as a classic example of a charismatic leader and the contemporary Habad movement as a personality cult.[11] The issue of his charisma must be a primary concern in any examination of the effect of his personality on the consolidation of his authority. Heilman argues that Schneerson's main strength was his ability to resurrect Hasidism after the Holocaust, at which he succeeded by speaking to people who had nothing in common with him or with Hasidism.[12] His success can be attributed to his charismatic personality, his unbending devotion to the cause, and his organizational ability. Chaim Potok also described Schneerson's charisma, and even expressed a fear of meeting him lest he be swept up in the cult of personality surrounding the Rebbe.[13] He notes Schneerson's power: "The slightest lift of a finger, the vaguest wave of the wrist. His was the mysterious ability to fill a room simply by being there."[14] All of these elements contributed to the Schneerson's charismatic authority, and explain, at least to some extent, the attraction he had for so many followers.

Friedman maintains that Schneerson's strength was in his understanding of the modern mind. He realized that the people visiting him, however successful, important, and wealthy, were often also lonely and afraid. They needed emotional support and someone to look up to, and he was able to satisfy this need through his charismatic personality.[15] It has been suggested that Schneerson was exposed to ideas about charismatic leadership and the effectiveness of simple slogans while in Berlin and Paris before the Second World War. Wherever he obtained his skill with people, it certainly contributed to his successful consolidation over Habad, and to the massive expansion of the movement.

The appearance and physical presence of Schneerson also contributed to his charisma, especially as he aged and became more majestic. Potok described Schneerson's appearance: "His blue eyes penetrated, he had a regal bearing and flowing beard."[16] This image of regality and majesty no doubt assisted in the presentation of Schneerson as wise and venerable, a figure of authority and maturity in whom others might confide. This is confirmed by the fact that Schneerson's popularity expanded as he grew older, and many Hasidim talked about his beard growing longer and becoming grayer. Some claimed this had occurred "overnight" or within an unusually short time, and attributed it to the mystical responsibilities that Schneerson took upon himself as Rebbe.[17]

Schneerson's physical impression of age and fragility was often contradicted by the movement of his hands and his brisk walk, which made him look as if he were actively defying old age. His schedule was that of a much younger man: he regularly delivered discourses of six hours or more, talking well into the night; stood for hours distributing money; and met with individuals at all times.[18] His perseverance when tirelessly greeting literally thousands of people, despite his advanced age and ailing health, impressed many onlookers and showed his great strength of character. That

Schneerson's apparent agelessness was primarily for public display is demonstrated by an account told by an eyewitness, who once saw him walking from his car to Habad central headquarters. He stepped out of the car vigorously, walked briskly and with strength, enthusiasm, and determination to the entrance to the building, then, believing he was unobserved, slowed down to a limp and hobbled into his office. That he understood the need of his followers to see a strong, energetic leader simply demonstrates the insight Schneerson had into the minds of his followers, and the burden of care he demonstrated, hiding his own humanity for the sake of his Hasidim.

Schneerson's activities, the demands he made of his Hasidim, his determination by force of his perceived mission (given him by Yosef Yitzhak and God) are all signs of the typical Weberian charismatic personality.[19] His evident humanity and his later physical suffering, his sheer determination and the success of his vision, are all indications of a leadership instinct beyond mere tactic or pretense. Schneerson was indeed a charismatic figure, and was fortunate to have had a platform that fully utilized his talent.

The Appearance of Suffering

Schneerson's charismatic authority was augmented in his later years by his increasing frailty and illness. The perception of suffering has endeared leaders to followers from time immemorial, particularly if the suffering was incurred for the sake of the faithful.[20] The situation was no different for Hasidism, as is especially evident in the imagery surrounding Schneerson in Habad. The ideological and emotional love the Hasidim felt toward their Rebbe was believed to be reciprocated, and indeed far surpassed, by that extended by the Rebbe, who was regarded as the life source of his Hasidim.[21] The Rebbe's very willingness to become a Rebbe was regarded as an act of self-sacrifice, engaged in for the sake of the Hasidim. When a Rebbe is seen to age, is burdened by his duties, or falls ill, this too is seen as evidence of his sacrifice for the Hasidim. A deeper commitment ensues on the part of the Hasidim when they believe that their leader is ailing, or even dying, because of their action (or inaction), and by their incessant need to be led.

According to later perceptions that arose as Schneerson aged, the Habad Hasidim had forced Schneerson to assume the role of Rebbe when Yosef Yitzhak died. He had acted dutifully, accepting the burden, and in his old age consequently suffered ailing health. The connection between the Rebbe's suffering and the burdens of his office awakened a sense of heartfelt love in many Hasidim, and fostered a willingness to deepen their dedication to the movement. This increased as he grew older and became more ill; as his sickness worsened, the realization that he was suffering for the Hasidim elicited greater appreciation for his sacrifice and further empowered his authority over the movement.[22]

In 1977, Schneerson suffered a heart attack, and it is surely no coincidence that during the late 1970s Habad activities throughout the world were strengthened.

Although the increased activism was also due to many other factors, the fact that Schneerson not only recovered from his ailment but enjoyed a restoration of health and vigor exceeding his pre-ailment condition no doubt contributed to the confidence the movement had in him. To many, the event was interpreted mystically, and led to more fervent messianic expectations. Indeed, from this time on a vocal messianic striving surrounded Schneerson, led by the Rebbe himself.[23]

The widespread practice of placing Schneerson's picture in homes and offices also appears to have become more popular from the 1970s onward. This is evident from the fact that in popular depictions of him, Schneerson is usually portrayed as an elderly sage in his seventies, eighties, and nineties. Before he developed the long white beard and wizened appearance that came with age, his picture was not conducive to wide appeal, and it would seem that his age and feebleness was more endearing to the Hasidim and the Jewish world than a youthful, vigorous Rebbe.

Messianic expectations grew as Schneerson aged, and when he suffered a stroke in 1992, many of his followers, influenced by the imagery of the Kabbalah, saw this as the birth pangs preceding the arrival of the mashiach.[24] By this time, the movement was familiar with the idea that the mashiach would have to suffer before he was revealed, and for many Hasidim, Schneerson's incapacitation was not a defeating blow but a verification of their belief that he would be revealed as the mashiach.[25] Suffering was therefore not only a part of Schneerson's charisma, but was understood as a necessary means for him to fulfill the messianic ideology of the Habad movement.

Other Personal Characteristics

Schneerson demonstrated many other positive personality traits, each of which contributed to his reputation and reinforced his charismatic leadership of the Habad movement. The loyalty to Yosef Yitzhak expressed immediately after the latter's death, on which his initial authority rested in part, never weakened. Throughout his life he attributed all of the movement's success to Yosef Yitzhak, who intervened from "on high." Evidence of this is the regularity with which he visited Yosef Yitzhak's gravesite to read letters to his Rebbe, to pray, and to commune with his predecessor. Over time Schneerson created a symbolism around Yosef Yitzhak's gravesite that compared it to Zion and the Holy Land.

Throughout his reign, Schneerson insisted that Yosef Yitzhak was in fact still the Rebbe of Habad, despite the fact that forty-five years had passed since his death. Schneerson's loyalty to his predecessor was endearing to the Hasidim, and became the standard format they used when expressing their own loyalty to Schneerson. Schneerson, through personal example, showed his Hasidim how a Hasid should behave toward his Rebbe, and by acting in this manner he ensured that others would follow. If the Rebbe acted in a certain way, then surely this was how it was to be done.

In addition to loyalty, Schneerson displayed a high degree of modesty over the years, despite his ever-increasing authority and stature within the movement, which only served to further enhance his status. Jonathan Sacks declared that Schneerson was the most self-effacing leader he knew,[26] and even though Schneerson may have developed delusions of his own messianic status toward the end of his life, we can see that he succeeded remarkably in maintaining a meek disposition.

He always gave deference to his mother-in-law, although it was known that there were some difficulties between them. She received a monthly stipend of $500 from the movement, and it always arrived promptly. Schneerson continued to eat in her home, and sat, as he had always done, on the left-hand side of Yosef Yitzhak's place, while Shemaryahu Gourary sat in the position of greater honor to the right. Throughout his leadership, he offered both public and private respect to Gourary, despite the ill will caused by the question of succession to Yosef Yitzhak. Schneerson retained Gourary in charge of the organizations over which Yosef Yitzhak had placed him, and allowed him to continue his residence in Habad's central headquarters building. He instructed his Hasidim that nothing bad was to be said about Gourary, and took steps to make sure they obeyed.[27] Indeed, the respect was mutual, and Gourary remained loyal to Schneerson, even siding with the Rebbe in a legal battle against Yosef Yitzhak's widow for possession of the latter's library.[28]

Schneerson lived in spartan conditions, and wore an old hat for many years until it was in tatters, although this was also to make a point. A Habad story tells how Schneerson purchased his hat from a Jewish store, the owner of which later began to open for business on Shabbat. In order to encourage the man to observe the Sabbath, Schneerson told him that he would not buy another hat until he closed his business on Shabbat. Many years passed, and both remained adamant. Eventually, the shop closed on Shabbat, and Schneerson changed his tattered hat. While this is illustrative of a point, and does not necessarily indicate modesty or frugality, Schneerson often wore his shoes until they had holes in them. He received only a meager stipend from his organizations, most of which he gave to charity. In his will, he left the little money he had to his educational organizations.

While many religious leaders and even Hasidic Rebbes take vacations and may even travel abroad, and also lead a comfortable lifestyle, Schneerson did not. He never left Crown Heights, except to visit the gravesite of Yosef Yitzhak. All of these traits seem to indicate a modest and humble personality, whose ideals were not tied to material gain. Strangely, the fact that a leader who was famous, internationally renowned, and perceived as superhuman by his followers acted with humility and lived with holes in his shoes increased his dignity, and drew many closer to him.[29]

Scholarship

Schneerson was a scholar before he assumed leadership of Habad. His interests were varied, and not limited to religious texts.[30] His personality alone served to attract many educated people to the movement. Doctors and scientists, mathematicians and intellectuals of all varieties (indeed, all who had sympathy for their Jewish roots but could not bridge the divide between what they perceived as the archaic law of their ancestors and their contemporary Jewish sentiments) were attracted to Schneerson. He was a paragon for these intellectual and educated people, and was known to be a scientist himself, who could converse on an array of different subjects and yet was firm in his commitment to Jewish religious life.[31] The importance to consolidation of Schneerson's interest in modernity and his knowledge of the contemporary world should not be underestimated. By virtue of the support of academics and educated activists, the movement had the resources to enter campuses and confront its hard-line opposition with people who had a personal sensitivity to the needs of those contacted through tactical outreach.

Schneerson's own scholarly style was debatable. Some might claim that he was intellectually dishonest and not concerned with the intellectual challenges or philosophic musings that scholarly pursuits are supposed to raise. While this subject is sufficiently complex to deserve further study, suffice it to say here that Schneerson's intellectualism was focused on and intended solely to complement his outreach ideology. He was able to quote secular sources to prove a point, and often did so, and used apparently contradictory positions to illustrate a point. Schneerson's scholarship, along with that of other Habad Rebbes, was often characterized by the use of a seemingly contradictory viewpoint in support of an ideological position. He exemplified this by his treatment of technology as a harbinger of faith, and used his secular education to advocate a religious lifestyle. Perhaps the best example of the use of opposition is seen in Schneerson's endorsement of Maimonides, who has long been considered the stalwart rationalist in Judaism, and was often criticized by Hasidism for his rationalism and lack of mystical knowledge.[32]

Maimonides' vision of the messianic redemption is quite non-mystical and was designed to reduce apocalyptical tension in Maimonides' own lifetime.[33] It is therefore ironic that Schneerson should have chosen Maimonides to provide the substance for a modern declaration of the imminent redemption, especially when there were other, more favorable sources available. Although it is possible that Schneerson employed a mystical reading of Maimonides, it may also be that his determination to render his critics partners in the redemptive vision was a motivation. Whatever the reason for his endorsement of Maimonides, it had the desired effect. The rationalist Maimonides became a defender of the apocalyptic, messianic worldview of the highly mystical Habad Hasidim.[34]

In the field of Jewish scholarship, Schneerson was known for his achievements in the study of Rashi, the great commentator and exegete of the Tanakh (Bible). He frequently used Rashi's commentary in his discourses, delving into it with sharp analysis and superimposing a mystical reading. Although this approach raised academic eyebrows, it has been seen as a contribution to religious commentary on the Tanakh.

In order to enhance Schneerson's scholarly status, his speeches were transcribed, edited, and annotated with footnotes by a team of editors to allow for verification of his ideas. In addition to helping readers to verify his references and pursue some ideas further than the immediate text allowed, the footnotes gave his words a degree of scholarly legitimacy, despite the frequent originality of the discourses. His innovative ideas were demonstrated thereby to be based on an interpretation of traditional sources, and were therefore less of a challenge to traditional thinking. During the peak of his scholarship, and before ill health and advancing age caused a decline in his memory, Schneerson was greatly respected for his intellectual competence. The editors who prepared his speeches for publication continued to be impressed by his mental acuity, despite the fact that they were confronted with evidence of his declining faculties.[35]

All of the above elements of Schneerson's personality contributed to his charismatic leadership and the adoration in which he was held by his Hasidim, and also by many outside the movement. He used his personal charm and aura of authority not only to establish intimate spiritual relationships with his Hasidim, but also to develop a public persona that contributed greatly to the success of the movement. Schneerson was regarded as a zaddik by his followers, and all who met him were impressed by his openness, sincerity, and humility. He came to represent the ideals of Jewish leadership, and thus it is understandable, given the cult of personality he attracted, that many of his followers came to believe him to be the long-awaited mashiach.

[1] Recounted by Jonathan Sacks, "When Mysticism Saved the Jewish People."

[2] See Jonathan Mark, "A Man of Letters."

[3] Jonathan Sacks, "The Man Who Turned Judaism Outward."

[4] Ibid.

[5] See Herbert Weiner, "Farewell, My Rebbe."

[6] See "Protocols": Menachem Friedman testimony, p. 1580.

[7] See Chapters 9 and 19.

[8] See Mark, "Man of Letters."

[9] See Jeannette Kupfermann, "How I Nearly Succumbed to the Charm of the Rebbe," Examples of important, nonpolitical visitors include the authors Chaim Potok and Elie Wiesel, Jacques Lipschitz, and the actor John Voigt, among many others.

[10] See Chapter 7.

[11] See Jerome R. Mintz, *Hasidic People*, pp. 168–169, 287–288.

[12] See Joseph Gambardello and Bob Liff, "A Potent Figure in Judaism."

[13] On the *Ted Koppel Show*, Chaim Potok said that he was afraid to meet Schneerson for fear of being overwhelmed by his presence. For other descriptions of Schneerson's magnetism, see Yehiel Poupko, "Of G-d and Man" (he compares Schneerson to the high priest, who was believed to be accessible to the whole nation), and Kupfermann, "How I Nearly Succumbed," among many others.

[14] Chaim Potok, "Rabbi Schneerson."

[15] See Laurie Goodstein, "Death of Lubavitcher Leader, Rabbi Schneerson, Stuns Followers."

[16] Potok, "Rabbi Schneerson."

[17] Habad oral tradition.

[18] See *Beis Moshiach* (April 26, 1996), p. 78, for a description of Schneerson's lifestyle, and the supernatural aura it gave him in the eyes of his Hasidim.

[19] See Max Weber, "The Sociology of Charismatic Authority."

[20] See, for example, the image of the suffering servant in Isaiah 52:13–53:12, the presentation of the life of Jesus in Christian tradition, and the life of Sabbetai Sevi. The messianic figure in particular is often characterized by suffering, and this was extended, at least by certain of his followers, to Schneerson in his role as the mashiach.

[21] See Chapter 2.

[22] See *Beis Moshiach* (April 26, 1996), p. 78: ". . . the Rebbe endured indescribable pain and suffering for over two years. In the Rebbe's life we find incontrovertible proof that the life of the tzaddik is a spiritual and G-dly one, completely transcending natural law."

[23] See Chapter 9.

[24] See, for example, Shmuel Butman, *Countdown to Moshiach*, p. 20; *Beis Moshiach* (April 26, 1996), p. 78.

[25] Butman, *Countdown to Moshiach*.

[26] Sacks, "When Mysticism Saved the Jewish People."

[27] According to a Habad oral tradition, Schneerson implied that the holder of portions of Yosef Yitzhak's diaries that were uncomplimentary to Shemaryahu Gourary would not prosper, and that possession of such information would be detrimental to the owners. This is one of the ways in which Schneerson discouraged the dissemination of unfavorable information, and serves as evidence of his desire to protect the reputation of his former rival for leadership.

[28] See Mintz, *Hasidic People*, pp. 281–297, for a brief summary of this case, and "Protocols" for a full transcript of the court proceedings.

[29] See Shmuel Boteach, "The Colossus and Me."

[30] It is even speculated that he read non-Jewish books in the bathroom, where it is disrespectful to study religious texts. This, to many Habad followers, is one explanation for Schneerson's knowledge of secular subjects, as he was never publicly seen to read a secular publication.

[31] It was observed in the *London Times*, for example, that Habad's use of the latest technology "contrasted strangely with the Rebbe's denial of evolution and his discouragement of University education—both the more bizarre since he himself had benefited from one of the most formidable courses of higher scientific study." See "Obituary: Rabbi Menachem Schneerson."

[32] Maimonides was bitterly criticized by many contemporaries and successors. His most contentious work, the *Guide for the Perplexed*, was often burned by Jewish opponents. Even his more acceptable work, the *Mishneh Torah* (particularly the first book, Sefer ha-Mada) was not permitted to be studied in some circles. Nahman of Breslav, among many other mystics and Hasidim, was known to be a harsh critic of Maimonides.

[33] See, for example, the interpretation of Maimonides' ideas on the messiah in David Berger, "The New Messianism," pp. 35–42, 88.

[34] See, for example, the references in Butman, *Countdown to Moshiach*; Haim Hillel Ben-Sasson, *Atah Yadati*; Shalom D. Volpa, *Yechi Hamelech Hamashiach*; Yosef Braun et al., *And He Will Redeem Us*.

[35] An editor of Schneerson's works, David Olidort, told how most of Schneerson's aides and editors adored him and saw him as virtually infallible, despite their numerous corrections of his failing scholarship (personal communication, Crown Heights, June 1995).

Chapter 9
The Ideology of Messianism

The Ideology of Redemption

Throughout Jewish history, there have been different strains of messianic thinking, and although these are often incompatible and philosophically at odds, they borrow ideas from one other. Many adherents of the utopian ideal represented by messianism do not have the insight, or perhaps do not care, to know whether they are more swayed by political or mystical ideals. They confuse their shared appetite for the redemption with the many different methods of achieving this social and ideological transformation, and thus many variants of messianism have arisen throughout Jewish history.

Jewish messianism had generally tended toward the ideal of a national redemption for the whole Jewish nation, and by extension for the entire world. This redemption, in its original conception, was not a mystical process but a political one, as described in detail by Maimonides in the Book of Kings section of his *Mishneh Torah*. Over the millennia of Jewish political disenfranchisement, the political ideals of traditional messianism became so distant and unachievable that the messianic goal could only remain relevant to the people and ideology of Judaism if they took on a mystical and religious form. This necessitated a transformation of the classical idea of national redemption to a mystical individual redemption. Lurianic Kabbalah served to popularize the notion of individual redemption in Jewish thought, a concept that had gained popularity with the emergence of Christianity over a millennium earlier. But even individual redemption can take on different forms. In another work, I have discussed the differences between political/rational messianism and mystical messianism.[1] While political messianism is more dominant in national redemptive ideals, mystical messianism is more prone to operate through the individual redemptive ideal. However, the opposite can also be true.

Habad under Schneerson fused these two interpretations of messianism in a way that perhaps puts them at cross-purposes. On the one hand, Schneerson's stated mission was to bring on the national redemption. This mission was dependent on the idea that personal piety and individual redemption would ultimately lead to the national and political salvation of the Jewish people, and through them of the world.

The national redemption that was vaguely formulated in Habad thought had a mystical form. Few people, including the movement's religious thinkers, invested sufficient time to understand or articulate the exact nature of the redemption they sought; if they had, they might have realized that their conception contained significant internal contradictions. The ideals they associated with redemption were holiness, proximity to God, ability to study Torah, and the absence of violence. Although superficially claiming to be working toward the national/political redemptive idea formulated in traditional Judaism, Habad's followers interpreted this with mystical notions. Despite this mystical bent, Habad employed politically and socially active methods of outreach, education, and raising community awareness. It used modern methods of action, such as lobbying, advertising, and fundraising, and many Habad messianists demonstrated great political and business savvy. Schneerson's own messianic rhetoric was political, and its symbolism was military: his chief aides were commanders, his followers were "soldiers," and the movement's children were organized into the Zivot Hashem, the "armies of God."

While the outer shell of Schneerson's messianic paradigm was political and military, in essence his concept of redemption was associated with mystical and religious ideals as an extension of the individualistic redemptive model. Hence, there was a significant contradiction between the redemptive ideal pursued by Habad and the method through which it was to be realized. Schneerson made over the national redemption into a mystical endeavor, instead of leaving it (as it should have been) as a national political redemption. The confusion of styles and ideology of messianic thinking in Habad should be kept in mind throughout the following discussion.

The Importance of Messianism

One of the major factors affecting Schneerson's later leadership of the Habad movement, and an important motivator in the expansion of the movement's activities and influence, was the emergence of a strong messianic element in Schneerson's teachings. While this had apparently always been present in Habad, the ideology of messianism was used much more markedly by Schneerson, first in his consolidation of power and influence, and later to enthuse his followers, possibly motivated by genuine messianic belief on his part. The effect this messianism was to have on the succession debate after Schneerson's passing will be dealt with later; for the moment, we will limit our consideration to the role of messianist ideology in the consolidation of Schneerson's authority and reputation in Habad and the broader Jewish world.

It is unclear when exactly Schneerson came to view his movement, his Rebbe, and later himself as messianic instruments, although it appears to have preceded his election to the office of Rebbe.[2] Although records are scarce, there is evidence to support the supposition that there was a group of mystically and messianically inclined Hasidim around Yosef Yitzhak, who had made predictions in the early 1940s regarding the imminent arrival of the mashiach. Schneerson, who was somewhat involved in the operations of the movement at the time and a figure of growing public prominence, was regarded as one of the people who identified Yosef Yitzhak as the prime messianic candidate. Although it is debated today whether he was, in fact, involved in these messianic predictions, he certainly seems to have been influenced by them.[3] In the years immediately after his assumption of office, Schneerson became a firm advocate of Yosef Yitzhak's status as the most suitable candidate to be mashiach, and also insisted that Yosef Yitzhak was still the leader of Habad after his death.[4]

To Schneerson, the hope provided by the messianic ideology justified the atrocities of the Holocaust, the growth of secularism, the decay of Orthodoxy, and the many other ills faced by the postwar generation.[5] The messianic redemption also explained to Schneerson many apparent irregularities in the world order and the eschatological realm. He could explain what looked like absurdities as pre-messianic birth pangs, events that were necessary precursors to the coming of the mashiach. Events that had seemed illogical or inhuman, such as the Holocaust, could be fitted into a messianic worldview. As part of the essential change that would occur in the cosmic nature of the world with the advent of the mashiach, they could be endured more easily.

Even such apparently illogical events as the election of Schneerson to the office of Rebbe could be explained in this fashion. For Schneerson, his leadership of Habad was an absurdity, not only because of the continuing leadership of Yosef Yitzhak, but primarily because it was a position that he felt he did not deserve. It was awarded to him because of the pre-messianic irregularities in the world,[6] and not because he was suited to the post or was endowed with special personal qualities.

Throughout his lifetime, Schneerson's messianism served to deepen the contradictory impression he left on people with whom he came in contact. The piety and increasing fervor of his messianic belief was often seen as being in opposition to the notion that he was a modern, university-educated, enlightened Hasidic maverick. The contrast of the two perceptions made him a curiosity, and served to increase his charismatic appeal for the masses of Habad. It also allowed Schneerson two public personalities, the mystic and the rationalist, each of which could be reconciled to the other.

Messianism contributed to Schneerson's consolidation of authority. Imbuing Habad with cosmic significance, it became the driving force of its outreach program and unified the movement behind a single overriding ideal. Thus messianism not only had ideological significance to the movement, but gave Habad a mystical and practical purpose, placing the movement at the center of the messianic redemption of world Jewry. In the early years, the goal of redemption enabled Schneerson to retain his popular support, which might have crumbled were there not a clear, challenging, and unifying goal to maintain the movement's focus. Later, it assisted in the development of a feeling of unity and commonality within Habad, as the disparate elements were united behind a single common cause.

The Effects of Messianism on Consolidation

The messianic idea, especially as it developed in Schneerson's lifetime, saw the presence of Habad in the United States as part of a Lurianic process to elevate the last sparks in the exile before the redemption.[7] It also explained the presence of the movement in the United States in the first place. While an impartial observer might view Yosef Yitzhak's escape from Russia in the 1930s as an act of desertion, leaving many of his most dutiful Hasidim behind in Russia to face persecution after exhorting them not to leave, and even swearing a blood oath himself to stay, Schneerson held that this was part of a supreme spiritual, messianic, and military mission. The mission involved Yosef Yitzhak's descent to the lowest spiritual sphere, the United States, to continue the struggle for Jewish survival and complete the last mystical mission preceding redemption. By this interpretation, Yosef Yitzhak was far from a coward; rather, he was a commander-in-chief coming to the ultimate battlefield.[8]

The idea of a messianic battle had other effects on the ideology, and especially the practice, of Habad worldwide. The Lurianic process described in the idea of the elevation of the sparks made the Hasidim essential tools in bringing the redemption, and there was even scope for them to become minor messianic figures.[9] In this manner, the ideology of messianism bolstered the self-perception of Habad's followers and enthused the movement to achieve Schneerson's outreach goals, which were themselves motivated by messianism. All of Schneerson's activities were seen by some of his most enthusiastic adherents as a cosmic strategy with extreme ontological implications. His campaigns were compared to military expeditions, his emissaries to soldiers, and his bad health to a spiritual suffering, designed to win the war against irreligion and bring the mashiach immediately.[10]

The belief that the Hasidim were acting on behalf of the *Moshiah* had an uplifting effect, not only on morale, but on the manner in which the Hasidim carried out their everyday activities. It was the main motivational force behind the frenetic activity surrounding outreach, gave comfort and encouragement to the emissaries sent around the world to establish Habad communities, and above all made the Habad Hasidim feel special. Schneerson's ideology of messianism borrowed heavily from the militaristic terminology and worldview of Zionism; the present-day Hasidim were soldiers of the ancient King David, fighting for Israel's spiritual independence and the long-awaited redemption. Spiritual militarism within Habad, which arose most notably after the Israeli victory in the Six-Day War in 1967,[11] was assisted by the victorious template of the fight for the State of Israel. The true battle, however, would not be over land, but over the spiritual heritage and future of Judaism in the world. Schneerson's presentation of the Hasidic mission was one of ultimate wartime urgency, a time when all effort and resources must be pulled together to ensure victory. Every man, woman, and child must come to the fight, to finally bring about the only solution to the world's difficulties—redemption.

The messianism of Habad was a force that endowed the movement with vigor and willingness for self-sacrifice to achieve the betterment of the Jewish world. For the

Hasidim themselves, messianic outreach combined elements of religious fervor and social activism; it directed energy, encouraged excitement, and, most important, brought fulfillment across the movement. Sacks has described the feelings of young Habad followers, male and female, who were sent by their leader on an adventure to new and strange places across the globe, to start Habad communities and thus hasten the redemption. He claims that there was nothing as exciting as this elsewhere in contemporary Judaism,[12] and for some at least, this adventure was sufficient reason to become a part of the movement. Rabbi Shmuel Boteach, for example, now a media-conscious public figure in Judaism,[13] has stated that he was motivated to join the Habad movement because of its grand vision.[14] The mission of redemption was so grand that it could contain even the most ambitious and energetic people within it, uniting idealists and scholars, fundraisers and activists, rich and poor, educated and uneducated. Through Schneerson's conception of the redemption, all segments of the Habad community were able to nullify themselves,[15] despite their own feelings of individual importance, to a sense of cosmic mission under his leadership.

Schneerson was clearly cognizant of the strong motivational factor that can accompany messianic euphoria, and it is probable that he encouraged the messianic enthusiasm that arose around him to encourage greater effort and striving to spread the work and influence of Habad. As the movement grew, and especially after certain events in world affairs and Schneerson's own life,[16] the messianic aim was institutionalized as a practical goal in the day-to-day work of activists throughout the world. Productivity and motivation were correlated to the ever more imminent arrival of the mashiach, which was brought closer by the increasing activity of Habad Hasidim. The anticipation of the arrival of the mashiach furthered the commitment and productivity of the movement's adherents, and it is clearly evident that the messianism surrounding Schneerson was one of the strongest forces in the consolidation of his Hasidic following, and in the expansion of the movement in both size and influence.

Messianism as a Motivational Device

Throughout Jewish history, it has not been unusual for rabbinic authorities to encourage faith in the messianic arrival.[17] Many leaders have employed the messianic hope to provide solace, encouragement, and hope to destitute Jews in times of oppression, and community depression or discouragement has frequently been alleviated by calculations of the precise time of the arrival of the mashiach. These predictive attempts (so far, at least!) have always gone by without event, but the communal benefit derived from the hope of expectation has often proved to be more important to the survival of the community than dealing with the consequences of later disappointment, which, although harsh, were surmountable. On a few occasions, of course, the messianic expectation has led to a massive schism, as occurred with the Christian, Sabbatian, and Frankist messianic movements, and some have expressed fear that Habad may go the same way with the messianic expectation held for Schneerson.[18]

While it is likely that Schneerson himself believed that the mashiach could and would come, as have many exponents of messianic euphoria through the centuries, the enthusiasm that the messianic hope imbued in the populace had an almost messianic and redemptive effect in itself. The messianic drive was both constructive and innovative, and as long as it lasted, it might be argued that the determination of Habad's followers might even have served to achieve its utopian goal. This is especially so if we adopt a rational, Maimonidean reading of the coming of the messianic era, wherein the efforts of the populace, led by a mortal leader, are a means to bring the redemption.

In this light, one may view Schneerson's references to the messianic time as a motivational and inspirational device. Perhaps he recognized that if, by the time of his death, his utopian ideal had not come to fruition, the Hasidim would have to suffer a period of remorse and crisis, schism and revision, until they could surmount their challenges. This, as we shall see, is what is currently happening within Habad. Until this event, however, the messianic spirit was recognized for its invaluable motivational effect, which facilitated the movement's expansion and encouraged its genuinely positive work within both Habad and the broader Jewish community.

Schneerson as a Prophet

The messianic ideal espoused by Schneerson was not directly explicit, and the precise nature and identity of the mashiach his followers were to bring was also never made completely clear. He did not specify a time for the arrival of the mashiach, and so was able to avoid the specific disappointment of a failed prediction, but he frequently exclaimed the arrival to be imminent.[19] There is enough ambiguity in Schneerson's teachings to allow for many interpretations of the identity and role of the mashiach in world events. What with the continuous failure of the "imminent" revelation, this ambiguity began to be used in support of the idea of Schneerson himself as the mashiach, both before and after his death. While this idea will be examined shortly, the notion of Schneerson as a prophet is important to the idea of messianism as it arose within Habad, especially for its role in consolidating his authority.

We have already seen the minor prophetic ability of Schneerson as experienced by his followers.[20] He would frequently give advice, in person and via correspondence, based on knowledge he could not have had, and was credited with possessing great and penetrative insight into the operations of Habad and of the world in general. This was to prove incredibly important to the development of his public, charismatic persona as Rebbe, and was only enhanced over the years as his advice was acted on and found to be sound.

He was also credited with predictions regarding world events, the fulfillment of which further enhanced his reputation. During the last years of his life, for example, he is credited by his followers with predicting the successful and speedy conclusion of the 1990 Gulf War, the failure of the attempted coup in the Soviet Union in August

1991, the collapse of Communism in Eastern Europe, and other major events of worldwide significance. His successful predictions, added to the personal insight into the lives and problems of his individual followers demonstrated by his responses to personal questions, heightened the perception of Schneerson as somewhat more than human. The events of the 1990s caused many in Habad to expect the coming of the mashiach, an idea into which Schneerson was able to tap.

Although Habad followers generally viewed Schneerson as the mashiach, they also viewed him as a prophet. The identification of a prophet as the mashiach is inconsistent with Jewish ideology on the issue, and so his later identification by his followers as occupying both roles is problematic. It is possible that Schneerson viewed himself as a prophet, and that his debated public silence on his status as mashiach was an acknowledgment of this inconsistency. He proclaimed, for instance, that his Hasidim should "go out and declare that a prophet has arisen and has said *Moshiach* is here," which is regarded by some as evidence of Schneerson's declaration of his prophethood.

This would be consistent with the traditional notion that Elijah the prophet would precede the messianic arrival and usher in the age. By this, Schneerson would not be the mashiach, but the prophet who proclaims him. While convenient, this theory does not entirely stand up; Schneerson himself made comparisons between Yosef Yitzhak and Eliyahu, which would place Yosef Yitzhak in the position of prophet, and might possibly elevate Schneerson himself to the role of mashiach *in potentia*. To confuse matters still further, Schneerson referred to the possibility that Eliyahu had already secretly arrived, but nobody yet knows about it.

Stories are also told in Habad of personal references or allusions that Schneerson made about his prophetic status. There is a recollection, for example, of a question asked by Leible Groner, to which Schneerson immediately replied, "Am I a *navi* [prophet] to answer?" Leible insisted, and Schneerson answered the question, thereby implying that he was a prophet. While it may seem that this conversation is being interpreted somewhat literally, the concept of Schneerson's response as an affirmative statement of his prophetic status might be better understood in light of one of Schneerson's own recollections. He recounted that Shneur Zalman, in response to a question, once replied as Schneerson himself had done: "Am I a prophet to answer?" after which he answered the questioner. Schneerson said that this proved that Shneur Zalman was a prophet, and so by extension Schneerson himself, by performing the same ritual, also acknowledged his prophetic status.

Schneerson as the *Mashiach*

Although there are difficulties in assuming that Schneerson viewed himself as a soon-to-be-revealed mashiach, there are a good many excerpts from his talks that intimate as much, at least according to his messianist followers.[21] Although often used out of context by messianist enthusiasts, these intimations nevertheless provide an insight into Schneerson's contemplation of the role of the mashiach, and give cause for speculation as to his self-recognition as a potential messianic figure.

Various views of the mashiach and his role are found throughout the history of Judaism. From an examination of traditional sources such as the Talmud, it is possible to identify a *cheskat* mashiach, or "potential mashiach," and Schneerson certainly accords with all of the hallmarks of this figure.[22] Linked to this concept is the mashiach *shebador*, or "mashiach in the generation," a concept that identifies a person with messianic potential in each generation.[23] Again, Schneerson's followers certainly came to believe that if any figure of the present generation of Jewish leaders was to be the mashiach, Schneerson was the most likely candidate. More distinctive than these ideas is the concept of mashiach *vadai*, or the "absolute mashiach," the final *Mashiach* whose coming has long been prophesied.[24] It is certain that Schneerson taught extensively on all of these concepts of mashiach, but the question of whether he identified himself with any of them (or even all of them) is another matter.

Although Schneerson may have sometimes alluded to his own messianic potential, his self-conception as occupying the role of mashiach is far from certain. It is definitely possible that he viewed himself as a potential messianic figure, and there are even indications that he tried to awaken his messianic potential by various means. Few figures in Jewish history, however, have laid claim to being the final and definitive mashiach,[25] as believed about Schneerson by his messianist followers during the last years of his life, and even since his death. It is difficult to reconcile this with Schneerson's continuous insistence that the present redemption is the true and final one, and that, after all promises and the many centuries of waiting, the redemption was at hand.

Whatever the motivation behind the later messianism, there were some in Habad who declared Schneerson to be the mashiach from the time he assumed the role of Rebbe.[26] He publicly rejected this notion at the time, but it is believed by some that his first Hasidic discourse alluded to his own messianic status,[27] and it certainly marked the commencement of Habad's messianic mission. Schneerson also made many references, especially in his later life, to the messianic status of Yosef Yitzhak, and intimated that the movement's present leader (whether himself or Yosef Yitzhak through him) was in fact the mashiach.[28]

Trying to be the *Mashiach*

It is possible, according to Kabbalah, for a messianic candidate to draw down the messianic soul into his own body and then be declared the mashiach. There is also reference to the difficulties in recognizing the redeemer:

The messiah . . . acquiring a holy *nefesh*, *ruah* and *neshama* [three different souls]. Then on the day appointed as the end, his *neshama* of *neshama* [the highest soul, called *yehida*], which was preserved in Paradise, will be given to this righteous man and he will become the Redeemer . . . receive more prophetic powers . . . and then he will recognize himself as the messiah. His messiahship had not been known (to him) before, but now it will be revealed. . . . Others, however, will not recognize him.. . . . he will be hidden away body and soul. . . . Then he will be raised to heaven, and thereafter the messiah will reveal himself fully and all Israel will recognize him and gather around him.[29]

This sentiment, with which Schneerson was doubtlessly familiar, could ideologically justify his own silence regarding his and Yosef Yitzhak's messianic status, and the insistence with which he demanded in later life that his Hasidim should demand the arrival of the mashiach. By involving his followers intimately in the bringing of the mashiach, Schneerson was not only able to unite the movement around a common ideology, but also gave it a powerful motivator for action. Habad itself, and every Hasid within the movement, was made personally responsible for the emergence of the messianic era. This was also a brilliant strategy for diffusing the possible failure of the messianic promises made by Schneerson: if the redemption did not occur as he had prophesied, it could be blamed on a lack of commitment by the Hasidim rather than a failure of vision or prophecy by their leader. This is a promise by which messianic movements have historically preserved their theological integrity despite the repeated failure of predictions of the specific time of the arrival of the mashiach.

Messianic Vacillation

Throughout his life, there were periods when Schneerson preached intensely messianic rhetoric and others when it was toned down considerably. This is not to say that he did not express extreme messianic expectations from the beginning, but rather that his emphasis and enthusiasm changed. Several events in his life are markers for the periods of most intense messianic preaching: the death of Yosef Yitzhak in 1950, the Israeli victory in the 1967 Six-Day War, his heart attack in 1977, the death of his wife in 1988, and his first stroke in 1992. The first three are discussed elsewhere for their impact on Schneerson's consolidation of authority, but the death of his wife and his paralyzing stroke evoked the most drastic changes in mood and ideology, especially in relation to messianism.

Even before his wife's death in 1988,[30] Schneerson engaged in strongly messianic rhetoric and made many references in his public talks to the notion of eternal life. These were understood at the time as references to the imminent death of his wife, and were no doubt a reflection of the pain he was experiencing at the prospect of her departure from the world. In the period before Schneerson's own death, the same comment were taken as supporting the popular messianist view that he would be granted eternal life, and would be able to lead the movement and the redemption despite his advanced years. In the period following his death, the same words have been used to support claims that Schneerson did not die, and some Hasidim still believe that he continues to lead the movement in physical form, albeit one not seen by ordinary eyes.

That the death of his wife greatly affected Schneerson and gave him cause to consider his own mortality is evident from several events precipitated by the death of Chaya Mousia. Immediately following her passing, Schneerson wrote his will, which was later amended, outlining his vision for the future of Habad in the event of his own death.[31] He also delivered discourses in which he spoke about his vision for the future management of Habad, and raised the possibility that his Hasidim should not consider him to be immortal. He gave fewer messianic discourses in this period, perhaps because he recognized the failure of his sincere desire for the advent of the mashiach and was coming to grips with the death of the person who had been closest to him. He was also faced with recognition of his own mortality.

The sobriety of Schneerson's messianic teachings continued until approximately 1990, when he again embraced a fervently messianic rhetoric in speeches that have come to be considered the most definitive pro-messianic and resurrection messages in the history of Habad. His teachings during this time resulted in an increase of aggressive messianic activity throughout the movement, and have been used to support much of the messianist ideology that has developed since his death.

Isolation and Messianism

After the passing of his wife, Schneerson was isolated as never before. Most of his few intimates had passed away due to advanced age, and with the passing of his wife he was left bereft of intimate companionship on an egalitarian basis. Those aides and friends who remained were for the most part members of the next generation, and shared little of Schneerson's background. One theory is that his aides, concerned about the mental and emotional well-being of their Rebbe, tried to shelter Schneerson from the outside world, especially given his increasing ill health. Despite his frailty and obvious signs of human fragility, Schneerson's Hasidim remained in sincere adulation of him, and did not dare question or doubt him. His aides, it seems, did not suspect that he experienced pain, suffering, or other emotions that normal humans suffer, and so he continued to maintain a superhuman facade, with the result that he became more isolated than ever. Certainly, he had less contact with the Habad community at large after the death of his wife, and this influenced his perceptions of the world.

It is possible that Schneerson had a false impression of the success of his messianic ideology and Habad's outreach efforts. In the isolation of his room, the reports he received from his aides and emissaries were no doubt very positive. Stories are told in Habad of how Schneerson used to parade children in front of Yosef Yitzhak's office in an attempt to make him happy and for the same reason reported positive things to his Rebbe; it is not unlikely that his own aides emulated this. The visitors he received especially in his later years were mostly in awe of him; stories of miracles and wonders resulting from his presence or blessings were doubtless reported back to him, perhaps cementing in his mind his identification as the mashiach.

The movement he led was meeting unprecedented success in its outreach efforts, fueled largely by Schneerson's messianic ideology. Larger crowds than had ever been seen regularly assembled at central headquarters to hear and see him when he made one of his increasingly rare public appearances. Prestigious people and representatives of political and social groups came to visit him, and hailed him as a hero of the Jewish people. No doubt, reports of the unprecedented growth of the movement and the success of the international Habad emissaries were reported to him, adding to the impression of the success of Habad in "elevating the sparks" and disseminating Hasidism to every corner of the world. This was, according to his own ideology, a major part of the messianic redemption, and a sign of the imminence of the coming of the mashiach. Other signs were also beginning to appear, in the form of historical events of near-apocalyptic proportions, including the Gulf War and the fall of the Soviet Union, the latter of which resulted in the exodus of Russian Jewry to Israel. This last was an event that Schneerson, himself a Russian Jew, no doubt found particularly poignant.

In the loneliness of his room, without any close companions to talk with, and insulated from any form of criticism, Schneerson may have given in to his grief and age, and come to view himself as the long-waited mashiach in person. The evident lack of another obvious messianic candidate or successor to the movement, and his own proclamation of the central role of Habad in the emergence of the mashiach, meant that he demanded of others that they insist and demand of God that the mashiach should be delivered immediately.[32] By assuming the role himself, he may have felt that he was simply fulfilling his own prophecy, and doing what he had preached, in trying to hasten the coming of the mashiach. Despite these efforts, two weeks before his first stroke on March 2, 1992, Schneerson admitted failure to his followers, confessing in desperation to them that he had done everything he could to bring the mashiach, without any sign of success. He expressed his confusion at the non-appearance of the mashiach, and turned to his Hasidim to complete the mission of bringing the redemption, demanding that they take on responsibility for this duty, and thereby bring the redemption themselves.[33]

At the time, Schneerson's admission of failure, both personal and of the movement, was interpreted differently by the various factions of Habad. Some used it as a directive to openly declare Schneerson the mashiach and crown him, in this way forcing God (who must act so as not to make fools of them) to bring the mashiach.[34] Others no doubt saw this as an empowering statement meaning that they now had explicit personal responsibility to bring the redemption, and should continue with their efforts in outreach and activism. As we shall see, the possible transfer of authority and responsibility represented by this event may have a bearing on the fate of the post-Schneerson Habad movement, as one of the spiritual functions of the Rebbe was given to his followers *en masse*.

Many of the Hasidim had in fact long believed that Schneerson was the mashiach, and as they saw it he had made direct and explicit reference to this time and again; his speech of transfer therefore simply confirmed what they had known all along. Even before his death, the proclamation of Schneerson as the mashiach was both popular and widespread, and many publications discussing the whole question of the mashiach and his identity were printed with Schneerson's tacit approval.[35] Admittedly, the most vocal and blatant proclamations of Schneerson's own messianic status did not begin until he was rendered incommunicative by the strokes in 1992, and increased more markedly after his death in 1996, but the idea was certainly to be found in the movement much earlier. If Schneerson had wished to deny his messianic status, he certainly had ample opportunity to do so before his strokes, and messianists have used this as evidence of his tacit approval of their activities and beliefs.

The role of messianic ideas and activity in consolidating Schneerson's leadership of Habad was perhaps one of the most important elements of his career. While messianism alone could not have given him control over the movement and the loyalty of his Hasidim, or assisted in the development of his charismatic persona, it played a major role in uniting Habad behind a common goal and ideology. By giving his followers a mission of superhuman and extraordinary proportions, Schneerson was able to unite the many disparate elements of the movement under one ideal, starting from his assumption of power in 1951 and continuing even after his death. Messianism assisted Schneerson in the initial consolidation of his leadership by allowing him to assert that his predecessor, Yosef Yitzhak, was still effectively in charge of the movement, thereby helping to win the support of his father-in-law's followers. Messianic ideas also enabled Schneerson to explain and incorporate major world-changing political and social events into the Hasidic ideology of Habad, allowing great occurrences to be proclaimed as a necessary part of the redemptive process. This in turn increased his power and prestige by heightening the perception of his prophetic abilities, which turned his desires for the coming of the mashiach into a prediction of a real and imminent future occurrence. While it aided Schneerson in consolidating his authority, the issue of messianism, as we shall see in Part Four, is now the foremost cause of division in the Habad movement, and threatens to tear the sect apart.

---

[1] M. Avrum Ehrlich, "Sabbatean Messianism as Proto-Secularism."

[2] See Avrum Ehrlich, *Leadership in the HaBaD Movement*, pp. 115–117.

[3] Naftali Loewenthal disagrees with this position (informal conversation, July 1996). He maintains that Schneerson was not behind these messianic predictions, since the language he used in the *reshimot* from this period was not the same as the terminology used in the Mahane Yisrael journal, *Ha-Kriah ve-ha-Kedusha*, which propagated them. Loewenthal argues that Schneerson's perspective of the Holocaust was different from that expressed by *Ha-Kriah ve-Ha-Kedusha*. The counter-argument would claim that Schneerson might have been involved with a group of people who held these sentiments, and may have been as influenced by them as they were by him. He did not necessarily have to have written the polemic himself. It is like-

ly that Schneerson's rhetoric regarding Yosef Yitzhak's messianic qualities and his posthumous presence among the Hasidim fell on the receptive ears of Mahane Yisrael's initiates, and thereby spread through the Habad movement.

[4] See *sachet* of Shabbos Terumah, 5710; also quoted in Yosef Braun et al., *And He Will Redeem Us*, p. 11.

[5] See Menachem Friedman, "Habad as Messianic Fundamentalism," p. 353.

[6] See the Kahn diary. He describes how Schneerson was uncomfortable acting as a Rebbe and apologized to elder Hasidim for his behavior. He did not begin his first *ma'amar* in the conventional manner, which Kahn interpreted as a sign of his unwillingness to assume the position of Rebbe too brashly. See *Torat Menahem* for the contents of this discourse. Schneerson's first *ma'amar* contains his own explanation; basically, his appointment rested on the fact that the seventh generation was so lowly and God so generous and forgiving that even someone of his low level of spirituality could assume the office of Rebbe. While much of this might be the result of either modesty or political expediency, it is clear that, at least publicly, Schneerson attributed his leadership to conditions in the world and the Habad movement, and not to his own qualities.

[7] See "The Fountains Have Been Disseminated," *Beis Mochiach* 42 (June 16, 1995), p. 60.

[8] See Friedman, "Habad as Messianic Fundamentalism," pp. 340 and 344.

[9] See "The Fountains Have Been Disseminated."

[10] See Friedman, "Habad as Messianic Fundamentalism."

[11] See Chaim Potok, "Rabbi Schneerson."

[12] See Jonathan Sacks, "The Man Who Turned Judaism Outward."

[13] He is the author of many books of a popular nature, including *The Jewish Guide to Adultery*, *Kosher Sex*, and *Dating Secrets of the Ten Commandments*.

[14] See Shmuel Boteach, "The Colossus and Me."

[15] The concept of *bitul*; see Chapter 2.

[16] These will be discussed below, but include the 1967 Six-Day War, his heart attack in 1977, the death of his wife in 1988, and his stroke in 1992.

[17] See, for example, Maimonides' twelfth principle of faith: "I believe with perfect faith in the coming of the messiah. No matter how long it takes, I will await his coming every day."

[18] See especially the opinions of David Berger in "Is the Rebbe Becoming God?" p. 19; "The New Messianism, pp. 35–42, 88; and *The Rebbe, the Messiah, and the Scandal of Orthodox Indifference*. See also Raquel Hasofer, "Messiah from the Living—Messiah from the Dead," which is concerned with the mashiach debate in the post-Schneerson Habad movement.

[19] He also frequently remarked that everything had been prepared for the mashiach: "He is standing at the doorpost and is just waiting for us to open the door and squeeze the redemption into the room."

[20] See Chapter 7.

[21] See, for example, Shmuel Butman, *Countdown to Moshiach*.

[22] Moses Maimonides, *Mishneh Torah*; see the section of this work published as *The Code of Maimonides, Book Fourteen: The Book of Judges*, trans. Avraham M. Hershman (New Haven, 1949), chap. 11, verse 4.

[23] Haim Hillel Ben-Sasson, in his *Atah Yadati*, derives this from Talmud Bavli: Sanhedrin 98b, where Rabbi Nahman states: "If [the mashiach] is from those living today it might be one like myself" (pp. 84–85). Ben-Sasson further quotes the responsa of Hatam Sofer (Hoshen Mishpat, Liqutim, chap. 98) as saying: "In every generation there is born a man from the seed

of Judah who merits to be the Mashiach of Israel, and when the time comes, God will reveal Himself to him and send him. He will then infuse him with the spirit of mashiach that was hidden and put away above."

[24] Rambam, *Mishneh Torah*, Laws of Kings 11:4 (*mashiach bevadai*).

[25] Among the few are Sabbetai Sevi, Isaac Luria, Abraham Abulafia, and possibly Jesus.

[26] When one of his Hasidim, Avraham Pariz, for example, printed a poster in 1952 proclaiming him as the messiah, Schneerson forbade its distribution.

[27] Some observers noted immediately after his first discourse that Schneerson had messianic delusions. See also the text of this discourse, *Sefer ha-Ma'amarim Bati le-Gani* (Brooklyn, 1977), for possible references to his own messianic role. Schneerson states, for example, that the seventh generation (he was the seventh Rebbe of Habad) was unique, emphasizing throughout the discourse that its special status was not due to its merits, and indeed that they did not deserve it, and "do not even want it," but nonetheless the generation is special. He compares the seventh generation to the final drawing down of godly light in a physical form, which is a necessary part of the messianic arrival. He clearly tries to explain to others and even to himself how and why he was placed in the position of Rebbe despite his unsuitability, and mentions the beginnings of a sense of mission, even a messianic mission, that would form the core of his leadership.

[28] See *sichot* for Beit Rabeinu Bavel, 5751; and Parshat Shoftim, 5751.

[29] Vital, as quoted by Abraham Abulafia in his commentary on the *Zohar*, entitled *Or ha-Hammah*, on *Zohar* 11, 7b. Cited in Gershom Scholem, *Sabbatai Sevi*, p. 53.

[30] Her funeral was held on February 10, 1988 (22 Shvat 5748).

[31] The wills and their part in the power struggle within Habad after Schneerson's death will be examined in Chapter 20.

[32] Joseph Caro, *Beit Yosef* on *Tur Or ha-Hayim*, chap. 188.

[33] *Sichah* of 28 Nissan 5751 (April 12, 1991).

[34] Ibid. See also "Rabbinical Ruling," p. 33, which contains a declaration of the Rebbe as *moshiach*, signed by dozens of leading Habad rabbis.

[35] See, for example, Butman, *Countdown to Moshiach*, pp. 57–59.

Chapter 10
Schneerson as a World Leader

Over the years of his leadership of Habad, in addition to consolidating his authority over the Habad community and the neighborhood of Crown Heights, Schneerson became a figure of immense significance to many outside the movement. As we have seen, he did this initially through the power of his office, but he built upon this base through the development of his natural charismatic leadership qualities, skillful administration, and the ideology of messianism. He built a corps of highly disciplined and ideologically motivated Hasidim across the world, through whom he had an impact, in varying degrees, on the broader Jewish world, the State of Israel, other world governments, and on various specific world audiences. Part of Schneerson's desire to become a figure of influence was no doubt derived from his concern for the dissemination of Habad ideology and religious observance to Jews dispossessed of their traditions and heritage. No doubt the role of this in the messianic process, at least according to Habad ideology, was also a contributing factor in his political and social involvement beyond the ultra-Orthodox world. The methods by which Schneerson became a figure of influence beyond his Hasidic dynasty, and the degree of his success in various political agendas, will be our concern in the next two chapters.

The Turning Point in Consolidation

Schneerson's popularity originally emerged from his post as the Lubavitcher Rebbe. From the time he assumed this role, he came to be known throughout both the Jewish world and, in time, throughout the non-Jewish community too. There appears, however, to be a complementary relationship between the strengthening of general Jewish and gentile support for Schneerson and his growth in stature within his own community. The Habad Hasidim, apparently, took pride in their leader's public popularity with dignitaries, parliamentarians, benefactors, and politicians, and came to view him more favorably with every successful encounter.

By the 1970s, Schneerson's popularity in the Jewish world was growing. His control over Habad was consolidated by this time, and the movement was internally strong and had a strong outreach ideology. Schneerson had already led the movement for twenty years, and he had aged, grayed, and become more distinguished in appearance with the passing years, looking more and more like the archetype of a wise and venerable elder. Moreover, there had been substantial natural growth in the Habad movement. Postwar children were growing up, the young and enthusiastic Hasidim of Schneerson's youth were already middle-aged, and their children were being edu-cated in the ideology of Habad. The movement's emissaries had met with tremendous success in the communities built that served to expand Schneerson's reputation as a visionary leader. It had become evident, even to outsiders, that Habad's beliefs and activities were a viable alternative to secularization and integration, offering a secure, stable future to those within the movement, and attracting even more to join it. The internal strength of the movement, by its very nature, had an effect on its public image and on the demeanor of Schneerson as its leader.

His reputation as a holy man, a prophet, and a miracle-worker considerably enhanced his popularity not only in Habad, but in the wider world.[1] He and the move-ment attracted the desperate and the optimistic, the curious and the superstitious, who came to ask his advice or simply to meet him. The increased receptivity of outsiders to Schneerson, evidence of his uniqueness of character, reinforced the Habad com-munity's commitment to him, and they more vigorously shouted his praises to the open ears of many segments of the wider Jewish population.

A Jewish Leader

Schneerson came to be known during his reign as a Jewish leader not only for Habad but for many observant and secular Jews across the world. How it was possi-ble to separate his personal reputation from the negative view of the Habad move-ment held in some quarters is not an easy matter to understand. The ideological rift between Orthodox groups often results in a total lack of communication between the various movements. Habad as a school has been criticized by many groups and indi-viduals who have nonetheless noted the significance and importance of Schneerson. Indeed, many were to observe throughout his reign that the leader was very different from his following, and therefore they were able to recognize his greatness as a man and at the same time to criticize his movement without personally attacking him. This is interesting, because his Hasidim were the conduit through which Schneerson was able to deliver his message and ideas to the wider world. His ability to be seen as sep-arate from his executive arm was a significant achievement, and contributed to Schneerson's image of being above involvement in political affairs.

Schneerson remained in the Crown Heights vicinity without leaving it for his entire time as Rebbe, not counting frequent visits to the gravesite of his predecessor, Yosef Yitzhak. Because of this, he did not visit dignitaries or attend meetings or leadership conferences on their "turf." Nor did he offer other leaders honors or deference, which would have served to put him on par with them as contemporaries. Rather, it was they who came to him. Rabbis, Hasidic Rebbes, spiritual leaders, politicians, and activists from across the Jewish world came to visit him in his own court, where he received them surrounded by his own people and on his own terms. The Hasidic enthusiasm and excitement surrounding these events, lending dignity and regality to his presence, would in all likelihood have been much less evident if he had held quiet meetings in distant places. It was this attitude, at least in part, which contributed to Schneerson's recognition as a Jewish leader of magnified stature.

Much of his reputation resulted from personal appearances and audiences attended by reporters, journalists, and writers who spread the image of Schneerson as a holy man to a far wider audience than the Habad community. Habad's media-oriented outreach strategy and its influence in non-Habad Jewish communities, the educational facilities established by the movement for the dissemination of its ideology, and a constant stream of propaganda from Habad served to widen Schneerson's appeal.

The general absence of leadership personalities in the secular Jewish world, especially sagacious and mystical figures like Schneerson, made it relatively easy to promote the Rebbe's appealing image throughout the Jewish community. Whether or not people liked him, knew what he stood for, or realized that he was the leader of a small movement within a multifarious Jewish life was rendered largely irrelevant. His advocates presented him as a general Jewish leader. For some time, his picture was the only likeness displayed in Jewish public places, which made him highly noticeable. Sermons and talks by his Hasidim, many of whom occupied synagogue pulpits in non-Habad congregations, referred to him as "the Rebbe" rather than by name, denoting his unique status and conveying a sense of comprehensive leadership. Hence, many Jewish laypersons came to see Schneerson as a Jewish leader par excellence, and the more curious among them wrote to him and attended his public appearances.

In Israel, the Habad movement has long been the most popular ultra-Orthodox group. Several factors made it appealing to the public despite the general segregation between secular and Orthodox communities. Perhaps most important, the Habad philosophy of tolerance and love for fellow Jews was markedly different from the insular orientation of many other ultra-Orthodox groups, who see anyone at variance with their ideals or practices as "the enemy," even if the opposition is Jewish. Moreover, Habad Hasidim were more inclined to join the Israeli army than other Hasidim.[2] Military service, from which most Hasidic groups seek exemption, is a sensitive issue, especially with secular Israelis, and Habad's participation in military activity has significantly bolstered the movement's favorable reputation as a part of Israeli society.

The Habad outreach presence in public places (bus stations, airports, and street corners) also served to make them a familiar sight to Israelis. Their friendliness and perceived integrity, despite their black garb and sectarian look, surprised many people, who began to believe that the Habad movement was different from other religious groups. Habad's outreach presence in the army was also an important contribution to its popularity. Emissaries were often sent to army bases in trucks known as "mitzvah tanks" to bring a reminder of Jewish culture and religious observance into the lives of soldiers. One of the most striking uses of these vehicles, and one that has provided an enduring positive image for Habad, came during the Lebanese war, when mitzvah tanks rolled into Lebanon along with the official armed forces, to lend assistance. The Habad movement was seen as sharing the burden of war with the rest of the Israeli populace, an action that was much appreciated and is still remembered.

Furthermore, the Habad presence in various countries outside of Israel often provided Israeli tourists with a taste of Jewish culture. Many Israelis, particularly after their compulsory army service, travel extensively overseas. Many of these tourists are in search of an identity or spirituality that they have not found in Israel, and so end up in India, Nepal, Thailand, and other so-called spiritual centers. Habad has established Habad Houses in all these places where otherwise secular Israelis encounter Jewish tradition in a different way from its institutionalized function in Israeli politics, through events such as the Passover seders in Kathmandu and Bangkok.[3] Because of Habad outreach, many Israelis have ironically begun to appreciate their Jewish culture outside of Israel, and some even become newly religious after encounters with Habad emissaries outside Israel. Whatever the effect, the Habad presence overseas further enhanced the Israeli secularist perception of Schneerson as a universal Jewish leader.

Despite this influence, or possibly even because of it, there was much criticism of Schneerson in the secular Jewish camp. Because of his public stature, he received disproportionate criticism from secular Jews as well as Reform and Conservative groups. Schneerson's public support for government funding of religious institutions, for example, was felt by many to impinge upon the separation of church and state; many Jewish secularists and reform groups opposed Habad's position, and were irritated by Schneerson's lack of conformity with mainstream opinion and culture. His hawkish views on Israeli politics and his involvement in the Israeli political debate over the "who is a Jew?" issue raised the ire of secularists and the Reform movement in the United States. These issues were also supported by other groups, but Schneerson was considered to represent a large following and thus was regarded as a chief proponent of these ideas. Thus he often received the brunt of criticism. This criticism might simply be perceived as another indication of his stature in the Jewish community, for the attention given him implied that his opinion was worth listening to.

Modern Orthodoxy

Even in some branches of modern Orthodoxy, Schneerson was perceived as an authoritative figure, or at least as a venerable sage and holy man. Modern Orthodoxy does not have a comprehensive, organized leadership structure, or a founding father or leader who is fundamental to its existence.[4] There is no predisposition to treat leadership figures with extreme veneration, as occurs in Hasidic communities. When Schneerson became Rebbe of Habad, there was a leadership vacuum in the Orthodox community, which served to deplete its sense of identity and the social and symbolic need for a figurehead. Even in the years since, there has not emerged a leader of prominence in modern Orthodoxy who could gain widespread popular support or who was even willing to seek it. Modern Orthodox Jews often sought out personalities from their own ranks to esteem, and there were attempts by more enthusiastic adherents to force two prominent Orthodox rabbis, Soloveitchik and Feinstein, into more universal leadership roles, but generally such efforts were unsuccessful.[5] Orthodox observance was therefore infused by Hasidic spirituality, which provided such leadership personalities, even though it did not necessarily adhere to most aspects of the Hasidic lifestyle.

Into this vacuum stepped Schneerson, of whom many stories had been told throughout the Jewish world. He was perceived from the outset as appropriately modern, yet was respected as an authentic Jewish sage. He also had one advantage over other Hasidic leaders: his invitation of correspondence from all who wished to write to him. Many in the Orthodox community took advantage of this receptivity, and soul-searching inquirers could communicate with what they hoped would be a truly "authentic" rabbi. He offered blessings and advice to all Jews, and was often able to assist them in their spiritual and personal problems. He was marketed in the broadest way, and hence was seen by many modern Orthodox Jews as a venerable leader who transcended his movement and his Hasidim.

Another area of influence for Schneerson in the modern Orthodox world was in the provision of religious training. Habad schools and yeshivot offered scholarships and evening classes; Schneerson encouraged the ordination of rabbis, and many people took advantage of the opportunities provided. After their training, many students joined the modern Orthodox camp while retaining a sympathetic affection for Habad. In this way, many of the younger generation of modern Orthodox rabbis were acquainted in some way with Habad and Schneerson, and inevitably offered deference to them. Moreover, Rabbi J. B. Soloveitchik, often considered a representative of the modern Orthodox movement, had known Schneerson from their youth. He spoke highly of Schneerson and even paid him a visit in Crown Heights.[6] This served to foster closer relations between the two camps and heightened Schneerson's standing among Soloveitchik's Orthodox associates. Rabbi Moshe Feinstein was also known to have paid deference to Schneerson. Habad sources recollect how Schneerson suggested that Feinstein don an extra pair of tefillin, a recommendation that Feinstein obeyed. Because of this, Habad followers described him as subservient to Schneerson. The notion that Schneerson was a mentor for even the most eminent Orthodox rabbis was carefully cultivated through stories such as these, and served to further embellish his status as a Jewish leader.

This is not to say that there was no criticism of Schneerson in the modern Orthodox movement. While many modern Orthodox leaders were either respectful toward Schneerson or careful to declare their indifference to him, other branches of modern Orthodoxy had fundamental ideological clashes with both Schneerson and the Habad movement. Most recently, David Berger, an Orthodox rabbi and academic, wrote a polemic accusing Habad of Christianizing heresies and calling for its excommunication from mainstream Judaism because of its messianic tendency. The polemics of confrontation between the two groups are often most interesting, and question Schneerson's Hasidic ideology, his strong political opinions, his mystical and superstitious orientation, the messianic fervor he encouraged, and various other issues of contention. Although this criticism has often served Habad unfavorably, it had nevertheless reaffirmed Schneerson's centrality in Jewish religious, political, and social life.

Sephardi Jewry

Other groups of religious Jews also began to see Schneerson as a towering leadership figure. Sephardi Jews, particularly those who migrated to Israel in the 1950s, thought highly of him because of the assistance they received from Habad. While other Hasidim and Lithuanian ultra-Orthodox groups are not very receptive to Sephardi culture and influence, the Habad philosophy did not depend on its Ashkenazi origins and had no problem welcoming Jews from other backgrounds into its ranks. Just as Shalom Dov Ber had sent emissaries to Georgia in his time and thus broke the ethnic lines previously associated with Hasidism, Yosef Yitzhak and Schneerson continued the same policy. Schneerson sent emissaries to Morocco and Tunisia in the 1950s, and established contacts with Jews in Yemen, Iraq, and Iran. The Habad movement was active in their integration into Israeli society after the establishment of the State of Israel, and many settled in Kfar Habad and other Habad neighborhoods there.[7]

The largely working-class oriental Jews who settled in Israel were both traditionalist and inclined to superstition. They were attracted by the stories of Schneerson's prophetic personality and miraculous deeds, and were deeply grateful for Habad's acceptance of them. Habad, in fact, claims the highest percentage of Sephardi initiates into any Hasidic movement. Although most of the Sephardi immigrants did not adopt the Habad lifestyle, they viewed Schneerson as a universal Jewish leader, as evidenced by the display of his picture in homes, shops, businesses, cars, and buses.[8] This facilitated Schneerson's influence on them, particularly in matters concerning Israeli politics.

The most significant factor in the Sephardi recognition of Schneerson as a supreme Jewish leader was the deference with which their own venerated leaders treated him. Baba Sali, the Moroccan Jewish mystic and popular leader, allegedly venerated Schneerson, visited him regularly, and spoke of him as a superior. His son, who heads the Moroccan community, has good relations with the Habad movement. Mordechai Eliyahu, a present-day Sephardi leader, also expressed great admiration for Schneerson. The perception that these esteemed community rabbis looked up to Schneerson further enhanced his reputation as a grand rabbi.

The Israeli political party Shas is at the forefront of Sephardi rights, education, cultural reawakening, and religious rededication in modern Israel. Although it has had little to do with the Habad movement, its strategy is remarkably similar to that of

Habad. It has a strong outreach program to attract secular Sephardi Jews. The program utilizes popular media figures and advertising, and has succeeded in drawing much support from mainstream secularism. Although Habad has little direct connection to this movement, it has apparently succeeded in changing the priorities of many religious groups to the practice of outreach.

Russian Jewry

Habad's affiliation with Russian Jewry dates from its very origins. Most Habad Hasidim are of Russian ancestry, and many Habad Hasidim, particularly of the older generation, still speak Russian. Habad Hasidim remained behind the Iron Curtain even as Yosef Yitzhak made his escape to Poland and later to the United States, and it was through these remnants of Habad in Russia that Yosef Yitzhak and then Schneerson maintained contact with Soviet Jewry. Habad is famous for its support of continuity in Soviet Jewish life. Emissaries used to smuggle ritual articles into the Soviet Union to facilitate the religious observance of Russian Jews, and many stories are told in Habad of the feats of bravery of Hasidim attempting to live in accordance with Jewish law and revive community life in the Soviet Union. Russian Jewish émigrés who have returned to their Jewish roots and chosen to live a religious life are overwhelmingly inclined to adopt Habad Hasidism as their religious preference.[9] Rabbi Lau notes that if any Russian Jews still identified with Judaism after the fall of the Iron Curtain, it wais certainly to the sole credit of the Habad movement.[10]

When emigration from the Soviet Union was possible for a time in the 1970s, and again in the late 1980s, the Habad movement helped many of those who left with their integration in Israel, America, and the other societies where they settled. There are Habad synagogues specifically established to accommodate Russian immigrants in most countries of the world. Habad has also sponsored other campaigns on behalf of Russian Jewry, such as the rescue and airlifting of one thousand Jewish children from Chernobyl to Israel after the nuclear disaster in April 1986. Russian children are trained in Habad schools and are supported by its institutions. Services ranging from religious education and free circumcisions,[11] to vocational training and mass bar- and bat-mitzvah ceremonies are also sponsored by the Habad movement. Joseph Gutnick, one of Habad's main financial benefactors, was deeply involved in the support of the latest immigration of Soviet Jews in the 1990s.[12]

Since the fall of the Soviet Union, other religious and Zionist organizations have come to the aid of Russian Jewry. Habad has established a yeshiva through the renowned talmudist Rabbi Adin Steinsaltz, and has sent emissaries to all the countries of the former Soviet Union. Beginning with the election of 1996, the Israeli government has had to reckon with the political power of the Russian émigrés. A pro-Habad sentiment is evident among a number of the Russian members of the Knesset.

Many academics and scientists, exploring their roots during the Jewish revival in the Soviet Union, developed an interest in Habad Hasidism because of its historical connection with Russia. When they migrated to Israel or the United States, they maintained their connections with the movement, and many became full participants in Habad activism, thereby strengthening its intellectual reputation.

Other Hasidic Groups

Other Hasidic groups treat Habad as a pariah, mainly because of its variant Russian origins, its intellectual ideology, and the unique qualities of many of its leaders, whose initiatives were often considered inappropriate or unduly progressive. Contemporary Habad communities that live among other ultra-Orthodox Jews, especially in Israel and New York, are treated cautiously by their neighbors. Their distinct identity, more modern yet recognizably traditional dress code, their meticulous obedience to Schneerson even after his death, make them stand out even in very conservative ultra-Orthodox neighborhoods. They are often criticized because of their modernity, the apparent laxity of their halakhic observance, their institutional preoccupation with outreach instead of learning, and their casual approach to esoteric literature.

Habad Hasidic literature, and most especially the works authored by Shneur Zalman, the movement's founder, is still studied and respected in other Hasidic circles, and because of this Habad's ideology cannot be ideologically shunned as heretical or inauthentic. Thus the Habad Hasidim are indulged by their Hasidic counterparts. Habad Hasidim, on the other hand, see their function in ultra-Orthodoxy as centering on outreach. There are emissaries whose prime occupation is the dissemination of Habad ideology. Many of the emissaries to the ultra-Orthodox are chosen because of their scholarship or familiarity with other ultra-Orthodox customs, and they actively try to attract Hasidim and mitnagdim from other communities to the ranks of Habad. Habad Hasidim feel that they are, in fact, the avant-garde of the religious world, and the trends they have started, ranging from political campaigning to outreach to the secular world, have all been adopted by other groups. Well aware that they are not appreciated or recognized by other Hasidim, they nonetheless see themselves as the most forward-thinking, progressive, and dynamic element of ultra-Orthodoxy, and therefore as having a decisive function to play even among the "converted."

In Israel, some degree of cooperation between ultra-Orthodox groups and Habad has come about because of political concerns and the need for alliances to further Orthodox influence in the country's life. Habad has forged alliances with the Ger Hasidim and other groups, and for some time they were active in the Hasidic political party, Agudat Yisrael, which had representatives in the Knesset. The alliance was reinforced when Joseph Gutnick, a multi-millionaire Habad Hasid, began to donate money to Hasidic organizations other than Habad, particularly Ger. This has created a friendly relationship between Habad and some other Hasidic dynasties, on the basis of shared interests and mutual dependence.

This is not to say, of course, that the opposition to Habad in the ultra-Orthodox community has been eliminated. Hasidic criticism of Habad has come primarily from the Satmar Hasidim of New York. Their objections to Habad's messianic fervor and perceived halakhic laxity is at the root of much polemic, argument, and even physical violence between the two groups.[13] The conflict between Habad and Satmar stirred up tensions in the Hasidic world, for other groups were compelled to side with one group or the other. These grievances reached a peak in the early 1980s, but eventually subsided. The tension at that time was aggravated by claims that Habad was missionizing in Satmar territory, and the rumor that some Satmar Hasidim were turning to Habad as a preferred ideology. Significantly, even at the height of this conflict, little personal invective was directed at Schneerson himself; rather, the Habad Hasidim were accused of misrepresenting Schneerson, and therefore bore the brunt of the criticism.

The Mitnagdim

The mitnagdic element in the United States and Israel kept its distance from Schneerson. Although its historical antagonism to Hasidism had, of necessity, calmed due to other, more pressing challenges, particularly postwar Jewish rehabilitation and opposition to the tide of secularism, there was still a sharp division between the two groups. The main point of contention was the messianic fervor surrounding Schneerson. Habad appears to have influenced the mitnagdim in some ways, especially concerning the priority for outreach. Whereas once Habad provided the sole outreach and educational services for secular Jews, today it has been surpassed by mitnagdic groups that have become extremely effective in their missionary work.[14]

The strongest expression of anti-Habad and anti-Schneerson sentiment is associated with Israeli mitnagdic circles, and particularly Rabbi Shach, who heads the elite Ponovitz yeshiva and is considered the leader of mitnagdic ultra-Orthodox Jewry. His criticism extended not only to Habad as a movement, as with the Hasidic groups discussed above, but also to Schneerson himself. Shach called him a false prophet and a madman, and even accused the Habad movement of heresy.[15] In mitnagdic circles, therefore, Schneerson was clearly a *persona non grata*, and did not succeed in establishing a favorable name for himself or his movement. The severe criticism and consequent schism between the groups reflected mitnagdic concern about Habad's increasing influence in the Jewish community and the need to put an end to it, or at least publicly express disagreement with its methods. The fact that Habad stood at the center of one of the most fierce Hasidic–mitnagdic confrontations in the twentieth century serves only to indicate the movement's strength and the fear of its spreading influence.

Religious Zionism

Habad's impact on the religious Zionist movement will be discussed at greater length in the next chapter. A word about the relationship between religious Zionism and Habad is necessary here, however, to illustrate the influence Schneerson had on the Jewish world. The full extent of this influence is still unknown, as future years may see a closer merger of the two ideologies. Despite the classical anti-Zionism of its early centuries, the present-day Habad movement has fully involved itself in the affairs and internal politics of the Israeli state. The movement justifies its engagement with the Zionist enterprise and the State of Israel on the grounds that the spiritual needs of the five million Jews who live in Israel, are not being met by the secular state. Officially and practically, the issue of statehood and the role of Israel as a nation are not in question. The central concern is the level of halakhic observance of the inhabitants of the Holy Land.

The religious Zionist movement comprises several different philosophic strands, the most dominant of which derives from the teachings of Rabbi A.Y. Kook. It is not the purpose of this work to discuss the similarities between the Habad movement's teachings and Kook's, but one may note that Kook's mother was from a Habad family, and much of his mysticism had its roots in Habad thought. Kook's outreach orientation, tolerance of secular Jews, and belief in their innate contribution to the eventual redemption were remarkably similar in many respects to the views of Habad. Kook's messianic fervor predated Schneerson's rise to power, and although this can only be surmised, may have stimulated and influenced Schneerson's messianism.

For many decades there was little formal ideological or religious cooperation between the two movements over the decades. Political necessity, however, has brought them to the negotiating table and forced them to recognize their commonality. This has taken place against the backdrop of the "land for peace" negotiations in Israel, which both Habad and religious Zionism strongly oppose. Habad had a long history of settlement in Eretz Yisrael before the establishment of the state, and the movement owned property in the Old City of Jerusalem, in Shechem, and in Hebron. These areas are the most sensitive areas in the Israeli-Palestinian peace talks, and Habad has allowed them to be settled and administered through the relocation of religious Zionists. Schneerson spoke out strongly in favor of Jewish settlement in Israel and against any retreat from captured territory. This included fierce opposition to the Camp David Accords in 1979.

Although Habad Hasidim did not actively settle in these territories, they were fiercely supportive of the right to do so, and also of the people who exercised this right. There was an unarticulated respect for the settlers, who despite their non-affiliation with Habad were seen as heroes by many in the movement. Although there was a sense of messianic mission in both the settler movement and the Habad outreach movement, this commonality was not appreciated by either group;[16] their cooperation and mutual appreciation was on a more pragmatic level.

The relationship became closer as the Habad movement began to fund advertising and propaganda campaigns against the Labor government of 1992–1996. Since many of the rightist parties were experiencing financial difficulties, Habad's financial support, activist initiative, and enthusiastic volunteers were much appreciated by the right-wing religious Zionist parties, and increased their appreciation of the Habad contribution to the Zionist cause. Much of the financial backing for these Habad campaigns came from Joseph Gutnick, who also gave money to settler initiatives, yeshivot, and settler industries. In this way, the alliance between the religious Zionist organization and Habad is ever increasing. With the death of Schneerson, the relationship has become stronger, and with the passage of time, an amalgamation of ideologies is certainly possible.

Israeli Personalities

Schneerson always took an interest in the affairs of the State of Israel . Many visiting Israeli dignitaries in the United States paid courtesy calls in Crown Heights, among them Ben-Gurion, Zalman Shazar, Menahem Begin, Yitzhak Shamir, and Ariel Sharon, as well as innumerable Knesset members, religious leaders, and generals. More leaders corresponded with him. According to Habad, Zalman Shazar's advisers allegedly told him that it was disrespectful to the office of President of the State of Israel for him to visit Schneerson, arguing that it would be more appropriate for Schneerson to visit Shazar at his hotel. Shazar responded that visiting the Rebbe was his honor, and continued to do so whenever he was in New York. The impression given by these visits was that Schneerson had the ear of Israel's leaders and, more important, that they listened to his advice, which of course served to enhance his stature in the Jewish world.

Throughout his reign, and through his connections to Israel's political and military elite, Schneerson maintained hawkish views on Israel's right to keep the conquered territories. Perhaps unexpectedly, however, he justified these views on purely military grounds, and not by citing scriptural sources or theological arguments. Schneerson maintained that, especially after the Holocaust, the existence of the State of Israel, and the retention of the occupied territories, was the best way to save Jewish lives. He met and corresponded with both Menahem Begin and Yitzhak Shamir, and advised them not to compromise on their "no negotiation" policy regarding the surrender of territory to the Palestinians.

Despite his efforts, though, Schneerson had little direct influence on Israeli politics. This is probably because its strongly democratic nature and stability effectively limits the impact of individuals. Other religious leaders, including Rabbis Shach and Ovadiah Yosef, had more political influential than Schneerson. The only time Schneerson appeared to affect Israeli politics was in the elections of 1988, when he instructed thousands of his Hasidim to return to Israel and vote. Additionally, he encouraged Habad sympathizers and his own personal admirers to support the Agudat Yisrael political party. Advertisements for the party even promised blessings from Schneerson for those who voted for it. Thanks to this campaign, so it is estimated, the party earned two extra seats in the Knesset, which equates to approximately 40,000 extra votes. This facilitated the rise of a Likud-led government. In later elections, Habad maintained this activity, although Schneerson reputedly delegated

Israel's territorial issue to Joseph Gutnick, who is a major funder of right-wing and religious political parties. He played a significant role in the rise of the Likud party in Israel's 1996 election.[17]

Because of his perceived interference in Israel's internal politics, even though he lived in another country and thus was not directly concerned, Schneerson was subjected to much criticism from Israeli parliamentarians who favored civil rights, secular statehood, and the pursuit of negotiations over territory. They pointed out that even though he professed concern for Jews throughout the world, and especially in Israel, he had never visited the Holy Land, accusing him of hypocrisy. When Habad began taking a more activist political stance in the early 1990s, leftist elements tried to prevent the movement from carrying out its activities in the army and at the national airport. They also advocated the cessation of government funding for Habad's charitable activities, claiming these were being conducted by a partisan political group.

Through such efforts, the influence and reputation of Habad in Israeli politics were reduced; the more blatant the movement's political activities became, the stronger the criticism of its activities, and the more marginalized it became. Hence, Habad's foray into Israeli politics although often politically successful, led to some erosion of its popularity with the Israeli public, and also with the many Diaspora Jews who feel that the movement's interference in Israeli politics is inappropriate.

Beyond the Jewish World

As we have seen, during the formative years of his consolidation of power, Schneerson succeeded in establishing his renown in the Jewish world, in most cases to a significant degree. He was recognized by informed Jews as a contributor to Jewish continuity and religious thought. The self-proclaimed aim of the Habad movement, however, was to bring on the messianic redemption, an event that would have profound effects on the whole world and not just its Jewish residents. There were attempts by Schneerson himself to influence world politics, and he initiated several programs to expand Habad's outreach to a non-Jewish audience. This was seen as a necessary, and indeed vital, stage in the messianic redemption, particularly by those Hasidim who viewed him as the *mashiah*. It was only through recognition of his messianic status that people would surrender to his leadership and facilitate the coming of the messianic era. To bring about this event, the Hasidim tried to forge an identity for Schneerson as one of the world's foremost leaders, but at this they were rather less successful.

This process is consistent with what Friedman has described as the transformation of the movement from local particularism to universal mission.[18] The declaration of Schneerson's leadership to the non-Jewish world was an essential element in the universalization of Habad. Over time, the Habad movement had taken on the burden not only of disseminating Habad ideology, but of expanding the influence of Hasidism in general. It did not stop with this, however, but saw itself as responsible for the dissemination of Judaism to those who were not observant, and still later its mission broadened to bring the gentile nations back to Godliness. Even this was not enough. The Habad movement saw itself as responsible for nothing less than the complete redemption and transformation of the cosmos into its ideal messianic utopian state. Schneerson was naturally at the epicenter of this equation as the messianic redeemer. He saw the world as his community, and sought to translate philosophic promises of redemption into practical programs whereby the redemption might be achieved.[19] His success in redeeming the Jewish people, while far from complete, had been rapid and significant, and by the 1980s, Schneerson headed a movement of possibly several tens of thousands of committed members, not to mention hundreds of thousands of sympathizers, and had wide influence in the worldwide Jewish community.

Weber notes that a charismatic leader achieves his status by virtue, among other things, of his mission. If this is so, then it becomes almost imperative for a messianic pretender in Judaism to broaden the scope of his mission. Schneerson successfully pursued the goal of the re-education of world Jewry, but if his messianic aspirations were to be recognized, he would have to extend his mission beyond Jewish spirituality to an all-encompassing revival of the spirituality of all humanity.

The Laws of Noah

Steps in this direction appear to have been taken in the later years of Schneerson's life. They are best illustrated by his campaign, initiated in 1983, to "influence the nations of the world." This was not an attempt to convert gentiles to Judaism; it was a program designed to explain the basic moral code expected of the gentile nations as prescribed in the seven Noahide laws.[20] This step was quite remarkable in that it was the first Jewish attempt at pseudo-missionary work toward the gentiles in many centuries. Schneerson's did not intend to make this new outreach a priority for Habad, or to detract from the more important goals that the movement was already pursuing. Rather, gentile outreach was presented as a means of utilizing free time (while traveling on public transport, for example, or on any occasion of interaction with the non-Jewish world) to remind the gentile world of its moral obligations.

The Noahide campaign led to large and costly advertisements throughout the world, proclaiming the imminent messianic revelation and calling on everyone, Jew and non-Jew alike, to participate. The advertising included the hanging of posters in public places that encouraged everyone to perform acts of goodness and kindness, in order to help prepare the world for the coming of the mashiach. The inclusion of the gentile world in Habad's messianic mission was not taken to extremes in Schneerson's lifetime, but was undertaken more extensively after his first stroke in 1992, when the Hasidim were no longer constrained by his veto. They felt that by publicizing the coming redemption to all humanity, they were forcing Schneerson to reveal himself as the mashiach, and for this reason it is possible that gentile outreach may develop into a central theme of Habad's outreach program in the years to come.

The impact of this media and public relations campaign on the world was relatively insignificant. The campaign attracted few gentiles and served primarily to anger Jews who felt that missionary activity was taboo and not part of the Jewish mainstream. The campaign was also ill conceived from Habad's point of view; since the movement did not encourage non-Jewish converts to join its ranks, it could not channel the energy of the gentile enthusiasts attracted by the campaign. A center for the dissemination of the Noahide laws was established, and non-Jews participated in its activities, but there was little else for these "converts" to do with their new faith. The traditional unwillingness to encourage conversion to Judaism, which Habad shared with other Jewish groups, served as a major obstacle to the success of this campaign, which was not intended to encourage conversion. The Laws of Noah are explicitly for non-Jews, and the adoption of Jewish halakhah was discouraged, except where it influenced observance of the Noahide laws. The rigorous conversion process required for an Orthodox conversion to Judaism was certainly not relaxed to accommodate gentiles interested in entering the movement, so this criticism is perhaps unjustified.

On a practical scale, the Noahide campaign under Schneerson might best be viewed as an unsuccessful aberration. On an ideological scale, however, it was extremely interesting, and carried within it a seed for the movement's possible future expansion into a universal religious system. It may also be an indication of Schneerson's perception of his own messianic status. In the short term, the movement's commitment to halakhah, its followers' sense of elitism, and its fear of estrangement from the Jewish mainstream, have kept even the more extremist elements within Habad from actively proselytizing or redirecting its outreach efforts to the non-Jewish world.

Schneerson and World Politics

Schneerson's influence on the world outside Habad was primarily obtained through his emissaries. The Habad communities around the world were all individually responsible for their own maintenance, financing, and programming, so winning local support was decisive in their success and growth. Habad representatives cultivated good relations with local Jewish and government leaders, and most particularly with the business sector. As a result, the many extremely wealthy Jews who have contributed regularly to Habad activities have had a vested interest in the movement's continuity. Often they have acted as lobbyists on behalf of the Habad movement to government bodies and to the non-Jewish world. Because of this, the Habad movement has come to wield power disproportionate to its size, with money available to obtain media access and influence political opinion.

Habad has achieved its strongest non-Jewish impact in the United States, but it has also been influential in other countries, including the former Soviet Union, South Africa, and Australia. In contrast to other Jewish organizations, its impact on American politics and government has been relatively minor. It has chiefly sought to influence American governmental policy by pressuring for a "moment of silence" in the nation's public schools, in order to facilitate religious awareness in American youth, an attempt that has not met with success.

The fact that Schneerson was honored on his birthday by every President of the United States since Richard Nixon is indicative of the impression he and the movement made on America.[21] The Rebbe had personal interviews with mayoral candidates in New York City, including Mayor Dinkins, an acknowledgment of the fact that the Habad population of New York was extremely disciplined in its voting turnout, with its adherents all voting as Schneerson directed. The movement claims to have been responsible for a number of electoral victories.

What emerges from all this is the fact that the need to present Schneerson as a world leader was important for the messianic aspirations of the Hasidim. After Schneerson's death, a great deal of lobbying energy was harnessed to win for him the highest award available to civilians in the United States. In late 1994, Schneerson was posthumously awarded the prestigious Congressional Gold Medal, with many powerful people attending the ceremony in Washington.[22] Turnout for his funeral also included large numbers of dignitaries, and telegrams were received from leaders across the globe.

Despite the attempts to present Schneerson as a world leader, however, his public appeal was not broad enough to attract wide popular support. He was respected as a great Jewish leader, and as an educator and advocate of ethics, but in Weber's terms, his mission was not sufficiently appealing to the gentile world to win him a significant following. For the Jewish world, the need for continuity after the Holocaust contributed to Schneerson's appeal, but the gentile world could not as easily identify with this need. The attempts to broaden his appeal came too late, with insufficient resources to make an impact and on the basis of a religious idea that would be rejected by most Christian Americans, namely, the emergence of a Jewish mashiach in the person of Schneerson. It must be concluded, therefore, that his role as the universal mashiach was not fulfilled during his lifetime, and that the world must await the messianic revelation a little longer.

---

[1] See Judy Noah Gothard, "The Wait Is Over." She recounts a miracle story about a hurricane that missed Miami, contrary to scientific expectation but as Schneerson had said it would; and Joshua Sandman, "Rebbe Played Profound Role in Judaism." See also *Prophecies Fulfilled*, a pamphlet published by Zeirei Habad. It claims that Schneerson predicted many occurrences in Israel, among them the Gulf War.

[2] Military service for Habad Hasidim is shortened to either one or three months, as opposed to the standard three years. Hasidim thereafter serve reserve duty. The high percentage of newly religious members, many of whom served in the army before joining the movement, gives Habad the positive public image of having many adherents who serve in the army like every other Israeli.

[3] See Jennifer Friedlin, "The Thais That Bind."

[4] See D. B. Soloveichik, *Divrei Hagut ve-Ha'archa*. He talks about the intrinsic role of leadership in differentiating modern Orthodoxy and ultra-Orthodoxy. He discusses various models of leadership and the relationship the masses have with them.

[5] Although they might have been able to recruit a more committed, disciplined following, the leadership style of these Orthodox figures did not encourage this type of adherence.

[6] Schneerson paid Soloveitchik the utmost respect, and in so doing forced a change in the way Habad adherents regarded Soloveitchik's school of thought.

[7] See Arieh O'Sullivan, "Jewish Leaders Praise Departed Rabbi." He quotes Rabbi Lau's praise of Schneerson for helping Iranian, Yemenite, North African, and Russian Jewries.

[8] The 1988 Israeli elections hinged on the vote of Agudat Yisrael, which considerably increased its constituency among Sephardi voters because of Schneerson's endorsement. Shas, the main Sephardi party, found that its support was significantly reduced, indicating how its natural constituency voted.

[9] See David E. Fishman, "Preserving Tradition in the Land of Revolution."

[10] Rabbi Lau, public lecture, Sydney, Australia, July 27, 1995.

[11] See Ashley Dunn, "Delayed Ceremony for Grown Men." He notes that the Habad-affiliated Bris Avrohom organization carried out over 4,000 circumcisions by 1995. One mohel (ritual circumciser) said he had personally circumcised about 8,000 Soviet Jewish immigrants since the mid-1970s, and in the period after 1991 he continued to perform approximately 500 a year.

[12] See *Jerusalem Post International Edition*, no. 1836 (January 13, 1996). The advertising section examines the activities of Rabbi Joseph Gutnick, a multi-millionaire Habad philanthropist noted, among other things, for his sponsorship of Russian educational programs.

[13] See Mordechai Moshkovitz, *Kuntres ha-Emet al Tnuat Habad be-Shnot ha-80*.

[14] The Or Sameach yeshiva group, the Eish Ha-Torah yeshiva, and the Shas movement are examples of this trend.

[15] See "You Felt Like the Space Around Him Was Holy." Rabbi Eliezer Shach described Schneerson as "the madman who sits in New York and drives the whole world crazy."

[16] The religious Zionist movement generally sees Rabbi Abraham Isaac Kook as its spiritual mentor. He advocated the idea that the return of Jews to Eretz Yisrael indicated the beginning of the redemption, the *hitchalta de-geulah*. Schneerson disagreed, and insisted that the redemptive process was immediate and did not have stages. He affirmed that the redemption was very near, and elaborated on the effects its nearness was having on the pre-messianic world. Habad Hasidim adopted the term *ikvita de-meshicha*, "the footsteps of the mashiach," as describing the time immediately before the redemption. Given the nature of the argument, these points are, in essence, polemical hair-splitting. The eschatological differences between the two views would be significant if the redemptive process could be quantified, but since it is not, they lead only to endless and largely fruitless discussion.

[17] See Sam Lipsky, "Interview with Gutnik."

[18] Menachem Friedman, "Habad as Messianic Fundamentalism."

[19] Jonathan Mark, "A Kingdom of Faith."

[20] These include prohibitions against killing, stealing, committing incest, blasphemy, idolatry, and eating the limb of a living animal. The seventh injunction is to establish courts of law. See David J. Davis, *Finding the God of Noah*.

[21] This date was declared "Education and Sharing Day" in American schools.

[22] President Clinton was supposed to come but was forced to cancel because of emergency trade talks with Japan.

Chapter 11
Habad Hasidism and Zionism

One final factor in the consolidation of Schneerson's authority over Habad requires our attention: namely, the curious relationship of Habad with Zionism and other forms of messianic endeavor not of its own instigation. This chapter will examine the parallel yet antagonistic courses taken by the Habad movement and Zionism. Whereas Habad yearned for a spiritual redemption and messianic fulfillment, and actively sought to achieve this by religious outreach, education, prayer, and increased commitment to halakhic observance, Zionism sought to achieve political "redemption," which was thought to be achievable through statehood via political means. Both, at some stage in their growth, were messianic movements, using messianic imagery and drawing support from enthusiasts with utopian, idealistic aspirations.

Whether Zionism and Habad are (or were) the redemptive movements their proponents believed them to be is immaterial to this discussion, so long as each maintained a belief in its own role and viewed itself as historically unique. Other religious, mystical, and Hasidic groups may have better exemplified the idea of spiritual redemption than Habad, and they may have done so in their own way independent of Zionism.[1] The Habad movement, however, seems to have responded to Zionism to some degree, and might have seen itself as almost in competition with it, trying to provide an alternative to Zionism's practical political program.[2]

The dynamic between the two groups began with the emergence of secular Jewish nationalism in the late nineteenth century, but the Habad movement has had strong ties to Eretz ha-Kodesh (the Holy Land) from its inception over a hundred years before the advent of secular Zionism. Under the leadership of Shneur Zalman, the first Habad Rebbe, it collected money for a charity fund (the *ma'ot*) that supported Rabbi Menachem Mendel of Vitebsk and his followers, who had earlier emigrated to the Holy Land and settled in Safed and Tiberias, and later in Hebron. Shneur Zalman's participation in collecting for this fund were one of the principal reasons for his rise to eminence.[3] He was even jailed for these efforts by the Russian authorities, on charges of supporting an enemy country, for Eretz ha-Kodesh was then occupied by Turkey, an enemy of Russia.

Shneur Zalman's successors, his son Dov Ber and his chief disciple Aharon of Staroselye, both continued to collect money for the Jewish communities in Eretz ha-

Kodesh. The prestige associated with the collection of this money made it a central issue in their own maneuvering for further authority among Habad and other Hasidic adherents. Dov Ber continued arduously in the collection of funds, and therefore was seen as continuing his father's mission and leadership. Consequently, he was portrayed as more than just a local leader; he was a zaddik who had a universal concern for Jews, particularly those in the Holy Land. Dov Ber's work on behalf of the collection earned him both local respect and the respect and loyalty of the recipients of these funds in Eretz ha-Kodesh. He started a new settlement in the holy city of Hebron, led by his son-in-law from the Slonim Hasidic dynasty, which further enhanced his image as a leader working for the return to Zion. The real estate and connection to Hebron is a motive in Habad's present-day political activities in that city. Dov Ber was eventually imprisoned by the Russian authorities for his work on behalf of the charity fund. As a result, like his father, he was seen as a leader ready to suffer for his mission. It should be noted that support for settlement in Eretz ha-Kodesh was motivated by strong religious reasons, and while there may have been nationalist undertones to these concerns, they did not carry with them the stigma of secularism, religious rebellion, and organized nationalist sentiments that later became the watchword of Zionism and one of the reasons for its rejection by pietistic groups.

Support for the Hasidim in Eretz ha-Kodesh and the building of new settlements continued throughout the leadership of the third Habad Rebbe, the Zemakh Zedek. His children and grandchildren, who were also Rebbes, supported these communities with varying degrees of enthusiasm, but it was only during the leadership of the fifth Habad Rebbe, Shalom Dov Ber, that problems arose from the vested interests of Habad Hasidism in Jewish settlement in Eretz ha-Kodesh.

As Zionism grew in popularity among many East European Jews, and its secular nationalistic ethos began to gain acceptance, Shalom Dov Ber took a decidedly aggressive approach. However important the Holy Land was in Jewish religious life and in Habad history, Shalom Dov Ber nevertheless articulated certain criticisms of Zionism, including a rejection of its emphasis on militant, political, and secular means to realize Jewish "redemption." He viewed the Habad approach of active pietism as the only solution to the Jewish people's misery and the best way to achieve the ultimate redemption. This is not to say that his movement was not political, or that it lacked militant organization and a well-conceived strategy, but that its formulated goal was spiritual and not political.

During the course of Shalom Dov Ber's activities against Zionism, the Habad movement came to represent the things that Zionism failed to represent for religious Jewry. Comparisons and antithetical distinctions were developed through this tension. Only during the last Rebbe's leadership, however, did Habad develop an awareness of what it believed to be its paramount role in the Jewish people's redemption. While it did not consciously compare itself with Zionism, one may nevertheless point to several Zionist influences on Habad. One can, as well, identify a series of common factors that contributed to Zionism's success and also to the growth of Habad's redemptive program. This was not due to coincidence but stemmed from the enthusiasm generated by their shared sense of mission.

Coincidental Timing?

The establishment of a yeshiva system by Shalom Dov Ber in 1897 provided the fifth Rebbe with a source of activist manpower from among the student body that was dedicated to Habad ideology and activism. Those who attended the yeshiva might otherwise have gone to other religious groups for instruction or have been drawn into a more exciting, proactive movement like Zionism. The creation of the Habad yeshiva was arguably the most important factor in making the Habad sect a political force in the political world. The yeshiva was one of the first such institutions in Hasidic history. Shalom Dov Ber named the yeshiva Tomhei Temimim, translated as "supporters of the pure ones." The first of several centers was established in the Russian town of Lubavitch, and served to attract Hasidim back to the traditional Habad town. Shalom Dov Ber groomed his students to become activists, not just scholars, and taught them his elaborate ideology and vision for the movement. He taught, for instance, that the institution had a divine mission to hasten the messianic arrival. The era they were living in, he said, was "the jubilee of the footsteps of the mashiach," referring, on the one hand, to the imminent arrival of the mashiach (and a return to the Holy Land), and, on another level, alluding to the failed messianic attempts of past ages, and the need to be wary of false promises of immediate gratification.[4]

While it is mainly coincidental that the first Habad yeshiva was opened only six months after the convening of the First World Zionist Congress in 1897, there are some historical links indicating that Hasidism was mobilizing itself in counteraction to secular enterprises.[5] In the early days of the Zionist movement, the possibility of secular and religious cooperation seemed plausible. The early Zionist Congresses had broad religious representation, and hence the opening of Habad's yeshiva was not so much a counterattack on Zionism as a sign of the times, where ideological factions were marshaling their forces and confirming their positions. Shalom Dov Ber's movement countered nationalist and secular messianic enthusiasm with a call to renewed religious service and missionary outreach, through the dissemination of Hasidic teachings as a prelude to the true messianic arrival. He argued that the messianic redemption was first and foremost a mystical process, and could not be achieved by force or political ventures. His uncompromising criticism of the Enlightenment quickly came to include Zionism, and he rejected its claim to have a solution for oppressed Jewry.[6] His criticism of Zionism intensified when he realized that the secular, non-halakhic Jewish identity it was attempting to forge would allow proponents to feel a sense of Jewish fulfillment without being required to subscribe to traditional values. Furthermore, political efforts in Eretz ha-Kodesh would substitute for the traditional messianic yearnings and transform them into a political agenda devoid of spirituality.

In the struggle against Zionism and secularism, the Habad movement united with its long-time Orthodox opponents, the mitnagdim as well as other Hasidic groups. Shalom Dov Ber established working relationships with many leaders and cooperated with them on issues of Hasidic education, unity, policy, and strategy. However, he opposed Agudat Yisrael for its support of rural settlements in Eretz ha-Kodesh, which he claimed lent legitimacy to the Zionist cause. By identifying a common enemy, a broad religious alliance emerged which might eventually have succeeded in thwarting the Zionists, if its constituent elements had not been put into disarray and effectively destroyed by the devastation of the Holocaust and the Communist oppression in Eastern Europe.

Shalom Dov Ber recognized that it was necessary to adopt modern techniques and understand the spirit and the needs of the age if he was to succeed in his campaign. He steadfastly set about building a modern, cohesive organizational structure. The better-organized the structures initiated by Habad, he felt, the more effective they would be. Shalom Dov Ber's yeshiva institutions were planned and put into effect within four years of his election to office, thus indicating the new approach he was taking. One of his practical concerns was the stream of emigration to Eretz ha-Kodesh among his followers, many of whom were choosing emigration instead of remaining in Russia to grapple with the difficulties there. Even if they continued to be religious after leaving Russia, their role in European Jewish life was too important to lose, and he insisted that they remain with him.

The nationalist fervor that spread through Europe during the nineteenth and twentieth centuries affected Jewry, even its fervently religious elements, as much as its gentile neighbors. Zionism enjoyed increasing popularity as a result. Shalom Dov Ber, perhaps acknowledging the spirit of the times, articulated a nationalistic, militant, and yet highly spiritual ideology of renewed piety as a substitute for the practical nationalism and militarism that Zionism offered. His program, therefore, catered to the nationalist spirit of the times yet maintained piety as its major theme. It endowed his idealistic young students, and an increasingly restless Jewish populace, with a sense of mission as well as a vehicle for expressing a newfound *zeitgeist*, while steering it clear of secularism, heresy, or the diminution of halakhic observance.

If a less articulate Rebbe had espoused Habad's brand of thinking, it might not have been received so favorably. Shalom Dov Ber, however, had a thoroughly elaborated ideological system that he advocated to the burgeoning class of enthusiastic emissaries that graduated from his new yeshiva. His teachings were intellectually profound, intricate, and attracted scholarly interest and a committed following. Shalom Dov Ber's vigorous and enthusiastic interest in and criticism of contemporary issues enthused his students, and fostered the growth of a class of Hasidim and activists with well-formed political and social opinions. Thus Shalom Dov Ber was the first of a new style of Habad Rebbe, outward looking and active in the political arena, and not limited to primarily spiritual affairs.

Opposition to Zionism

Because of the messianic fervor surrounding Schneerson, or perhaps in line with Schneerson's own thinking, Shalom Dov Ber's antagonism to Zionism was to develop into a posture of great ideological significance in the modern Habad movement. Schneerson viewed Shalom Dov Ber and the other Habad Rebbes as role models, and while it is not unusual for an incumbent Rebbe to hold up a predecessor as a model of perfection and at the same time abandon or change his program, this raises the possibility of cognitive dissonance. The threat of such dissonance in the modern Habad movement appears to have motivated Schneerson and his teachings, and therefore his adherents assumed an exaggerated feeling of grandeur and superiority to Zionism.

Whereas Zionism objectively succeeded in most of its practical goals and had become a source of pride for both secular and religious Jews, the Habad movement's goal of messianic redemption had not come about. Habad leaders and adherents could therefore either concede to Zionism's universal success and acknowledge Shalom Dov Ber's misjudgment in opposing it, or they could attribute his seemingly poor judgment to a sublime understanding. The former would implicate him and his son and successor Yosef Yitzhak as misguided leaders who were partly to blame for the demise of the many Hasidim whom they encouraged to remain in Eastern Europe instead of emigrating to Eretz ha-Kodesh. By impeding Zionism in Russia, they prevented action that might have saved many Jews from death. Because of the impossibility of any such acknowledgment, a belated acceptance or recognition of Zionism was unlikely. Continuing to stand aloof and adopting an attitude of superior wisdom served to steer the movement away from internal confrontation, and obviated any cognitive dissonance in relation to opposition to Zionism.

Schneerson steered an interesting course that maintained the integrity of the Habad ideological resistance to Zionism. On one hand, he distinctly changed Habad policy toward the new State of Israel, and worked for the welfare of the nation within its political structures. On the other hand, he remained aloof from acceding to Zionist ideology or respect for the state per se. Support for Israel was advocated purely on the grounds that Habad had always supported Jews in the Holy Land; how much more so when a large population of Jews needed support and assistance, as was the case after the establishment of Israel. Habad participation in Israel's politics was thus legitimized, and discussion with its leaders, collaboration in education, army service, and political representation were condoned, and even advocated by Schneerson, with a remarkable forthrightness unprecedented in Hasidic relations with the new state.

On the face of things, Habad's activities in Israel seem to be aligned with the principles of Zionism, but in fact the opposite is true. The fact that Zionism's version of redemption succeeded led to another dilemma: Habad adherents could either reject their faith as invalid and their leadership as misguided, or they could strengthen their faith by asserting that the Habad formula for redemption was purer than and superior to Zionism. The movement as a whole, when it addressed the issue of the success of Zionism, claimed that secular Zionism's undermining of piety and religion had thwarted Habad's attempt to usher in the messianic age, and thus the Zionists were partly responsible for the Holocaust. However, in due course the "true" redemption will win out, and Habad's vision will be fulfilled. Zionism's temporary success is but a hollow reflection of what might have been if the Habad approach had succeeded, and the achievements of Zionism will pale into insignificance once the messianic age is upon us.

Zionist Influences on Schneerson

Schneerson was undoubtedly exposed to Zionist ideas in his youth. Rabbi Shaul Shimon Deutsch, a revisionist Habad historian and self-proclaimed Habad Rebbe, has explored Schneerson's youthful influences. He argues that Schneerson's younger brother Yisrael Arieh Leib (1908–1951) was a Zionist and later a socialist.[7] He immigrated to Israel and lived there for a time before moving to Liverpool, England. Deutsch describes how the Schneerson family employed Zionist teachers for Menachem Mendel, Yisrael Arieh Leib, and its other children, and ingratiated itself with the Zionist elements in its hometown of Yakatrinolava, thus ensuring the elder Schneerson's position as rabbi of the city. When Yisrael Arieh Leib became a Zionist, his parents were not pleased, but tolerated it. Menachem Schneerson, however, although he studied modern Hebrew literature and culture, did not become a Zionist in the classical sense. Since he was introspective, stubbornly determined, inspired by messianic dreams, and oriented in favor of activism, he probably found Zionism attractive. His commitment to the then contemporary Habad ideeology, however, led him to formulate his own views on the issue, negotiating a system of thought that merged traditional Habad ideas with the changing times, and addressed the appeal of Jewish activism.

Schneerson often claimed that his immediate predecessor and father-in-law, Yosef Yitzhak, was the mashiach. Yosef Yitzhak's outreach and religious-renewal activities, therefore, became a standard component of the messianic process perpetuated by Schneerson, and were not replaced by explicitly political activism or other activities pertaining to Israel or important for Zionism. Schneerson did not recognize the establishment of the State of Israel as part of the messianic process, and he bitterly criticized religious Zionists who proclaimed statehood as *reishit zemichat geulateinu*, "the beginning of the process of our redemption." Despite what he must have seen as a wondrous achievement, Schneerson resisted being drawn into an ideological acceptance of the state. Stubborn in his refusal to be second fiddle, he advanced his agenda as the most important issue to the survival of world Jewry. His admiration of Zionism and its success is evident, however, in his utilization of Zionist imagery and techniques in pursuit of Habad's ambitions.

Schneerson endeared himself to Habad Hasidim by his grief at Yosef Yitzhak's passing in 1950. He frequently visited his gravesite in Queens, New York, and coined the term "Zion" in reference to it.[8] Thus reverence for the movement's former leader and his goals became associated with reverence for Zion, the Holy Land, giving it mystical, and even messianic, importance. The use of the term "Zion" implied that Yosef Yitzhak was the embodiment of the holy mountain of Jerusalem, the Temple site, and other such messianic images. It is probable that the use of Zionist imagery was deliberate, to emphasize that the Zionist love for the physical land was a misplacement of spiritual commitment to the establishment of the Holy Land in the messianic era. Over the years, Zionist imagery was increasingly utilized by Habad, and the central headquarters of the movement at 770 Eastern Parkway in Brooklyn became associated with the Temple in Jerusalem and was considered by many to be *Yerushalaim delaila*, the "Higher Jerusalem." It was also termed the *Beit Mashiach*, the "house of the mashiach," and pictures of the building are common features in Habad households. Hasidim traveled to Crown Heights for holy days from around the United States, and even from Israel, to visit the Rebbe. This resembles the traditional obligation for Jews to travel to Jerusalem on the pilgrim festivals, in order to fulfill their obligations at the Temple.[9] This is simply one more comparison to be drawn between Habad practice and Zionism.

In a letter to Chaim Weizmann, Israel's first President (in Hebrew, called simply *nasi*, meaning "leader"), Schneerson expressed his disappointment at the quality of leadership in the Jewish state: "I always imagined a *nasi* of Israel to be pious and learned."

It is no coincidence therefore, that Schneerson coined a new title for the Habad Rebbe. He called his predecessor the *nasi ha-dor*, or "leader of the generation." This term evoked the regalia of ancient Jewish leadership, obtained through piety, scholarship, and supreme authority. The title was probably intended to contrast with the State of Israel's highest office, the presidency. Schneerson was implying that the Habad Rebbe was the true President of Judaism, and not the holder of the Israeli political office.

Schneerson clearly respected the aggressiveness of the Zionists in establishing their own country. Deutsch argues that he took an interest in nationalist movements, leaders, leadership style and techniques, and military strategy. While Schneerson may have copied other leadership models, he most directly emulated the Zionist version of nationalism, and particularly the organization of the Israeli army, for which he had special praise, respect, and affection. This affection was not a result of the soldiers' Zionist beliefs, but arose from their dignity, self-assurance, and readiness to fight and sacrifice for the survival of Israel. He recognized, however, the ideological difficulty of admitting that so important a breakthrough in Jewish history had been achieved by secularists.

Whatever the reason, Schneerson used Zionist and military symbolism in Habad. He set up the Zivot Hashem ("Armies of God") youth movement, which endowed Hasidic youth with a sense of mission and identity as soldiers in God's army, much as he thought the Israeli army endowed soldiers with mission, identity, pride, and unity. In the Israeli army, women were soldiers who held guns and fought alongside men. They were the focus of world media attention, which depicted Jewish women as bearing arms in readiness of the need to fight for Israel.

In times of war and national emergencies that challenge survival, women and children are often called upon to support the physical struggle. Schneerson used this argument and encouraged women to participate in the Jewish people's struggle for religious survival. Hence girls as well as boys participated in the Zivot Hashem, were able to earn equal rank, wore uniforms, and carried out "missions" of good deeds and mitzvot (commandments). Equality between the sexes, albeit in this somewhat limited context, was virtually unprecedented in the history of Hasidism. Schneerson used other forms of military imagery that may have been inspired by his interest in military history and in Israel. Motivational and inspirational songs played on Hebrew words and acronyms of military significance; as an example, "the emissaries of our master will bring the righteous mashiach, with tanks and guns in our hands from 770." In Habad, the Hebrew words for "tank" and "gun" became acronyms and wordplays for various religious duties; "gun," for example, is *NeSHeK* in Hebrew, understood to be an acronym for *ner Shabbat kodesh*, the commandment to light Shabbat candles on Friday night. The employment of military terminology for docile religious practices is clear. Practices like this illustrate the influence Zionism and Jewish nationhood had on Schneerson, implicitly if not explicitly, and the ideological empowerment Israeli statehood had on Habad's messianist mission.

Habad saw itself as the true spearhead for the redemption of the Jewish people, and considered Zionism a superficial alternative. The Habad approach to redemption was seen by its exponents as the true and more perfect solution to the woes of Jewish history. This was the view of the Ba'al Shem Tov, and Habad philosophy further reinforced it. Support in the movement for secular Zionism was inconsistent, and rarely extended beyond giving aid in practical matters. The small, ultra-conservative Hasidic group known as the Malakhim, once a splinter movement from Habad but now strongly associated with the Satmar Hasidim, is a testament to Habad's ideological potential for extreme anti-Zionism. Its anti-Zionist activism and rhetoric represent the most radical in the Satmar community.[10]

The Six-Day War and After

Schneerson's views on Israel appear to have changed after the Israeli victory in the Six-Day War in 1967, which resulted in the capture of Jerusalem and the Temple Mount. Along with other religious groups, Schneerson was taken aback by the historic significance of the victory, and began to attribute importance to Zionism's achievements as a sign of the impending messianic era. This did not involve accepting the Zionist program, but was a recognition that these achievements would have been impossible without Zionism.

When Jerusalem was captured, Schneerson was inclined to adopt the biblical precepts that applied to Jerusalem, including the giving of tithes. To avoid the problem, he suggested to his Hasidim that they not remain in Jerusalem over the pilgrim festivals, because if they were there they might be obligated to bring gifts to the Temple, according to halakhic instruction. Most rabbinic leaders believed that this was not necessary, but Schneerson was more literalist and messianic than other leaders, and thus more inclined to view the capture of Jerusalem as significant in the messianic process. Schneerson also expressed great pride in the successful rescue of kidnapped Jews by the Israeli military with the Entebbe raid in Uganda in July 1976. He called it a miracle and considered God to be working through the Israeli army, something that led to criticism by his Satmar opponents, who believed that it was forbidden to consider the actions of secular Israeli heretics to be the will of God.[11] Despite these events, however, when Israel seemed to be ignoring the messianic opportunity he felt it had, Schneerson reverted to his regular program advocating religious renewal, perhaps benefiting from seeing that the Israeli victory, for all its historical significance, did not bring on the long-awaited redemption.

Never Set Foot in the Holy Land

It is curious that Schneerson never visited Israel, despite the relative simplicity of such a visit compared to the difficulties experienced by past leaders, and an examination of his reasons for refusing to do so reveals his perception of himself and his role as a Jewish leader. While Hasidim have given religious explanations for Schneerson's reluctance to move to or even visit Israel, Schneerson's own comments are more revealing. It is only through conjecture that one might probe the real issues behind Schneerson's refusal to visit a land that he clearly loved and acclaimed as having the highest importance and holiness.

When Chief Rabbi Shlomo Goren asked him why he had not visited Israel or settled there, Schneerson answered to the effect that the majority of Jews were in the Diaspora, and his responsibility was to them and their return to religious observance. While ideologically this answer makes sense, it is noteworthy that while just about all present-day Hasidic Rebbes, even those who are notoriously anti-Zionist, have visited Israel, Schneerson never did. Some settled in the Holy Land, but most other Hasidic Rebbes have spent various lengths of time there, not only to be with their Israeli Hasidim, but also to be in the land of Jewish origins, visit the graves of saints, and meet the holy men and scholars who reside there. At one point, Schneerson indicated that his reluctance to visit might be a form of emulation of the actions of earlier Rebbes. Since Shneur Zalman, the first Habad Rebbe, had not gone to Israel although he dedicated his life to helping the Hasidim there, Schneerson too felt no compulsion to visit the Holy Land.

The previous Satmar Rebbe, Yoel Teitelbaum, visited Israel and was later buried there, as is the desire of many God-fearing people. It is no small issue, therefore, that Schneerson refused to even visit the state. Some have attributed this refusal to the human qualities of insecurity, stubbornness, or arrogance. Perhaps having to wait in lines, fill out visas, pass through customs, and be treated like other people, without the adoring crowds that usually accompanied him, was too daunting. Being a tourist in another country, and having to visit the highly respected rabbinic figures and saints who lived there and would not leave for religious reasons, might have been seen as lessening his dignity, and could have lowered his stature in the eyes of his community. The power gained by remaining in Crown Heights and having the world come to him might also have been jeopardized by a visit to the Holy Land. There may have also been practical considerations; if he could visit Israel, then his excuse for not attending rabbinic conferences, visiting other Hasidic Rebbes, and becoming more directly involved in the contemporary Jewish religious scene would disappear.

The concept of a zaddik taking a vacation or a personal trip seems inappropriate, given his role in securing Godly grace and ensuring the continued existence of creation; a vacation would detract from his cosmic duties. While many other Hasidic Rebbes did vacation and travel abroad, Schneerson did not. Perhaps this was due to his view of the Habad Rebbe as the *nasi ha-dor*, or "leader of the generation," and therefore as a person who could not indulge in pleasures like others do. As noted previously, he attributed his success in the role of Rebbe to the relationship he had with the gravesite of his predecessor. Leaving New York for gratuitous vacations might therefore have been inappropriate. His refusal to leave the New York–based gravesite for the Holy Land, however, was a departure from Jewish deference toward the Land of Israel, which is the home of abundant gravesites. Figures from the patriarchs to the prophets and the famed rabbis of ancient Israel, as well as kabbalists and Hasidic masters, are buried in Israel. Refusal to go there using the above argument betrays Schneerson's highly partial view that his was the true Zion, his court was the holiest and most important place in the world, and the Holy Land played only a supporting role to the gravesite in Queens.

Perhaps Schneerson simply had no opportunity in his first years as Rebbe to visit Israel, being concerned with reconstructing a community devastated by the Holocaust and forced migration, and consolidating his own rule. By the time he had consolidated his authority, the fact that he had not visited the Holy Land had become such a point of interest and intrigue to people that going there would have been anti-climactic, and might possibly have dampened the messianic speculation surrounding him. The casual nature and ease of flying could threaten to normalize his relations with the yearned-for Holy Land, or he might simply have enjoyed the idealization of Israel as a spiritual goal, and did not want his mental image of it tarnished by reality.

There were certainly unarticulated ideological considerations involved in Schneerson's decision to avoid Israel, particularly as critics in religious Zionist and secular circles in the United States and Israel urged him to visit and thereby give his endorsement to the national Jewish effort. Both intrigue from within the movement and criticism from without grew, as Schneerson involved himself increasingly in Israeli politics and successfully swayed the balance of power in Israel's government by his influence over sizable segments of Israeli Jewry. The ability of a person who had never set foot in the country to affect it to the degree that he did inspired awe in some quarters, but bitterness in others, because it was felt that he was interfering in matters outside his direct interests.

The Habad movement's parallel course to Zionism and Schneerson's struggle with Zionism indicate that difficult psychological issues were at work. Schneerson saw himself as heading the movement that would be the main tool in bringing the messianic redemption. He saw Zionism, which has been described as a political messianic endeavor, albeit with a secular bent, as his greatest competition, and he refused to defer to it, or even to recognize its authority over Habad's activities.

In the post-Schneerson era, Habad's ideological opposition to Zionism may undergo yet another transformation. While many Habad adherents still advocate outreach and education, the inculcation of Jewish values and unity, they also seem to be undergoing a process of normalization. Elements of contemporary Habad seem to have realized that the movement is no longer the superstructure for Jews to work within, for Israel has taken on this function. However, as we enter the post-Zionist era, where Israelis are becoming less utopian, less patriotic, and less united by a shared vision of Zionism, Schneerson's desire to supersede Zionism is becoming a more realistic goal. The failure of Zionism and the post-Zionist culture to unite Jews across the globe has contributed to the burgeoning of other messianic movements, which view themselves as an alternative to state-sponsored secular Zionism. Habad is no longer the only active combatant in this struggle, and will have to compete with many other groups if its vision of Judaism is to bring the unity inherent in the advent of the messianic era.

---

[1] For example, the sixteenth-century mystical settlement in Safed and Jacob Birav's attempt to reconvene the Sanhedrin.

[2] Satmar is more distinctly anti-Zionist than Habad, so much so that it is sometimes said to have only one major focus, anti-Zionism. The anti-Zionist emphasis reflected a personal predilection of its former Rebbe, Joel Teitelbaum, and was not found among his predecessors or supported by his successor.

[3] See Avrum Ehrlich, *Leadership in the HaBaD Movement*, pp. 131, 150, 152.

[4] See A. Morgenstern, "Messianic Concepts and the Settlement of Israel." He discusses messianic attitudes and predictions among certain mitnagdic elements in the Zemakh Zedek's time. When these predictions failed to materialize, some mitnagdim converted to Christianity. Hence, messianism can be shown to have affected the mitnagdic camp more than the Hasidim, despite mitnagdic suspicions of Hasidic heresy.

[5] The yeshiva was established primarily to counteract the threat of the Volozhin yeshiva, which was depleting Habad and the Rebbe of their best men and drawing resources to the mitnagdic camp. Habad youth were beginning to accept mitnagdic leadership and were losing their sense of Hasidic identity. Particularly painful was the fact that these scholars were to be the future leaders of Jewry and would have, under mitnagdic influence, only a minimal affiliation with Habad.

[6] In *Kol ha-Yoze le-Milhemet Beit David*, Shalom Dov Ber bitterly condemns Zionism, the Enlightenment, secularists, and Hasidic pretenders. His criticism of the Enlightenment is especially strong (he states in unambiguous terms that he "hates" those "enlightened" people).

[7] According to Zvi Hakarvi, Yisrael Arieh Leib defected from mainstream socialism and became a follower of Trotsky. Despite the fact that he abandoned Orthodoxy, he lived with Schneerson for some time in Berlin, but was eventually forced to flee Eastern Europe, using the name Mark Gourary. See Shaul S. Deutsch, *Larger Than Life*, vol. 1, pp. 101–103, and vol. 2, p. 118.

[8] See Kahn diary.

[9] There are other implications to these similarities beyond comparisons to Zionism. For instance, Scholem argued that the transformation of physical redemption into ritual and spirituality in early Hasidism neutralized the messianic element. See Gershom Scholem, "The Neutralization of the Messianic Element in Early Hasidism."

[10] See Jerome R. Mintz, *Hasidic People*, pp. 21–26, for a good description of the Malakhim. Also see Bernard Sobel, *The M'lochim*.

[11] *Sichos Kodesh*, vol. 2, 5736.

Part Three
The Institutions

Chapter 12
Initial Consolidation

Introduction

As we have seen, Schneerson maintained a low public profile from arrival in New York in 1941 until his succession to authority. He had been given official control of three fledgling organizations aimed at outreach and education, but played a much more hands-on role in the running of Habad worldwide when he assumed leadership of the movement. The comparatively minor institutions he administered before his elevation to office became the backbone not only of his rise to power and consolidation of leadership, but also of his vision for the Habad movement. During the lifetime of Yosef Yitzhak, Schneerson's control over these institutions helped him to establish a position of activism within the movement that seems to have made him attractive to many young Habad enthusiasts. His tangible achievements made him appear to many to be the most effective administrator in the movement, and assisted in developing both his leadership qualities and the popular support to take over as Rebbe of the community upon the death of Yosef Yitzhak.

After his selection as Rebbe, Schneerson continued to expand these institutions to further consolidate the movement and his leadership of it. While his duties as Rebbe began to reflect a more personal commitment to his Hasidim, Schneerson made it clear from the first that his prime commitment was to the instructions that he as a Hasid had been given by his own Rebbe; namely, to fulfill Yosef Yitzhak's goals of educational outreach. This commitment was repeatedly stated by Schneerson, and he remained true to his Rebbe's vision throughout his life. This is best demonstrated by the fact that the three organizations originally led by Schneerson are at present among the most active institutions in the movement.

Schneerson's obsessive determination to carry out the will of his father-in-law and Rebbe Yosef Yitzhak, even if posthumously, was noticeable to all. Both before and after the death of Yosef Yitzhak, Schneerson concerned himself with the expansion of these organizations through quiet achievement. Over time, they became the *de facto* official tools of the Habad movement and the means whereby its leader could implement his vision of the world.[1] Especially after the death of Yosef Yitzhak, when Schneerson began to attract more widespread attention and popular support, many enthusiasts and skilled ideologues who shared this vision and wished to contribute to its implementation were attracted to these organizations. When Yosef Yitzhak died, many of those who had the ideals of the Habad movement at heart saw in Schneerson and his work the embodiment of these ideals and hence supported him as Rebbe.

These institutions allowed Schneerson to express in a practical, nonpolitical way his enthusiasm, dutifulness, innovation, and genius, which not only bore fruit but also served Yosef Yitzhak's goals of outreach. The organizations themselves functioned as focal points for voluntary action and activism within the ranks of the movement, especially by the younger members of the community, and helped them maintain a connection to Habad and Hasidism. The organizations also provided employment for many, catering to the economic needs of highly qualified Hasidim who might otherwise have had to look for employment outside the community. In short, the organizations made Schneerson the focal personality of Habad, and attracted the attention of many eager and enthusiastic participants to do practical work to further its goals. Because of this, Schneerson was seen as the active achiever within the Habad movement, consolidating support of his appointment as Rebbe. As his influence spread, particularly after he assumed the mantle of leadership, Schneerson began to attract gifted individuals from around the world to work with him in Crown Heights.

Success of Institutions

It may be argued that the primary function of a leader is to bring about the prosperity of his following, and Schneerson was no exception to this standard. Success and prosperity are the litmus tests of most forms of employment, and Schneerson gained support through the success of his leadership over the primary organizations responsible for outreach. Weber's charismatic leader was compelled to provide for his constituency or suffer the fall from grace associated with failure to provide. The Habad Rebbe, too, was implicitly required to provide for his flock and ensure their success, prosperity, and well-being both physically and, in many ways more important, spiritually, even if this was not his explicit responsibility.

In the Hasidic tradition, the role of the Rebbe to guide and instruct his following, to offer advice that would better their lot and provide them with a sense of security and fulfillment, distinguished him from other models of leadership. The Habad Rebbe, additionally, had a conception of mission and responsibility as part-and-parcel of his office, derived from the teachings and actions of his predecessors. Schneerson in particular felt that, beyond the call of his Hasidim's welfare, he had a mission to complete, given him by Yosef Yitzhak. The achievement of this mission through the institutions under Schneerson's guidance became a barometer of his success as a Rebbe. The spiritual success of the Rebbe in the fulfillment of his duties could be seen in a clear, tangible form through the output of the publishing houses and the social and educational programs initiated by the organizations in Schneerson's charge. In effect, the level of worldly success reflected the righteousness not only of the vision of Habad, but also of its leader.

The success of Schneerson's institutions was an important encouragement for the Hasidim. Since the institutions were the tools to achieve the divine mission laid out by Yosef Yitzhak and the previous Rebbes, their success demonstrated that this mission was under divine inspiration and protection, and their activities became even more important in the eyes of the Hasidim. In a perpetuating cycle, each institutional success attracted more voluntarism, more enthusiasm and increased faith in Habad's vision, leading to greater dedication and still greater success. At the forefront of all of this was Schneerson, who served as the creative impetus and inspiration. In time, and especially with the increasing emphasis on messianism that developed under his later leadership, to work under him was to work in the fulfillment of a cosmic mission.

Employment

A sense of accomplishment and idealism is important in the effort to rally dedication around a cause or a leader. Useful employment provides needed services for the community, as well as a sense of personal accomplishment for the employed.[2] From the outset of his reign as Rebbe, Schneerson was in a fortunate position in that his institutions could employ people, his enthusiasm could ensure success, and his Hasidic vision could create a feeling of satisfaction and fulfillment for his community. All this was done through the institutions over which Schneerson had been appointed by his predecessor. Most important for his rise to power, he did not have to win control over these organizations at his inception as leader, because they had been under his control for the better part of a decade. It is evident that his leadership of these institutions contributed greatly to his election, allowing him a power base from which to garner support and public recognition within Habad.

With the growth of these organizations, Schneerson could afford to employ even more people. They grew and diversified so that people with many different talents could be employed. Hasidim could earn their livings while contributing to their religious ideals of outreach. As these institutions grew larger, a greater portion of the Habad community came to rely on them for a portion of its income. Many associated their personal well-being, economic success, and continued employment with the success of the institutions and Schneerson's authority. Again, support for Habad was maintained through appeal to a sense of divine mission and personal reliance on the spiritual guidance and inspiration of Schneerson.

The projects undertaken by these institutions, especially outreach and publication, spread the work and mission of Habad beyond the confines of the local community in Crown Heights. The impulse toward universal mission, which will be elaborated in a later chapter, meant that more Hasidim were needed in the Diaspora Jewish communities, both throughout the United States and abroad. More emissaries were sent to start new communities and projects outside Crown Heights, often thousands of miles away. Connection to Schneerson and to Crown Heights as the spiritual and geographic center of Habad was maintained by the regular assembling of Hasidim for festivals and gatherings. Those working or living near Crown Heights would come to see the Rebbe or participate in events after a day's work elsewhere in the city.

The consequences of sending people as emissaries of the educational wing of the movement to university campuses, businesses, community synagogues, and indeed anywhere that a significant population of Jews might be found (including locations outside the United States), served to further strengthen the influence of the movement.[3] Although this will be discussed in greater detail later, it should be noted that outreach, as Habad came to call its community work, served to expand the movement beyond imagination. The leadership vacuum in the religious life of Jews throughout the world left Habad emissaries well endowed to swiftly fill it, and as a consequence further "employment" and demand for the products provided by Habad (literature, kosher food, religious paraphernalia, and the like) were found. A vast range of new professions and work opportunities were opened for the Hasidim, attributed by many to have arisen directly from the direction provided by Schneerson. This worldly success served to reinforce the belief that their path was correct and the Rebbe's decisions were right and even prophetic. Their worldly success through living according to Schneerson's vision was identified with the need for obedience to Schneerson's instructions and dedication to his vision.

Especially in the initial stages of the movement, this was especially comforting for parents who had concerns that the New World of America would not facilitate religious life as they had known it in Eastern Europe. The general mood in the immigrant community, and not just in Judaism, in the United States of the 1950s was one of assimilation into mainstream American life.[4] Religious education as found in traditional European communities was generally frowned upon by the mainstream Jewish population, and tolerated only in small, pluralistic doses. In the religious community, it was perhaps understandably feared that exposure to the world might lead to a diminution of religious observance. To avoid this, there was an attempt to minimize the impact of secularism and the broader American culture on the religious community by retaining a traditional Jewish educational system. During his leadership of Habad, Yosef Yitzhak's policy had been that traditional Jewish education would continue regardless of any outside or communal influence, a stance that Schneerson was careful to retain in his administration of the educational organizations of the movement. Religious education was pursued uncompromisingly with little or no secular study included in the curriculum. Before the success of Schneerson's outreach, the traditional yeshiva education given their children caused Habad parents to worry for their children's livelihood and ability to integrate into their new world. Conversely, the education of the new generation of Habad Hasidic children left them with such a severe secular educational handicap that they had little alternative but to pursue religious-clerical professions, in which there was scope for neither integration nor material success.

The parents of this generation were somewhat pacified by the success of Schneerson's outreach efforts and by the evidence that their children could be employed as rabbis, teachers, ritual functionaries, activists, and in other community-oriented professions. In fact, many of the new generation of Hasidim were getting high-profile employment as rabbis of important non-Habad synagogues and were successfully entering and prospering in the educated middle class.[5] Their worldly success and community recognition encouraged the Hasidism of this generation to continue enrolling their children in the Habad educational system, which in turn continued to prosper. Even those who shared little of the zeal or ideology of the movement, despite growing up in the community, could find employment and livelihood according to their talents, and this in turn helped retain their support for the movement.

As a means of developing the community and retaining members, the role of employment in the leadership consolidation of Schneerson and the overall success of the Habad movement cannot be overemphasized. It not only encouraged people to remain religiously, or at least communally, active affiliates of Habad, when many Jewish communities were being dissolved by assimilation and secularization, but it also helped to maintain the diversity of the movement, finding employment for those who were not inclined to scholarship. This demonstrated the universal applicability of the religious life even against the backdrop of a nontraditional culture, and served to solidify the community under the leadership of Schneerson. As a consequence of his guidance and the programs he established, many Hasidim came to look to their leader for their financial, as well as spiritual, well-being.

A War Economy

The best way to describe the Habad movement's activities and tremendous rate of growth is through analogy to a war economy, however incomplete it might be. A war economy occurs when a government at war (or planning to be) invests a tremendous amount of money, often either borrowed or printed, in certain key military industries, with the focus mainly on the manufacturing sector. By this means, the government is able to create near full employment, with the resultant increase in prosperity and ideological fulfillment that come with economic satisfaction. The artificial economy creates a massive demand from industry, which in turn is financially successful because of the war effort. The overwhelming urgency inspired by the existential threat of war often serves to unite the threatened population, and an increase of national spirit increases the enthusiasm of the labor force. All workers function in a spirit of voluntarism and unity in the face of a shared struggle. Often, women take care of domestic services, and if need be even take an active combat role. In a desperate struggle, children, too, bear arms.

This analogy is similar in many ways to Schneerson's strategy for Habad, which is unsurprising given the fact that his formative years were spent in a Europe ravaged by the Second World War. His rhetoric and institutions, his interpretation of the heroic acts of his predecessors, and his urgency in regard to the completion of the mystical mission assigned Habad by his predecessors were all harnessed to bring about victory. The songs he introduced, the slogans he used, the employment of men, women, and children of all ages and dispositions, served to express the urgency of his goals. It is quite likely that Schneerson was familiar with the theory behind a war economy, and with the propaganda tactics employed by nations at war (or preparing for conflict). He had lived through the First World War, the Communist Revolution in Russia, and the Second World War, and thus had access to many examples of the theory and application of leadership techniques. His exposure to the intellectualism of universities in Berlin and Paris at this time also no doubt exposed him to discussion of military issues.

Whether or not he was familiar with the idea, the manner in which Schneerson encouraged full employment in his movement and the ideology he fostered by pseudo-military means in the war against secularism and assimilation bear many parallels to a war economy. His tactics were very successful in unifying Habad, and in increasing his own prestige and authority in the movement through creating opportunities for gainful employment.

Institutions and the Dissipation of Opposition

Schneerson's success in education, publishing, and outreach under the leadership of Yosef Yitzhak served to cement his leadership of the movement after the death of the previous Rebbe. The institutions headed by Schneerson had inherently greater productivity and success than those administered by Yosef Yitzhak's other son-in-law and rival for leadership, Rabbi Shemaryahu Gourary. This is not to say that Gourary had no role to play in the development of the movement after the death of Yosef Yitzhak, but Schneerson's role was the more public one, and the one whereby material success was more easily quantifiable.

The institutions Gourary controlled were largely either political or of an honorific nature. His primary responsibility was the administration of AGUCH, the Union of Habad Hasidim. As we have seen, AGUCH was originally established by Yosef Yitzhak in 1940, but had functioned unofficially since the 1930s in Russia. Its constitution, although drawn up later, advocated the renewing and retention of Habad Hasidic consciousness in the New World and promised help to organize study groups for Habad affiliates. As it originally functioned in Russia under Yosef Yitzhak, the organization collected money for his work on behalf of Soviet Jewry, and assisted him in obtaining public support during his arrests by the Soviet authorities. The institution was instrumental in bringing Yosef Yitzhak to the United States in the first place, and under his leadership became the basic instrument for Habad's activities around the world. After the assumption of office by Schneerson, the movement was more or less deactivated, and certainly played a smaller role in the evolution of the movement after 1951 than previously. The movement was revived in the 1980s, however, and may contribute to the question of succession within the movement, as we shall see.

After 1951, Gourary continued to head the United Lubavitch Yeshivot, which provided services to yeshiva students, and the organization responsible for supervising the burial customs of Habad, but the standards for success in these organizations were not as readily measurable as in those under Schneerson. Hence, Gourary had few supporters, and they were not given the economic incentives that involvement in Schneerson's initiatives provided. True activists, even if they liked Gourary, would find it difficult to express themselves while in his employ. Thus the support he received as a potential rival to Schneerson, and, with it, his profile in the movement, continued to decline.

The same held for other possible rivals and critics of Schneerson, who had no real way in which to express their own initiatives or win support, and so remained largely ineffective as an opposition to him. This left the movement's posts and positions free to be filled by enthusiastic supporters of the new Rebbe, increasing his popular support and further consolidating the basis of his power. Hence, the fraying of opposition to Schneerson's succession as Rebbe was not so much the result of a crushing blow by his supporters as simply a "drying out" of opposition. Those outside the Schneerson camp did not have the resources to energize themselves as an effective opposition, for the "action" was happening elsewhere. Anyone who wanted to participate in the growth of the movement had to do so through Schneerson.

Fundraising

Fundraising is probably the most important element of Habad's functioning, and lies at the core of the movement's outreach potential. The public relations image that Habad cultivated throughout Schneerson's leadership had a great deal to do with fundraising. Shneur Zalman, the movement's founder, was an excellent collector, as shown by his management of the *maot* charity fund for the Hasidim in Israel.[6] So, too, were the other Habad Rebbes, who raised money for the extrication of those imprisoned for Judaism and for other charitable works. Shalom Dov Ber and Aharon were imprisoned because of their fundraising activities. Dov Ber endorsed Shemaryahu Gourary's marriage to Chana (Yosef Yitzhak's daughter) because of his long-term friendship with the Gourary family, who were renowned as both devoted Hasidim and wealthy benefactors of the movement. Yosef Yitzhak's leadership in Soviet Russia was due in large part to his ability to get funds from the United States and France in support of his educational initiatives. Hence fundraising has played a significant role in the perception of a Rebbe's leadership throughout the history of Habad.

The Habad movement worldwide is dependent on its ability to draw funds from individual donors in each local community. Habad has been organized such that community initiatives are mostly locally sponsored, so each community must cultivate capable individuals and teams for fundraising purposes. The mentality of many Habad Hasidim and the indication of success within the movement is therefore often focused on fundraising ability. There are stories of young, inexperienced Hasidim, newly arrived in an area, who have both naively and brazenly approached wealthy individuals for sponsorship, with remarkable success in raising exorbitant amounts of money for their projects. This success has created a cargo-cult mentality, whereby the community relies heavily on funding that often arrives unexpectedly or from unusual sources, and huge projects may be started with no idea of where the funding for their completion will come from. The success of this outreach technique has contributed to the sense of a divinely ordained mission, as unexpected sources of funding often turn up to cover expenses when needed.

The lucrative potential of religious fundraising has made Habad activists sensitive to fundraising issues, with the result that for many, fundraising has developed into a way of life. The Jewish world has been more inclined to donate to Habad projects than to other Jewish causes because of the success of the movement and its high public profile. The appeal of Habad to many wealthy Jews with post-Holocaust guilt and distant nostalgia for the "old life" was a result of Habad's ability to mix tradition with innovation, modern ways. Even benefactors inclined more to the Conservative or Reform segments of the Jewish world preferred to support Habad institutions because of their noticeable difference from the more modern Jewish movements: the "produce" was more distinct, more tangibly "Jewish," and more appealing to donors who wanted to see hard results from their charity dollars.[7] The image of Habad as a modern form of Hasidism appealed to donors, and conversely helped cement these images into Habad's own sense of identity.

Because the movement had solid achievements to show, and was seen as acting for the benefit of Judaism as a whole, it attracted more donations from the local community and from wealthy donors. The donors were impressed by the results achieved by Habad's outreach projects, and many who had often desired to give were now able to do so, secure in the knowledge that their money would not be wasted.[8] The cycle of donation that Habad has been able to establish began with the enthusiasm of Habad emissaries for hard work and their willingness to support ideals without remuneration, and ended in the strategic donor's recognition of the solid investment he was making to a truly charitable cause. In a domino effect, the availability of funds attracted more voluntarism and more activities as well as larger, more ambitious ventures. In 1992 alone the movement as a whole is believed to have received over $100 million in contributions.[9]

The Habad policy of free services, free seating in synagogues, and free food at events was appealing to many donors.[10] The services provided by Habad survived on the generosity of satisfied patrons, and therefore were a refreshing change from the distasteful practice in many synagogues of charging for these things. To many donors, the break with moneymaking religious practice was attractive for the resulting sense of spirituality and the refreshing separation of religious services and money. For wealthy donors, the issue was not the money but the cause. The spiritual appeal of Habad for many donors did not result purely from its refusal to charge for services.

The sense of authenticity and the unapologetic Jewishness of the movement appealed to those who did not feel able to be as committed or open about their own observance of Jewish tradition.

The movement's activities were carried out on a shoestring budget, fired by an ideology that inspired a sense of true commitment and self-sacrifice. As Habad became more prosperous, and the availability of funds increased, the expansion did not create laziness, but opened up more opportunities for determined, trained, experienced activists. The movement's executors were not merely bureaucrats, but ideologues who would seek to utilize the charity in the most effective and innovative ways, with the consideration not based so much on impressing the donor, but on carrying out the will of the Rebbe and his mission.

Unlike earlier generations, where fundraising was a specialist activity, in Habad even community rabbis and activists have had to become proficient in the pursuit of funding for their projects. The fundraising concept became a part of the consciousness of Habad, and was not an activity reserved for the Rebbe. The effect of fundraising on a large scale, with individual communities responsible for their own budgets, had a consolidating effect on Schneerson's authority. He provided the inspiration and ideology that united the movement behind the fundraising drive, and individual communities were united in their efforts to self-fund. Schneerson was almost always credited with any successful campaign to raise funds, as the embodiment of all fundraising efforts, and hence became the generation's "super fundraiser" and the grandest, most successful of Rebbes in this respect.

Schneerson himself was adept at fundraising. The image he presented to the public was quite different from his image among Hasidim, most probably due to the public relations needed to raise funds from a broader constituency. He often appeared more pluralistic than one might expect from the Rebbe of a traditional Hasidic dynasty, with his black clothing and flowing beard. His conviviality paid off, as he gave audiences to numerous dignitaries and potential benefactors to the movement, including many contacts established by Habad emissaries worldwide, who were honored with an opportunity to meet Schneerson personally. His awe-inspiring charisma and personal stature encouraged more donations from personal visitors, who had often been prepared for the audience by enthusiastic Hasidim with their reverence and respect for the Rebbe.

The physical, economic, social, and ideological effects of fundraising on Schneerson's consolidation of the movement has already been demonstrated. The overall effect of his fundraising ideology was a belief that financial success was a sign of the action of divine grace. This was heightened by the domino effect, whereby success attracted funding that led to greater success and enthusiasm, in a self-perpetuating upward spiral. The high employment rate of Habad activists in respectable, high-income jobs with a strong sense of achievement and religious, cultural, and ethical fulfillment made the Habad Hasidim grateful to Schneerson, who was credited with their upliftment in every sense of the word. Over time, more people were attracted to Habad centers because of the sheer economic success and charisma of the movement. All this was attributed to the wise leadership of Schneerson.

The Negative Effects of Fundraising

As will be discussed later, for every successful technique utilized by Habad in its outreach and consolidation, there was a price to pay. Fundraising, for example, led to the emergence of a duplicitous group personality. While rabbis throughout Jewish history had been spiritually generous, welcoming all Jews as equals regardless of their backgrounds and religious caliber as part of an extended family, this changed in Habad. Some Habad rabbis, due to the necessity of raising funds to support themselves and their communities, began to view some Jews as more equal than others. The lucky ones who got special attention were all too often wealthy.

In Habad, fundraising was (and is) often the subject of intense conversation at Shabbat tables and gatherings. While this is not an uncommon situation in non-Habad synagogues and communities, in the Habad movement it was an obsession which underlay the community's ability to function and earn wages. Because the main ideological thrust of the movement lay in outreach, and there was strong encouragement for everyone to set up an independent "Habad House," every Habad activist became concerned with making money, raising funds, or developing wealthy acquaintances to obtain money for the realization of the movement's goals. Obviously, those members of the movement who assisted in alleviating the community's financial burdens were appreciated and respected. Dependence on charitable funds for livelihood, both individual and collective, carries significant risk, however, especially if events occur to place a personal blemish on either the movement or its individual members. The needs of fundraising, therefore, led to the development of a utilitarian streak in even the best and most loyal Hasidim, and challenged the ability of the movement to publicly express more controversial elements of its ideology. Those unconcerned with the ideal of outreach were not as affected by this, and ironically the Hasidim most dedicated to carrying out Schneerson's program were most prone to develop duplicitous characters. In some instances, the development of institutionalized duplicity had serious ramifications for the integrity and character of both individuals and the movement as a whole.

The obsession with fundraising created an aura of awe around the wealthy. Those known to give money became figures of respect in the local synagogue and were talked about with reverence, whether or not their other accomplishments justified it. Other qualifications of success became less important to many in Habad: the scholarly, the pious, the cultured, the artistic, or the sensitive effectively became second class in comparison to the wealthy. In time, all effort within Habad came to revolve around gaining favor with the wealthy members of the community. The partiality toward wealthy people created a culture centered on financial gain, at the cost of the purportedly spiritual nature of the religious interests of the Hasidim. Wealthy Jews, businesspeople, and others with influence were often specifically targeted for fundraising, and in the event that they entered a Habad House or synagogue, their concerns become the concerns of every potential fundraiser. Deferential attention was commonly paid to them, they were given precedence at the dinner table, and their spiritual concerns were given far greater attention by funds-dependent Hasidim because of their wealth or influence. Time was invested in the wealthy by fundraisers, allegedly because they were Jews and therefore important in the coming redemption, but in reality because they were able to make a financial difference to the movement and its programs.

When any friendship is made between people on the sole basis of financial gain, it results in a degree of duplicity. A wealthy person seeking spiritual guidance is encouraged to develop what he assumes to be a spiritual relationship with a Habad teacher, but for some in the movement, the opportunity is not so much one of spiritually uplifting a fellow Jew as of developing a donor who will finance further outreach. The consequences of this to honesty and trust are devastating not only for the deceived benefactor, but also, spiritually, for the Habad Hasid. When occurrences of this kind are not just passing incidents, but become a regular phenomenon in the movement, as occurred over time in Habad, it reflects an entrenched duplicity whose consequences are manifested in different ways. Certainly, the degree of spiritual cohesion in the movement is diminished.

Ideology and the methods by which Habad rabbis addressed problems were often tailored to the wealthy segments of the community, one result of which was an increasing appeal to populism. We might attribute the choice of terms, the unacademic nature of discourses, and the employment of analogies and metaphors to the desire to appeal to the wealthy merchant class, a segment of the population important to Habad's survival. Interestingly, this took a toll on the quality of Habad theology, which over time began to accommodate and attract the more financially lucrative segments of the community. Use of analogies and language appealed to this popularism, and the issues examined by rabbis in the community were often those of concern to the merchant classes, in distinction to other segments of the community. This occurred even in the discourses of Schneerson himself. Many of the books written by Habad adherents seem to have been tailored to appeal to a specific audience with which the authors seek to enamor themselves. Thus, one result of the need to raise funds was a widespread and institutional descent into populism.

In the long term, the price paid for Habad's emphasis on fundraising and outreach was a sacrifice of intellectual honesty, veracity, and scholarly endeavor. As we shall see, Schneerson's involvement in political issues was later to be moderated by his followers, who were concerned about the popular appeal of Habad as a tool for attracting money to the movement. The more a movement depends on fundraising, the more popular it must of necessity become. Perhaps it is in the sense of a need to appeal to populism that the decline of what originated as a scholarly ideology began. Because it occurs among the spiritual cream of the movement (its emissaries, educators, and rabbis, all of whom are reliant on funding provided by benefactors) it has the potential to spiritually impoverish the movement in the long term.

[1] For example, Schneerson used Mahane Yisrael to purchase property for the movement, and was able to control the publication output of Habad through his influence over the Kehot publishing house.

[2] See, for example, "Walls of Ivy," the story of Elie Silberstein, in Edward Hoffman, *Despite All Odds*, pp. 65–76.

[3] Menachem Friedman, "Habad as Messianic Fundamentalism," pp. 345–354.

[4] See Jerome R. Mintz, *Hasidic People*, pp. 18–20.

[5] For example, in Australia, Habad emissaries are rabbis of synagogues with distinctly Anglo congregations, including the largest mainstream conservative synagogues of Sydney. This situation is mirrored across the Jewish world.

[6] See Avrum Ehrlich, *Leadership in the HaBaD Movement*, pp. 131, 150, 152.

[7] See Kimberley Lifton, "Judaism's Foot Soldiers."

[8] See ibid. Lifton tells how Habad functions attract many dignitaries, who in turn attract other important guests, and so on in a domino effect. She notes that Habad is self-declared to be apolitical. A case study of the Detroit Habad community illustrates this, describing how donors to its institutions feel that Habad activists are "good people," and that while "others talk, they do."

[9] See Jonathan Mark, "The Last Dance," and Ari Goldman, "The Nation." Yehuda Krinsky is quoted as saying that Habad collected over $200 million that year, but as most communities are self-funded, it is very difficult to verify the figure.

[10] See Lifton, "Judaism's Foot Soldiers."

Chapter 13
Consolidation of Local Authority

The New Rebbe

Economic success and employment greatly assisted Schneerson in his consolidation of authority over Habad, but another factor, the establishment of a center and headquarters for the movement, was to prove vital for the ideology of Habad, and especially for the sense of community that was to develop throughout his reign. By the time Schneerson succeeded Yosef Yitzhak in the office of Rebbe, the Habad movement had already moved to Crown Heights, a well-to-do neighborhood of Brooklyn, New York. The Jewish community around Crown Heights was composed mainly of immigrants who had fled Eastern Europe and the Nazi persecution of the Jews, and contained a small core of Habad Hasidim, followers of Rebbes from other Hasidic dynasties, non-Hasidic observant Jews, and secular Jews.[1] Habad's presence was reinforced by its new yeshiva, which attracted around twenty students in its early years. In short, the community inherited by Schneerson was small, dispirited, disunited, and faced with many challenges. As in so many other areas necessary to the survival of Habad in the United States and worldwide, Schneerson rose to the challenge, and over the years not only consolidated the Habad community in Crown Heights, but expanded its influence outward, across the country and the world.

The small size of the community in the early years of Schneerson's leadership may actually have assisted him in his assumption of leadership. Members of the stalwart old guard of Yosef Yitzhak were not regularly in Crown Heights, and so there was little local opposition to Schneerson's election.[2] Had they mustered more of a presence, they might have been less willing to welcome a new, young, and modernist leader as their Rebbe, for he would surely mold the movement's aims in his own image. However, the relative weakness of the community-in-residence in Crown Heights made it easier for Schneerson to establish his mark in the area, and hence to dominate the central headquarters of Habad. In those early days, the community was small enough for Schneerson to personally know most of the residents and Hasidim, and more important, the enthusiastic students who helped to build his public profile before the election. Even before he became Rebbe, he had guests for Shabbat, officiated at weddings, and was regularly available for consultation by all who desired his advice.

137

Schneerson's election enabled him to replace Yosef Yitzhak as the Hasidic focus in both the community and the neighborhood. This served, in time, to attract many enthusiasts from outside the neighborhood to see him. As the Habad movement expanded under his leadership, new people began to move into Crown Heights, attracted by the desire to be in the presence of the new Rebbe and to pay him their respects. These people, in distinction from many of the old residents, were considered Hasidim of Schneerson (as opposed to those of Yosef Yitzhak) and contributed to his consolidation of the whole neighborhood. In time, the new arrivals be gan to outnumber the old guard and those who were resistant, suspicious, or undecided about Schneerson's appointment, including many who had studied under Yosef Yitzhak. As we have seen, one feature of Hasidism is the unique relationship that develops between a Rebbe and his students or followers, and many followers of Yosef Yitzhak initially found it difficult, if not undesirable, to embrace the new Rebbe.[3] However, as they became the minority in the Habad movement and found little in his leadership to complain about, many embraced him as their Rebbe. A similar attachment to Schneerson will make the task of replacing him very difficult, if ever such an attempt should be made.

As the community grew and naturally attracted new people, the members of the old guard who were ambivalent about the new Rebbe were outvoiced. While some of the old Hasidim were strongly supportive of Schneerson and put their energies into working with him, others waited to see what would happen. When they saw that he was successful and that new people were moving into the area, they ceased to have any real contention with him. The Hasidim who had originally supported Shemaryahu Gourary eventually either recognized Schneerson's qualities or saw that they were outnumbered and decided to join the majority, especially when Gourary himself expressed support for Schneerson as successor.[4] Some members of the hardline opposition to Schneerson left the neighborhood and aligned themselves with anti-Habad elements in Williamsburg and Borough Park.[5] Others remained passively critical of the developments in the movement, but most were eventually won over by Schneerson's dedication. Whatever the reasons, most opposition to Schneerson in Crown Heights disappeared within a few short years after his succession.

The Postwar Period

The postwar period saw new East European arrivals into Crown Heights, starting from the late 1940s and early 1950s. A second wave of immigration commenced in the 1970s, when the Soviet Union temporarily allowed Jewish emigration, an opportunity of which many Russian Jews, with help from Habad and other groups, were happy to take advantage. Additionally, as the fame of Schneerson spread, Israeli Hasidim came to the United States to study at the Habad yeshiva, and many either remained in Crown Heights or later returned there permanently. Hasidim from communities around New York and around the United States came to visit, work, study, or live in the Hasidic community in Crown Heights.

Some key figures in the movement's present leadership came to Crown Heights in these years, and were chosen to work in Schneerson's institutions or in the administration of various Habad projects. The presence of these institutions did much to attract young people to the neighborhood, especially as operations expanded and there was an increased demand for labor.[6] Additionally, the fact that Crown Heights was (at least once) an upper-class neighborhood made it an attractive choice for people who desired a comfortable Hasidic lifestyle. Many new residents of Crown Heights were American Hasidim from the younger generation, or migrants who had not known Yosef Yitzhak intimately and accepted Schneerson wholeheartedly as their Rebbe. With more people moving into the area, and the neighborhood getting stronger, the critics could not complain that Schneerson's leadership was failing the movement. By 1988, an estimated 20,000 Habad Hasidim lived in the greater Brooklyn area, with Crown Heights as the epicenter of the movement.

At the same time, the departure of other Jewish residents from the neighborhood, including Orthodox groups and Hasidic Rebbes,[7] left a power vacuum from which Schneerson emerged as one of the few leadership figures in the area. The remaining Orthodox Jews were naturally drawn to the strength of the Habad movement and its new leader. Their children were particularly influenced, for many of them attended the only remaining Jewish schools in the area, which were sponsored by the Habad movement. Hence, in time, Crown Heights came to be synonymous with Habad territory.

Challenge and Response: The 1970s and After

In the early years of his assumption of leadership of the Habad movement, Schneerson's consolidation of the local community was accompanied by population fluctuations due to immigration, the mass migration of Jews from Crown Heights, and the appearance of an African-American community in the Brooklyn neighborhoods surrounding the Habad enclave. While these occurrences might have meant trouble for the still-settling Habad community, under Schneerson's leadership the movement used them to its advantage, thereby enabling him to further consolidate his authority.

It is impossible to know what might have occurred to the Habad movement had it relocated to Borough Park, Williamsburg, Long Island, or elsewhere, as many other Orthodox and Hasidic communities did in the 1960s and 1970s. What is certain is that the determination of Schneerson to remain in Crown Heights consolidated the community in its formative stages, and assisted in the future growth of the movement under his leadership. The changing ethno-demographic variations in a Brooklyn neighborhood might not immediately be seen as a cause for Hasidic solidarity, but the composition of the neighborhood surrounding Crown Heights appears to have affected many aspects of the movement's worldview. As we shall see, the location of the central headquarters of Habad in Crown Heights became one of the principal causes of Habad's strength as a movement.

In the 1960s and 1970s, the more conservative and wealthy segments of the population of Crown Heights, including many Jews, started to leave for more affluent and pleasant neighborhoods.[8] The mass emigration of Jews from Crown Heights caused a dilemma for the Habad Hasidim and its leader. Habad institutions had purchased property in the area, and were beginning to achieve hard-earned results in outreach and consolidation. A relocation of the entire movement would have put the growth of Habad back a decade, if not terminate its achievements completely. On the other hand, the real estate crisis was such that if Habad organizations and individual Hasidim did not get out soon, they might lose the value of their houses, investments, properties, and savings.

The basic decision to be made pitted the quality of life for the Hasidic population, which might be improved by leaving the area, against the integrity and solidarity of the community, which might be shattered if the locality were abandoned. Were Schneerson to chose incorrectly, the decision could prove disastrous to the efforts of Habad, and undo the decades of work that had already contributed to the consolidation of the movement. A bold solution was required, and Schneerson gave instructions that his followers were not to leave Crown Heights, but to remain firm in their resolve to stay put.[9] The impetus behind Schneerson's strategy is unknown; it may have been influenced by Yosef Yitzhak's example of perseverance despite odds in the face of the massive Jewish emigration from Russia, which he had vigorously opposed, or by Schneerson's own stubbornness when facing opposition.

The decision to remain in Crown Heights indicated Schneerson's preference for the physical sense of community, togetherness, and unity that Crown Heights provided, although by this stage Habad had become an international community held together by ideology and technology. If his Hasidim were to leave the geographic proximity of his influence, the very fiber of their Hasidic lifestyle would be profoundly affected, and the personal and direct influence the Rebbe had on them as a community might be diminished, if not lost. If they were to relocate, the whole community might not be able to move to the same location, so that regrouping and reconsolidation after a move would detract from the explicit goals of outreach established for the movement. Schneerson also probably realized that condoning migration from Crown Heights would lead to a domino effect; the first to leave would cause others to do so, with chaos and economic ruin for the movement, as well as for individual Hasidim, the most likely result.

The only effective way that Schneerson could prevent the mass migration of his followers from Crown Heights, and avoid a complete landslide of real estate prices that would financially ruin many of his followers, was to steadfastly refuse to leave the neighborhood himself, and to demand the same of his followers. For this decision to have any effect, it had to occur on a communal scale. Through implicit instruction by Schneerson, strict orders for obedience and community discipline conveyed by his aides, and appeal to the community's religious sentiments,[10] calm was eventually restored, and the threat of exodus was averted. For many people this was a relief, as they could allay their fears concerning livelihood and lifestyle and demonstrate their commitment to the Rebbe. For others, however, the decision no doubt presented a challenge to their ideological commitment to remain behind in what they feared was a trap. In either case, the decision to remain demonstrated the resilience of the movement to meet challenges and withstand them. Schneerson had decided that the Habad responsibility for outreach and the importance of remaining a tightly knit community superseded the individual wealth or comfort of his followers.

Once the decision to remain had been made, the Hasidim adopted a siege mentality, united against opposition, which deepened their commitment to Schneerson and Habad. It made good economic sense to faithfully carry out Schneerson's instructions, so that Habad real estate, business, and other enterprises could maintain their self-reliance and stability. The holiness of Schneerson's instructions was no longer simple polemic; indeed, many people's livelihoods depended on it, and many realized that they had a vested interest in the observance of Schneerson's instructions. Everyone was encouraged, pressured, socialized, and religiously compelled to carry out his directive to remain in Crown Heights, for the good of everyone else in the community. Personal welfare was linked to Hasidic piety and obedience to the zaddik, in order to secure the community's support for the decision to remain in Crown Heights.

These events brought about a landmark change in how Schneerson was perceived in the Habad movement, and altered the manner in which his future instructions were received. In order to allay uncertainty about the correctness of the decision against leaving the neighborhood, everyone clung on in desperation to Schneerson's instructions, hoping that he would lead them out of the difficulties they were in and that real estate prices would stabilize.

Initially, the decision to remain in Crown Heights enabled those who remained in the area, including the Habad community, to take advantage of lower property prices, and the movement was able to greatly expand its operations, especially through the acquisition of property for schools and other space-hungry institutions. Lower property prices also meant that rent became affordable for Habad émigrés on a lower income. More Habad supporters were therefore able to move closer to Schneerson and 770, not only adding to the size of the Habad population in the neighborhood, but enhancing the sense of solidarity and community. When people began to feel secure that no one else would leave the area, house prices stabilized because property could not be bought at any price. Although feelings of uneasiness about the situation continued, the resilience of the communal decision not to budge had created an increased sense of cohesion.

However, the lowering of property prices had another effect, which also affected the Habad community: the influx of substantial numbers of African-Americans into the neighborhood. From the 1970s, African-Americans and Hasidim shared the streets in distinct economic inequality, and the influx of poor African-American families into the neighborhood was one of the reasons contributing to the decision by

other Jewish groups to leave the area. For Habad, the presence of a culture so different from their own in the local area was an additional challenge to their identity, and
further strengthened the community's sense of solidarity and commitment to
Schneerson.

The effect of these changes on the Habad Hasidim was interesting. They had
remained behind but had watched all their Jewish friends and neighbors leave. The
decision to remain was, for some, brave and an expression of loyalty to the movement
and their Rebbe. Although there was an economic strategy involved in their obedience, it was nevertheless justified religiously. The effect of the migration of Habad
Hasidim into Crown Heights created an atmosphere of communal self-reliance and
Hasidic fellowship centered around the Hasidic headquarters at 770, and focusing on
the Rebbe and his teachings. The community had made an articulated decision to
obey its Rebbe, and had therefore thrown in its lot with his vision for them.

The relative isolation of Habad from other Jewish communities and from the
African-American presence meant that the economy of those who remained was
based on supporting one other, and accommodating the new residents who had
moved into the area. As they were now the only Jewish presence in the neighborhood,
the culture of the Habad movement was articulated and explored in isolation from
major physical interaction with other traditions of Judaism. Habad's difference from
other Hasidic groups was now not only cultural and ideological, but geographical,
which had further effects; where once Habad Hasidim might have considered integrating with other Orthodox communities or Hasidic dynasties, their geographic isolation now prevented this and assisted in the creation of a unique Habad identity. The
migration of other schools of Hasidism from the area made Schneerson the sole voice
of Jewish leadership in the neighborhood.

The act of self-isolation as a means of demonstrating the distinctiveness of the
movement was a practice followed by earlier Rebbes of the Habad movement, and
had helped them to consolidate their authority. Schneerson's decision to remain in
Crown Heights was compared to the demand by Yosef Yitzhak that his Hasidim
remain in Soviet Russia.[11] Schneerson was seen as a leader and pioneer like Yosef
Yitzhak, although his decision, unlike that of his predecessor, served to preserve their
identity, and rather than eventually abandoning his followers to their fate, Schneerson
remained with them. He was respected for his determination and the wisdom of his
decision, for he had faced the challenge to the movement with distinction. Faith in his
judgment was enhanced and encouraged, and the period of the 1970s marked a cross-
roads for the community, a time of testing and increased expansion.

However, the growing racial tensions of the 1990s between the Hasidim and their
African-American neighbors, and the growth of incidents of violence in the neighborhood, raised questions as to the prudence of Schneerson's decision.[12] The original dilemma he faced was difficult. Schneerson chose the temporary benefit of communal cohesion in a state of siege, while perhaps recognizing that one day things

would reach a crisis point for the faithful. The cultural and communal insulation and the development of a siege mentality, despite its obvious drawbacks of isolation and growing insularity, nevertheless produced intense feelings of identity and belonging. These were harnessed by the Habad Hasidim in their outreach work.

The Crown Heights of today is a Hasidic enclave consisting of a number of blocks surrounded on all sides by a population overwhelmingly African-American. Within Crown Heights, the vast majority of the residents of several square blocks are members of the Habad movement. The neighborhood is not well groomed, although some streets have vestiges of their more affluent past. Since the death of Schneerson, the neighborhood has been somewhat renovated, with public garbage collection and the planting of trees contributing to a more pleasant environment for the Hasidim and their neighbors. Eastern Parkway distinctly divides the Hasidic and black neighborhoods. Habad's central headquarters, situated at 770 Eastern Parkway, is a distinctly unremarkable building given its influence on the Jewish world and the focus awarded it by Habad adherents worldwide, as will be discussed below.

What If Schneerson Had Relocated?

One must consider what might have happened to Habad had Schneerson decided to leave Crown Heights in the 1960s, as did other Hasidic Rebbes. There are large ultra-Orthodox communities of faithful Hasidim who follow Rebbes whose standards of learning and popular appeal are remarkably mediocre. However, because they inherited the mantle of leadership in their community, these Rebbes, as a matter of course, attracted large numbers of people to their court for Shabbat activities. The role of the Rebbe in many of these movements remains primarily that of a figurehead; they are the centers of large ultra-Orthodox communities, and their courts provide a focus for their community.

It may be argued that if Schneerson had moved to such a neighborhood, he would still have attracted very large numbers of people to his talks on Shabbat afternoon, and in turn, because of his charismatic personality, many would have become his loyal adherents and activists anyway. It is even possible that he could have taken over significant segments of other ultra-Orthodox neighborhoods just by moving into them, through force of personality and charisma. This would have served to bolster his own following and take support away from his ultra-Orthodox detractors.

On the other hand, if he had designed his leadership personality and his rhetoric around these large ultra-Orthodox constituencies, he would have had to speak to their interests and needs, and might never have developed a strong appeal to secular Jews and the international Jewish world. As this is conjecture we may speculate only so far; however, it is interesting to imagine how he might have molded a much larger ultra-Orthodox flock in his image had he had the opportunity and been less insistent on remaining in Crown Heights.

Crown Heights: Religious Significance

Although the neighborhood of Crown Heights, in itself, was not the force behind the Habad movement's success, it played a significant role in several ways. Most important, it served as the home of the community's principal member, the Rebbe. It thus served as the spiritual and communal focus for the movement not only locally but also internationally.

Further, the area accommodated one of the main Habad populations in the world, attracted not only to the presence of the Rebbe but also by the sense of community that developed around him through the communal activities over which he presided.[13] Many of the movement's major organizations were located in Crown Heights, and 770 served as the central headquarters of the movement, prompting those most active in the administration of the movement and its programs to remain in the area. It is also significant that the largest Habad presence in the world, and the focus for its activism, was located in the city containing the largest Jewish population in the Diaspora, New York.[14]

So far as localities have significance in the minds and lives of Hasidim, Crown Heights took on a symbolic significance beyond its municipal limits. This significance, along with the gradual transformation of Crown Heights from an affluent neighborhood to an African-American ghetto, cultivated an atmosphere in Crown Heights that fostered its outreach spirit and strengthened the connection between Schneerson and his constituency.

Although much of the publicity and outreach work of the Habad movement takes place far away from Crown Heights, the movement's membership look to this locality for inspiration. Eretz Yisrael, the Holy Land, although still a prominent theme and source of symbolism for Habad Hasidim, nevertheless takes second place to Crown Heights in terms of news, gossip, politics, and general interest within Habad. The town of Lubavitch in Russia, where the movement was born and from which it draws one of its names, became a relative irrelevancy to the life of Habad Hasidim once the movement's center was moved to the United States. The fact that the town is the location of the gravesites of the early Rebbes has not been forgotten, [15] but in the last two generations, Crown Heights has come to serve as the locus for the Habad community. This is especially so now because to the proximity of the graves of Yosef Yitzhak and Schneerson.

Crown Heights has remarkably taken over as the central symbolic locality in Habad. Today, pictures of the movement's central headquarters at 770 Eastern Parkway are a fixture in Habad homes and offices, and stand alongside pictures of Schneerson as symbols of its strength, ideology, and unity under a charismatic leader. Replicas of the building at 770 have been built in Habad communities around the world, including Israel and Australia. As described by Friedman, the tendency to attach to a locality, be it Eretz Yisrael, Lubavitch, or Crown Heights, is an expression of "local particularism." The movement's transition to a more universalistic expression as it shed its dependence on the city of Lubavitch appears to be retrogressing with its newly emergent attachment to Crown Heights. [16]

Although one might presume that modern communications systems would remove the need for travel and therefore make the Hasidic pilgrimage to Crown Heights religiously redundant, this presumption would prove incorrect. In fact, the use of modern transportation meant that personal physical contact with the Rebbe and with Crown Heights could be maintained even among Hasidim living abroad. The personal dimension of regular visitation to the Rebbe's court, the personal and communal spiritual experiences that took place there, and the memories exported to the communities in the Diaspora by the participants, comprised a religious and cultural message for the worldwide Habad Hasidic network. Events at 770 were spread across the world through personal contact with those who had originally participated in them, lending immediacy to the experience that assisted in the furtherance of a feeling of community and unity. This further strengthened the association and commitment to the Crown Heights locality for followers of Habad in the Diaspora. Over fifty years of continual focus, despite (or perhaps because of) challenges from outside the community and occasional difficulties with surrounding neighbors, Crown Heights became an essential part of contemporary Habad life. Even after the death of Schneerson, the area serves not only as a center for pilgrimage, but as a focus for the movement, and communication with his gravesite continues through letter, fax, and even e-mail.

Administratively, Crown Heights was and is the headquarters of the movement and its many appendages. The outreach, educational, financial, and communal life of the community are administered from 770 and other buildings in Crown Heights, and most of the movement's administrative hierarchy were (and still are) resident in the area. The centralization of administrative and executive authority in the area resulted in Crown Heights being treated very much like a capital city by followers of Habad. Although individual communities were administered locally, they all looked to Schneerson and his organizations for direction and inspiration, and so cemented the centrality of Crown Heights in Habad's ideology.

With the development of the messianist trend within Habad, 770 and Crown Heights both took on messianic associations as the workplace and central command of the mashiach. The street address of the movement's central headquarters at 770 Eastern Parkway has even taken on numerical significance. The number 770, according to the Jewish system of *gematria*, is the numerical equivalent for the words *Beit Mashiach*, "house of the mashiach," and there are other numerical correspondences that indicate to Hasidim the divinely inspired nature of the headquarters. [17] A replica of the building at 770 Eastern Parkway has been constructed in Israel, to accommodate the mashiach when he is revealed; the reason for the construction of replicas in other locations remains unclear.

Even after Schneerson's death, the locality has retained its significance. Many places in the neighborhood hold religious significance for Habad Hasidim because they recall the life and works of Schneerson, his places of residence and prayer, the paths he walked and the many events that he presided over. Yearly visitations and "pilgrimages" to Crown Heights have maintained their numbers, although how long this can last without the presence of a Rebbe is still to be ascertained.

The future of Crown Heights as the spiritual and physical center for the Habad movement depends, among many other things, on the movement's inclinations toward local particularism or universalism. The neglecting of the traditional town of Lubavitch by the Hasidim of Shalom Dov Ber was indicative of Friedman's idea of transformation into universalism.[18] However, the reattachment to Crown Heights under Schneerson could be an indication of the movement's retrogression into a local-particularistic mindset, where the focus is on a location rather than the idea of a universal message. The inability to make the final step in severing local-particularistic ties is apparent in the movement and is reinforced by its still strict halakhic observance. These conservative tendencies in the movement can be interpreted as a basic rejection of universalism, particularly in its long-term implications.[19]

[1] Jerome R. Mintz, *Hasidic People*, pp. 139–140.

[2] See Avrum Ehrlich, *Leadership in the HaBaD Movement*, pp. 398–399.

[3] Ibid., pp. 338, 385–387.

[4] Ibid., p. 399.

[5] Ibid., pp. 398–399.

[6] See Bonnie J. Morris, "The Children's Crusade," p. 334.

[7] For example, the Bobover Rebbe. See Mintz, *Hasidic People*, p. 141.

[8] Ibid., pp. 139–153.

[9] See Joseph Gambardello and Bob Liff, "A Potent Figure in Judaism."

[10] See testimony of Mendel Shemtov, in Mintz, *Hasidic People*, pp. 142–143.

[11] In Yosef Yitzhak's case, the consequences of staying in the Soviet Union were disastrous for the obedient Hasidim; moreover, as there was little for those who stayed to do, their sacrifice was largely in vain. While he prevented his followers from leaving Russia, Yosef Yitzhak himself eventually migrated to the United States, long after it became impossible for many of his followers to escape Communist persecution.

[12] The racial tensions between the two communities came to a head in 1991. On August 19, two seven-year-old African-American children were struck by a car driven by a Hasid in Schneerson's entourage. One of the children, Gavin Cato, was killed, and the other, his cousin Angela, was critically injured. Later that night a twenty-nine-year-old Australian rabbinical student, Yankel Rosenbaum, was stabbed to death, apparently in retaliation for the death of the child. Following this, there were a series of marches, riots, and looting, and a great deal of resentment against the Habad community, which was perceived by vocal elements of the African-American population as receiving preferential treatment from police and other city officials. See Mintz, *Hasidic People*, pp. 328–347 for a detailed account of these events and their aftermath.

[13] See Chapter 7.

[14] Schneerson also observed with symbolic intent that New York was the seat of the United

Nations, and thus the center of the effort to unite humanity under one banner and ensure human rights and justice for everyone.

[15] The Iron Curtain prevented pilgrimage to the town of Lubavitch for a half-century, but the opening up of Eastern Europe has not brought about a resurgence of Habad visits to Lubavitch and other "holy" sites. Many *shluhim* to Russia do make the pilgrimage to Lubavitch, but few Habad Hasidim visit Russia specifically for this purpose. Many other Hasidic schools, by contrast, have taken the opportunity to reconnect with their roots; the Breslav dynasty, for example, has renewed its connection to the town of Uman, and Breslav Hasidim have made pilgrimages there throughout the last half-decade, made easier by the relaxation of travel to the former Soviet Union.

[16] See especially Friedman, "Habad as Messianic Fundamentalism," and below.

[17] See Shmuel Butman, *Countdown to Moshiach*, p. 3. Gematria games are often used to supplement ideological positions in Habad and in Hasidism generally. A relevant example derives from the name Habad. The numerical value of the words *hokhmah, binah,* and *da'at* from which it is derived is 770. Mitnagdic opponents of the movement have wryly noted that Habad is also an acronym for *hamor bli da'at* ("a senseless donkey"), which also adds up to 770.

[18] Friedman, "Habad as Messianic Fundamentalism," p. 337.

[19] It stands to reason that universalist movements would incline to antinomianism, and this probably gives them broader appeal. Christianity is an example.

Chapter 14
Administration and Bureaucracy

The Rebbe as "Chief of State"

In every school of Hasidism, the hierarchy of command officially starts and finishes with the Rebbe. This was the case with Habad in which, as we have seen, the Rebbe was given control over all aspects of the running of the movement, and especially over the administration of its activities. Theoretically, the Rebbe had veto power over all the actions and plans of all of the movement's organizations.[1] In the United States before the arrival of Yosef Yitzhak, the Habad movement had a more democratic style of leadership, which deferred to Yosef Yitzhak's control via correspondence before his arrival, and in person after he immigrated. A sense of this independence of spirit may have lingered in the hierarchy of AGUCH, which existed before Yosef Yitzhak's arrival in America, and this may have contributed to the organization's effective termination soon after Schneerson's election.[2]

All Habad organizations officially execute the will of the Rebbe, and during his period of leadership were either given instructions by Schneerson himself or through his aides, who usually functioned as the practical administration. Rabbi Hodokov, for example, who was formerly Yosef Yitzhak's chief aide, was given the title "Chief of Staff" in the movement, and had far-reaching executive authority in representing the "Chief of State," Schneerson.[3] As Rebbe and Chief of State, Schneerson was formally and legally the President of many of Habad's official institutions, including AGUCH.

Yehuda Krinsky, one of Schneerson's top aides and a key player in the administration of the movement after his death,[4] described Schneerson's authority as emerging from his position as leader of the community:

> . . . as such he directs the general organization's work [and] the outer structure of the organization. . . . he doesn't get involved in every detail of every organization, but he heads dozens of organizations. . . . he would have veto power over every case because of the reverence held for him. . . . His word is like dogma. . . . he knows the people and his community intimately. . . . he chooses the organization's heads because he knows who is appropriate for what position.[5]

148

Schneerson's responsibility for the pursuit of the mission and goals of Habad as established by Yosef Yitzhak further contributed to the solidification of his authority over the daily affairs of the movement. It also gave him the ideological basis from which to most effectively judge the success of the movement's outreach and other activities. His position of Chief of State of the Habad movement assisted Schneerson in his consolidation of authority, allowing him complete control of the actions taken by his followers.

Schneerson's Administrative Qualities

Schneerson's administrative authority developed over time. The administrative skills that he employed in his institutions both before he became Rebbe and as Rebbe were the key to his success. This is not to say that he was familiar with the subtle nuances of accountancy or tax law, or with the right systems for distribution of funding or the reshuffling of organizations, that are often characteristic of efficient administration. At the beginning of his leadership, Schneerson was dealing primarily with ideologues and religious students, individuals who were intelligent and perceptive individuals but had little formal training in business, administration, law, publishing, or any other skill involved in the movement's enterprises. His staff, like Schneerson himself, had to learn the practical skills necessary for the performance of their duties, an action made easier by their education and intellectual training.[6]

Schneerson's contribution to the activities of his staff lay primarily in his ability to enthuse them and enlist them in his vision for the movement, to direct their efforts into areas that he considered to have priority, and to pass on his determination to expand operations. In this sense, he was a supreme administrator and motivator, directing his subordinates to take over the more menial functions of administration and the paperwork involved in running large organizations,[7] especially in his later life.

During his time in office, Schneerson developed his own strong and distinct managerial skills and techniques. From the outset of his rule, he demonstrated an insight into the minds and hearts of his new constituency, and knew how to motivate them into useful production. He was able, for example, to mobilize the Hasidim out of their despondency after Yosef Yitzhak's death, and this proved to be one of the most important things he did in consolidating his election and increasing his appeal to the Hasidim. The methods he employed are discussed elsewhere;[8] they showed great administrative skill in knowing his constituency and easing their minds so they could function more efficiently.

Schneerson recognized the merit of full employment and ideological fulfillment for all his Hasidim—men, women, the elderly, the scholarly, the unscholarly, children— in the various countries where Habad communities resided. He recognized that the skills of the Hasidim were varied, but that they needed expression and could be directed for the benefit of the whole movement. Were it not for Schneerson's utilization of their skills inside Habad, they might have gone elsewhere to express themselves. Instead, others came to Habad to be able to utilize their skills, and to find fulfillment of their talents in a powerful ideological framework.

Schneerson's motivational "war cry" was none other than a call to achieve the ultimate mission of redemption. This represented a marked departure from other motivational incentives, which generally advocate personal gain or financial profit. Schneerson did this not in his own name, but on the authority of Yosef Yitzhak. He was determined to fulfill the mission given him by his predecessor by fostering daring expansionist tactics and moving beyond conventionally wise business practices. By this intentional overreaching, drawing an increased commitment to the movement by all concerned was not only desirable, but essential. Beyond all expectations, Schneerson succeeded, and with every success, the belief grew that the mission given to Habad was so large that cosmic, super-rational tactics could work. What at first seemed an over-optimistic belief that financial and other obstacles to expansion and mission would be overcome was for the most part justified.[9]

One strong administrative skill that Schneerson possessed was his open-mindedness, which in turn led to his receptivity to innovative, non-traditional ideas and originality in his outreach programs. Although Schneerson did not personally espouse the use of innovative technology,[10] philosophy, or ideology in his own private life, he encouraged the pursuit of anything that might increase the effectiveness of Habad's outreach. The technology used was often cutting-edge, and changed as technology developed. Telephone, fax, radio, television and satellite communication, tape-recording of talks, use of computers and the Internet, high-speed travel, modern printing machinery, and the like, all became a part of the outreach efforts and organizational structure of Habad during Schneerson's reign. Throughout his leadership, communication facilities were established to make the distribution of material and internal communication more efficient.[11] Modern technology was utilized to build upon the old system of correspondence established by the earlier Habad Rebbes, and the increased speed of communication enabled the transformation of the widespread Habad communities into a global village.

Schneerson's effective use of modern technology was often criticized by other Hasidic groups that saw the use of technology, even in the dissemination of Hasidism, as posing a threat to their traditional way of life.[12] For Schneerson, the use of technology demonstrated that being traditionally observant did not mean giving up the modern world, but rather embracing it in furtherance of the spread of the Hasidic message. It is unclear whether Schneerson himself initiated the use of technology and innovative techniques of outreach, or agreed to them when others suggested them. Whatever their origins, however, these innovations were perceived by his followers as directed by the Rebbe, and the praise for their success was his. He was required to defend his innovative methods to the movement's more conservative ultra-Orthodox critics, and explain why they were legitimate tools for use in Habad's outreach programs. As his critics were many, and came from different segments of the wider

Jewish community, his willingness to defy them showed strength of spirit, open-mindedness, and determination.[13]

His amenability to technology was one of his most important innovations. Considering the newness of the instruments and their often difficult operation and expense, as well as the cultural taboo against them throughout the ultra-Orthodox community, this move was all the more impressive and unprecedented. Technology became a basic tool in the operations of Habad. Many innovations were adopted on the initiative of emissaries exposed to modernity (through education or environment) and their largely secularized congregations and audiences, or were suggested by Hasidim who came from secular backgrounds and were newly religious. Either way, new ideas eased their way into Habad organizations.

Delegation of Authority

Schneerson's method of delegation was different from that of his predecessors. It was common practice for Rebbes to employ the services of male family, usually sons and sons-in-law. As befit their family connection, they would often be given highly sensitive and responsible work, and would be in close contact with the Rebbe and come to know him intimately.[14] In Schneerson's case, because he had no family or children, he was forced to delegate authority to his Hasidim. He was therefore able to choose the most skilled and suitable people for each position, and could dispense with them if they proved unsuitable or ineffective, actions difficult to undertake with family. The effectiveness of Schneerson's leadership is further demonstrated by his ability to turn a necessary break with tradition into a sense of equal opportunity. It was felt by the Hasidim that everyone could join Schneerson's mission and serve a useful function in Habad's infrastructure, which was not a nepotistic system reserved for family or a select group of intimates.

Schneerson's ability to delegate authority was a primary organizational skill at which he excelled. He cultivated Hasidim who demonstrated talent, and even before he assumed leadership of the movement, he utilized his close contact with the yeshiva students to encourage suitable people to take up positions in the organizations under his direct control, so as to best utilize their talents. Schneerson's technique of delegating authority was famed, particularly as part of the outreach program that sent emissaries and activists to communities around the world. Habad emissaries frequently became highly public and responsible figures in the communities to which they were sent, and helped increase the presence and importance of the movement throughout the world. Although the emissaries frequently reported to Schneerson with information and requests for advice, his ability to maintain a remote level of control over his delegates arose mainly from his trusting them. He recognized their need for autonomy, and the importance of allowing them to decide important local issues for themselves. This is not to say that he did not provide detailed plans to his emissaries, or give concrete and direct advice, but he recognized that there was only so much he should do, since he was unaware of the intimate details of local conditions.

Schneerson's emissaries frequently described his involvement with their outreach work as total. All positive achievements were attributed to him and his direction, but Schneerson more accurately involved himself in what have been described as "thousands of pinpoint surgical interventions [while] remaining sensitive to people's needs."[15] He was known to answer questions put to him in meticulous detail, no matter what their relationship with the community or level of authority or prominence; a student or a housewife would frequently receive the same level of consideration from Schneerson as the leader of a major institution or community.[16] Often Schneerson extended advice that referred the writer to the local rabbi, sometimes providing his name. A story is told that in one case Schneerson contacted the local rabbi he had recommended, telling him how to respond to the question that would soon be put to him.[17]

By the extensive delegation of authority and the trust he vested in his emissaries, Schneerson fostered the development of a generation of leaders in Jewish communities all over the world. He delegated authority for answering simple inquiries to those who were best suited to answer them: community rabbis and local authorities. In doing so, he not only fulfilled the goals of outreach and redemption laid out by Yosef Yitzhak, but ensured the legitimacy, independence, and loyalty of his emissaries, and made them an integral part of Habad's self-appointed mission to the world.

Throughout his early years as Rebbe, Schneerson was involved in the active, hands-on administration and general supervision of programs, and the establishment of organizations, projects, and campaigns to ensure the survival and expansion of Habad. In later years, burdened not only by age but also by more Hasidim turning to him from around the world, he continued to initiate projects, but did not directly implement their fulfillment. He relied on others to do so, but was always careful to maintain his supervisory role. He received letters from administrators both requesting and giving advice concerning projects, and received regular progress reports from Habad institutions. These were not part of the formal organization of the movement, but were written voluntarily by the Hasidim out of a desire to keep the Rebbe informed, and perhaps tacitly to attract his attention or approval.

Schneerson retained his power of veto over the activities of the movement throughout his reign. Before a project could be launched anywhere in the world on behalf of the movement, Schneerson would first be called upon to give his approval and blessing to the venture. In the early years of his leadership, he personally gave directions to those he desired to carry them out, but as the autonomy and initiative of his representatives increased, new action plans arose from the suggestions Schneerson made in his weekly *sichot* talks. Through these talks, which in later years were communicated worldwide by telephone and satellite hook-up, Schneerson would communicate his vision of the movement. He would suggest an idea, and some forward-thinking, innovative, and enthusiastic Hasid who wanted to please the Rebbe and distinguish himself would conceive of a way in which it could be practically executed. An outline of the plan would be sent to Schneerson, who would recognize the initiative and bless its success, or point out flaws in its conception. The credit for any successful action was attributed to Schneerson, but in effect the middle hierarchy and the enthusiasm of the Hasidim in adapting Schneerson's *sichot* into practical, realizable stages of action was the primary cause of their success. In later years, Schneerson did not have to involve himself with the logistical aspects of new initiatives. Competitiveness and self-propelled eagerness to do what they were told allowed Schneerson to merely acknowledge the initiatives of institutions and individuals through the act of giving his blessing, which was requested of him before any initiative was undertaken.

Aides, Secretaries, and Assistants

Throughout the history of Habad, the Rebbe's secretaries, assistants, and aides were traditionally his closest associates. They were often called upon to represent the Rebbe and the movement to important dignitaries or government officials, and were therefore required to have extensive authority and an intimate understanding of the Rebbe's ideas and the movement's vital interests. In past generations they were expected to visit Habad communities, often remote from the residence of the Rebbe, and enthuse the Hasidim with the Hasidic spirit by recounting stories of the Rebbe's greatness, esteemed qualities and the wonders he worked. Because these accounts were allegedly from their own first-hand experience, they served to authenticate and legitimize the power and authority of the Rebbe more than the stories told by other people, who were less intimate with him. Their role was therefore one of consolidating the authority of the Rebbe helping to bind the community together around him. Whenever there has been a debate over the succession in Habad, the candidates under consideration often came from the ranks of the Rebbe's aides and close associates.[18]

The aides had a tremendous responsibility for protecting the Rebbe's privacy. Traditionally, they were members of the Rebbe's extended family—his brothers, sons, sons-in-law, and cousins—where the restraints of privacy came more naturally. As Schneerson did not have an extended family, his aides came from the general membership of Habad. Early in his leadership, he retained many of the aides who had served Yosef Yitzhak;[19] he appointed others who had worked with him in the past, and still others from the ranks of Hasidim who had proven themselves in the service of Habad.

Schneerson's predicament was unusual for a Rebbe, for the absence of extended family required him to maintain the professional status of a "flawless leader" even to his closest associates. Throughout his life there was no one, except his wife, with whom he could be other than "The Rebbe," a factor that no doubt made a deep impact on his psychology and required him to internalize his true personality. This fact alone might have contributed to the uniqueness and loneliness of his leadership, and perhaps to the development of the messianic element, especially in his later years.

Ironically, the very people who were most aware of the Rebbe's faults, that is, his aides and intimate associates, were most sought after to recount stories of his "blemishless" existence. Their dilemma makes for an interesting study, and is the subject of much curiosity. It is inevitable (although unprovable) that some resorted to complex psychological acrobatics involving denial and cognitive dissonance to reconcile their Hasidic conceptions of the flawless Rebbe with their observations of the real person. They would tell stories of the Rebbe's wondrous actions, balancing delicately between fantasy and reality, but would do their best to explain away any discrepancy between the two. This approach reflects the reverence for the zaddik in Hasidism, which requires that his actions, even if unhalakhic, are not to be understood in purely human or mundane terms, but as part of some deeper mystery. It might be further theorized that other, perhaps more realistic aides would incline more to insincerity. Their recognition of the Rebbe's humanity would not prevent them from supporting the image of their leader's loftiness to other Hasidim, perhaps because they saw the necessity for continuity in the movement as more important than accuracy about the leader's humanness. This is, of course, speculation; the only certainty is that the privacy of the Rebbe was always protected, and the flawless image was perpetuated throughout his lifetime. This protectiveness was not demanded by Schneerson himself but was something the Hasidim wanted. They would have been enraged by compromising stories about Schneerson, and no aide would have been able to retain his job if he had spoken critically about their Rebbe.

Historically, the classification of the Rebbe's associates and assistants was subject to a number of variations and levels of hierarchy. This remained true of Schneerson's aides, and thus composition of his staff changed as the movement expanded and new needs developed.

The School of Assistants

When Schneerson assumed the leadership of the movement, it was effectively administered by the "old school" of assistants. This comprised the early Habad activists in the United States, augmented by those who came from Europe with Yosef Yitzhak. As such, they were primarily the Hasidim of Yosef Yitzhak. The former Rebbe's ill-health and his practical, nonmystical approach to business made him a less awesome figure to work with than his successor, and flawless standards, approaching mystical ability in their effect, had not been expected of him by his aides.[20] Yosef Yitzhak had earned their respect by the sheer tenacity of his character, not for his flawless decisions or mystical connection with the Divine. For many of these men, Schneerson was not expected to be perfect, just competent to the task.

Yosef Yitzhak had been accompanied from Europe by some aides who were university educated and thus of a rationalist disposition, such as Rabbis Hodokov and Liebman.[21] American aides like Rabbis Jacobson and Simpson were concerned about the continuity of the movement that they had helped build, and less worried by the question of whether or not Schneerson was a zaddik. These men continued to work for Schneerson until their deaths, as did Rabbi Nissan Mindel, the only man of this generation of leadership still alive in early 2002. They were considered his closest associates. It was unlikely, given their connection with the previous Rebbe, that they would have a problem with the inherent difficulty in the idea of a "flawless Rebbe"; their thinking was less mystical and more social and pragmatic. Over the years, the aides who continued to work for Schneerson after Yosef Yitzhak's death were all highly supportive and respectful. At the time of writing, only one of them was still alive, and although it might seem that he would have a unique position in the modern movement, he is practically irrelevant to the leadership and daily affairs of Habad.[22]

With the passage of time (as older aides died, activities expanded, and internal hierarchies developed) the need arose for a larger staff that would report directly to Schneerson, or at least receive instructions and discuss ongoing administrative issues with him. Several people slowly made their way up the loosely defined hierarchical ladder to become regular aides and assistants to Schneerson, including Rabbis Leible Groner, Yaakov Kline, and Yehuda Krinsky.[23] The latter's role in the movement was primarily as secretary and spokesman for the largely inactive AGUCH organization, and by his own claim, he was also spokesman for the entire Habad movement. Each of these men came to his office in a different way, demonstrating that there was no single road to a position of prominence in the movement. These men were educated primarily under Schneerson, and would therefore have had to come to grips with the dissonance created by increased exposure to the human reality of the Rebbe, as opposed to his public persona.

The image of Schneerson as a "superman" was influenced by Schneerson's romanticization of his predecessor, Yosef Yitzhak. Over time, these projections were also applied to Schneerson, only in his case the idealization and mythologization of the Rebbe occurred while he was still alive. The disillusionment experienced by close aides of Schneerson is illustrated by a personal communication to the author. One Shabbat, in the early hours of the morning, a Hasid was studying in the hall adjoining Schneerson's study. He heard noises emanating from the room and heard Schneerson go to the toilet, break wind, groan, and flush the toilet. Because of this evidence, the student realized that the Rebbe was in fact human, and not a supernatural being, and from this point on, his religious commitment and Hasidic worldview were shattered. Although Schneerson's humanness would appear to be self-evident, for those who idealized him, and especially his close aides and associates, recognition of it through everyday contact no doubt caused a change of perception.

The difference between public persona and private man became more evident as Schneerson grew older. As time passed, he slowly became less able to carry his public image as flawlessly and superhumanly as before. He more frequently made mistakes, was more prone to give inaccurate references or misquote sources in his discourses, and became more insensitive and dogmatic about issues that required public sensitivity.[24] His aides, for the most part, treated him with absolute respect and caution, not daring to contradict, correct, or question him even within their own hearts. Some of his aides, whose responsibility it was to prepare transcripts of Schneerson's talks for print, found incorrect references and were forced to correct them.[25] For some, this aroused philosophic doubt about his status as a zaddik, while others maintained their conception of him as a flawless zaddik despite their personal experiences to the contrary.[26] For the most part, their avoidance of the issue of the increasing unreliability of Schneerson's faculties meant that, toward the end of his life, his statements, teachings, advice, and policy went unchecked by his aides, beyond the correction of obvious technical errors.

Even medical issues may have been dealt with inappropriately, for there are some who claim that as Schneerson became more physically infirm with age, the medical attention he received was affected by his status as a zaddik.[27] The aides had their Rebbe's best interests in mind, but some of them believed that he was omniscient and knew the true outcomes of his actions better than any medical experts. For this reason, and because they did not wish to contradict him, they did not force Schneerson to undertake therapies if he refused or make him take medications that he did not wish to take. The issue of the medical care of the aging Schneerson became the focus of intense dispute within the movement, and even attracted outside media interest as Schneerson had first one stroke, and then a second.[28] Seeking the best care for the Rebbe, aides argued over his treatment and were separated into two camps, identified by the names of the two chief secretaries, Groner and Krinsky. The latter advocated more professional, scientific treatment of Schneerson's illness, the former allegedly hesitated to accept this approach.[29]

The Bureaucratic Hierarchy

The role of the Hasidic Rebbe is to ensure a direct relationship between himself and his Hasidim. Most do this through *yehidut*, the writing of letters, the distribution of charity, and by means of Hasidic gatherings. Despite the comparative rarity of these occasions in the lives of most adherents of a Hasidic movement, Hasidim believe that their relationship with the Rebbe is direct and without an intermediary, and in traditional societies this was often the case. With the advent of the modern era, and the adoption by Habad of modern methods of communication, even communities separated by continental distances were enabled to maintain this sense of personal contact. The delays inherent in the delivery of mail, the interference of aides, distance, language, and other potential obstacles did nothing to reduce the perception of personal contact and attention afforded by Schneerson to his Hasidim. His personal attention to the difficulties of his followers led early on to the belief that there was no need for an intercessor, administrative control, or middle management in Habad. The Hasid and the Rebbe were at one with each other. This was the strength of Schneerson's charismatic authority and the general principle of Hasidic leadership.

However, with this principle of leadership, the growth and expansion of the movement were limited by the number of people with whom Schneerson was able to personally communicate. While Schneerson dealt with much of his own correspondence, the numbers of people visiting him, even before his final election to office in 1951, necessitated the imposition of some form of central coordination. Several secretaries were appointed for this purpose, and in addition to arranging interview times, the Rebbe's secretaries would oversee the people going into and out of his office. As the conduits by which access to Schneerson was granted, they had a far-reaching authority beyond their apparent duties, because every visitor would need to be allocated a time by the secretaries. The process of booking and waiting for an audience created a sense of division and distance between the Rebbe and the ordinary Hasid. The secretary became an integral link between the two, perceived as a conduit to get the Rebbe's ear, and at times acting as his voice.

The necessity of balancing Schneerson's public accessibility with the needs of the movement at large led to the imposition of an administrative bureaucracy. It seems to have also been recognized that the absence of an organizational structure to deal with the complexities of expansion were likely to spell the decay of the movement, or at least retard its growth. The challenge for Habad was to juggle these two considerations, maintaining high administrative performance and allowing accessibility to the Rebbe. Excessive bureaucracy would interfere with the public perception of Schneerson as charismatic and divinely inspired, whereas keeping the distance between Schneerson and his followers would foster the mystique that was building around him, and prevent any but his closest aides from seeing beyond the desired public persona.

Schneerson's aides, assistants, and emissaries filled the administrative/organizational role required by the movement for growth. Thus they served to a large degree as senior and even middle management for Habad, but this was perceived in purely administrative terms. Despite their physical proximity to Schneerson, as a group they were not considered any closer to him spiritually than anyone else, except inasmuch as they were able to spend more time in his physical presence than the average Hasid. Religiously, therefore, the members of the managerial elite were not awarded hierarchical status and had no spiritual authority except as representatives of the Rebbe. Since all administrative and spiritual levels of the Habad organization received advice and instruction from Schneerson equally, the notion of an administrative hierarchy that responded through levels of seniority to Schneerson does not apply to Habad's managerial structure. All of his staff members, far from being an elite within the movement, effectively held the status of middle management.

This is not to say that some operational areas and the individuals in charge of them did not hold more power or attract more notice than others. Schneerson's aides, despite their physical proximity to him, were not all able to publicly represent Schneerson or the movement as a whole, but some, particularly those who were associated with public relations, had his trust and were able to do so. During the early life of the movement, they were skilled at advertising the successes of the movement and the wise guidance of the Rebbe, and did much to attract a great deal of desirable attention and publicity to both Habad and Schneerson. As his leadership advanced, however, and some of his publicly declared positions became more extreme or expressed a viewpoint likely to damage the fundraising ability of the movement, some of his aides were accused of attempting to modify Schneerson's public image, or at least lessen the impact of his controversial views. They were opposed within the movement, and some of Schneerson's secretaries were criticized for detracting from the Rebbe's effectiveness as a representative of Judaism and Habad by their attempts to moderate him or his message.[30] By doing so they opened themselves to charges of disloyalty and lack of faith in the Rebbe.

Krinsky is often said to have been the main perpetrator and therefore serves to illustrate the phenomenon. His position as spokesman for AGUCH and the Habad movement, although originally not a commanding duty, increasingly grew in scope and importance as Habad became a more public-oriented and media-centric organization, reliant on outreach and fundraising for its impact. Public relations duties became a highly responsible and sensitive job. Were it not for Habad's expansion and the growth of its influence in Jewish and even general political circles,[31] the spokesman and public image considerations would not have become such important issues. Krinsky might have been left as a relatively insignificant member of the movement's bureaucracy, in charge of a largely defunct appendage from the founding days of the movement's presence in the United States. However, Schneerson's popular charisma and leadership practices became increasingly important as his reign continued and Habad grew in size and influence. Everything from internal matters of fundraising and interaction with the broader Jewish community to more contentious issues, such as involvement in Israeli and American politics, was based on the public perception of Schneerson and the movement he headed.

The approach taken by the Krinsky faction to present the most positive face of Habad to the public appears prudent in the eyes of the rational onlooker. The attempt to moderate Schneerson's more extreme statements in his later years, in order to ensure that the movement continued to be acceptable to the non-Hasidic public and the Jewish world, was effective. It was to the credit of such pragmatists that the Habad movement, until the last years of Schneerson's rule and in the period following his death, maintained such a solid and favorable public portfolio despite its heavily mystical undertones and extreme religious elements, especially messianism.

The public relations machine combined the mystical charm and obsession of a charismatic leader with the modern marketing tools of public relations, in accordance with the dictates of market forces and public opinion. It preserved both Schneerson's personal stature and Habad's reputation, and thus ensured its fundraising strength.[32] The service it provided to Habad may well have been recognized by Schneerson, and perhaps it was for this reason that its exponents maintained their power base in the movement and even received his tacit support. The difficulties the movement experienced with its public image after the death of Schneerson were due, at least in part, to the weakened position of the Krinsky camp, and the strengthening of more extreme, and especially messianist, elements of Habad.

The friction between the Rebbe's will and the activities of some of his assistants developed into an interesting relationship, where the administrative bureaucracy was at once disliked as an impediment to Schneerson's leadership and tolerated as a necessary instrument for the implementation of Habad policy. Some Hasidim were enraged at the audacity of the aides in their attempts to impede the Rebbe in his role as leader of the movement. For them, Schneerson was the only true authority and master of Habad and its activities, as befit his position as zaddik and Rebbe. They saw the public relations effort to quiet Schneerson as an expression of a severe lack of faith in Schneerson's supremacy and ability to define a true and workable strategy for his Hasidim and their fulfillment of the mission of Habad.

The perception of administrative opposition had the effect of further strengthening Schneerson's popularity in the movement. He was seen, no doubt, as tormented by his associates, isolated, misunderstood, and muted by people with a narrow partisan interest in their own security and success. Gossip and rumor in the community indicate that there was even a feeling that Schneerson had been betrayed by those who should have been his closest and most trusted associates. As a consequence, the Hasidic following rallied in Schneerson's favor; his personal, direct leadership was enhanced just because he was perceived to be at odds with the bureaucrats who had compromised his Hasidic vision and the mission given to Habad by Yosef Yitzhak.[33] Some Hasidim have even gone so far as to say that these people were one of the major impediments to Schneerson's revelation as the mashiach.[34]

The effect of this conflict on the Hasidic following is interesting. On the one hand, Schneerson's perceived struggle with the bureaucracy allowed him to maintain his image as the underdog, loner, and crusader hero, and on the other, he was able to enjoy the benefits of an organized bureaucracy. If he had planned it this way, the strategy could not have been more cleverly conceived. It could be interpreted as a prudent strategy in social-scientific engineering, a tactic to preserve Schneerson's charismatic authority in the face of Habad's massive institutional expansion. In this way, the fervor generated by the charismatic leader could be channeled, organized, and institutionalized for the expansion of the Habad movement. This synthesis is somewhat paradoxical, but it is consistent with Habad's notions of spirituality. In this case, the development of a hierarchical organizational structure and the institutionalization of Schneerson's leadership through formal means of rule, fund collection, supervision, and reporting proved mutually beneficial to the Rebbe and the movement's consolidation.

The Last Years

During the forty-five years of his reign, Schneerson suffered a number of major health crises that affected his physical ability to administer the movement and necessitated modification of public access to him. The first such event was his heart attack in 1977, blamed by many on overwork and lack of rest for a man of advanced years. The impact of this event on his health induced him to refrain from many public responsibilities, apparently much against his will but at the insistence of medical practitioners.[35] He ceased to give *yehidut*, and was subsequently seen less in public. This served to further increase the authority of his assistants, who already controlled access to their leader and now became more instrumental in running the movement and in the process of communicating with Schneerson. The perception of Schneerson as a more distant, unreachable figurehead made his public demeanor more impressive, his appearances more exciting, and communications with him more significant to many of the Hasidim.

In the last years of Schneerson's life, particularly after he lay paralyzed by a series of strokes beginning in 1992, a debate raged within the senior administration over who would have access to him and at what times. Whoever had access, or at least whoever gave the appearance of having access to the Rebbe, would be widely perceived as his mouthpiece and his ears, and thus as acting with his authority and by his permission. The question of access to Schneerson in the last years of his reign touched on the issues of succession, and represented the onset of an internal power play for leadership that has still not been resolved. Practically speaking, the secretaries of Habad, as the major body with access to Schneerson, ran the movement during the last years of the Rebbe's life.

The perception of direct communication between Schneerson and his Hasidim was continued even after he suffered his paralyzing strokes; letters were read to him, and certain bodily movements were taken to indicate his responses. These movements were interpreted by the secretaries, and formulated into responses to the questions posed. In this way, issues of importance were often considered, including questions concerning the administration of the movement, the granting of advice, direction of business activities, and even permission to marry. Through these communications, the direct link of the Hasidim with their Rebbe was maintained, and it is not entirely surprising that at first the secretaries, as accessories to the Rebbe-Hasid relationship, were trusted to be representing the true thoughts of the Rebbe, as expressed through his bodily movements. In time, some Hasidim began to feel that these men were misrepresenting Schneerson. Whether this misrepresentation was willful or not is a matter of personal opinion, but certainly the power of the secretaries increased with the infirmity of Schneerson.

The importance of the secretaries in the daily running of the Habad movement increased steadily, because questions concerning the administration and activities of the movement needed to be answered. There was no discussion of the question of succession in case of Schneerson's death,[36] and so there was no second-in-command, or even a prominent candidate, to take over the administration of the movement after his infirmity. All questions about the running of the movement, and all requests for direction, were still directed to Schneerson. The interpretation of his bodily signs was often vital, therefore, in getting answers to important questions. Over time, some Hasidim began to feel that certain secretaries were preferable to others when it came to posing questions to Schneerson; some were seen to get better responses than others, and the way the question was formulated was also considered to be important. In this way, the various assistants to Schneerson maintained both his authority as well as their own.

The running of the movement during the last years of Schneerson's life and the uncertainty about who held the reins of power at the time raises fundamental questions about the nature of leadership in Habad. The events of the period make one wonder to what extent and for how long Schneerson was a mere figurehead, a "rubber stamp" for his executive bureaucracy, and which of his aides gained power during the years immediately preceding his death. The issue would prove important to the question of succession.

The Relationship Between Power and Discipleship

As mentioned above, many highly ambitious and accomplished people worked loyally under Schneerson, viewing him as the ultimate sage and leader. They declared their undying commitment to him and were, at least by their own declarations, obedient to his will. This phenomenon is curious in itself. Why would people freely give up their liberty and right to self-determination to serve another person's will? Curious as this phenomenon is among ordinary, humble, and non-ambitious Hasidim, it is even more remarkable when one considers the many ambitious and powerful people who either grew up in the movement or joined it as adults and achieved eminence therein. Superficially, at least, these were the most unlikely people to become obedient, subservient, self-nullified disciples to any human, and yet in practice they were chiefly responsible for the public image of Schneerson's unmatched grandeur.

A governing dynamic must be sought to explain the social phenomenon of ambitious people offering lip service to a charismatic leader, and in all probability this dynamic will reveal a mutually beneficial relationship between leader and follower. Several factors are evident in the dynamic. If ambitious followers become obedient to someone, he must be a very special individual. If he were a figure of ordinary ability, they would either be forced to abandon him as unworthy of their commitment or would present him to others as great in order to justify their status as follower. Another key in this leader-follower dynamic is that the participants must gain something, even if at a subconscious level, from the relationship.

History indicates that powerful and ambitious people, even of the most diabolical, egotistical, and self-serving type, have risen to eminence in religious institutions in disproportionate numbers and often to the detriment of the truly pious and spiritual. A list of such people would include Catholic popes, Eastern gurus, would-be prophets and other self-appointed interpreters of God's will, and messengers of various mashiachs or demigods. The existence and eminence of such persons in religious hierarchies across the globe is an historical fact, so we must try to understand why certain "disciples" are drawn to certain "leaders," and examine the nature of the presumably mutually complementary dynamic between them.

The dynamic in these relationships is no doubt one in which the disciple is a disciple in name alone. Due to his apparently close relationship with the leader, the disciple is able to assume increasing powers of leadership during the leader's own life, as a spokesman, an emissary, or a missionary, and thereby is able to wield great influence. Without the outer perception of closeness to the leader, the disciple would be unable to gain influence. Through (conscious or unconscious) manipulation of his relationship with the charismatic leader, the disciple enhances his own influence over the masses that adore the leader, for without their adoration the disciple would have no sway over them. Examples include Paul of Tarsus (who never knew Jesus), Nathan of Gaza (who barely knew Sabbetai Zevi), and other spokesmen who presumed to speak in the name of their chosen religious leader, thereby claiming to interpret God's will. The ability to become the voice for a charismatic force is power in itself, albeit indirectly wielded.

If this theory has validity, it helps to explain why so many ambitious and powerful people have been willing to pay the price of subjugating themselves to religious discipline, "annulling" themselves to their leader and abiding by his rules and dictates. This seems, in the long run, to empower them in the eyes of the masses, and puts them in position to assume leadership in the absence of the leader, whether because of distance or death. This is especially evident in the case of followers of a messianic leader. When the leader cannot express his own will, especially if he is dead, the power and influence of the spokesman are greatly amplified, and he often becomes the new leader of the movement.

A general theory of leadership may be suggested whereby the middle management of a movement seeks influence over its power base via connection to the leader the masses adore. By making themselves indispensable to the leader during his life, the middle managers solidify their own positions. They may even create a leader of their own design, building and perpetuating his image, disseminating stories to support it, and perhaps even coming to believe it themselves, as an instrument of their own survival needs and striving for power. The more powerful the leader is, the more powerful the middle managers become. If, as is certainly possible, the charismatic leader is a genuine pietist who believes in his own connection to God and his need to act in accordance with a divine calling, then very often his managers maneuver him more than he maneuvers his disciples, encouraging his inspired ways and indulging his beliefs, because they attract discipleship. The less able the leader is to express his own views, the more influential the spokesman becomes, because he stands between the leader and the followers, and he becomes the voice of both interpretation of doctrine and of authority. As in the case of Habad, the more ill the leader grows, the greater becomes the opportunity for middle management to assume power. Speaking for a "mashiach awaiting resurrection" is a perfect opportunity for such *de facto* leaders. On the one hand, they are able to maintain the expectation and excitement of the masses, and keep the leader's charismatic hold over them which is essential for their own authority. On the other hand, they are able to serve simply as caretakers for the movement, with almost unlimited license to interpret doctrine.

It is no accident that ambitious players were able to find a home in the Habad movement. Because Schneerson's vision for the movement and its mission was so grandiose, he believed in decentralization of authority, and not only allowed but encouraged leaders to take on their own fiefdoms, as long as they advanced the outreach agenda of the movement. Schneerson's personality was an easy one on which to heap praise, and his image was easily "doctored" to reflect the desires of his spokesmen. Praising Schneerson did not detract from the reputation or the prestige of the one giving praise, but enhanced it by giving the appearance, if not the actuality, of devotion to the Rebbe. Schneerson is said to have "made leaders," and indeed he did. Due to the rapid expansion of the Habad movement across the globe, there was a significant vacuum of power to be filled, and a lot of influence was for the taking.

While this is a highly skeptical reading of the power dynamics within Habad, it does not by any means detract from the leadership qualities of Schneerson. To the contrary: a true leader intuitively understands these natural laws, and benefits from them. Likewise, many of the Hasidim who comprised this group acted intuitively, with a natural sense of leadership dynamics, taking advantage of the fact that their best opportunity to achieve something outstanding was under the patronage of a Rebbe who not only empowered them, but seldom interfered with their own leadership roles.

---

[1] See "Protocols": p. 35.

[2] See Avrum Ehrlich, *Leadership in the HaBaD Movement*, pp. 398–399.

Ibid., pp. 265–288.

[3] See "Protocols": Yehuda Krinsky testimony, p. 685.

[4] He is now head of AGUCH, and is trying to establish himself as the "official" voice of Habad, with varying degrees of success. This will be discussed in Chapters 19 and 20.

[5] See "Protocols": Intervenor-Defendant testimony, p. 143. Krinsky's account of the hierarchical structure is interesting because he is a key player in it and a powerful force in the ongoing administration.

[6] The rejection of television and other Western cultural media, together with the absence of secular studies from their educational curricula, has contributed to a unique intellectual disposition among Hasidic groups. Western cultural exposure fosters the development of valuable social and cognitive skills that are often surprising and refreshing. There are many Habad Hasidim who have learned complicated skills despite having had no formal training in them. Many excel at computer programming, business, or other professions. The Habad organizations in Crown Heights are run competently by Hasidim of this type.

[7] See Schneerson's reaction to the pressure to take on roles other than those given him by Yosef Yitzhak, in Ehrlich, *Leadership in the HaBaD Movement*, pp. 370–371.

[8] See Chapters 5 and 6.

[9] See the figures in Gershom Gorenberg, "Get a Job."

[10] Ironically, Schneerson personally did not use modern technology, nor did most of his assistants. His office was spartan, the only concession to the modern world being a telephone. He did not use a computer, nor did his secretariat until the last years of his life. Hence, visitors to his rooms could still appreciate the simplicity of a technology-free environment, no doubt somewhat unexpected in the command center of a movement that had so enthusiastically embraced the modern world.

[11] See "Protocols": Immanuel Schochet testimony, pp. 2612–2614. He notes that the World Learning Communication Center (WLCC) was established in 1976. Its offices were (and still are) at 770 Eastern Parkway, and it is responsible for the broadcasts of Schneerson's *sichot* and *ma'amarim* delivered at *farbrengens*. These were disseminated both live and in recorded form throughout the worldwide Habad community.

[12] See Mintz, *Hasidic People*, p. 377, n. 16.

[13] One should keep in mind that Habad Hasidism could have developed on the same lines as the more conservative, insular Hasidic groups in the vicinity. Remarkably, Schneerson was able to draw many potentially dogmatic Hasidim into the era of modernism while still maintaining many elements of East European Hasidic culture. Schneerson's chief critics harped on his modernism. Kahn notes that even taping his talks, if known, would have enraged conservative elements in the community. Orthodox critics complain about Habad's laxity of observance, late prayer times, praying without a minyan, and Western influences. Satmar Hasidim criticized Schneerson for allowing his lectures on the *Tanya* to be broadcast on the radio. Schneerson's ability to weather the criticism and bring his flock to a general consensus on its approach to modernity was no easy task and remains an impressive accomplishment.

[14] See Chapters 1 and 3.

[15] See Marc Wilson, "The Rebbe's Counsel."

[16] See, for example, Susan Handelman, "Chicago Native Reflects on Her Experience with the Rebbe." Handelman tells how Schneerson made detailed suggestions on corrections to an article she had written, and later provided career and academic advice. There are many such stories; they all reflect Schneerson's attitude and, more important, its impressive effect on people.

[17] Habad oral tradition.

[18] This is seen most obviously in the Staroselye model of succession, and to a lesser degree among the Malachim. Aharon of Staroselye was the primary competitor to the leadership of Dov Ber, the second HabadRebbe. He had been Shneur Zalman's closest disciple for over thirty years. Aharon eventually moved to a town call Staroselye, where he set up his own Hasidic court. See Ehrlich, *Leadership in the HaBaD Movement*, pp. 160–192, esp. pp. 167–172. Chaim Avraham Dov Ber Levine HaCohen, known as the Malach, was a Hasid of Shalom Dov Ber, the fifth Habad Rebbe. He apparently had a falling-out with his Rebbe, and consequently emigrated to the United States in 1923. His breakaway movement attracted a small number of Hasidim who call themselves Malachim and at present reside in Williamsburg, Brooklyn. They opted not to appoint a successor after Avraham died. They are antagonistic toward the Lubavitch-Habad dynasty and to the successors of the Habad movement after the Zemakh Zedek. For a more detailed exploration, see Mintz, *Hasidic People*, pp. 21–26; B. Sobel, *The M'lochim*; Ehrlich, *Leadership in the HaBaD Movement*, pp. 269–271.

[19] Nissan Mindel is one example; a Hasid of Yosef Yitzhak, he was also trusted by Schneerson, and was mentioned as a possible source of leadership after Schneerson's death.

[20] Ehrlich, *Leadership in the HaBaD Movement*, p 262.

[21] See Shaul S. Deutsch, *Larger Than Life*, vol. 2, pp. 27 ff., for an account of Hodokov and his former position as a high-level bureaucrat in an East European government.

[22] This refers to Rabbi Nissan Mindel.

[23] See "Protocols": Yehuda Krinsky testimony, p. 112. Krinsky began his career as Schneerson's driver; his early education in a secular primary school in Boston gave him an educational advantage over other Hasidim, and his contribution was valued as he rose through the organization's ranks. He worked with Schneerson from 1955 and became secretary of AGUCH in 1976. He served as one of Schneerson's aides until the latter's death.

[24] For example, Schneerson's conservative approach to the question of "who is a Jew?" (an ongoing issue in Israeli politics), dismissing the validity all but Orthodox conversions to Judaism, stirred up much contention in Israel and among the American Jewish establishment. The issue was eventually quietened so as to protect Habad fundraising interests. Likewise, controversial issues such as territorial compromise in Israel that might have estranged benefactors from giving much-needed funds to Habad, were often moderated, particularly by the AGUCH organization under Krinsky. Rabbi Immanuel Jakobovits (personal interview, Sydney, June 1996) said that Habad moderated its presentation of anti-Zionist ideology and right-wing politics in England. It also downplayed its messianic fervor in order not to antagonize large parts of the English Jewish community.

[25] Interviews with Levine and D. Olidort (Schneerson's editors).

[26] Lecture by and interview with Leible Groner (Israel, 1995, and Sydney, 1996); and interview with Yaakov Kline (Sydney 1996).

[27] This position was supported primarily by Groner and the messianist faction.

[28] The first stroke occurred on March 2, 1992, the second on March 7, 1994.

[29] See the report by the Crown Heights Beit Din on the issue of irregularities in Schneerson's medical treatment. Groner is often seen as supporting Schneerson's messianic claims. His position on medical treatment reflected this idea.

[30] Messianic elements in the movement accused Krinsky of this alleged offense.

[31] The power of Schneerson to influence the voting patterns of his followers was recognized by many politicians who courted his support. See, for example, Jonathan Mark, "A Kingdom of Faith."

[32] Fundraising is often a barometer of theological stability. The messianist-resurrectionist element in the movement is concerned not with the validity of the theology but its conduciveness to fundraising.

[33] Habad oral tradition.

[34] See *Beis Moshiach,* an internally circulated magazine designed to promote the messianic-resurrectionist doctrine. Many articles blame the messianic failure on a lack of faith among the Hasidim. A particularly interesting term was coined for such faithless people: *Hasidische Amalek*, that is, an Amalekite who appears to be a Hasid.

[35] This is well known in Habad oral tradition.

[36] For reasons that will be discussed below.

Chapter 15
Community Services

Unlike many of the major central organizations responsible for the running of Habad's daily affairs, such as the Merkaz L'Inyanei Hinukh and the Agudat Hasidei Habad (AGUCH), which are administratively centered in Crown Heights, many other Habad organizations are far-flung, with locations throughout the world. This is especially so of the many groups responsible for the social activism of the movement, which often have only local impact and influence, and are administered independently of the central organization. In this way, the Habad technique for management of its social services, including political impact and financial control, is very decentralized. On the other hand, social and outreach initiatives are often highly centralized in motivation and ideology, with activities often initiated by the direction of Schneerson, who was had ultimate control of the movement and its activities. His approval and blessing were sought by all who desired to initiate activities, and, most important, he provided the ideological and motivational impetus in which such activities were to be directed. Schneerson therefore often personally encouraged the outreach actions of his Hasidim, even if he did not direct their initial setup and implementation. Central approval also included, from time to time, a financial contribution to encourage the project in its initial stages.

The Outreach Concept

"Outreach" is a term coined by the Habad movement that refers to missionary work aimed solely at Jews.[1] Sacks says of Schneerson that he "not only came to embody the concept of 'outreach,' he very nearly invented it."[2] The goal of Habad's outreach was to reawaken the soul of every Jew, especially the majority who were secular and nonreligious, to God, religion, and the observance of Jewish law. The idea was to be found in embryo in the origins of the Habad movement, whose Rebbes had always concentrated on educating and sending emissaries to remote Jewish communities to facilitate the observance of Jewish law and custom. It was only under Schneerson, however, that the concept was institutionalized as the prime characteristic of Habad's social activity.

The concept of outreach gave the impetus for all of the other initiatives undertaken by the movement during the period of Schneerson's leadership, and became the primary cause of his fame throughout the world but especially within the general Jewish community. Outreach was the driver behind the *shlihut* (emissary/missionary) program, the most effective tool in the consolidation of Schneerson's leadership.[3] The promotion of outreach through *shlihut* made many of the services of the movement possible and helped support many of its institutions. So important and effective was Habad outreach for the growth and consolidation of the movement after the death of Yosef Yitzhak that some observers have called for its tactics, initiatives, and methodology to be adopted in rehabilitating all of Diaspora Jewry.[4]

During the period of Schneerson's leadership, Habad became the fastest-growing Jewish subcommunity in the world. While the Habad movement is not the largest Hasidic sect,[5] it is certainly the best-known, and the noticeable presence of members of the movement served to promote its name and ideology in overt disproportion to its numerical size. Without the willingness of many thousands of young men, newly married couples, and larger, more established families to move to cities and even foreign countries at the request of Schneerson, the movement would not have been as effective as it has been in bringing many to return to Jewish observance. At present, Habad is not as well known for its mystical philosophy and ideology as for its outreach efforts.

Schneerson dispatched his emissaries to all areas of the world where Jews might be found, but concentrated the movement's efforts on several key targets: university campuses, non-Habad synagogues, and remote areas that lacked an effective infrastructure for Jewish observance.

Campus Outreach

As a former university student, Schneerson no doubt recognized that outreach would at some stage need to reach the secular Jewish intelligentsia, and he wasted no time in doing this. He instructed emissaries to focus on university campuses throughout the United States, where study houses and lectures were initiated for the benefit of Jewish students.[6] It was felt that young, intelligent, idealistic Jewish students might be attracted to the movement, and might be able to find purpose and direction through the practice of Hasidism. The comparative modernity of Habad was an attractive factor in the success of campus outreach. The movement demonstrated that Judaism did not have to be a European, "Old World" phenomena, as many of the students' parents might have felt, but could be practiced in a modern context, using advanced technology and providing material opportunities not traditionally associated with Hasidism. Sacks has compared Habad's outreach activities to those of the early days of Hasidism, during which the Hasidim were eager to convince the mitnagdic intelligentsia of the Hasidic way,[7] although undoubtedly there was more in common between the Hasidim and mitnagdim than between Habad and secular Jews.

The efforts of Habad in campus outreach were effective not only in attracting "converts," the ba'alei teshuvah,[8] but, possibly more important, in exposing a high proportion of future academic, business, and political leaders to Habad and its ideas, and for familiarizing many with the image of Schneerson. It was no doubt hoped that those exposed to Habad on campus might later, when they had become respected members of the general community, be able to support the legitimacy of the movement, whether financially, politically, socially, or otherwise.

Synagogues

From the origin of his leadership, Schneerson encouraged all his Hasidim who were able to study so as to pass the *semichah* examinations and become rabbis. Until 1983, these ordinations were carried out under the old criterion of scholarship and intellectual ability, but from that date Schneerson began to actively encourage the mass ordination of rabbis.[9] Consequently, the standards required to become a rabbi in Habad were lowered, and the emphasis moved from being able to pass examinations to the possession of piety and an inclination to the job. This is not to say that there were not many highly learned students in Habad who were encouraged to study for *semichah*, but rather that what was looked for was enthusiasm and suitability for the position of rabbi more than traditional scholarly achievement.

This change was implemented in order to ordain rabbis who would serve primarily as religious functionaries and community leaders, and thus it can be seen as a political tool to increase the influence of Habad in the broader Jewish community. Due to their generally poor academic competence, these Habad rabbis would defer serious halakhic and religious matters to more competent rabbinical authorities either within Habad or outside the movement.[10] This is not to say that the movement did not produce some "old-style" rabbis, academically gifted and scholarly,[11] but rather that the minimum standard for ordination had been lowered to accommodate the less academic members of the community. A disproportionately high percentage of Habad Hasidim were consequently ordained into the rabbinate, and many began to take up rabbinical positions in synagogues across America and the world.

Although these new rabbis were often younger than their congregants and less educated in worldly issues, they were often respected by their communities by virtue of their religious studies and their commitment to spirituality. When it became evident to their congregations that these rabbis turned for advice and counsel to more senior rabbis, who in turn revered and respected Schneerson, it fostered the impression that Schneerson was a grand rabbi, a "rabbi's rabbi," to whom all turned for clarity and guidance. This enhanced the reputation of the Rebbe, and elevated the status of the Habad movement, wisely led by such a respected and venerated man.

The work of Habad rabbis in non-Habad synagogues popularized Schneerson's status and the Habad system. People interested in pursuing a more committed Jewish life were encouraged to do so through Habad educational facilities, and hence the movement attracted many newly repentant Jews to its ranks. The distinctions between Habad and normative Judaism were increasingly blurred, especially in the minds of newcomers, who frequently were unaware of the differences between the two. Habad community rabbis, believing that their traditions were superior, did not call attention to these dissonances.

Ba'alei Teshuvah

One of the most significant developments in the Jewish world in the past fifty years has been the dramatic rise in the number of Jews adopting the religious lifestyle.[12] At the forefront of the movement encouraging the newly religious, known as ba'alei teshuvah ("masters of repentance") has been the Habad movement, which has not only actively sought out converts from the nonreligious Jewish community, but has also greatly assisted those who wish to spiritually reconnect with their Jewish ancestry.

Like many other new religious movements, the Habad outreach seems to have developed with a specific target demographic in mind: single, educated, Jewish, college-aged, spiritual seekers. The movement's first active recruitment centers were primarily located in college towns, in houses close to campus, with the assumed intention of attracting young, idealistic, and easily persuaded Jewish youth to the religious lifestyle. These early Habad centers provided a "home away from home" primarily for students, and for many often represented the first contact with ultra-Orthodox Judaism. As we will examine below, the "Habad House" did not simply serve as a forum for the exploration of Jewish tradition, for it also served a social purpose in bringing together people of similar backgrounds and ideas.

As with fraternities and other student societies, the primary activities of campus outreach were the organizing of social functions, but in this case they had an educational purpose, and offered lectures/classes connecting various aspects of Jewish theology to practical concerns in the lives of the audience. While lectures provided an ideological framework for the incorporation of Jewish spirituality into the everyday experience of potential recruits, the most important "conversionary" tactic was the social experience of inviting the curious into everyday Hasidic life. Central to this was the "open-house" policy maintained by Habad surrounding the observance of Shabbat. The opportunity to participate in one of the foremost religious practices of observant life, in a spiritual and family atmosphere (the Habad Houses were often run by young married couples), was an exceptionally successful recruitment technique, and remains so to this day.[13] The experience of Shabbat represented a golden opportunity to expose the unobservant not only to theology, but also (and most important) to the everyday practice of Jewish spiritual life. It was an exceptional tool for the exploration of religion, in a friendly setting where questions of a practical nature could be explored at leisure. The experience permitted the full range of issues surrounding religious life to be examined: ritual and tradition, law and custom, dietary laws (*kashrut*), family relations, prayer and traditions of worship, and perhaps most important, the inculcation of the Hasidic devotional spirit through singing and storytelling.

The Habad House also served as a center for learning and for training those who wished to adopt a religious lifestyle. While the social complexities of Hasidic custom were important in developing an emotional attachment to the movement, connection to Schneerson also played a major role in the religious life of many, if not all ba'alei teshuvah. The implications of this will be explored more fully later. However, attachment without proper education in its practical use and direction was discouraged by the movement, as it has been by traditional Judaism through the centuries. In order to assist newly observant followers to develop a lasting commitment to Jewish observance, and incidentally to the Habad movement, Habad Houses and representatives frequently lectured or led seminars in which ideological and practical issues were discussed. While at first these classes were small and designed to instruct on a basic level, as the movement grew in size and influence, the demands of recruits necessitated the development of special educational programs for ba'alei teshuvah. In time, this was to develop into an organized curriculum in local communities, and eventually led to the establishment of several yeshivot, located in key locations around the world. The purpose of this education was quite different from what is found in traditional yeshivot, where the emphasis is on studying Talmud. The emphasis at first was on communicating basic knowledge regarding Jewish custom, culture, and law, as well as Hebrew language, and the basics of Habad philosophy. Most classes therefore, at least in the initial training, were concerned with ethics, kashrut, observance of Shabbat, and other practical matters essential to the observant lifestyle. Of course, the hope was that by the end of the training, men at least would be able to commence the study of Talmud, and women would be able to maintain an observant home.

This last was to be one of the central elements of the Habad recruitment strategy, because once the basics of Hasidism had been learned, the emphasis was on encouraging recruits to marry and establish observant families of their own. Once married, usually arranged through a matchmaker, the ba'alei teshuvah were encouraged to establish Habad Houses of their own and commence the recruitment of further followers. This was to be done through the same tactics by which they themselves had been recruited (a socialization process directed at nonreligious Jews).

One may add that there is now a substantial representation of university-educated ba'alei teshuvah in the Habad movement; also, that many students and researchers who initially came into contact with Habad for the express purpose of objective research have been inspired to join its ranks. Since Habad was an accessible Jewish group, open to contact with the outside world, favorably disposed to technology and publicity, but still distinct and exotic, it attracted the interest of sociologists, theologians, and others drawn to research a cultural or religious phenomenon. There are a number of prominent cases where researchers were touched either by the local Habad rabbi they contacted or by Schneerson himself, or by both. This is not an unusual occurrence in religious ethnographic research.

The attraction of these academics to the movement added to the intrigue surrounding Habad, and tales of the "university professors" (actually, usually graduate students) who had discovered the greatness of the Rebbe spread in the movement. These stories validated the beliefs of Hasidim, and gave hope for the ultimate success of the Rebbe's outreach programs. Academic converts to Habad also enhanced the movement's reputation in the outside world. These ba'alei teshuvah academics disseminated pro-Habad sympathies through their writing, teaching, and other academic work, and helped create a positive image of the movement as a living philosophy rather than solely a religious or doctrinal system. Later, some Habad rabbis were to earn academic degrees, so that Habad became even more appealing to the educated segments of the broader Jewish population. The presence of academic Hasidim also assisted the movement to avoid being classed as a form of fundamentalism, with the negative connotations of narrow-mindedness and naiveté implicit in such a classification.

Emissaries / Missionaries

Schneerson's emissaries were the executors of his outreach campaign. They were characterized by enthusiasm for Schneerson and strict obedience to his directives. Sacks claims that few international organizations could have been more tightly led by a single individual on the most slender of resources,[14] namely, the stream of communication he maintained with the emissaries through correspondence and later more modern methods. Despite their dispersal to most places on earth where Jews reside, the emissaries kept in touch with each other, and discipline and morale remained high, mainly thanks to the personal contact each had with the Rebbe.[15]

Schneerson's discourses, ideas, suggestions, and campaign initiatives were communicated almost immediately to the emissaries, who in turn obediently communicated them to congregants, students, and children in their respective communities. The purpose of having emissaries throughout the world, and of the organizations and services they founded, was to instill the spirit and practice of "authentic" Judaism into the life of Jews wherever they may be. According to one observer, "the Rebbe built Lubavitch into the most powerful Hasidic movement in history. . . . tens of thousands around the world feel and act a little more Jewish because of him, no one else comes close to that achievement."[16] This was one of the fundamental goals of the Habad movement under Schneerson, and guided much of its outreach work.

Currently, there are an estimated two thousand official Habad institutions worldwide, staffed by more than eight thousand emissaries,[17] and innumerable Habad Houses (on which more below), with representation on six continents. Schneerson encouraged his emissaries to wear their distinctive Hasidic clothing at all times if possible, but certainly when they were representing the movement, believing that this would arouse feelings of familiarity and warmth in nonobservant Jews, and remind them of their parents or ancestors. It also served as a kind of uniform for the movement, by which its members could be identified, and thus acted to unite the Hasidim wherever they might be, through a sense of common history and tradition.

Habad emissaries in countries with few Jews have often taken advantage of the reputation of Jews as powerful, wealthy, and influential to further their outreach work. There are stories told in Habad of emissaries to Asian and South American countries who were able to cultivate high-profile business leaders and politicians because of the belief that the Habad movement was an influential a Jewish lobby with good business connections.[18] Whatever the reasons, many close political and social alliances were formed by Habad emissaries worldwide, and the idea that Habad was a representative of Judaism itself grew with its increased public profile through these alliances. Schneerson's status as leader of the movement was also enhanced by this type of activity, further consolidating his authority.

Public Relations

We have already discussed the role of the public relations arm of the Habad movement in the consolidation of Schneerson's control and its effect on the expansion of the movement. It must be kept in mind that Schneerson himself was extremely effective in the area of public relations. From the time he assumed the position of Rebbe, he encountered a wide and often influential range of individuals who afterwards spoke highly of him.[19] Some of these were important personages, but many were not, and it is significant that there are few articles and reports of encounters with Schneerson that do not describe him favorably. One might think it possible to glimpse the true person behind the public face of the Rebbe through accounts by non-Hasidic and even non-Jewish people who met him, people unbiased by any emotional connection to him as Rebbe and zaddik, but all the reported encounters seem to have been perceived through the same filter of adulation through which the Hasidim perceived their Rebbe. This influenced even non-Habad visitors.

The movement's official spokesman became ever more important, both in Habad and in the world at large, with the rising importance of public relations to the movement. The role of spokesman was assumed by Yehuda Krinsky long before Schneerson's death, and so it might be safely surmised that he had the Rebbe's support, tacitly at least. His high public profile has been important to the question of succession since the death of Schneerson, as will be discussed further on.

The public profile of Habad was also heightened by the use of billboards, by full-page newspaper and magazine advertisements in major publications like the *New York Times*, by the appearance of members on radio and television programs, and in books and movies. Until the 1990s, Habad was the only Orthodox Jewish religious group to embrace technology as an instrument for Jewish revival.

The movement attracted more attention as it entered the political arena, both in the United States and in Israel. Apart from the power and influence to be gained by giving public support to a successful political issue or personality, the movement's media image was heightened by its expression of political opinion. As Israeli and general Jewish political issues are often disproportionately covered by the media, the existence of a distinctively dressed and articulate Jewish group willing to present a firm ideological viewpoint attracted media attention to the movement, its ideas, and its projects.[20]

In addition, the growth within the movement of messianic speculation and ideology throughout the reign of Schneerson provoked a great deal of attention and interest within the general Jewish community and from the media. Chaim Potok has argued that the media-conscious orientation of the Habad movement, starting with the arrival of Yosef Yitzhak in the United States, may have been a key factor in its promulgation of a strongly messianic ideology. Messianism may have been seen as a device to attract more media attention to the movement and its outreach goals.[21] While this idea may be a little cynical about Habad's sincerity, messianism certainly drew media attention to the movement, and provided a framework in which Hasidim were able to missionize to nonreligious Jews worldwide. Outreach campaigns such as public donning of tefillin (phylacteries), the sukkah-mobile (a mobile sukkah used during the festival of Sukkot), and public celebrations of Hanukah drew public interest to Jewish issues and in the movement that was behind these activities.

The success of Habad's public relations enterprises was most graphically demonstrated when Schneerson died in 1994. Many important political and civil dignitaries attended his funeral,[22] which was also widely covered on television and in the print media worldwide. Indeed, a collection of over 200 articles and obituaries for Schneerson was published shortly after the event, with stories taken primarily from American newspapers.[23] That such a large number of articles was written in so short a space of time is an indication of the huge public interest in the movement and in Schneerson himself. His death even made it onto international television news broadcasts, demonstrating the breadth, if not the depth, of interest Habad and its messianic ideology had attracted worldwide.

Modern Technology

Public relations for Habad were amplified manifold through the efforts of many technologically conscious Hasidim who, because of their exposure to the modern world and the university, had flirted with these media well before they became essential household tools. While still influenced by modernity, Habad Hasidim were strongly discouraged from studying at university, in accordance with the ethos of ultra-Orthodoxy. Particular opposition was directed against study of the humanities, which was felt to pose the greatest threat to religious life. The advent of modern technology, particularly the computer and developments in communications, was therefore a blessing for many otherwise outwardly directed people. There are a number of reasons why modern technology was embraced so quickly by Habad: it was new, and so its use was not tainted with stigma; rejectionist religious views had not yet been developed in relation to the latest technology, and so its use was not forbidden. Technology allowed Hasidim to access the modern world without reliance on formal study of the forbidden humanities.

Habad was the first ultra-Orthodox Jewish group to take advantage of such technology. As the Internet became a medium to access secular education, it came to the attention of non-Habad ultra-Orthodox religious legislators, who subsequently condemned it and in some instances outlawed its use by their adherents. In Habad, however, technology was adopted so quickly that by the time Habad's religious authorities became fully aware of it, the use of modern technology was so widespread in the movement as to make a prohibition all but impossible to enforce. Indeed, technology had become so indispensable a part of the movement's activities that its use was accepted in rabbinic circles because it was accredited with disseminating Torah.

Use of the Internet and of e-mail in particular was to prove essential to outreach, and also to the cohesion of the movement. Both official and unofficial Habad Web sites began to appear shortly after public access to the Internet was available, and in time many local communities and organizations supported sites of their own. These sites served to inform community members of important events, provided access to teachings, and offered the opportunity to disseminate the teachings of Habad to a new and educated audience. One of the most important consequences of the use of the Internet in Habad, however, was its use as a tool for networking. E-mail lists of community members and activists were developed; religious teachings were disseminated, including calendars and reminders of events important to the world Habad community, such as birthdays and anniversaries of the passing of the Rebbes. Weekly biblical readings were distributed directly to Hasidim electronically, with commentaries by learned scholars, and online learning was developed, whereby someone new to Hasidism could move from the basics to the most abstruse theology and ideology. Most important for Habad, pictures of and discourses by Schneerson were also available online, as well as by satellite, television, radio, and on audio and video recordings, enabling the worldwide community to have instant access to Crown Heights and the court of their Rebbe. Religious books and other products could be purchased via the Internet, a useful feature for small and geographically remote communities. The worldwide Habad movement was therefore reinforced by the World Wide Web, and the challenges presented by its international character became more easily negotiable and surmountable.

At present the Internet is one of the main forums for discussion of Schneerson and the significance of his passing, utilized by messianist, non-messianist, and anti-messianist Hasidism. There is even a Web site for ex-Habad Hasidim, who have left the movement for various reasons but nevertheless wish to stay in touch with one other and offer mutual support. Thus, despite geographical separation and lack of wide numerical support, these groups are able to survive and cohere across the world, and the debates in which they engage may well prove determine the future direction of Habad in the post-Schneerson era.

Habad's embrace of technology and the Internet has had other positive effects for the reputation of the movement in the wider community. Apart from its direct use in disseminating the ideology of the movement, many Habad Hasidim who did not choose careers as emissaries have become computer technicians, programmers, and professionals in related technological industries. This not only enhances the future survival of the movement by ensuring that it has a presence in the modern world, but also serves to advance Habad's reputation as a movement that embraces modernity.

The Drawbacks of Outreach

Despite its many achievements, the outreach program has also had some drawbacks. These were primarily the result of the time and effort required by Habad's innovative techniques of outreach, which diverted funds and energy from other projects,[24] and of the challenges to the movement's ideological system raised by exposure to the world at large. These influences have had a negative effect on the education of the next generation of Hasidim, but have also contributed to the uniqueness of a movement that would not have succeeded were it not for the perceived aberrations it practices.

The practice of outreach has earned Habad a reputation like that of the Jesuits in Catholicism, for the movement's missionizing has given it wide influence and has disseminated its teachings throughout the world.[25] Missionary activity to non-Jews has generally been considered taboo throughout the history of Judaism, which has developed an ideological and practical opposition to the conversion of non-Jews to the faith.[26] The term "outreach" was coined by Habad to avoid the negative, Christian-centered connotations of the concepts of "missionary work" or "missionizing," and even within Habad's outreach effort, the emphasis has been on returning nonreligious Jews to the religious observance practiced by their ancestors. Nevertheless, the zeal of Habad for outreach, and its aggressive marketing techniques, have provoked a certain wariness toward the movement among secular and religious Jews alike, who do not care for the notion of Jews engaging in missionary activity even within the confines of the Jewish community.[27]

The obvious challenges for the movement are caused by developments in Habad's ideology. Issues of ideological dissonance are generally not talked about in the community, or publicized outside it, in order to avoid negative attention to the movement, and to lessen the potential for ridicule and humiliation. For this reason, contentious issues are difficult to source if one is not involved in the community, and it has been impossible thus far to examine their true effects, let alone their long-term impact on the movement. Habad's dependence on fundraising for its sustenance has occasionally meant that it has had to compromise or to water down its position on some issues, especially in relation to its interaction with the outside world and sources of funding.[28] The dichotomy between ideas that could be expressed only to other members of the movement and those that could be expressed to outsiders caused problems for some Hasidim. This is especially the case with Habad community rabbis of non-Habad congregations; they often teach views that agree with mainstream public opinion to their congregation, but hold divergent and possibly more controversial views in private. One of the prime examples of this became commonplace after Schneerson's death, when the messianic teachings of Habad led to the rise of a "resurrectionist" doctrine to the effect that the deceased Schneerson would return from the dead and reveal himself as the mashiach.[29] The effect of the messianist belief on the question of succession will be dealt with later. It is sufficient to say here that Habad community rabbis and members of the movement as a whole often hold controversial ideas such as this as a private ideology, and present more digestible ideas to others.

The movement has changed in other ways as a direct result of outreach activity. The Habad Hasidim sent around the world as students and emissaries have themselves been exposed to new ideas and practices to which they would not have been exposed in a more traditional Hasidic sect. One consequence is that Habad youth are often far more worldly than other Hasidic or Orthodox youth, many of whom have grown up in ghettos or sheltered communities with only intermittent or controlled interaction with the outside world. Familiarity with slang and popular culture among modern Habad youth is no doubt a cause for concern to the religious leaders who are responsible for the preservation of the movement's identity and piety.

Familiarity with the outside world has also led to an increase in the number of Habad students pursuing a secular education and attending university. While there are no exact figures, the perception in the community is that growing numbers of Hasidim are reading secular newspapers and purchasing television and video equipment, the use of which was once taboo in the community.[30] These influences may be attributable to the exposure to outside influences often encountered in outreach work, although the example of Schneerson himself may be the causative factor. He pursued university studies, lived and worked in the secular world on coming to the United States, and emphasized the use of the latest and most advanced technology in Habad's outreach efforts. This being the case, it is perhaps understandable that Habad's disparagement of secularism has gradually lessened over time.

As a further consequence of outreach, and one that may ultimately prove more damaging to Habad's future, the Habad emissaries, whose primary function is to impart Jewish education and spirituality to those without it, are often doing so at the expense of their own education and spirituality. Habad students are often so preoccupied with their outreach and teaching work that they are unable to concentrate, as a priority, on their own piety and spirituality. The emphasis on outreach has deflected attention from other areas of Habad religious practice, and has effectively led to the spiritualizing of outreach as the most effective religious technique in the movement. This was particularly emphasized in the last decade of Schneerson's leadership, when outreach was empowered as the means through which the mashiach would be revealed.[31] All other activities, therefore, have second place within the mission of Habad, resulting in a lowering of the movement's scholarly standards. The lax levels of scholarship in Habad are also a by-product of Schneerson's insistence that all able men should be trained as rabbis, in order to reach more Jews through positions of influence among the Jewish populace.

Much of the free time of Habad Hasidim is spent on outreach. Festivals, school holidays, most Fridays, and other opportunities that previously would have been used for study are now occasions for outreach, and even Shabbat has become an opportunity for Hasidim to share a meal with visitors and recruit for the movement. Mitnagdim and other Hasidim scoff at Habad's growing reputation for scholarly ineptitude. The situation is even more embarrassing for the Habad movement because it was once distinguished from other schools of Hasidism specifically because of its scholarly slant.[32]

In addition to its role in consolidating Schneerson's leadership and disseminating the movement's teachings, outreach also served to introduce new ideas and influences into the community. Habad could have taken precautions to shelter itself from these influences, as other Hasidic groups have done, but instead chose what it sees as the greater path of dissemination over insulation. While the movement is certainly the most influential and most well known school of Hasidism in the modern world, outreach and its effects may prove detrimental to its survival in the long term.

Habad has paid a considerable price in earning the kudos of a range of Jewish leaders for its hard work and accomplishments in instilling Jewish pride and culture into Jewish youth. Habad is often said to have influenced the secular world, but the influences are all too often mutual. Exposure through outreach has adversely affected its religious standards. From the use of foul language to heresy, outreach is proving to be a double-edged sword. The contact between the secular world and Habad's outreach communities has had a direct impact on the more insulated Habad communities and on other ultra-Orthodox ghettos. This has become a source of great consternation within the other groups, and is one of the main reasons for their criticism of Habad.

The Satmar Hasidim are perhaps the most forceful in condemning Habad, and have published many volumes of polemic against Habad and its heresies. They attack Habad for being to close to secular influence and adopting the habits of the secular world, thereby detracting from the purity of Orthodoxy across the world. One subject of criticism, for example, is the Habad encouragement of newly repentant Jews (ba'alei teshuvah). Satmar Hasidim maintain, and not without considerable justification, that Habad's ba'alei teshuvah and converts have imported undesirable habits and an outside worldview into the "pristine and pure" world of ultra-Orthodoxy. Habad has therefore compromised the study of Torah for the questionable benefits of outreach.

One could make the argument that Habad is no longer ultra-Orthodox because it is no longer insular, and ultra-Orthodox exponents might be the first to agree. If this claim is so, Habad's transition from one type of movement to another has been very rapid. The reason for the rapidity of the transformation seems to be that the change occurred among the movement's principal exponents (the emissaries, rabbis, and educators) who were its strongest elements. While employed by Habad in these functions they were influenced by the outside world because of their constant exposure to it. Like bees returning to the hive, they imported information and habits into the previously closed sanctuary of Hasidic life, and in this way the entire ultra-Orthodox community has been influenced by modernity. This is especially evident in the United States; in Israel, Habad Hasidim are distinctly more conservative and "ultra-Orthodox."

Further, as will be discussed later, there has been significant defection from the ranks of Habad since the death of Schneerson, creating an ex-Habad community, the full extent of which is still not known. This group of ex-Habad Hasidim will no doubt bear further observation in the years to come, as part of a phenomena with many interesting ramifications. While there has always been a flow of people exiting the movement and rejecting religious observance, the exodus from Habad began to pick up momentum as the messianic element intensified. Some began to reconsider their association with the movement after the death of Schneerson. Their departures from Habad were made considerably easier and more viable because of their previous outreach activities outside of the ultra-Orthodox ghetto. Many people leaving Habad had once been emissaries, and had established business contacts, friends, and other support mechanisms independent of their primary religious associations. This made leaving religious life easier, and is one reflection of the price Habad is paying for its modernity and outreach practices.

Another curious consequence of outreach is the mutual support network established by those leaving Orthodox groups. Ex-Habad Hasidim have been observed with ex-Satmar Hasidim, forming friendships and supporting one other, something they did not do in their traditional communities. Most other schools of Hasidism, and many segments of the broader Jewish community, greatly dislike Habad primarily because of its outreach work. Habad's leaders often send students to synagogues in a given community over festivals and holidays. The motivation, according to Habad, is to enliven the synagogue with a Hasidic spirit. This practice, however, has often infuriated local non-Habad rabbis, who commonly feel that the Hasidim are encroaching on their territory. They view these activities as patronizing because of the implicit message that Habad believes its brand of Judaism is superior to all others. Similarly, offers of help (financial, educational, and otherwise) made by Habad to local communities are seen as a form of colonization, and have caused rifts in some communities. Activities such as these, which arise directly from Habad's policy and practice of outreach, have produced a strong dislike among many segments of the Jewish community, and an antipathy to Habad and its goals.

The Habad Yeshiva System

The idea of a specifically Habad yeshiva was initiated by Shalom Dov Ber, the fifth Habad Rebbe. The system of Hasidic education it represented may very well have been responsible for the Lubavitch dynasty's survival despite persecution in Eastern Europe, especially during the reign of Yosef Yitzhak. It was also a central part of the re-emergence of Habad in the United States. The first Habad yeshiva in America was founded as soon as Yosef Yitzhak arrived in 1940. His experiences in Russia very probably had convinced him that the successful transplantation of Habad into the New World was dependent upon the establishment of a yeshiva to train and teach the next generation.

The same principle was applied throughout the United States and around the world under Schneerson. As more children grew up within the movement and more students arrived in Crown Heights to study, it became a routine part of the Habad educational policy to spend some time after high school in a yeshiva. This became even more the case as the educational facilities of the movement attracted more committed people and better teachers, and as the infrastructure grew. Although not a common expectation in the early years of the movement, by the 1970s it was practically a basic requirement that every Habad boy study at least for a time in a Habad yeshiva, especially when Schneerson encouraged rabbinic ordination for all men who were able.

A yeshiva is best compared to a theological school. Although the subjects of study vary from community to community, it is generally assumed that the Talmud and other halakhic texts occupy most of the curriculum, which comprises a total of approximately sixteen hours of study daily. In Hasidic yeshivot generally, and Habad yeshivot in particular, the study of mysticism is an added feature of the curriculum, generally occupying two or three hours per day. The trend in contemporary Habad yeshivot is for students to break from their studies regularly on Fridays, and less regularly on various occasions throughout the year, to dedicate time to outreach programs. This practice has earned the movement severe criticism from other streams of Orthodoxy, which claim that this practice takes students away from their primary duty of study to less important pursuits. Habad yeshivot have developed a reputation in the Jewish scholarly world for weak scholarship, and therefore do not attract the better talmudic students. Exceptional Habad students who are serious about learning often continue their studies at non-Habad Lithuanian yeshivot, where the study regime is more traditional and much more rigorous.

The yeshiva system was the backbone of Schneerson's popular support even before he assumed the post of Rebbe. It continued to be his main support throughout his reign, and still is years after his death. Schneerson was always careful to maintain ties with the movement's students, whose rebelliousness, enthusiasm, imagination, vigor, and free time made them a valuable (and vocal) resource to be channeled into useful initiatives. As these students grew older, they became the next generation of leadership of Habad, all intensely committed to Schneerson and his vision for the movement.

As school students, Habad boys learn both secular and religious subjects; the yeshiva system is somewhat different. Attendance is voluntary, and therefore students are generally more serious and committed to study and the development of their spiritual life. While attending yeshiva many students begin to mature in their observance, developing a deeper religious commitment. In Crown Heights, yeshiva students were often the most fervent supporters of Schneerson. Part of their curriculum was spent studying Schneerson's writings and teachings, which further developed their commitment to him. They were often the most earnest members of the audience at Schneerson's talks. He was the primary reason they were on their "mission," and their attachment to him was palpable. Much of the messianic fervor evident throughout the history of the movement, especially in the last decade of the Rebbe's life, was fostered in the yeshiva.

As the movement became larger and more influential, the cream of the students were chosen to go overseas. At first, only specially selected students were given the honor of serving the Rebbe abroad. In time, though, it became commonplace, especially as more Habad yeshiva students became available. Today, it is standard procedure for Habad students to travel on *shlihut*, where they undergo an active apprenticeship in the mission of the movement, under trained, experienced leaders in real-life circumstances. Most yeshiva students emerge from their experience as seasoned missionaries, ready for a more committed career within the movement.

Originally, it was mainly students from the central Habad yeshiva, Ohelei Torah, in Crown Heights, who were sent to the movement's centers around the world.[33] By the time of Schneerson's death, the Habad movement had opened dozens of yeshivot around the world, and in most countries where there was a sizable Habad community, there was a yeshiva.[34] Students were frequently sent to these smaller yeshivot for one or two years as emissaries of the movement in order to perform outreach and strengthen communities that lacked human resources and educators. In turn, many Habad students from around the world spent a few years of study in the central Habad yeshiva in Crown Heights. This central meeting point has often been described as an officers' training corps for emissaries.

To be sent on *shlihut* was and is considered an honor and a privilege. It is usually very exciting for students, who get to travel the world, meet new people, and practice their outreach skills. Often the period of *shlihut* gives the young student his first exposure to secularism and other perceived vices outside of his previously sheltered Orthodox lifestyle, but it is impossible to determine how many have been tempted to leave Habad as a result of this exposure. The sense of being on a mission as an emissary of the Rebbe no doubt lessens the desire to adopt "outside" ways too strongly.

Many emissaries developed a strong sense of responsibility for the education of the communities as they came to realize the full extent of Jewish assimilation and cultural ignorance. Students became teachers or took on other roles in the community, and many decided to settle in the location permanently, often marrying a local girl. In this way, Habad developed an international flavor, with relatives and friends throughout the world and a network of contacts focusing on Schneerson, Crown Heights, and the achievements of the movement. Many students developed a new appreciation for the Rebbe and his interest and concern for the well-being of far-flung international Jewish communities. His personality became larger than life, because their only contact with him was via stories, satellite hook-ups, and video. As a result, his significance as a leader seemed even more imposing abroad.

The results of this worldwide educational enterprise are varied. The exposure that outreach provided to non-Hasidic Jewish communities throughout the world made the Habad movement one of the best-known ultra-Orthodox groups. While most ultra-Orthodox sects are little known outside their home territory, living as they do in isolated communities in Israel, Belgium, the United State, and other countries, Habad is a familiar force throughout the Jewish world. This has enabled the movement to influence the very concept of Orthodoxy in the broader Jewish community, and to establish cross-cultural relationships with a wide cross-section of the Jewish world.

The work of yeshiva students over the years has been invaluable to the expansion of the movement. Apart from the fact that students give their time and effort to outreach with no expectation of pay, which has saved the movement vast amounts of money over the decades, the yeshiva has provided an organized reserve of activists who can be mobilized for especially worthwhile causes. The independence and initiative of the students, doubtlessly a result of their youth and idealism, spurred many new ideas for effective outreach on behalf of the movement. This human reservoir could not have been maintained in other, less homogeneous and ideologically united organizations. Its group cohesiveness, coupled with the image of activists as tireless walking advertisements for Schneerson and Habad, had an effect on Jewish communities abroad. To many in the broader Jewish community, Habad became the a paragon of Orthodox observance.[35] It stood out as an identifiable movement, separate from other Orthodox schools, and escaped being identified as one strain of Orthodoxy among many. This reappraisal of Habad within the spectrum of Judaism facilitated the appraisal of Schneerson as the grand rabbi of Orthodoxy, and not simply another Rebbe of a small subsection of the Hasidic community. Schneerson's position in world Jewry was greatly enhanced by the disproportionate representation of Habad throughout the world, through its emissaries and their role in the revival of religious observance.

The Habad yeshiva system is a good example of Schneerson's centralized-decentralized method of administration. Under this system, the local community took responsibility for the financial and other burdens of its ongoing work, and the central administration provided broad ideological guidance. The yeshiva system is controlled partly by Merkaz and partly by the United Lubavitch Yeshivot. During the reign of Yosef Yitzhak, the United Lubavitch Yeshivot was run by Shemaryahu Gourary, and under Schneerson he continued to do so, no doubt in part because of Schneerson's desire to change nothing established by his predecessor. Gourary was an excellent manager of the yeshiva system, and a gifted orator and fundraiser, continuing throughout his life to collect money for his yeshivot.[36] The yeshivot that were opened throughout the United States and internationally during Schneerson's leadership, were sponsored primarily by Merkaz and the local communities, although they were administered in conjunction with Gourary's organization. The yeshiva system was a highly effective instrument in establishing Habad influence in mainstream Jewish Orthodoxy and strengthening its influence on world Jewry, as well as providing a considerable tool for Schneerson's consolidation of leadership.

The Habad House

As part of its aim to spread the observance of religious law throughout the Jewish world, the Habad movement established the institution of the Habad House. Unlike the yeshiva system, the primary aim of which was the further education of those who were already observant, the Habad House aimed to provide education, training, and guidance to facilitate the religious observance of those new to Habad, and to provide a living example of observance for the Jewish populace worldwide. The idea of the Habad House was initiated by Schneerson in 1959 with a call for all Habad families to open their homes to the general Jewish community.[37] There was both a personal and an institutional call for homes to be opened for hospitality, education, and prayer, with every family personalizing this principle into their daily routine and welcoming fellow Jews into their lives and homes.[38] Because of this program, there are currently thousands of Habad Houses around the world, providing education and hospitality to those interested in seeing the religious life in practice.

In addition to families opening their homes, a number of Habad Houses were opened by young emissaries who targeted a particular demographic, usually the student body on a university campus or younger Jews in a major city.[39] These target-focused Habad Houses eventually expanded their operations to smaller areas and localities, to better serve the needs of the broader population. Habad Houses are often run by a dynamic husband-and-wife team, the wife often becoming indispensable in attracting female interest, as well as providing the hospitality services that are an important element in attracting visitors.[40] The establishment of a Habad House is often financially aided by Merkaz L'Inyanei Hinukh, the central Habad agency, and by the local Habad community, but it is expected to achieve independence and do its own fundraising within a short space of time.

The role of the Habad House in the expansion of the movement is best demonstrated by its operation in smaller communities. In areas with a small Jewish population, and therefore with no synagogue, the Habad House frequently becomes the place for religious services, especially on Shabbat. As a focal point for community building and activity, this often leads to the development of a large local Habad community within a few years. The Habad House thus serves to fill a religious vacuum in the chosen locality.

The practice of sending emissaries into areas and setting up Habad Houses to encourage locals to become part of the movement often leads to complaints about Habad. It has embittered non-Habad community leaders who feel that the movement is encroaching on their territory. In some ways, they are right. The movement has an abundance of eager, efficient, enthusiastic emissaries who are willing to work for little or no money, which makes it difficult for those outside the movement to equal the activities or interest generated by the Habad House. As many of the emissaries are also rabbinically qualified, Habad has tended to take over communities in need of rabbis or other religious functionaries.[41] On the other hand, the fact that Habad has been able to do this indicates that there is a need in the local communities that is not being met by other organizations.

Thanks to their central role in their communities, the Habad Houses worldwide have provided self-generated employment for Habad Hasidim, as well as massive public relations activity. They are often the only Orthodox presence in many Jewish communities around the world, providing essential services to those they have encouraged to join the movement. As well as bringing many non-religious Jews to observance, the Habad Houses and Hasidim disseminated the teachings of Schneerson and Habad, and helped to build the cult of personality that surrounded him. This in turn further popularized him in general Jewish circles and increased his influence worldwide.

The conception of opening up branches of hospitality and outreach is not new to Judaism, and has long been a feature of many Jewish organizations.[42] However, the scale on which Schneerson implemented the Habad House was unprecedented. The idea that *every* Habad household would be actively involved in outreach and public dissemination of Habad ideology and observance meant that the entire movement was drafted into the outreach effort. Whether an activity as simple as offering hospitality to strangers or visitors for a Shabbat meal, or as complex as studying with a less committed Jew to teach the heritage, the community was put to work. Business and professional Hasidim were not exempt from this, and outside of their work hours they were often involved in some extracurricular outreach program.

The involvement of every Habad family was encouraged not only by the Rebbe's directive, but also by peer pressure from the community. Commitment to the movement was further demonstrated by the "Habad House" sign affixed to the front doors of many homes, an advertising directive issued by Schneerson to signify the presence of a Habad House in a community. The pressure to affix the sign to their homes challenged the apprehensive to make up their minds and commit more fully to the leader of Habad. Through symbolic gestures such as signs and community activities, those who were loosely affiliated with Habad were encouraged to deepen their commitment and articulate their connection to the movement.

The Habad House spearheaded Habad's outreach enterprises and activated all the followers of Habad in the movement's activities. It also attracted many newcomers into the religious lifestyle, through commitment to the principles of Habad. In this way, Schneerson further consolidated his authority and translated the Hasidic outreach mission into a format for every individual to participate in, even those outside the institutionalized community.

Other Organizations

During his years as Rebbe, Schneerson initiated many other projects and organizations to expand the movement and serve the general Jewish community. The nature of these initiatives indicates his concern for the advancement of Judaism worldwide, beyond the world of his Hasidim. Many of the programs he established reflect the strategy that characterized Schneerson's institutional policy and work ethic, evident from the very early days of his leadership. Unlike other religious groups, many of which focused their attention on the religious elite and the yeshivot, Schneerson also catered to other segments of society.[43] He was particularly concerned with developing employment opportunities for as many people as possible, and with using employment not only to help the Hasidim support themselves, but to advance the cause of the movement.[44]

In 1954, in accordance with these ideas, Schneerson established an agricultural school in Kfar Habad in Israel, one of the movement's main centers around the world. The aim of this school was to help the community sustain itself economically through agriculture, and to provide self-reliant labour for the Habad community in Israel. The training of young Habad Hasidim as agricultural laborers, as opposed to sending them to study in a yeshiva, was at the time quite a revolutionary thing to do in the Israeli Hasidic world.[45] The school established under this initiative provided vocations for Habad Hasidim and others who might not have had an aptitude for the yeshiva environment. Schneerson was visionary in seeing that all the members of the community could play a role of some kind in building the movement, and indeed that in order to grow, Habad needed more than scholars and rabbis. His policy of agricultural education permitted people to work the land, support their communities, and yet still play a role in the Hasidic community.[46] The school reflected Schneerson's realistic concern about the needs of the Israeli Habad community. It also demonstrated a concern for the non-scholarly that was somewhat lacking in other branches of Hasidism.

Apart from catering for the committed Hasidic community, the facilities established under Schneerson's direction drew many immigrants to the movement, especially in the early years of his leadership. They came initially to learn a useful profession in a familiar environment, with others from East European backgrounds who spoke their language, but they were also exposed to the Habad philosophy and lifestyle. In addition to learning new professions, many also adopted the ideology of the movement and joined its ranks. In the early days of the movement, many new members were attracted in this way. In later years, the practice of training immigrants was effectively applied in Israel to large numbers of Sephardi Jews, many from Arab countries and largely discriminated against by both mainstream society and the predominantly Ashkenazi religious establishment. Habad was the only group to receive them with open arms. To this day, many older Yemenite and Moroccan Jews in Israel remain indebted to Habad and Schneerson for this, and many became committed Hasidim as a consequence of this outreach. The same is true of the many thousands of Russian Jews whom Habad helped to emigrate during the 1970s and the 1990s.

Other community efforts supported or proposed by Schneerson include the establishment of a vocational school in Kfar Habad for young adults, and the creation in 1952 of a Women's and Daughters' Association. Schneerson also encouraged activities for the elderly, and opened a number of study halls particularly for them.

Worldwide, Habad's policy of self-sufficiency and self-employment led to a large number of innovative employment opportunities, many either previously unavailable or unnecessary.[47] As local communities grew because of the work of Habad emissaries, it became necessary to provide certain necessities for the religious. Opportunity therefore existed for the establishment of kosher food outlets (including restaurants and fast food), matzah-baking programs, stores selling religious literature and paraphernalia, wig-makers, providers of kosher childcare, and so forth. All of these services were necessary for the maintenance of a religious community, and were frequently previously unavailable in many areas. Such initiatives made it easier for non-Habad Jews to maintain a level of religious observance even if they did not subscribe completely to the Habad ideology. Schneerson was thus able to commence the "elevation of the sparks," a necessary component of the messianic doctrine at the core of Habad's outreach momentum.

Habad also contributed to the Jewish community by providing new synagogues, women's centers, yeshivot and study houses, drug rehabilitation centers, Internet services,[48] summer camps, and public celebrations of Jewish festivals such as Hanukah, Pesach and Lag Ba-Omer. Outreach efforts included mitzvah-mobiles,[49] worldwide public seders,[50] Shabbat candle-lighting campaigns, toll-free telephone lectures,[51] and holiday gifts and religious services for Israeli soldiers. Since all of these outreach efforts required people and money to implement, they brought employment for the community. Such efforts have given Habad a massive and powerful influence worldwide, quite disproportionate to its size.

The above-mentioned organizations established by Schneerson during his early years as Rebbe were attempts to mobilize all segments of the worldwide Habad community, and to utilize each segment of the community (men, women, and children) in accordance with its capability and needs. He tried to provide employment and self-fulfillment, Jewish education and a sense of community, while remaining steadfast to wider outreach goals. The strategy he undertook indicated that he did not demand a uniform brand of dedication or effort, but desired different Hasidic communities and individuals to participate in his movement and vision according to their disposition. This pluralism was evident in many of his projects.

---

[1] See Jonathan Sacks, "The Man Who Turned Judaism Outward." He notes that Schneerson virtually invented the idea of outreach and the modern ba'alei teshuvah movement.

[2] See "The Rebbe."

[3] Menachem Friedman, "Habad as Messianic Fundamentalism," pp. 345–357.

[4] See "The Rebbe's Empire."

[5] Although the exact figures for other dynasties are not known, it is generally agreed that the Satmar, Ger, and Belz dynasties are numerically larger than Habad.

[6] Friedman, "Habad as Messianic Fundamentalism," p. 346.

[7] See Sacks, "Man Who Turned Judaism Outward."

[8] These will be discussed below.

[9] See Sacks, "Man Who Turned Judaism Outward"; and idem, "When Mysticism Saved the Jewish People."

[10] Schneerson himself referred matters of halakhah to the Beit Din, and advised the movement to do likewise in the event of his death. See Chapter 19 for more details.

[11] Many of the extreme messianists demonstrate a high level of scholarship in support of their position. See especially Yosef Braun et al., *And He Will Redeem Us*.

[12] M. Herbert Danzger, *Returning to Tradition*, pp. 58–62.

[13] Lis Harris, *Holy Days*, esp. pp. 54–76.

[14] See Sacks, "When Mysticism Saved the Jewish People."

[15] See "Rabbi Schneerson Led a Small Hasidic Sect to World Prominence." The article describes how widespread Habad is, claiming that there are few places in the world where one will not find at least a small Habad family. A common Habad adages holds that "Wherever one travels, one can find two things: Habad and Coca-Cola." Another says: "Join Habad and see the world."

[16] See Yossi Klein Halevi, "Can Chabad Outlive the Rebbe?"

[17] See Jeffery L. Sheler, "A Movement Goes On Without Its Leader."

[18] See *Beis Moshiah*. This weekly magazine publishes numerous stories and accounts of Habad emissaries in various countries, their achievements, and miracles that allegedly occurred for them as a result of Schneerson's divine intervention.

[19] See Herb Brin, "Through the Night." Brin, the editor of *Heritage*, a prestigious magazine, recorded an emotional account of his encounters with Schneerson. He says that his coverage of Schneerson in 1954–55 inspired Ben-Gurion to visit Schneerson. Attracting Ben-Gurion to his court, as noted, might have been decisive in the growth of his public popularity, for a flow of Israeli politicians and generals followed.

[20] See David Landau, "His Influence." He notes that the distinctive clothing, beards, and behavior of Hasidic Jews, as well as their ability to articulate themselves, makes them camera-attractive, media-viable subjects. He surmises that the Rebbe of Satmar's visit to Israel had wide coverage on CNN and the front page of the *New York Times* because of the photogenic qualities of the Hasidim.

[21] See Chaim Potok, "Rabbi Schneerson." The view proffered by Potok is consistent with a story told in Habad of Yosef Yitzhak. According to the story, Yosef Yitzhak expressed satisfaction that the messianic ideology in his time had called attention to the idea of redemption. On one occasion he gave a talk about the imminent arrival of the mashiach, then asked Schneerson how the Hasidim had reacted. Schneerson replied that many had somewhat skeptically asked whether Yosef Yitzhak thought himself the messianic candidate. Yosef Yitzhak is supposed to have retorted, "Nu, at least they are thinking about the *moshiach*." This story can be seen as an indication of the desire in Habad to call attention to the idea of the coming of the mashiach; even if it is controversial and no specific messianic candidate is mentioned, at least people are thinking of mashiach.

[22] See "Menachem Mendel Schneerson" (*Lubavitch in the News*, p. 9). The author notes the presence of, among others, Governor Mario Cuomo, New York Mayor Rudolph Giuliani, Senator Alphonse D'Amato, and Israeli politician Benjamin Netanyahu.

[23] *Lubavitch in the News*.

[24] Including education and building renovation. After Schneerson's death, the movement had time to renovate 770, for example, and to generally improve the appearance of Crown Heights, which had until then not been possible because of the emphasis on outreach.

[25] "Obituaries: Rabbi Menachem Schneerson" (*Lubavitch in the News*, p. 30).

[26] See J. Rosenbloom, *Conversion to Judaism from the Biblical Period to the Present*, esp. pp. 74–78; Danzger, *Returning to Tradition*, p. 198, n. 1.

[27] See Jerome R. Mintz, *Hasidic People*, p. 50; Danzger, *Returning to Tradition*, pp. 300–303. Religious Jews, especially Satmar Hasidim, resent being told to do what they are already doing by people whose learning and ideas they do not respect. Outreach is one of the main causes of friction between Satmar and Habad, as it is between Habad and other Hasidic courts.

[28] These issues include, for example, Schneerson's refusal to compromise on the surrender of Israeli territory to the Palestinians, his stance on the "Who is a Jew?" issue regarding both Reform and Conservative converts to Judaism and the question of Ethiopian Jewry; his messianic rhetoric; and his support for government involvement in religious education in American schools.

[29] See especially Braun, *And He Will Redeem Us*.

[30] This is still so to a certain extent, and few will publicly admit to watching popular television programs, claiming they use TV only to obtain news or for educational purposes.

[31] See Chapter 9.

[32] As might be observed, for example, by the adoption of the name Habad itself, the derivation of which has already been discussed.

[33] Recently, the Morristown yeshiva has also begun to send out emissaries.

[34] A yeshiva was opened in Toronto in 1957, and *kollelim* (colleges) were established throughout the United States and Israel in the 1950s and 1960s. Yeshivot were opened in Melbourne in 1967, Miami in 1974, New Haven in 1976, Seattle and Caracas in 1977, Los Angeles in 1978, Buenos Aires in 1980, and Johannesburg in 1984.

[35] Sacks, "When Mysticism Saved the Jewish People."

[36] Gourary's position in the movement was delicate. He continued to live in 770 among Schneerson's fiercest supporters. He continued his work in the movement's organizations as before. He did not challenge Schneerson's authority and became a dedicated Hasid. In the court case fought by his wife and son against the Habad institutions, he supported Schneerson against his family.

[37] Ari L. Goldman, "The Nation."

[38] See Lis Harris, *Holy Days*, for an account of life in a Habad household.

[39] Mintz, *Hasidic People*, p. 92.

[40] This emphasis on the domestic role of women is an important element of Habad's ideology. See Chapter 17 for further discussion.

[41] It has been doing this since the time of Yosef Yitzhak, who sent rabbis and other religious functionaries to remote Jewish communities that lacked qualified human resources. The practice was therefore not an innovation of Schneerson's reign or the institution of the Habad House concept.

[42] Similar services for Jewish students on university campuses are provided, for example, by the Hillel Association.

[43] Hasidic leaders are characterized by their readiness to initiate social projects and training for the betterment of the physical existence of their followers. This practice was common in Eastern Europe, but in Israel Hasidim usually pursued ascetic religious lifestyles and were not trained or encouraged to do physical labor. Even today, many Hasidim are exempt from the compulsory military service enforced on other Israeli citizens. Habad, however, actively

encouraged nonclerical pursuits in both Israel and the United States for those who did not wish to take on scholarly pursuits. This appears to have influenced other groups. The Israeli political party Shas applied this principle of social and educational support in developing its Sephardi following, and achieved political success in the 1990s, including an electoral victory in 1996, and constant growth since then. It has come to be known as the Habad of the Sephardi world. Islamic organizations, particularly Hamas, have also used this principle to rally support, with significant success.

[44] See Chapter 12.

[45] See Yishayahu Leibowitz, *Yehadut Am Yehudi u-Medinat Yisrael*, and *Ha-Olam u-Melo'o*. He asserts that post-Holocaust Orthodoxy was (and is) focused on the re-education of its rank-and-file. Youth are expected to spend many years in religious and scholarly training, and consequently the yeshiva has become a primary focus of their lives. He claims that there are more yeshiva students and yeshivot in Israel than at any time in the history of the Jewish people. See also Gershom Gorenberg, "Get a Job."

[46] The idea of physical labor is compatible with the general Hasidic attitude toward the simple life; additionally, it can be seen as complementing the Habad idea of spiritual growth brought about through interaction with the physical world. Schneerson may have been inspired to some degree by the perspicacity of the Zionist movement and its stubborn struggle to "redeem" the land. Schneerson's brother had been swept away by the Zionist idea and had emigrated to Israel.

[47] See Sacks, "When Mysticism Saved the Jewish People."

[48] See Lesley Pearl, "Cyber-matza?"

[49] Vans with students that park in public places, especially during festivals such as Sukkot and Lag Ba'Omer, to encourage passing Jews to keep at least a part of the festival. In New York and other major centers, the mitzvah-mobile is a permanent fixture on the streets, encouraging religious observance.

[50] See Jennifer Friedlin, "The Thais That Bind." The author discusses Habad seders in Nepal and Bangkok that attracted 600 Israelis, drawn to an appreciation of Judaism unknown to them in Israel. The article notes that Israeli travelers plan their trips around the seder, which has become an annual tourist event. See also "Worldwide Seders Set by Chabad."

[51] The caller accesses a lecture, changed regularly, on a variety of religious subjects. There are also stories for children and other inspirational subjects, free of charge to the caller.

Chapter 16
Publishing Houses and Libraries

Dissemination through Publication

The Habad movement has traditionally been very active in its use of the medium of print to advance its ideas and program. Shneur Zalman's printing of the *Tanya* set a precedent that later Rebbes were determined to emulate. Throughout the history of the movement, the use and distribution of publications of various types to disseminate ideas established a precedent still followed by the movement. Public relations with the outside world, communication between the communities of Habad associates across the globe, and most importantly the unabashed utilization of the latest technology to advance the Hasidic way of life were all part of the Habad practice of publication. Present-day Habad outreach tactics still include massive publication endeavors as part of the movement's effort to reach the widest possible audience.

Even before he became Rebbe, Schneerson was put in charge of the compilation and publication of Habad works. He was given valuable manuscripts to transcribe and publish, had access to the considerable resources of Yosef Yitzhak's library (on which more shortly), and attracted a circle of scholars and assistants. He was also put in charge of the movement's publication program by Yosef Yitzhak, and effectively appointed himself *de facto* Habad archivist after the death of his father-in-law. His position as scholar and disseminator of Habad material made Schneerson an attractive candidate for the succession. The continual publication of works that catered to Habad Hasidim, the general Orthodox population, and the broader Jewish public served to consolidate Habad's literary domination of much of the Jewish world. Moreover, it ensured the centrality of Schneerson as a general Jewish religious leader, educator, and link to the ancient chain of tradition.

In his capacity as Habad's publication manager, Schneerson was able to consolidate his authority over the movement more rapidly and effectively than might otherwise have been possible. The role put him in a position of contact with a wide cross-section of the movement, from scholars to students, and this enabled him to influence many followers who would rally to his support when he assumed leadership of Habad in 1951.

Schneerson's administration of the Merkaz L'Inyanei Hinukh, which was responsible for the educational activities of the movement, became the means by which he consolidated his authority over Habad. The success of Merkaz in carrying out the aims of Yosef Yitzhak, who had appointed Schneerson to head it and determined its initial direction and goals, would become the primary barometer for Schneerson's success as the movement's leader. Throughout his life, Schneerson claimed that he was merely the administrative director of the organization, the executor of Yosef Yitzhak's instructions. As the chief executor of his father-in-law's ideals, in the execution of which he was highly successful, Schneerson established his reputation, and throughout his life he kept close control of the organizations given to him by Yosef Yitzhak. He remained a manager of the educational arm of the movement, and was effectively in charge of Habad's publishing houses, activities that probably meant more to him than the post of Rebbe.[1]

Throughout his reign, Habad scholars and learned people served Schneerson by publishing scholarly and educational works to further the Habad ideology. Their aims coincided with his and, through him, Yosef Yitzhak's. They had varied qualities and qualifications that brought them to the publishing world; some had scholarly backgrounds, others were inclined to teaching, speaking, writing, or were active in other fields, and hoped that their message would be heard both within the Habad community and outside.

These men became assistants to Schneerson, and in time some of them became quite influential in the movement.[2] Their great respect for his scholarship and dedication to his goals were important for his election to the position of Rebbe in the first place, and their loyalty to him and words of adoration to others assisted in the development and dissemination of his reputation as a great leader. The aura of mystery that surrounded Schneerson was partly due to the legendary proportions in which these associates described him. Their role in establishing his public persona was very important; endorsements of Schneerson could not have come from finer, more educated and idealistic people. Indeed, they formed the future of the movement.

The educational and publication branches of the Habad movement became a vehicle through which these active individuals, including Schneerson, could work to change the world. They participated in Schneerson's vision and served as his main instruments of expression, at first in the publishing organizations given him by Yosef Yitzhak, most notably Kehot, then to an outer group of scholars, rabbis, teachers, and activists. Through these connections, the influence of Schneerson was spread around the world Habad Hasidic community, and to at least a part of the general Jewish world.

Within the movement, and even in the outside scholarly community, the publishing efforts of Habad also had an effect. The appeal of unpublished Hasidic works and scholarly texts becoming available to the reading public created a heightened awareness of their existence, particularly in educated circles, and scholarly interest in Habad was heightened by the new publications. The appointment of Schneerson to the publishing arm of Habad coincided with a growing academic interest in Hasidism and Hasidic culture.[3] The increased interest in the Habad movement in scholarly circles slowly spread into the non-academic community.

The publications produced by Schneerson would be the primary source of learning activities for Habad communities around the world. Until the movement began to print its own books and other materials, there was little non-specialist literature available to those interested in Habad, and what was available was difficult to acquire. The publication of Hasidic works by his predecessors made Schneerson a vocal spokesperson for Hasidism, and a voice for Jewish revival.[4] This was underscored by the continuity represented by the publication of Hasidic works in the United States, an uncommon phenomenon at the time. The merger of traditional philosophy with modern technology utilized in the publishing efforts was also to emerge as a pattern in Schneerson's career.

The existence of Habad Hasidic books allowed religious students to further involve themselves in the study of the ideology and philosophy of the movement, which had the effect of increasing their commitment to it. The publication of works of philosophy also contributed to the dissemination of Habad ideology. The most famous printing campaign in contemporary Habad was seen with the mass publication of Shneur Zalman's distillation of Habad philosophy, the *Tanya*. Schneerson directed that this seminal work was to be printed wherever Jews lived, and Habad activists consequently traveled with portable printing presses, producing bilingual editions of the *Tanya* in thousands of cities and dozens of countries throughout the world.

Schneerson actively campaigned for the publication of a number of other works on subjects of relevance and interest to the religiously observant. As a result, Habad now runs the largest Hasidic printing company in the world.[5] The movement has succeeded in making the *Tanya*, among other Habad works, a household book in the scholarly secular and religious communities. Considering the relative size of the movement and its modest start in Brooklyn in the 1930s after dislocation from Russia, this increase in the prominence of an obscure mystical work is all the more remarkable. No other Hasidic movement has matched Habad's major philosophical impact on the broad Jewish community, largely due to the publishing efforts of Schneerson.

Internally, the effort of publication solidified the movement's philosophical and ideological base, and served as a source of unity and consensus. The practice of publishing several works in one volume, such as the combined edition of *Humash*, *Tehillim,* and *Tanya*, elevated the significance of the late-seventeenth-century work to the same level as the Psalms and Torah.[6] By adding a schedule for the daily study of each of these works, the link between these texts was forged even more closely, and the movement was unified behind a single guided system of study. While the practice of single-volume publication has opened Habad to the charge of attempting a form of *de facto* canonization of its texts,[7] such publications consolidated the Diaspora of Habad communities into one disciplined, homogenous community, and promoted *Tanya* as a mainstream Jewish scholarly work.

In addition to these book-publishing efforts, Schneerson supported many innovative means of reaching the public, including the broadcast of radio lectures and the distribution of videos. Although these methods of disseminating his teachings had been in unofficial use for many years, and his lectures reached many communities without Schneerson's encouragement and often without his knowledge, it was decided in 1978 to establish an official organization to do this more effectively.[8] The motive for this consolidation may have been the growing demand for his teachings, related to a tremendous surge in the movement's popularity. Whatever the reasons for the initiative, the establishment of a central organization to distribute Schneerson's teachings in recorded and transcribed formats allowed both internal consolidation and the ability to supervise the distribution to ensure that there were no mistakes in the texts of his talks. The increasing attention the movement was attracting was accompanied by a large and scholarly audience for Schneerson's talks, and accuracy was therefore imperative. Perhaps the success of the movement persuaded Schneerson that his teachings were making a difference to outreach, and that self-promotion was therefore of value to the achievement of the movement's goals.

The AGUCH Collection

Books play a significant role in Jewish religious life, and throughout the history of Habad, they have been important to the development and perpetuation of the movement. Habad Rebbes both collected books and wrote down their own ideas, essays, letters, and other works. Often, these texts were not published, but were handed down from generation to generation, usually to the succeeding Rebbe or through the family line as a form of inheritance and sign of transfer of authority. As they were not published, however, many of these works were lost in a series of fires suffered by several of the Habad Rebbes.[9] Despite this, Yosef Yitzhak inherited a sizable and valuable collection of rare books and manuscripts from his predecessor, and built upon it during his own lifetime. Unfortunately, though, he was unable to rescue this collection completely when he fled Eastern Europe for the United States. What he was able to save was made virtually priceless by the destruction of Jewry occasioned by the Second World War and the Communist suppression of Judaism, but eventually some parts of the collection were released by the Soviet authorities and preserved in the cellar of Habad's central headquarters.

The ownership of these books and manuscripts has been a divisive issue in the Habad movement.[10] Yosef Yitzhak left no known will that alluded to the future of the books. Since the collection was located in the home of Yosef Yitzhak, it might be assumed that the library belonged to his family or his designated successor. The difficulty in determining ownership came from the fact that Yosef Yitzhak lived in the building that was the central headquarters of Habad, a building owned by AGUCH, and so the matter was undecided until 1985, when a federal court case ensued over the ownership of the book collection.

The books were described in court as a symbol of leadership, representing the very office of Rebbe. On this basis, a federal court decided that by virtue of Yosef Yitzhak's relationship with his Hasidim, his property became their property after his death, and his books should remain the communal property of the Hasidim. This decision was seen as a victory for the Habad movement against personal interests that were trying to gain possession of the library. Indeed, the legal struggle came to symbolize a struggle for Schneerson's leadership, represented by the importance of the traditions embodied in the book collection and the significance of books as representative of the movement's glory. Ironically, one of the primary arguments used in court in favor of Habad's retention of the library was the fact that the books had been passed down from one Rebbe to the next in a regular chain, indicating their significance as property of the leader of the movement.[11] This symbolism was ended, however, when the court decided that the collection belonged to the movement as a whole and gave it into the administration of AGUCH, the legally registered parent organization behind Habad. Consequently, when Schneerson died, the collection was not passed on to a successor, but remained in the hands of AGUCH, the symbolic heir to his authority.

Schneerson and others often alluded to the symbolic value of books. Before his death, Yosef Yitzhak had given Schneerson a number of manuscripts, with the idea of having them published by the Habad publishing organization administered by Schneerson. At his death, Yosef Yitzhak's wife was eager to retrieve these manuscripts from Schneerson because she understood their symbolic value to leadership status in Habad. She favored the succession of her other son-in-law, Shemaryahu Gourary, and feared that his claim would be weakened if someone else controlled the library. At the time, Schneerson is recorded as having told his mother-in-law that he had already returned the manuscripts to Yosef Yitzhak's book cupboard, but he later said, "They gave me the key, can I let the books be stolen?"[12]

During and after the court case, Schneerson repeated his view that the books belonged to Yosef Yitzhak and perhaps to the Hasidim but not to the Gourary family or to any individual, including himself.[13] He supported the movement's position in regard to the lawsuit, and he attributed much symbolism to the legal victory. Indeed, he composed a victory song to be sung on triumphal occasions to mark the success of the court case, which became, among other book-related occasions, a minor festival for the contemporary Habad movement.

Whatever its symbolic significance, the library was economically valuable and academically impressive. It contained over 40,000 books and 1,750 manuscripts, including 1,400 Habad manuscripts that had never been published.[14] Its was one of the biggest Hasidic libraries in New York, and certainly one of the largest private libraries of its kind in the world.

The strength of the library lay in its ability to support independent research through its collection of publications and manuscripts of historical, academic, and political interest. Because it contained irreplaceable material and texts, since most other copies had been destroyed in the Second World War, it had a major scholarly monopoly and became the envy of many people. Its contribution to the strength of Habad lay in the desire of scholars to gain access to the collection, and the movement's right to deny access to anyone who was not to its liking. Many of the finest Jewish scholars in the world, including Gershom Scholem, the noted historian of Kabbalah, were denied access to important resources.[15] At present the book collection is guarded with maximum security, and access to the archives is given on a selective basis. Many potential critics of the movement have become wary of openly speaking against Habad for fear that they too may encounter problems with the movement's leaders. Even at present, scholars of Habad history and ideology must be careful about how they describe the movement for fear of vindictiveness and an informal (but effective) ban on providing material or help to their work. The most notable instance of this is the research of Rabbi Shaul Shimon Deutsch on Habad's history under Yosef Yitzhak and the early life of Schneerson.[16] Political pressure has apparently also been brought to bear on non-Habad clergy and communal leaders, who are careful not to criticize Habad because of the movement's influence in the broader Jewish community and religious hierarchy.[17]

The Merkaz Library

Quite apart from the many thousands of volumes in the AGUCH collection, Schneerson also began to build his own library. Officially organized in 1968, and known as the Merkaz Library or simply as "the Rebbe's library," the collection served him and the movement as a sister library to the collection of Yosef Yitzhak.[18] The materials it contained were largely acquired under the auspices of the movement's educational organization, Merkaz, of which Schneerson was director. Yehuda Krinsky, one of the Rebbe's chief aides, was instrumental in establishing the collection, from the initial fundraising to secure the premises at 766 Eastern Parkway,[19] to the collection of books from individuals and organizations.[20] Some of the most important works in the collection were recovered from the hidden library of Yosef Yitzhak, which had remained in Eastern Europe, and other rare manuscripts and books were given to the library by interested donors. In time, an impressive Judaica library was built, especially after a public call for books to be donated.[21]

Librarians and scholars were employed to edit and collate the material for publication, among them Rabbi Levine, who became the librarian, chief scholar, and senior editor. In addition to cataloguing the collection, Levine edited a regular journal, *Yigdal Torah*, edited a number of manuscripts for publication, and wrote his own works on the history of Habad. The library also ran a small in-house publishing company that published these works and gave a medium of expression for many talented people within the movement.[22]

The Merkaz Library was instrumental in solidifying Schneerson's reputation as a major educator and facilitator of outreach programs for Jews everywhere. It provided Habad scholars with a local outlet for the expression of their scholarly interests, and it served the broader needs of the education of the Hasidism. Symbolically, it declared Schneerson's independence from the AGUCH Library, over which there was so much dispute, and established his leadership in its own right, rather than relying on the authority of his predecessors.

Community Libraries

The establishment of community libraries and collections for general Jewish use was a commonplace program of every Habad community. These libraries provided a place where curious people could read and research Jewish culture. Schneerson's emphasis on book collections expressed itself in a directive that every Hasid should aspire to own as many books as possible, stressing certain works as absolute requirements for every home. The existence of Habad libraries with their careful selection of literature and theological leanings catered to the needs of the diverse communities, and served the additional function of disseminating the ideology of the movement. Control of the community libraries increased the public presence of the movement, and served in many instances as a focus for community building.

The use of publishing and the control of knowledge available through access to Habad literature and libraries were fundamental not only in Schneerson's consolidation of authority over the movement, but in its dissemination across the world. The centrality of libraries and books to the issue of power and authority in Habad is demonstrated most clearly by the legal battle over ownership of Yosef Yitzhak's library. The need Schneerson felt to establish his own collection independent of his predecessor's demonstrates more than the power of access to the manuscripts contained within the library (it raises fundamental questions about the nature and symbolism of authority in Habad).

[1] Because they were given into his charge by *his* Rebbe.

[2] Nissan Mindel, for example, is a well-known Habad scholar and author, and was also one of Schneerson's assistants.

[3] The founding of the Hebrew University in the 1920s along with other Jewish studies programs in later years led to a growing interest in Hasidic literature and ideology. The works of academics like Gershom Scholem, who opened up the academic study of Kabbalah, and Martin Buber, who popularized Hasidic life, created an awareness of these subjects.

[4] The call for the publication of the *Tanya* in all countries of the world caused a huge resurgence of the Hasidic kabbalistic text, and many commentaries and explanatory books on the *Tanya* were also published.

[5] See "Protocols": Intervenor-Defendant testimony, pp. 139–140. Kehot's publications include the writings of all the previous Habad Rebbes, other unpublished Hasidic literature, philosophic manuscripts, books, pamphlets, and quarterly, monthly, and weekly journals. Jacobs notes in "Protocols" that Kehot is the world's largest publisher of Hasidic literature.

[6] Jewish custom encourages the respectful treatment of holy works. An example of this is the order in which they are stacked; generally, this is done in descending order of holiness, with the Torah on the top. Habad Hasidim, however, would allow or even require the *Tanya* to be given deference and placed on top.

[7] See Alan D. Crown, "Jewish Roots of Christian Liturgy," for a similar example of such canonization. The early Church was significantly influenced by Jewish custom. Hence, it might be argued that Jewish movements such as Habad, which resemble Christianity in some respects (most notably their messianist expectations and missionizing), were not influenced by Christianity per se, so much as they preserved in their own system of beliefs and practices the original Jewish tendencies that had influenced Christianity. Additionally, one notes the beginnings or early signs of a new canonization of Habad literature, similar to the Christian canonization of the New Testament, that puts Habad works on par with the generally accepted canon of sacred books.

[8] See Kahn diary.

[9] Habad has had a history of fires, first in Liozna, then Liadi, and later in Lubavitch. Stories tell how the Rebbes took precautions to preserve their books from fire or calamity. Shmuel, the fourth Rebbe, was said to have had chariots on call for the evacuation of books in time of fire. When a fire destroyed part of the library, he berated the Hasidim for not having stolen his books before the disaster and thus saved them from destruction. This story is often used to justify the theft of religious objects, which is called *hasidische ganeiva*, a Hasidic theft.

[10] See Jerome R. Mintz, *Hasidic People*, pp. 281–297, for a description of the legal battle for the ownership of Yosef Yitzhak's library.

[11] See "Protocols": Memorandum Decision and Order, pp. 28–29.

[12] See Herbert Weiner, $9\frac{1}{2}$ *Mystics*.

[13] See "Protocols": Zalman Posner testimony, p. 932. Schneerson spoke harshly of the books being in foreign hands. He used symbolic language to indicate that they were holy, that they represented Zion and Jerusalem, and that they still belonged to Yosef Yitzhak, and certainly not to Barry Gourary. He is quoted as saying, "Anyone who still holds any of my father-in-law's books in Israel must immediately return them to my father-in-law's house."

[14] See "Protocols": Shalom Ber Levine testimony, p. 1051.

[15] See "Protocols": Yehuda Krinsky testimony, p. 694. Krinsky describes how the Habad librarian, Rabbi Chaim Liberman, denied Scholem access to the AGUCH library.

[16] See Shaul S. Deutsch, *Larger Than Life*.

[17] See Binyamin L. Jolkovsky, "The 'Messiah Wars' Heat Up."

[18] See "Protocols": Intervenor-Defendant testimony, p. 106. Rabbi Shalom Ber Levine is the librarian of the Merkaz library, otherwise known as the Rebbe's library.

[19] The location was next-door to the central headquarters of Habad at 770 Eastern Parkway, and in his later years the Rebbe used to sleep at the library over Shabbat, rather than return to his more distant home on President Street.

[20] See "Protocols": Yehuda Krinsky testimony, pp. 639 and 642.

[21] See "Protocols": Shalom Ber Levine testimony, pp. 1138–1139. It describes how the Merkaz library was founded in 1968, how books were sought, and the systematic and organized assembling of the collection.

[22] See "Protocols": Shalom Ber Levine testimony, pp. 1050–1062.

Chapter 17
The Role of Women

Women's and Youth Organizations

The importance of Schneerson's views on women and their role in Hasidism was vitally important to his leadership, not so much practically as ideologically. They demonstrate most emphatically his ability to present old ideas as new and desirable; repackaging what was already found in the tradition without essentially changing its composition. Schneerson displayed his genius regarding the place of women by ideologically elevating their status within Habad while effectively doing little to change the actual nature of their roles or the activities with which women in patriarchal cultures are centrally concerned. While the "advanced," "enlightened," and "modern" status of women in the contemporary Habad movement was widely publicized, thereby presenting a face of egalitarianism to the world, the women of Habad essentially continued their traditional activities under the patriarchy as housewives and mothers. Women in Habad certainly enjoyed a freer lifestyle than women in other schools of ultra-Orthodoxy, and by this standard Schneerson's progressive attitude was truly unprecedented. Nevertheless, his attitude to women was far from modern by the standards of the outside world. As we shall see, while he theoretically acknowledged the spiritual equality of the genders, he did not extend this idea to equality of power, influence, or activity within Habad.

The place of women within Habad was seen as dependent on the essential difference between men and women. As expressed by Rabbi Manis Friedman, the head of the Beis Chana women's yeshiva:

> . . . men and women generally have two fundamentally different approaches to life: the man yearns to "slay the dragons" of injustice and inequity, to bring about perfection through his labors. The woman, in contrast, seeks to protect, nurture, and sustain the godliness and perfection that already exist on earth. Both are needed. . . . Both are equally important.[1]

While this is hardly an official Habad policy statement, the thinking it expresses is found throughout the movement and its approach to the role of women; the two gen-

ders have equally important roles, complementary and mutually supportive, but distinctively different.

The Influences on Schneerson

The Habad movement has traditionally boasted that Torah and Hasidic spirituality
are readily available to women as well as to men, and throughout its history, the
movement has recorded to their credit the role of women in its annals. One such story
is the legend of Menucha Rachel, the daughter of Rabbi Shneur Zalman, who, it is
told, sacrificed her own life in place of her father so that he could continue to lead the
movement during a time of widespread disease. Women have also involved themselves in matters of succession and authority, often supporting one claimant over
another, and the support of the wife of the deceased Rebbe has often been influential
in appointing his successor.

The status of the Rebbe's wife throughout Habad history has often been compared
to the royalty of a queen. In linking women to the princess/queen archetype, Habad
succeeded in psychologically empowering traditional female roles, as we shall see.
The role of the wife of the Rebbe in the contemporary movement is due mainly to
descent from Schneerson stock; the wives of Yosef Yitzhak and Menachem Mendel
were not just women, but women with fine Hasidic lineages, the importance of which
in the question of succession should not be overlooked. It is perhaps because of their
special status that the Schneerson women have been known for their independence.
It is told of Yosef Yitzhak's wife that she was fiercely stubborn and made decisions
for herself,[2] and Schneerson's wife followed in her footsteps. She was the daughter
of Yosef Yitzhak and was evidently independent: she married late, studied at university, drove a car, and worked in a secular environment. These attributes are all
extremely uncharacteristic of Orthodox women, and particularly of a Rebbe's wife,
but once Schneerson became Rebbe, she effectively had no role in Habad, losing
much of her independence and wielding no power, except that of any wife over her
husband. She had no real public function, and did not occupy a position of authority.
In fact, while volumes have been written about her husband, little is known of Chaya
Mousia beyond her name.

The fact that Schneerson's wife had no children was no doubt an important factor
in the relationship of the couple, and perhaps lessened her role in the movement. She
had failed to attain one of the major status symbols for Habad women: namely, the
production of children. The absence of ordinary family life and the company of children no doubt left Schneerson with more time and energy to devote to the direction
of Habad; it also had other effects on his thinking about women.

Schneerson's exposure to the modern world before becoming Rebbe and his university studies no doubt influenced his ideas concerning women and their place in the
Habad movement, although a more pervasive influence was probably the role of
women in traditional European, and specifically Jewish, culture. His advocacy of tra-

ditional roles, albeit viewed from a different ideological vantage influenced by modern public relations and advertising techniques, was a much more significant part of his message in Habad.

The fervor with which Schneerson extolled the virtues of traditional female activities in Habad was surely influenced by the struggle for the State of Israel and the participation and dedication of women there.[3] While the enlistment of women in the army was controversial at the time, Schneerson must have seen parallels with Habad's messianic mission. If women could be mobilized in military action under emergency circumstances, so they not only could, but also must, be enlisted into the ultimate battle for the spiritual survival of Judaism. This military imagery would be used explicitly in Schneerson's youth program, as we will see, but had the more important effect of empowering the traditional roles of women as mothers and homemakers. These were presented time and again as vital fields for the survival of Judaism against the attacks of modernism, secularism, integration, and feminism. The Habad House, under the care of a dedicated Jewish female homemaker, was the most important battlefield for Jewish survival, and the Habad women were in many ways the most important soldiers.

Women's Initiatives

Schneerson, aware of the role of his wife and other women in his own life, was sensitive to women's issues and the potential contribution of women to outreach. He saw a practical role for women in the vital work of outreach, centered largely around their traditional roles of housekeeping, child-rearing, and providing moral support to their husbands. He was able to move these ideas beyond the ideological, and empowered these roles for women so that women themselves became their strongest advocates. Under his guidance, Habad created a network of women's organizations and activated women's consciousness toward religion, spirituality, and outreach, focused largely on a return to traditional values and a rejection of modernity. This proved to be one of his greatest organizational successes, and it became evident that the women of the movement were able to be more than housekeepers and appendages to their husbands. Their work in the home could be expanded into the community through education, hospitality, clerical work, and other activities that have characterized the movement's strengths, particularly in terms of community building and outreach. The power and authority of women remained, however, largely in the home, or in their relationships with their husbands, and little real organizational authority was given them.

Whereas other schools of Hasidism encouraged women to remain at home in the traditional roles of child-rearing and housekeeping, Schneerson encouraged Habad women to expand their activities outside the home and become active in outreach programs. Many of the activities they were encouraged to pursue were devoted to teaching the virtues of traditional values to a new generation of Habad women, especially the influential ba'alei teshuvah. A supportive infrastructure was developed, and from the early 1950s, Habad women's organizations and schools for religious girls were established worldwide.[4] Women were encouraged to study certain Jewish texts, especially those essential to the keeping of Jewish tradition, but they were discouraged from studying Talmud and philosophical/theological texts, in accordance with traditional Orthodox culture. Apart from learning practical laws and observances necessary to their roles as homemakers and mothers—family purity and kashrut, for example—ethics and the *Nach* (i.e., the biblical prophets and writings other than the Pentateuch) form the main part of a woman's education in Habad. Women study practical or inspirational literature, and are not encouraged to study Talmud and halakhah as the men do. In the religious schools, the subjects learned by boys and girls were (and are) different, illustrating the reality behind the myth of intellectual or ideological equality between the genders in Habad.

Even women employed outside the home in outreach functions did not have extensive authority within the movement, and were limited to publishing cookbooks and magazines for women, with spiritually uplifting stories and advice on how to raise children. This is a reflection of the prevalent view in Habad of the essential difference between men and women. Schneerson's token encouragement of mass bat-mitzvahs for girls, a ceremony not commonly observed in mainstream ultra-Orthodoxy, was primarily a publicity stunt, designed to give the appearance of equality but without real significance. Indeed, the celebration of the bat-mitzvah was only common among the newly religious, and did not attract wide support among long-term Habad followers.

Of much greater significance to the women of Habad was Schneerson's empowerment of their active role as the preservers of Jewish tradition. Throughout his reign, he initiated specific campaigns targeted at Jewish observance in the home, for which the woman was given responsibility. Noting the importance of the home in the preservation and continuation of Jewish religious life, Schneerson empowered the role traditionally played by women in Judaism. Elements essential to family observance of religious law were the responsibility of women. The maintenance of a kosher kitchen, the education of children, the observance of family purity, lighting of Shabbat candles, and many other details became the mission of Habad women. There were specific campaigns to publicize the importance of these things for the preservation of Judaism, most significantly the mikvah campaign to encourage ritual bathing after menstruation, and the candle-lighting campaign designed to emphasize the importance of lighting candles on Shabbat night. These campaigns not only gave ideological direction to women but were largely organized by them. This fact is not in itself a demonstration of the power and authority of women in Habad, but simply signifies the emphasis on certain prescribed areas of activity for them.

Schneerson's consolidation of control of Habad through the activation of women had a twofold effect. First, it attracted women into a more committed Jewish life, by making them responsible for maintaining standards for the entire household. They were given ideological responsibility for the preservation of Jewish tradition and practice, and thereby an opportunity to deepen their own commitment to the movement. This commitment was further enhanced by the practical effect of involving women in the vital work of outreach and the administration of the movement, albeit only over aspects of Habad deemed the responsibility of women. Women were not only given an elevated ideological status, but were able to play a part in the redemptive mission of Habad through the dissemination of that mission to others throughout the Jewish world.

The Family

While some women became involved in organizational and administrative work, took positions in the publication arm of Habad, served as counselors or teachers, or took other jobs, many others remained in the home, raising large numbers of children. The role of mother was the primary one women were expected to adopt in Habad, and many Habad women embraced the role enthusiastically. In a literal interpretation of the biblical injunction to "be fruitful and multiply," some families in the movement have up to twenty children, all from the same mother and father, and many parents have between eight and twelve. Indeed, it is considered somewhat irregular within Habad for a family to have fewer than four children, indicating the importance of childbirth and the home in the Habad movement. It also indicates the centrality of the role of motherhood for women; those with a half-dozen or more children generally have little time for anything else, so motherhood has been elevated to something of a status symbol.[5] Motherhood is understood as the primary duty of a Habad woman, and other career decisions may be made, but only after a woman's duties to her family have been completed.[6]

Schneerson often spoke about the evils of family planning as not only against nature but, more importantly, against Torah. He declared:

It is an unfortunate fact that all too often people are influenced by popular opinion rather than by what is right. While many social issues are nothing more than harmless trivialities, there is currently one issue of vital significance that is being treated casually: family planning. It is a destructive practice that has become so widespread as to affect all but the strongest individuals. The ills of family planning cannot be overstated, for it involves such crucial issues as emotional stability, marital harmony, and the entire husband-wife relationship. Ironically, the practice of family planning masquerades under the guise of benevolence, proclaiming concern for the well-being of married couples, and indeed, all humanity.[7]

The movement strongly discourages the use of contraceptives of any type, and except on medical grounds, many Habad rabbis are reluctant to authorize them.

Schneerson condemned family planning on practical as well as ideological grounds. He refuted the view that child-rearing is an expensive undertaking, often cited as a reason for modern families to limit the number of children they produce:

> An appraisal of real motives might be in order. Is it possible that the concern of financial limitation may be a rationalization for living in a particular lifestyle? Contemporary society demands a material standard that is, to say the least, excessive. Is it possible that we have adopted indulgences as necessities and this causes our worry about finances? . . .
>
> The real problem is not one of insufficient personal resources, but rather one of priorities. In many other aspects of life, such as careers and personal achievement, people accept inconvenience and even self-sacrifice to attain their goals. The real problem is that children are regarded not as sources of joy and happiness, but as burdens and impediments to pleasure and "fulfillment."[8]

In Schneerson's own case, the expense or difficulty of raising a family was moot, for two reasons: he did not have children of his own, and he had access to a practically unlimited source of money.

The prevention of pregnancy, whatever the reason, was viewed as inherent evil, or at least as strongly against the will of God, a fundamental act of opposition to the action of the divine:

> A child is not a faucet to be turned on at will. No power on earth can guarantee the birth of a baby. . . . such power is God's and God's alone. . . . the blessing so disdained earlier may not be available later. Take His blessings when He offers them, gratefully, and rest assured that this third Partner is benevolent . . . and can be trusted to know the best time.[9]

Rhetoric of this kind formed a major part of the ideology of Habad toward its women, and is indicative of the idealization of parenthood by a man who did not have any children himself.

The fact that Schneerson did not have children most certainly colored his view of parenthood and the challenges it presents. While it no doubt gave him an appreciation of the negative aspects of life without children, especially as a source of solace and comfort in old age, his lack of a family of his own led to an obvious lack of practical knowledge about the effort involved in raising children and caring for a large family. While many women are able to care for large numbers of children, this lifestyle is not for everyone, but the idealization of motherhood in Habad left few other options.

A "Fresh Approach"

The open approach toward the position of women served to attract them in numbers to Habad ranks. The schools and women's yeshivot that the movement opened attracted not only Habad students but also non-Habad Orthodox, Conservative, and secular girls. This was, in the main, due to the attraction of a private Jewish education, the popularity of which was enhanced by the Habad practice of giving scholarships, thereby providing a free education to a new generation of Jewish women. Many were grateful for the opportunity the scholarships provided, and for the exposure to religious traditions and ideology, and therefore subsequently remained committed to the movement. Secular students often had preconceived notions of Orthodoxy as rigid and inflexible, especially regarding the status and role of women, and were surprised by the openness and spirituality of these institutions. While the main focus was very much on the necessity to marry and produce children, the idealization of these traditional roles served to make them attractive to many who might otherwise been turned away from religious observance. Through Habad, many women were able to find emotional and spiritual expression without being deprived of a traditional family life and a sense of religious fulfillment.[10]

In an era characterized by universal initiatives for female liberation and rejection of old social systems and values, the Habad women's organizations stood firm in presenting a vision of tradition that was positive and progressive, no doubt encouraged by Schneerson. Their claim that the roles of women in Habad were not stifling or oppressive, and in fact served to defend Judaism from dissolution, brought down much feminist criticism.[11]

Beyond the public relations "scoop" of women defending traditional social roles, the activities of Habad women served other purposes for the movement. The involvement of women in the outreach initiatives of the movement was particularly influential. It allowed many women both within the movement and outside to feel comfortable and legitimized in the roles they felt had been assigned to them by nature. One result was a quantitative increase in women's activities in Habad, and an increase in the number of women recruited into the Habad community. On the other hand, it increased the pressure on some women to produce and raise more children than they desired, limited career opportunities, and denied many who wanted something more from life than decades of household tasks. Many of these women no doubt drifted to the periphery of the movement, having an emotional or social connection with Habad, but unable (or unwilling) to fully participate.

As Judaism is in many ways a home- and family-oriented culture, and is focused around communal celebrations, festivals, rituals, and customs, the women's active participation in these events, combined with a growing sense of personal mission, made the culture richer for many. Visitors to a Habad household are frequently impressed by the activity of the women of the family beyond their child-rearing skills. Children growing up in a dynamic female environment, active in the ideology of Habad, often develop a unique identification with the movement, and in the years before his death they developed a love of Schneerson and his mission that was imbued in them from a very young age. Thus, the socialization of the next generation of Habad Hasidim could not have been carried out as effectively without commitment from the women of the movement. Habad's enterprising spirit and sense of uniqueness could not have been achieved without the active socialization of women into active, rather than passive, roles.

Today's Habad women are at the forefront of the movement's ideological bandwagon, and are vocal on many issues, albeit only those considered to be of interest to women or pertinent to their role in the movement. They plan children's educational curricula, or at least those for the girls, and advertisements for the movement,[12] and have been involved in politics and demonstrations for government support of parochial schools, in particular the schools for religious girls.[13] The addition of women into the outreach ranks served the practical purpose of doubling the human resources available to the movement for outreach and other activities. Women were sent on emissary work, not only accompanying their husbands but also teaching classes to women on women's issues in the communities to which they were sent. According to one of these women,

> My work complements my husband's, but we do different things, reflecting the local need and our own personal interest.
>
> I teach two classes each week for women. One class is studying *Pirkey Avoth* (*Ethics of the Fathers*) and the other revolves around the Torah portion of the week. We also do frequent hospital visitations and have a monthly program with a different woman speaker for each occasion. . . . We reach out through programming by women, about women, and for women.[14]

Teaching (and learning) is not equivalent to what men do within Habad because the needs of women are regarded as being different from those of their husbands. Philosophy and theology are rarely discussed, except where they touch on the role of the woman in a Jewish household.

The importance of women in Habad's outreach efforts is evident from the fact that many of those sent as emissaries of the movement are rabbi-rebbetzin teams.[15] The rebbetzin is particularly useful to the movement by attracting the women of the local community by organizing social functions, women's lectures, providing hospitality (especially on Shabbat), and cooking. Many fledgling communities have rapidly become dependent on the rebbetzin because of the increasingly important role they have molded for themselves in the building of the community. On many occasions, a rabbi's appointment in a synagogue has been dependent on the amiability of his wife, although the desire to marry a well-connected woman (i.e., one from a distinguished or powerful family) betrays the true value of women within Habad. As Schneerson rose to prominence at least in part due to his marriage to Chaya Mousia, others have sought to marry into important Habad families to secure positions or power and influence.[16]

When Schneerson died, the preservative role of women became obvious to everyone, for Habad women's organizations demonstrated a united front in encouraging continuity of activity, and proposed practical strategies for achieving this. Many of the movement's men, by contrast, entered into debate about the best course of action, and effectively decided nothing. This, more than anything else, perhaps best demonstrates the different roles assigned to the genders in Habad: the women are active and action-oriented, and are concerned for the continuity of the tradition; whereas the men concentrate on learning and debate.

As a consequence of more than a generation of education and socialization, many Habad women feel completely natural in their social and family functions. Indeed, the female role in Habad is so firmly consolidated that many young girls would not consider marrying outside the movement, because this would necessitate an end to the expression of their identities through outreach.[17] Within the movement, the role of women as the anchor to their family is a significant part of their identity. Stories are often told of devoted women ensuring the continuing observance and deepening commitment of their husband and family,[18] and thus in many ways women are the backbone of the movement. Because of their importance to the survival of Habad into the next generation, Schneerson always insisted that women should never forget the traditions of modesty, observance, and dedication to the family.

Habad's treatment of women opened the way for other Orthodox groups to recognize the importance of actively integrating women into most aspects of Jewish life, at least ideologically,[19] through recognition of their central role in the continuity of Jewish observance. While many women in the broader Jewish community are deferring marriage and family in favor of the pursuit of a profession, Schneerson placed marriage and family as the first priorities of a woman's life. Through this, he ensured that the movement he led would continue to be a force in future generations, and he solicited the support of a generation of dedicated women.

Educational Contributions

The involvement of women in the education of Habad youth led to breakthroughs in Orthodox teaching techniques. One example is the creation of the Zivot Hashem (literally "Armies of God") youth movement, which was strongly supported by the women's organizations. Observant women went from door to door to less religious households, distributing educational material for children designed by Zivot Hashem and encouraging them to send their children to religious schools.

Much discussion took place in the movement in the 1960s concerning the future of religious education. Some critics raised the issue of the lack of Jewish role models for children, and the implications this had for Jewish education and the development of awareness of Judaism among the movement's children.[20] Many ways of rectifying this problem were discussed. The Habad women's organization proposed the creation of educational material celebrating Jewish values, and also put forward the idea of tapping into the infatuation of American children with superheroes by developing a Jewish equivalent.[21] The result was a series of comic books, the most famous being *Mendy and the Golem*. Mendy, a common name in Habad (it is a diminutive of Menachem Mendel, the Rebbe's name), was a strictly religious boy who had many adventures, and always emerged victorious without sacrificing his religious commitment.

These works were the fruits of women's initiatives, produced by mothers who best understood the needs of their many children and needed suitable literature to help them instill traditional Jewish values in the next generation. The comic books and other educational literature, presented women in equality to men and treated them respectfully; the women and girls in the stories could do everything the boys did and still hold to their religious commitment.[22] In this way, the principles of equality and female activism entered the consciousness of the next generation of Hasidim.

Youth Organization: The Principle

The principle of youth education is a common rabbinic requirement and important in Jewish tradition. Its techniques are addressed in talmudic, halakhic and moral works.[23] However, little is known about the intricacies of the educational system in early Jewish history, or whether there were youth movements and organizations for youngsters.

Youth education was imperative in the development of Hasidism. The Ba'al Shem Tov himself, who was described as a schoolteacher, told tales to his students and influenced them from a very young age to become Hasidim. Shneur Zalman, the founder of Habad, wrote on the psychological development of children and the importance of education in their foundational years.[24] Shalom Dov Ber, the fifth Habad Rebbe, dedicated himself to developing techniques of education for children to meet the challenge of modernism. All of this shows that throughout the history of Hasidism and Habad, the leaders were aware of the processes of change and the impact of outside influences on their children. In Europe, the focus was largely on limiting the influence of the outside world on the education of Hasidic children, but the challenges faced by Habad in the United States were much greater. American leaders, including Yosef Yitzhak and Schneerson, were forced to confront a challenging, secular environment, where the pressures to assimilate were great, even from within the broader Jewish community. They needed to consolidate the hold of Hasidism on the youth of the movement, lest they leave the faith and destroy the future of the movement.

East European Jewry was famous for its heder system of education, which generally involved a small group of male students taught by a teacher; only the more fortunate and gifted children would continue their studies in a yeshiva.[25] Transplanting this system to the United States and the Diaspora was a challenge, especially with the expansion of the population, and it was not known whether the system could be orchestrated on a large scale. Indeed, many believed the system was doomed to failure in the early stages of multiculturalism in America. State curriculum standards had to be maintained, and assimilation was a buzz word for immigrants.

In the face of secular and assimilationist pressure, new methods were required to attract the youth to retain their Orthodox observance. Although the heder system was retained, new methods of education were clearly necessary if Hasidism was to have a future in the modern world. Yosef Yitzhak was not opposed to the introduction of modern educational techniques in theory, but Schneerson was quick to put them into practice. He appreciated the absolute priority that needed to be given to the education and socialization of proud Hasidic youth.

Within a year of his election, Schneerson established a Habad youth movement called Tzeirei Habad in Israel, in order to give structure to Israeli Hasidim who were suffering adjustment problems in Israel in the wake of national independence.[26] He also started a string of institutions and schools for boys and girls worldwide, including the Zivot Hashem youth movement. Translated as "Armies of God," the name empowered Hasidic youth to fight for spiritual values against secularization, modernism, and assimilation.

Symbolism of the Organization

When the secular State of Israel was created by irreligious soldiers and secularists, many Hasidim, especially those living in Israel, suffered from disillusionment. The Orthodox tradition had largely opposed the secular Zionists before the establishment of Israel, and Habad was a strong voice in this criticism. Hasidim worldwide could not help but rejoice in the almost miraculous War of Independence in 1948, but they suffered a subtle humiliation. They were unable to openly express their joy in Jewish triumph, because the victory was not theirs but had been won by the secular Zionists. Despite their intensely anti-Zionist ideology, many Hasidic groups retained a quiet admiration for the Israeli army, idealized as proud Jews fighting against all odds in a desperate fight for Jewish survival. The idea of a strong Jew was made especially attractive by the long history of Jewish persecution and helplessness culminating in the Holocaust, for which religious authorities were at least partly responsible.[27] The news of Israel's military victory stirred up images of redemption and seemed to foreshadow the advent of the long-dreamed messianic era. Clearly, there was a deep-seated admiration felt for Israel's defenders, even if the irreligious nature of the state prevented formal expression or acknowledgment of this admiration. Hence they remained in a state of ideological limbo vis-à-vis the new State of Israel.

The Zivot Hashem movement founded by Schneerson, with its military uniforms, hierarchy, bravado, and promotion system, was something of a reenactment of the

Zionist battle, indicating the waging of a spiritual struggle for Jewish survival to parallel the physical fight for Israel. This war, however, was far more important than the physical battle for statehood. The struggle for Jewish survival was the true battle, and its success would be achieved through emergency Jewish education and re-awakening. In this way, the Hasidic vision of complete spiritual and physical redemption would be achieved. The Habad movement adopted the methods of the Israeli youth movements for all Habad communities worldwide.

Zivot Hashem had clearly military overtones in name, content, award system, and imagery. Physical militarism was, however, far from its intention. Habad Hasidim are pacifists in everything but ideology; the only militancy they imagined was the army led by the mashiach-king, a military general who would take them to the Holy Land and fight for Hasidism. The military imagery of Zivot Hashem made it possible for a downcast people, victims of post-Holocaust persecution, to feel like victors. The organization embodied the Habad ideology of spirituality acting in the world and the pursuit of achievement. Moreover, the military imagery imbued Habad's youth with a sense of emergency and immediate danger to the Jewish people that required a battle of cosmic proportions. It required the mobilization of the same resources, dedication sacrifice, and heroism needed for a real battle. When critics denigrated the organization's military trappings, Schneerson explained that for him the movement's sole purpose was to bring children closer to God and obedience to Jewish tradition.[28]

By imbuing the military organization, motivation, and paraphernalia of the Zivot Hashem youth movement with spiritual symbolism, Schneerson legitimized the interests and activities of religious youth.[29] They could proudly identify themselves with religious observance, and enlist in the ranks of a visionary army fighting the war for Jewish survival, like the envied Israeli soldier. Now young religious Jews could proudly wear uniforms and fight with unbridled pride for Jewish values.

The Growth of Zivot Hashem

The American obsession with the military assisted in the success and expansion of the movement, and Zivot Hashem quickly became one of its most effective institutions. Schneerson launched a newly revised Zivot Hashem program in 1980, to cope with the needs of expansion. The youth group was run with military efficiency, and so was tightly structured and well organized. The aim of the group was to bring the long-awaited messianic redemption by doing good deeds and mitzvot as commanded by Jewish law.

The rewards and motivation for doing good deeds was promotion to ever-higher ranks in the Army of God. Members received identification cards and uniforms, including hats. They were asked to perform missions for the preservation of Judaism, such as studying Torah and writing essays on Jewish history and genealogy. Projects involving American politics and lobbying were also undertaken by the movement's youth,[30] to give them an idea of their place in the modern world.

Over time, and with Schneerson's encouragement for Habad followers to have large families, the Zivot Hashem grew considerably. Although it is difficult to estab- lish accurate statistics for the movement, official figures estimate that within six months of its founding 40,000 children had joined the movement, and by 1988 this had grown to an estimated 300,000 children.[31] It has branches in 234 cities around the world,[32] ran radio programs, a telephone dial-in for Jewish information and sto- ries, homework assistance groups, and provided scholarships for members to attend youth camp. It organized rallies and festival gatherings for large numbers of people, had its own publishing company, and communicated with its membership with a jour- nal called the *Moshiah Times*.

Zivot Hashem took instructions from Schneerson. He was the head of the Army and its military commander-in-chief. As with other branches of the Habad movement, Schneerson's regular *sichot* were used to derive the movement's orders and strategies. After being given their initial direction by Schneerson, the leaders of the movement began to develop their own missions within the ideology of Habad's outreach and educational goals. Missions were derived from Schneerson's ideology, and cam- paigns were initiated to implement his vision for Habad and Judaism.

Schneerson expressed his respect for the Army on a number of occasions, and sup- ported its goal of instilling pride in Judaism and Hasidism. He spent a great deal of his time meeting children, handed out dollars or coins to them, and saluted his Army in street parades. A story is told of parents who wrote to the Rebbe for advice about their son, who had been stricken by illness. Schneerson reputedly promoted him in the Zivot Hashem, and explained to the boy that his new rank entailed new and holy responsibilities. God would grace the boy with health and blessings so that he could achieve his mission.[33]

Parents and teachers were actively involved in propagating Zivot Hashem, and thus it served to bind parents more closely to their children and involved them in their chil- dren's lives much more deeply. Parents were often given hints by the leaders of the movement on how to encourage their children to do mitzvot. They were advised to tell certain types of stories to their children, provide them with appropriate play items including toys and dolls, and provide pictures of role models for their children to emulate. They were encouraged to endorse heroes who kept Jewish law,[34] employ army themes in discipline, military/religious jargon in speech, and so on.[35] In time, Schneerson developed a policy calling for all playthings to be educational and suit- able for use in Jewish households. By this means, he sought to lessen exposure and attachment to non-kosher animals such as teddy bears, and characters like Porky Pig and Mickey Mouse, replacing them with kosher substitutes.

In order to help parents find religiously acceptable playthings for their children, a Zivot Hashem shop was opened in Crown Heights in 1983. It stocked Kosher Kids toys and clothes, Jewish games, puzzles, pencils, books, videos, stickers, posters, T- shirts, educational materials, and children's fiction. The items sold by this store, and encouraged throughout the Habad movement worldwide, served to provide parents with guidance as to which toys were appropriate and enabled children to develop strong role models. In addition, the store served the social role of giving employment to sales personnel and production assistants. The demands of an in-house publishing industry, toy manufacture, and production of other educational devices for children provided jobs for many Hasidim worldwide.

The most important effect of the Zivot Hashem for the long-term survival of the Habad movement was its role in the consolidation of many tens of thousands of Hasidic and non-Hasidic youth to the service of Schneerson's ideals from a very young age. For the children growing up in the movement after his election as Rebbe, Schneerson played the role of general, hero, and chief of staff, further consolidating their connection to him as they grew to maturity, adopted more of the movement's religious ideology, and participated in its outreach efforts.

For non-Hasidic youth, the Army of God movement in their communities exposed them to an exciting military/religious hierarchy, fired their imaginations, and offered a dynamic picture of Hasidic life. In many cases Schneerson remained an important figure in their lives even after they had grown up and moved into non-Hasidic professions and lifestyles. While they may not have formed a lifelong devotion to Habad during the years of their membership in the Zivot Hashem, some were later moved to contribute to the movement for sentimental reasons.

[1] Edward Hoffman, *Despite All Odds*, p. 83.

[2] See "Protocols": Hana Gourary testimony, p. 2846. "My mother was a very proud woman. She didn't consult with anyone. She didn't let anyone make decisions for her in anything that she did."

[3] The desperate military struggle that brought Israel into existence involved the enlisting of women into the army, an event practically unprecedented in modern military history.

[4] The Beit Rivka School in Melbourne, established in 1953, was the first of these.

[5] See Hoffman, *Despite All Odds*, p. 89.

[6] Ibid., pp. 92–93.

[7] Ibid., p. 90.

[8] Ibid.

[9] Ibid., pp. 89–90.

[10] Something of the spirit of this fulfillment is expressed by Jeanette Kupfermann in "How I Nearly Succumbed to the Charm of the Rebbe." She observes: "By night I studied a sort of modified cabbalism. . . . By day, I watched women peel onions, cope with nine or 10 children, and take part in door-to-door campaigns to revive symbols such as Friday-night candles. . . . I remember one woman, a convert, arriving late for the study group, wig askew, milk leaking, but radiant, having just given birth to her sixth or seventh baby, and apologizing for not having studied the appropriate text the night before." This sort of breathless enthusiasm seems to be commonplace, especially among female converts to the movement.

[11] See ibid.

[12] A massive media campaign in Israel in support of the messianic arrival was carried out in 1993, and was partly planned and executed by Mrs. T. Bolton, wife of a yeshiva dean. The liberal attitude toward working women is unusual for the ultra-Orthodox community.

[13] Bonnie J. Morris, "The Children's Crusade." Morris notes that the lack of alternative funding for the Habad religious girls'schools was a motivating factor behind the pressure on the government by Habad women. This surely indicates the Habad view on the education of girls; funding is available for the education of boys, whereas their sisters have to rely on government support.

[14] Hoffman, *Despite All Odds*, p. 86.

[15] A rebbetzin is the wife of a rabbi.

[16] One example of this is the minor dynasty of Pinchus Feldman, Schneerson's original emissary to Sydney, Australia. Feldman built the community in Sydney from practically nothing, and he, his sons, and his sons-in-law now control most of the city's Orthodox, and not just Habad, synagogues. This situation is mirrored in many other communities worldwide.

[17] Other Hasidic groups allow Hasidic intermarriage, and it is quite common. Habad women, by contrast, rarely marry non-Habad men.

[18] See *Jerusalem Post International Edition*, no. 1836, advertising section. Joseph Gutnick describes his wife as the primary force behind his charitable work. She constantly encourages him to give more than he otherwise would.

[19] See Netty Gross, "Tradition Can Wait."

[20] Morris, "Children's Crusade," p. 340.

[21] Ibid., p. 339.

[22] Ibid., p. 341. Morris notes that the Habad comic book *Mendy and the Golem* often portrays women in a very positive and complimentary light. In one story, a mother is studying Kabbalah, an occupation traditionally reserved for men.

[23] See, for example, Deuteronomy 6:7: "Teach them to your children when you rise and when you go to sleep." See also Pirkei Avot, Maimonides' letter to his son Avraham, and Shalom Dov Ber's *Hanoch Le-Na'ar*.

[24] See Moshe Hallamish, *Netiv Le-Tanya*.

[25] See David E. Fishman, "Preserving Tradition in the Land of Revolution." He discusses Yosef Yitzhak's leadership tactics in Soviet Russia.

[26] See Mordechai M. Laufer, *Yemei Melech*, vol. 3, which contains a series of letters from Israel asking Schneerson to solve their problems and take over the leadership of their community.

[27] Many Hasidic rabbis advised their followers to remain in Eastern Europe and opposed the Zionists. A famous adage of these rabbis played on the name *Polin*, "Poland," as meaning *Po-Lin*, "here we will sleep."

[28] See Morris, "Children's Crusade," p. 339. She quotes Schneerson's letter in *Di Yiddishe Heim* 24:2 (1984).

[29] Morris, "Children's Crusade," p. 343.

[30] Ibid., p. 335. She points out that the movement involved itself in American political issues, such as prayer in the public schools. Members of the Zivot Hashem youth group were told to write to President Reagan to lobby for this purpose.

[31] Ibid. Morris quotes the *New York Times* (February 7, 1989).

[32] See *Zivot Hashem Handbook*, p. 13.

[33] Morris, "Children's Crusade," p. 338.

[34] Ibid., p. 341. She describes how the market for children's educational items, particularly comic books, expanded beyond the Habad community.

[35] Ibid., p. 339.

Part Four
The Succession

Chapter 18
The Issue of Succession

The Passing of the Rebbe

Although Schneerson was ninety-two when he passed on June 12, 1994, and his health had been steadily decreasing for many years, his death sent shockwaves through the worldwide Habad community. The idea that Schneerson could or would die was not one that had been entertained by his followers before its occurrence. Mere mention of the possibility of the Rebbe dying was akin to heresy of the worst kind. Schneerson was spoken of only in terms of his imminent revelation as the mashiach, and the announcement of his messiahship was what was looked forward to each day, not his death.

When he finally died, a siren was sounded in Crown Heights, the same siren that had once called the faithful Hasidim to the headquarters at 770 Eastern Parkway for *farbrengen* or other public events with Schneerson. Due to his illness and incapacity since suffering a stroke in 1992, the siren had not been heard for years. When it was sounded in the early hours of the morning, amidst the anticipation of redemption for which the followers had waited so long, many believed that it was the sound of the shofar[1] and the call of the mashiach. When people arrived at 770 and were told that Schneerson had passed, most not could immediately comprehend. They had been fervently awaiting his arrival as the mashiach, and his death simply could not happen. The immediate reaction for some was to consider it a sign; every other world event until this time had been considered a step on the way to mashiach, so now that Schneerson had seemingly died, this marked the final test to be endured before his imminent arrival.

Nevertheless, the people were confused; there was no word or public statement from the rabbis, and there was only silence from the leaders of Habad's various organizations. The only action possible was to attend the funeral and await guidance from their leaders as to its long-term implications. The feeling at the funeral was confused. While most people walked in procession in the silence of mourning, broken occasionally by the loud wailing of individuals overcome with grief, some stood in small groups on the sidelines, dancing, drinking, and rejoicing: the mashiach, after all, was on his way.[2] The juxtaposition between these two groups foreshadowed the wider rift between messianists and non-messianists that has developed in the years since.

The funeral itself was the traditional funeral of a Hasidic Rebbe, albeit much larger in size and prominence, for Schneerson was an established Jewish leader, a man respected and admired worldwide. Tens of thousands of Hasidic Jews flocked to New York to attend the funeral. In Israel, the United States Embassy opened on Sunday to provide visas,[3] and Israel's national airline, El Al, scheduled an extra flight so that 450 Israeli Habad followers could attend the funeral.[4] Ben-Gurion International Airport, outside Tel Aviv, swarmed with Schneerson's followers, willing to pay cash for tickets in order to arrive in New York in time for the funeral. Beside the thousands of Hasidic mourners, major dignities from the United States and Israel also attended, and dozens of others sent messages of condolence and sympathy for the loss suffered by the Habad community. New York's mayor, Rudolph Giuliani; Benjamin Netanyahu, leader at the time of the Israeli opposition party, Likud; Gad Ya'acobi, Israel's ambassador to the United States; Colette Avital, Israeli consul general in New York; and Lester Pollack and Malcolm Hoenlein, the chairman and executive vice chairman, respectively, of the Conference of Presidents of Major American Jewish Organizations, were among those personally present in New York.[5] Israeli Prime Minister Yitzhak Rabin and Yisrael Lau, Chief Rabbi of Israel for the Ashkenazim, both sent public statements of condolence.

The funeral came at a time of great confusion and trial for Habad, for its members were trying to deal with the question of how to proceed without a Rebbe. As we shall see, some searched Schneerson's discourses for clues as to his intentions for the movement; others planned to carry on outreach and other activities as though no change in direction was necessary. Still others awaited his imminent return from death and assumption of the mantle of mashiach. "The Rebbe will arise soon . . . just wait and see," was a common sentiment in a community inculcated in the spirit of messianic expectation. Initially, he was to have arisen on the day after his passing, but when this did not eventuate, predictions were extended, first to the next week, then a month, a year, and some messianists now proclaim that he will rise sometime before the passing of the current generation. The fact of the matter remains, however, that Schneerson did not rise; the Habad movement's hopes, dreams, and beliefs were shattered, and there was no clear successor to the leadership. Even now, almost a decade after the event, many issues surrounding the question of succession are still unresolved, and the Jewish world is keenly watching to see whether the movement will survive the death of its Rebbe, who for many of its Hasidim was also their mashiach. How the question of leadership is being resolved by the Habad movement is a complicated matter, and the patterns of leadership and continuity that are emerging are complex.

When Prophecy Fails

The following are three personal accounts of the disappointment and reconciliation experienced by Habad Hasidim. The first account relates to the night of the expected messianic coronation of Schneerson. He was expected to stand up after the evening prayers and reveal himself as the messiah.

I was a guest in the home of one of the Rebbe's secretaries but was not at all familiar with Hasidic behavior so I was not sure if it was normal or not. That night there was to be a big gathering—an event—the Rebbe was going to be coronated and declared the king messiah by his followers. Though he was already crippled by a stroke for a few years he was expected to stand up out of his wheel chair after the evening prayers and declare his status. It appears that this event had been arranged by a faction within the community and there was some disagreement over it. There was excitement in the street, the secretary's home was full of people and there was a live link to 770 where the Rebbe was praying the evening prayers with thousands of Hasidim.

The streets had a carnival atmosphere about them, venders were selling trinkets, key rings and the like with the Rebbe's picture attached. Everyone was expectant. The Rebbe was wheeled out in his chair to evening prayers and when it concluded there was great expectation in the home as we watched the screen to see if he would stand up. After the prayers he was wheeled back out without event.

People's reactions were subtle. I expected a stronger reaction to the disappointment, discussion and debate. Though there was clear disappointment, no one wanted to show it. It was a bit like your team losing a football game; they still supported the team, still loved and rooted for it and did not wish to criticize its performance but they were obviously upset. The subject of their gathering there that evening was not mentioned, people moved around the house for a bit longer and then left.[6]

Another example was the day after the news of the Rebbe's death.

I was sitting in the shul and a friend of mine, a young rabbi of around thirty, the dean of the yeshiva came in. He was a big meshichist although opposed to the coronation ceremony led by strongly theatrical messianists of a different political camp. A few days earlier he had told me how the Rebbe was Moshiach and will not and could not die, quoting sources for it from his writings and other places. He came straight up to me and said "The Rebbe is going to arise soon . . . just wait and see." . . . to expressions of doubt that I raised and that it sounded nearly perfectly like what Christians speak about Jesus, he entirely disregarded the comparison and insisted that this view is possible and supported in the Talmud. He looked quite determined and upbeat. People were looking for direction, not really knowing what to think and waiting for someone to come up with a bright idea. This one did not really seem to be it, although it began catching on in the absence of anything else. . . . I am not sure when I heard the next proposal ("The Rebbe is not dead, he is still alive, it's all an illusion, just as the children of Israel thought that Moses was dead and so they built the golden calf, we have to have faith, the Moses of the generation is not dead"). It could have been the same day but perhaps a few days later. I remember thinking to myself that the young and ambitious emissary that espoused this view was more uppity, somehow his demeanor more reassuring. He was a scholar and was thrashing a path for those who didn't know what to think, his view was odd but somehow potent and either before hand or as a result of this, he began leading a distinct camp in the city. . . . That evening we gathered into the house of the leading Habad rabbi of the city, my friend's father. He spoke about how the Rebbe had predicted this occurrence and played us a tape of the Rebbe speaking and how he instructed that the Hasidic rabbis of every city should form a beis din who should answer all the questions and problems of the Hasidim of that city. He also spoke about how there can be a private theology and a public theology in regards to the Rebbe, he seemed to be pleading with a group of hard line meshichtim not to make their views public. He told us that even if we believed the Rebbe was the messiah the best thing was to keep this as a private theology. . . . Later, his son, my friend, changed his views again. . . . "The Rebbe was the potential messiah, the Talmud recognized the possibility for zaddikim to rise from the dead and it was possible." But he didn't necessarily commit to any one view. I assumed that whatever view he really believed, he would not make it public and then observed over time that his public persona just took over and he ceased to be troubled by it too much.[7]

A final example of the difficulty for one Hasid after Schneerson's death is as follows:

Following a pleasant family Sunday, I'd made my way to synagogue for evening prayers. I noticed a younger friend sitting giving a shiur, he seemed to have been crying in the past few minutes as his eyes and nose were red, however he ignored my inquiry as to his well-being. On entering the study hall, the mood was morose but there was nothing I could pin this down to, no one seemed to be willing to inform me as to what was wrong. Finally a rabbi a few years my senior informed me "The Rebbe is back in 770." At first I could not understand why this would be a cause for depression, it took him a few repetitions of the same phrase before I could understand that the impossible had happened. It was still an unthinkable mental leap to associate death with the Rebbe, we sat around theorizing, would there be a funeral? How could there be? One cannot simply bury the Rebbe! How could one, he is an immortal, the Moshiach! As news filtered in that a funeral was scheduled for the following morning Australian time, those of us who would have tried to fly to New York at any expense groaned inwardly, as the short time interval would have made this impossible. Not that I felt I was going to a funeral at all, rather I had a feeling of being in a limbo even worse than the previous few years had brought. Years where the Rebbe's health had teetered to and fro, with our hopes clinging to daily faxed reports and a telephone hotline news service established in Crown Heights, where we would avidly check updates, expecting any moment for the Rebbe to simply "snap out of it" and proclaim his revealed status as the messiah. For too long now things had remained static, and while in one way the sense of uncertainty had been heightened by this unexpected turn of events, I remember assuring friends that "the only predictable thing about the Rebbe is his unpredictability," and that here it seemed we were faced with an event, the only possible closure to which would have been an utterly miraculous one. I wandered in a shell-shocked daze, I left synagogue and drove homewards, remembering I'd left a coat behind, I turned back towards shul, only to drive three times around the block. I was so utterly shattered that each time, after remembering my coat and turning the car, I had already forgotten where I was going and why, only to remember once again on the way home.

I went to sleep that night heartened by my wife and children, who had laid out their Sabbath best to go to a television station early the next morning where a satellite link of events would take place. I waited for sleep feeling that we stood at the brink of a moment which might well change the course of human history—the Messianic redemption, yet the world seemed so familiar, so mundane, unaware of the cataclysmic events embracing it. The satellite linkup destroyed me emotionally. After watching the doors of 770 intently, the doors through which I'd seen the Rebbe stride so many times, the sight of his study table, cut up into a coffin and topped by his *kapote* [black Hasidic garb] and hat was too much to bear. I remember giving a cry of pain and dissolving in tears. The rabbinic leadership present seemed surprisingly devoid of emotion, and later that day at a private function, I was horrified that out of keeping with practice of hasidim worldwide and many in Australia, were not wearing the torn lapel of the mourner, but had changed into fresh clothing. As I and my friends sat, still stunned by events, we were amazed to hear this rabbi announce that the entire Moshiach campaign had been a mistake foisted upon the Rebbe by his hasidim, who in their overconfidence had built expectations to an unreasonable extent which they would now have to come to grips with. I and those of my friends who had kept up with the Rebbe's talks over the past few years were aghast. It had been the Rebbe himself who was the most militant and controversial messianist. It seemed incredible that within a day of his burial, his stated desires could be so totally, dishonestly and disingenuously misrepresented to the majority of our community, who not having learned the material themselves accepted this rabbi's version as correct. I undertook to become a rallying point. I would study the Rebbe's talks of the past few years obsessively, underlining, learning by rote, looking up the cited sources, and would become the avenue of honest information regarding the Rebbe simply through knowledge of primary sources, for those people whom this rabbi obviously wished to keep from accessing such knowledge. This I achieved, but nothing solved the aching underlying question which time only served to heighten. Where was the Rebbe? Not the physical body, that we knew, but where was our immortal spiritual guide?[8]

What Is Transfer?

Over the millennia, there have developed a variety of formulas for the appointment of leaders in Judaism, from the elders of the original twelve tribes to the appointment of rabbis to the Sanhedrin. In the main, the methods of appointment elevated the middle rung of the religious hierarchy to positions of greater prominence, but, especially in the history of Hasidism, the method of "transfer" to the highest echelons of leadership is not yet clear. One thing, however, is clear, and that is that stronger groups, movements, and cultures throughout history have developed a successional mechanism of one sort or other, so as not to exhaust their energy and resources in a power struggle in the event of the death of a leader.

In the Habad movement, there still is no defined pattern of transferral and succession to the position of Rebbe, apart from the fact that leadership largely appears to emerge from within the Schneerson family. From the origins of the movement, Habad Rebbes often succeeded to the leadership by virtue of their family heritage, supported by factors such as scholarship and organizational ability. While not the only definitive pattern of transfer in Habad, this method was the primary one until the current generation. The reasons for its breakdown in the contemporary movement are many, but hinge primarily on two factors: the presence of a highly charismatic leader in the person of Menachem Schneerson; and the dilemma presented by a leader who dies without producing an heir or nominating a successor. Such factors as messianism, diffusion of authority, and other elements of ideology and administration only serve to further complicate matters.

Quite apart from the question of succession, the nature or extent of the authority of the Rebbe was not always clearly defined in the movement. Shneur Zalman, the founder of Habad, delegated authority to a close circle of family and disciples. Menachem Mendel Shachna, known as the Zemakh Zedek, gave the license and privilege of interpreting Hasidic teachings in public to important Hasidim, and thus delegated some of his own authority to a wider circle of initiates. Shalom Dov Ber started to train and delegate authority to his son and successor, Yosef Yitzhak, from the age of thirteen, and also trained scholars and rabbis for other public positions. The practice of delegating authority to subordinates continued under the leadership of Menachem Mendel Schneerson, who lived and died without progeny, but delegated authority to a wide circle of activists throughout the world. He also broke precedent by encouraging the mass ordination of rabbis and training of religious functionaries. The question of succession is therefore made all the more ambiguous by the nature of the authority inherent in the position of Rebbe.

When Does Transfer Occur?

The nature of the zaddik, the important role played by the intended successor to the leadership of the movement while under the guidance of his predecessor, and what might be considered in many ways the gradual transfer of authority from one generation to the next—all these factors sometimes make it difficult to determine when a transfer of authority takes place.

In Habad thought, the zaddik is not seen as inheriting his status at some point in his lifetime, but is endowed with it at birth.[9] If this is the case, then the act of accepting the mantle of Rebbe after the death of his predecessor does not endow him with additional spiritual force, potency, or authority. Rather, the acceptance of authority symbolizes the social and spiritual commitment the zaddik has taken upon himself to guide the movement. Its public nature also serves to reveal this commitment, and the incumbent's true "saintly" nature, to the Hasidim.[10] The act of receiving the mantle is usually signified by the public recitation of the new Rebbe's first Hasidic discourse, as occurred when Schneerson was appointed.[11] This is the first of many acts that are part of the communal responsibilities of public office.

The acceptance of public office, and hence the succession, can stretch over a period of time, a fact that is generally ignored by Hasidim who prefer to see the act of taking on the leadership as a supernatural event that occurs immediately with the carrying out of certain prescribed rituals. However, the reality behind the succession throughout the history of Habad is one of gradual acculturation and acceptance of the burden of the role. Shneur Zalman did not ascend to prominence immediately after the death of his predecessor, nor did Dov Ber, Shmuel, or Shalom Dov Ber. As we have seen, Schneerson himself for some time rejected all suggestions that he assume the leadership after the death of Yosef Yitzhak, and spent a year building support in the movement until most factions of Habad accepted him.

The act of acceptance, whether sudden or gradual, would therefore appear to be the decisive factor in the transfer of authority. Obviously, transfer only takes place with the acceptance of the authority of the new Rebbe by the Hasidim, and even then requires the candidate to accept the duties attendant to the position. According to Habad theory, the process of acceptance by the Rebbe is necessary in order to prove his worthiness; when finally he annuls himself to the will of the people and the will of God, he becomes a conduit for godliness to sustain the life of his community. By accepting the yoke of leadership, the zaddik signifies the complete nullification of his own will to that of God. His lack of ego, acquired through the process of *bitul*, makes him an ideal vessel for the manifestation of godly light.

Whatever the situation, the ultimate transfer of authority is only made possible by the death of the previous Rebbe. According to the *Tanya*, the death of a zaddik has a significant impact on the material world, far greater than his impact during his lifetime.[12] After death, the zaddik's bodily limitations can no longer restrict his influence, and it is dispersed throughout the world by means of a mystical transformation occurring at the time of the zaddik's death. This indicates the significance of the death of the previous Rebbe before his authority can be transferred or assumed by a successor. While he is alive, the Rebbe cannot be argued with or questioned, and this status continues after death. Thus, any partial delegation of authority or responsibility during his lifetime is dependent on the will of the Rebbe, and does not necessarily imply a right to succession on his death. It also explains the connection Hasidim often feel to their Rebbe even after his death, and is a way to understand Schneerson's insistence that Yosef Yitzhak was still in charge of Habad after his death. The idea poses problems for the question of succession in the contemporary movement as well; if Schneerson is still able to influence the movement, what need is there for a successor?[13]

The Need for Succession

The question of succession is of the utmost importance to the future of the movement, and the institutions of Habad face different problems resulting from the question of authority and succession. After the death of Schneerson, the distinct interest of the institutions was to ensure continuity of activity, to which a struggle for power over the movement would be detrimental. The ideological construct of a Rebbe who continued to lead despite his death and demise was thus attractive, and seems to have been imposed on the movement, ensuring institutional and doctrinal continuity while the deeper question of succession is resolved.[14] The precise nature of Schneerson's role post-death is still a matter of heated debate, but is accepted in one form or another by most, if not all, Hasidim.[15] One result of this continuation of administrative function and remote authority by a deceased figurehead is the perpetuation of the institutions of Habad, and the continued, unopposed influence of those Schneerson placed in charge of them. The effect of this on the current direction of the movement will be examined at greater length below and in the following chapters.

The notion of a remote-controlled movement has offered a workable solution for the continuation and administration of the movement so far, and it appears that the idea has also found its way into the belief system of the individual Hasid. Offered the choice of continuing the mission set for the movement by Schneerson (primarily outreach), and the desire for a Rebbe of flesh and blood, many of the Hasidim have chosen to internalize their attachment to the person of the Rebbe. They have done so because of the need for activism and to perpetuate his program. It may also, at least in part, be the result of a refusal to accept the fact of his death—as long as his work is carried on, then Schneerson will never die. This idea has taken on popular form in the emergence of a strongly resurrectionist/messianist belief in the movement.

As has already been noted, messianic fervor, especially after the onset of Schneerson's illness, has been one of Habad's primary motivational tools. It has not only encouraged enthusiasm for the work of the movement, but has assisted many people to explore and transcend their own limitations. The messianic idea, with

Schneerson as the potential mashiach and the essential role of the Hasidim in the revelation of his messianic status, helped push people to the far reaches of the earth to assume an awesome responsibility. In short, it enabled otherwise simple people to become extraordinary. For many, the inner security that they are working for the messianic incarnation is reassuring. To take this away from them might have negative effects on their functionality within Habad, and therefore, however ironic, it may be necessary, in the short run, to maintain the belief in Schneerson's messianic status in order to save the movement. In the long run, however, the messianic ideal could also cause the collapse of the movement, or at least its irrevocable change; the Habad way of life has heretofore needed a physical Rebbe.

The choice of succession has parallels with the two alternative conceptions of redemption in kabbalistic and Habad thought, the *geulah pratit* ("individual redemption") and the *geulah klalit* ("general or national redemption").[16] On the one hand, the present Habad movement as a whole seems to be opting for the ideal of general redemption, as expressed in its outreach and institutional apparatus. A direct, physical mentor or Rebbe is not as critical for the purposes of general redemption as it is for individual redemption, so long as the goals set down for the movement are pursued.

This is opposed to the quietistic ideal of personal redemption achieved with the assistance of the Rebbe through an individual's spiritual quest. The spiritualization of the office of Rebbe in the minds of present-day Habad Hasidim, wherein the office need no longer be held by a physical entity, may indicate the emergence of the individual redemptive perspective suggested above.

In reality, the spiritualization of leadership in Habad appears to be occurring as a means of deferring a decision over succession, and in order to stabilize the movement's institutions. It has so far prevented a massive rupture of faith, the emergence of cognitive dissonance, and the resultant fallout from the ranks. In doing so, the goals of activism and outreach have been prioritized, and the ideal of general redemption has been put forth as the primary goal of the movement. This trend of the supremacy of general over personal redemption commenced during Schneerson's early leadership, became more pronounced after his heart attack in 1977, and assumed supremacy after his incapacitating stroke in 1992. After his death, few seem determined to reverse a trend established by the Rebbe.

One of the primary challenges to the future of the Habad movement and the question of succession will arise from the traditional centrality of the Rebbe in the lives of his Hasidim, preferably as a physical being. The principal innovation of Hasidism was its notion of the Rebbe as teacher, guide, and zaddik. The relationship between Rebbe and Hasid is arguably *the* defining feature of the Hasidic idea. As we have seen, the strength of the Hasidic movement as a social and spiritual force, and its primary attraction to the East European Jewish masses, was largely due to the popularity of the movement's charismatic leadership. In time, there emerged a need for a spiritual bond between the semi-divine zaddik and the very mortal Hasid. An attractive enticement to the dejected Jewish masses in the era when Hasidism began was the individual attention and care the Hasid received from a divinely ordained spiritual master and sage. The Rebbe also served an important social function for his community by inducing fraternity and cohesion among his disparate followers. Since all of these elements helped to make Hasidism the most successful Orthodox movement in modern Judaism, it is possible that the absence of a Rebbe figure will challenge the cohesion of the Hasidic community, and possibly its very future.

Many of the functions of the Rebbe in Hasidic life were more than merely spiritual or ideological. Most of the comfort and solace he offered could only be effectively carried out in person, or at the very least by personal and individual contact. The Rebbe answered questions, gave advice and encouragement, and distributed blessings to his followers. He prayed for them, and was believed to be able to successfully intercede with God on their behalf. Socially, the Rebbe was the epicenter of the community, its focal point, and the source of its petty conversation and gossip. His public appearances, whether speaking, meeting people, or simply going about his everyday activities, provided material for the community to talk about and fret over. His age, health, idiosyncrasies, and teachings were the entertainment of the community, and in many ways the center of its spirituality. This was especially evident in the person of Schneerson, in whom the Habad Hasidic community found its heart and focus.

The superiority of the zaddik to his Hasidim facilitated a sense of equality and commonality among the members of the movement he led. It seems to be true that the size and importance of the community affects the image of its Rebbe; the larger the community, and the wealthier, more dignified, and more egocentric the Hasidim of whom it was composed, the greater the need for its zaddik to be recognized as superior to all. The ideal superiority of the Rebbe became a sociological device that served to humble even the most powerful of adherents into equality with their peers. The elevation of an individual to a position of ideological and even physical supremacy over his Hasidim (and the rest of humanity) facilitated the harmonious integration of the diverse elements that composed his Hasidic following. It might even be argued that the idea of the greatness of a Rebbe was an outgrowth of his community's success, which resulted in a corresponding need to expand the Rebbe's authority so as to facilitate communal harmony. In other words, the greater the community, the more awesome and impressive its Rebbe had to be. If this is true, then the death of a powerful Rebbe would leave a power vacuum in which his most influential followers competed for his authority. This seems to be occurring within Habad since the death of Schneerson; a successor could neutralize the inevitable clashes of interests and prevent a power struggle that would only result in disillusionment and the loss of the movement's spiritual mission.

Aside from these social functions, the principal role of the Rebbe in Habad was in his capacity as a guide and example for his following. This idea was initiated by Shneur Zalman, and has been preserved ever since in Habad thought and practice. A practical guide in spirituality is needed to enable humanity to advance on both an intellectual and a pragmatic level. Without a Rebbe, the highest levels of contemplation cannot be achieved,[17] and therefore the basic principles of the movement cannot be instituted. Adding to the spiritual need for a Rebbe is the fact that Habad philosophy can only be expounded and interpreted by the Rebbe himself. The absence of a Rebbe would therefore mean the stagnation of Habad Hasidut, and its eventual descent from a living and vibrant tradition to an anachronism.

The role of the Rebbe as an interpreter of Hasidism for the modern world was also exemplified in his function as an administrator and strategist, able to guide the movement's practical activities because of his higher spiritual disposition. He divined the needs of the world, and developed appropriate methods of Hasidic service to meet them. Habad teaches that each generation presents its own challenges, and the role of the Rebbe is to tailor his strategy to match them. Without his interpretation, which of necessity must be based on accurate and timely information, the movement would not be able to meet the needs of future generations, leading eventually to its administrative and strategic decay.

Apart from the ideological and practical motivation provided by the Rebbe through the application of Habad philosophy to contemporary affairs, there are also possibly far-reaching implications on an ideological level. Especially under Schneerson, it was taught that spreading Habad Hasidut was a necessary precursor to the impending arrival of the mashiach. If anything were to interrupt the flow of Habad ideology, the messianic redemption might be slowed or even stopped, and the messianic age itself would be endangered. As the Rebbe was believed to be the source of all spiritual sustenance, it is through him that the existence of the world was made possible,[18] and without him, the world would be starved of its spiritual force, and would consequently collapse physically. Thus the absence of an incumbent successor conduit seems to mean that the world would, in effect, no longer exist, although the persistence of the world after the death of Schneerson apparently rules out the actuality of this event.

For all of these reasons, the ideological and practical teachings of the Habad movement indicate the importance of finding a successor to Schneerson as Rebbe of the movement. Apart from the practical need for a physical person with whom interaction is possible to serve as figurehead for the movement, the ideological gap arising from the absence of a successor is so evident that it cannot easily be ignored. Were Habad Hasidim less scholarly or ideologically conscious, this dissonance could possibly be overlooked, but such a situation is not likely.

The only alternative to finding a replacement to Schneerson is to argue that his leadership needs no replacement. This solution, accepted by some in the movement, has forced the Hasidim to adopt more mystical justifications for the absence of a successor, including the belief in an impending resurrection. Other solutions involve Schneerson's temporary disappearance and impending return, or an impending eschatological change that will override the rules of the universe as they are now understood.[19] The need for a successor is so important to the Habad movement that the absence of any clear method of succession has necessitated the construction of extreme ideological justifications. These offer solace in the short term, but most probably will create expectations that will remain unfulfilled and possibly lead to disillusionment and defections.

The Difficulty of Succession

Habad's present successional difficulties surpass in complexity any similar problems in the history of the movement. This is so not only because of the impact that Schneerson had on the movement over the forty-five years he was Rebbe, but even more because of the system of beliefs and expectations which he and his Hasidim jointly built around him. His charisma and the cult of personality his Hasidim constructed make it difficult for any potential successor to compete with the deceased Schneerson, whose every action was perfection. The messianism he fostered built an ideological prison from which it is difficult to escape: he promised the redemption, and many still await its coming, and a vocal minority, now rapidly emerging as the mainstay of the movement, has proclaimed the resurrection of Schneerson as the mashiach. Even the usual method of succession, through the progeny or relations of the Rebbe, cannot be applied because Schneerson died without producing children. The problem of finding a successor is therefore greater than it might otherwise have been, and each of these obstacles needs to be explored further to understand the complexity of the issue.

Unrivaled Personality

Schneerson's leadership was highly charismatic, and throughout his reign his idiosyncratic ways, dedication, and charm were much loved by his Hasidim. Although it is impossible to quantify, the succession crisis may indicate that the commitment of Hasidim to Rebbe was stronger in the case of Schneerson than for any earlier Habad Rebbe. One might imagine that his effect on his followers was so powerful because he was a better leader than his predecessors. More likely, the ideological prism Schneerson created for the movement in the historical, and specifically post-Holocaust, context under which he assumed leadership of Habad led to the emergence of a difficult paradigm, and produced a dependence on the continued stability provided by his leadership.

One result of this attachment to Schneerson is that many Habad members have not only refused to accept the idea of replacing him, but also deny the fact of his death. This strongly resembles the denial syndrome experienced at the passing of loved ones, only on a mass scale. Although Schneerson was not related biologically to his Hasidim, the emotional dependency that many of them felt was more significant than the ideological or religious commitments of other Rebbe-Hasid relations.[20] The emotional "childishness" of this denial has been condemned by some of the more rational elements in the movement, but has largely fallen on deaf ears.

The commitment of his followers to Schneerson appears to have gone beyond what was generally required of his office. Schneerson effectively raised and guided two generations of Hasidim, and was instrumental in the educational and social programs that implanted the Habad ideology on the majority of the movement's current leaders. Many of them, and a vast proportion of the followers of Habad worldwide, were educated and inculcated into a movement that idealized its leader to superhuman proportions. Their dedication to Schneerson has since become intensely personal and emotional, beyond the ideological commitment due his position, and makes the task of finding a replacement for him virtually impossible.

Ideological Prism

Another, more ideological and less emotional reason for the refusal to recognize a successor to the movement arises from the belief that the Habad movement was spearheading the much-awaited redemptive process, a point greatly emphasized by Schneerson, especially in his last years. The messianic fervor encouraged in the movement, focusing on the person of Schneerson, and the emphasis on redemption that underlay the movement's outreach, made it difficult to accept his death. For many, acceptance of his death would be an acknowledgment that the movement he led had failed in its task of ushering in the messianic era.

The apparent failure of the movement led to other ideological crises, and some very interesting methods and explanations have been utilized to deal with these. The perception of Schneerson as perfect and without flaw encouraged a completely literal interpretation of his promises, messianic beliefs, and fervor in the collective ideology of his followers. Schneerson's insistence that the mashiach was soon to arrive resembled the promises made throughout the generations by biblical and rabbinic personalities. Although the failure of the mashiach to arrive on these earlier occasions disappointed many, it did not generally precipitate a crisis of the magnitude of the one in contemporary Habad.

The ideological crisis in Habad is the result of a chain of circular logic. Schneerson, idealized as a true prophet by his followers, had promised the advent of the mashiach in his own lifetime. The failure of this promise implied that Schneerson was a failed prophet, and this in turn meant that Judaism was a failed religion. Since everyone knew that this was not possible, another explanation was sought in the form of messianist and resurrectionist ideology. The crisis was a further result of the attachment of the Hasidim to their Rebbe. If they had not idealized his ability and seen him as a prophet, the failure of his messianic predictions could be explained as a result of human error or wishful thinking by Schneerson. Some have no doubt arrived at this conclusion, but for many, denial of his death seemed a more comfortable and theologically more logical idea. Schneerson had prophesied the redemption, and it was assumed that he himself was the mashiach; since the redemption had not occurred, he could not logically be dead. More moderate elements accepted the fact of his death, but the same logic and faith in Schneerson's prophetic skill led to the hope of his imminent resurrection, and did not indicate false prophecy. The only alternative to these justifications and loopholes, for some, was rejection of the faith, and resulted either in their leaving the community or their continuing frustration within it.

These simplistic formulas are the fruits of rigid, literal, and fundamentalist thinking, and emerge primarily from either a denial of the humanity of Schneerson or a fundamental flaw in Habad's teachings. Rather than acknowledge these possibilities, many of the Habad Hasidim have preferred to adopt a logically consistent but purely hypothetical (and rather unrealistic) construct requiring supernatural intervention for the completion of the stated mission of the movement, namely, the fulfillment of the redemption and the messianic arrival.

Some have raised the stakes and hinged their faith in Hasidism, and even Judaism, on another logical construct to explain the failure implicit in the death of Schneerson. If Habad was spearheading the redemptive movement, but was on the verge of collapse due to the absence of a successor, then the only logical conclusion would be the belief that the redemptive process had already started, either during Schneerson's lifetime or immediately after his death. This, by their logic, would enable the movement to complete its mission even without Schneerson, and would save Habad from demise. Those who have adopted this position claim that if they are wrong, this would indicate a fundamental flaw in their way of life and everything they have ever stood for. In this game of "double or nothing," many were setting themselves up for continued hard work as missionaries, or else laying the ideological groundwork for leaving the religious life.

Another messianist explanation for the death of Schneerson may provide a mechanism whereby the messianists can be reconciled with the non-messianists, and selecting a successor might be permitted even though Schneerson retains his messianic status. The problem can be resolved by the messianist recognition of Schneerson as the *mashiach ben Yosef*, the mashiach son of Joseph, who according to the Talmud is to die in the course of his messianic mission. This death is simply a prelude to the coming of *mashiach ben David*, mashiach son of David, who is the final mashiach.[21] Thus, Schneerson can remain a messianic figure, and his death could become a part of the messianic redemption, removing the necessity to deny it. This view has been used throughout Jewish history to neutralize messianic speculation and curtail the growth of messianic movements. The position does not appear to be gaining widespread support, but has emerged as part of the messianist debate within Habad.

No Obvious Replacement

The difficulty of replacing the unrivaled figure of Schneerson with another person might have been counter-balanced by the availability of an unambiguous successor from his progeny, as had often been the model for succession in both Habad and other schools of Hasidism. Schneerson, however, produced no children, and therefore left the arena open for much confusion and speculation. The very absence of a successor served to mystify some Hasidim, as if Schneerson's not having had children were part of a predestined plan wherein a successor to him was not required. The failure of Schneerson to produce a biological successor was a primary contributor to the messianic fervor that arose around him; if there was no successor, then there must be no need for a successor—Schneerson was the mashiach, and would usher in the messianic era himself! And then there would no longer be any need for a Rebbe. Moderates within Habad might have been induced to accept this view, not only by the messianic ideology fostered by Schneerson during his lifetime, but by the realistic fear of not finding a replacement of his stature after his death.[22]

An Extreme But Active Minority

A fundamental element of Habad ideology, especially because of Schneerson's leadership, is that a minority can defeat a majority by the force of its conviction and willingness for self-sacrifice. This idea was a working principle throughout his leadership, and at present it is found most vocally among the messianic lobby of the Habad community. As we have seen, a strong and politically significant messianic element emerged in the Habad movement under Schneerson, and its influence became more noticeable in the later years of his life.

Belief in Schneerson's messianic qualities was a strong component of Habad's outreach work. Schneerson himself emphasized a messianic strategy for the outreach program, which was undertaken in anticipation of and preparation for the messianic era. Even if we understate the messianic expectation of Habad activists, it can safely be said that those Hasidim who dedicated their lives to outreach and communal activities did so under the guidance and inspiration of Schneerson. Thus they were less willing to accept another Rebbe in his stead, as compared to those who were not as active in the movement, and therefore demonstrably less committed to Schneerson's program.

Commitment to Schneerson and his outreach mission may have been more strongly identified with the messianist element of the movement because of the more active self-publicity carried out by the messianists. Their publicity often depicted non-messianists as less committed to outreach and Schneerson's policies, making them less attractive to the committed Hasidim who wish to continue the mission and outreach established by Schneerson during his lifetime. The non-messianists are generally less ideologically motivated than the active and vibrant mission-minded zealots of the messianist faction, but unlike the messianists, they are more practical, and usually include the ba'alei batim[23] who make up the majority of most congregations. People of this sort tend to be less vocal and occupy positions of less importance than the messianists, so while they might support the election of a new Rebbe, or at least do not support the messianist rhetoric, they have little influence on the course taken by

Habad. With no capacity or basis to draw converts to their way of thinking, their viewpoint remains largely unvocalized.

The messianist elements have employed hard-sell marketing tactics even in the Habad community, making dissent from the messianist program look like an act of heresy or impiety. An illustration of such a tactic is the comparison between a Hasid who doubts Schneerson's messianic status with Korach, the rebellious relative of Moses who was eventually punished.[24] A more extreme comparison likens the non-messianists to Amalek, the archenemy of the Jewish people, irredeemably evil beyond the help of repentance. Enemies of the messianist ideology have been called *hasidishe amalek*, the Hasidic Amalek.[25] This comparison internalizes the traditional mission of the Jewish people within the Habad movement; all of the elements once opposing Judaism or the Children of Israel are now ranged against the Habad movement. The fight against Amalek in the modern world is not against a gentile nor Jewish Amalek, but rather against the Hasidic Amalek. This intimates that the redemptive process will occur only through Habad, and that the force for redemption is at work therein, facing opposition not only from outside, but, more disturbingly, even from within the movement.

This extremism leaves moderate Habad Hasidim in a dilemma. An expression of doubt regarding Schneerson's resurrection or messianic status is deemed a heresy of the worst sort, which estranges the non-believing Hasid from the Habad messianist leadership in the local community. Support for the messianist ideology is garnered from biblical, rabbinic, and mystical sources that serve not only to support the position, but silence less learned opponents who are unable to express a contrary opinion with the same textual weight.[26] The messianists' piety, scholarship, and dedication to Schneerson is usually of a high order, and at least in the years immediately after Schneerson's death, they attracted wide and popular support. Thus a vocal minority provided a transitional ideology for the movement based firmly on Schneerson's message, giving hope and comfort to many, and above all insisting on the continuation of the mission and activities he had instigated. If only for this reason, the messianist faction of Habad has been instrumental in the survival of the movement after the passing of its leader, and may provide the emotion and drive required to move Habad into the next generation, whatever the its ultimate leadership and direction.

---

[1] Ram's horn.

[2] Michelle Bearden, "Lubavitchers Mourn and Ponder Future."

[3] Arieh O'Sullivan, "Jewish Leaders Praise Departed Rabbi," p. 34.

[4] Susan Birnbaum and Pamela Druckerman, "Thousands Mourn Lubavitcher Rebbe."

[5] Ibid.

[6] Anonymity requested.

[7] The author.

[8] Personal account by Michael Lever.

[9] *Tanya*, pt. 1, chap. 1.

[10] There is a Habad story that likens the burden of becoming Rebbe to an actual physical

weight. Menahem Nachum, the first son of Dov Ber, the second Habad Rebbe, is believed to have felt a supernatural weight when he was selected as the new Rebbe after his father's death. He understood this as a sign that he was not strong enough to bear the burden entailed by the position, and so he refused the leadership of Habad. See Avrum Ehrlich, *Leadership in the HaBaD Movement*, pp. 195–196, for more details.

[11] The *ma'amar* (long Hasidic discourse) that is given, for example, marks the beginning of a Rebbe's reign, and indicates his acceptance of his position of authority over the Hasidim.

[12] *Tanya*, pt. 4, chap. 27b, in the name of the *Zohar*.

[13] That he is able to influence the decisions of his followers even after death is made most evident by the practice known as *iggerot kodesh*, by which answers to questions are derived through mystical consultation of the published collections of Schneerson's letters.

[14] Of course, the question need never be positively resolved, and there is a Hasidic school that has never replaced a deceased Rebbe, namely the Breslav Hasidim. Despite the fact that it did not replace its Rebbe, the Breslav movement has not only survived, but even flourished.

[15] Resurrectionist messianists believe that he will return from the dead to continue where he left off; other messianists that he continues to lead personally, although by spiritual rather than physical means. Still others believe that his influence and ideology will continue to guide the movement after the loss of his physical presence, but accept the fact of his death. These are just the main factions that have emerged after Schneerson's death.

[16] There are different strains of general or national redemption. The type referred to here is influenced by religious pietism as opposed to nationalist aspirations (as might be found in secular Zionism). For a more detailed discussion of the varieties of redemption, see A. Ehrlich, "Sabbatean Messianism as Proto-Secularism: Examples in Modern Turkey and Zionism." See also Naftali Loewenthal, "The Neutralization of Messianism and the Apocalypse."

[17] See Samuel H. Dresner, *The Zaddik*, pp. 128–132.

[18] The incumbent Rebbe inherits, by means of an unexplained cosmological process, the function of *zinor*, or "funnel," through which the world receives its vitality. See ibid.

[19] Schneerson used this argument in discussing Adam and Eve, and the change in the nature of the world. The concept would be consistent with this logic. Some followers claim that as the redemption is upon us, the ontological order of the universe has changed. The impending redemption allows for godliness to pervade all aspects of existence equally. The final step is moments away, when Schneerson will return in body to inaugurate the messianic era.

[20] One Hasid told me that his motive for joining the messianist campaign was not so much to bring about the redemption as to be able to see Schneerson again.

[21] Suggested by Isser Weiberg, in a letter to *Jewish Action*, Fall 1995.

[22] Rabbi Jack Luxemburg, head of the Washington Board of Rabbis, has been quoted as saying that the messianic fervor may have been driven "not only by veneration of the Rebbe and his great piety but by the underlying concern that the community needs an extraordinary type of intervention to maintain itself because its internal dynamics seem to be headed for a real difficult period." Quoted in Caren Benjamin, "Succession Question Downplayed." The idea seems to be a common one in Habad.

[23] Congregants who visit a Habad shul for Shabbat and festivals, but work and earn their livelihoods outside the community.

[24] See Numbers 16:1–50.

[25] See Zev Goldman, "Geulah Insights on Torah." This is a radical position to take, because it indicates a change in the ontological root of their opposition.

[26] See Raquel Hasofer, "Messiah from the Living—Messiah from the Dead."

Chapter 19
Schneerson's Intentions

The Question of Intention

One of the foremost difficulties in establishing the process of succession, or even in determining whether a succession can take place within Habad, is the question of Schneerson's intentions for the movement in the event of his death. While knowing his opinion would probably not alleviate the dilemma, nevertheless all of the factions in the succession debate trace their main points of support to either his actions or his teachings, if not both. The multiplicity of positions on the succession dilemma is due in the main to the complexity of the Rebbe's life and teachings, and the possibly intentional ambiguity of what he said on the issue.

Schneerson established the precedent early in his reign of leading through suggestion, rarely giving explicit instruction or orders until after a project had been proposed. We have already examined this phenomenon of interpretation and its role in the dissemination of Habad ideology through outreach, and the same practice has had a direct impact on the current leadership debate. The question of succession, therefore, can be better understood in light of Schneerson's attitudes and practices regarding the need or way to replace him as Rebbe. There has been a great deal of debate and discussion on the subject. Some Hasidim believe that Schneerson never alluded to the movement's leadership after his passing, others that he offered various alternatives to the appointment of Rebbe. This debate rages throughout the Habad community, and has even found its way onto the Internet via online discussion groups.

Succession and continuity are basic issues for the movement's existence. Throughout the history of Habad, none of its Rebbes has ever explicitly identified his future successor. This had sometimes led to fragmentation within the movement,[1] but it apparently seemed a better alternative than the appointment of an ill-suited or undesirable successor, which might have led to disobedience of the will of the preceding Rebbe. In most cases, the Rebbe did not leave a legal will outlining the disbursement of property or authority to successors, although Shalom Dov Ber wrote a letter instructing his son to serve the community diligently. Perhaps he believed that the community would accept his son Yosef Yitzhak as his successor, but this is not explicit. In the instructions he left, Shalom Dov Ber gave no express instruction in favor of

Yosef Yitzhak's appointment, leaving it for the Hasidim to decide. In so doing he may have set a precedent for the current successional situation. Schneerson gave some indication of how to ensure organizational stability and local order within Habad after his death,[2] but he left the issue of succession open for the Hasidim to decide. Before his death, Schneerson nominated three individuals (Hodokov, Pikarski, and Mindel) as the primary authorities in Habad's administration, and perhaps intended the community as a whole to select one of them as its new leader. On the other hand, he may have intended for there to be no single leader, and instead a scenario wherein many minor Rebbes would emerge, as in the early days of Hasidism.[3]

The election of Schneerson himself had partly hinged on the question of continuity, an issue that was a concern even in the 1950s. Some Hasidim claim that Shemaryahu Gourary was found unqualified to inherit the post of Rebbe because his only son was deemed an unfit successor.[4] The alternative to Gourary, however, was Schneerson, who presented the equally troubling circumstance of having no progeny at all. A story is told in Habad about Abraham Hirshle, who came to congratulate Schneerson at his inception. They hugged, and Hirshle is understood to have given Schneerson three pieces of advice. One of these was that he have a child, perhaps implying advanced knowledge of the difficulties to succession that would arise should Schneerson die childless. Onlookers report that Schneerson burst out crying at the suggestion. Visitors to Schneerson over the years who posed questions regarding succession were met with the same response, deferring the future course of Habad to the messianic arrival. In light of these events, and the importance of the issue to the future of the movement he led, it is inconceivable that Schneerson, as a visionary, highly intelligent, and organized person, did not seriously consider the issue.

Schneerson's refusal to publicly speculate about the continuing leadership of Habad after his passing was probably a tactic designed to heighten the messianic fervor he fostered in the last decade of his life. From this perspective, the absence of a successor was a primary proof and motivation for the messianic drive; if there was no successor, then there must be no need for one because the arrival of the mashiach was imminent. Schneerson's silence on the issue of succession is therefore as important as his explicit instructions would have been, had he given any. He did not, but many Hasidim believe that by example throughout his life he provided implicit direction about the course of the movement in the event of his death.

Yosef Yitzhak as the Rebbe

As we have already seen, Schneerson, from the time of his election to the leadership of Habad, adamantly insisted that Yosef Yitzhak was still the true Rebbe, and that the movement's every success was attributable to his continued leadership.[5] At the time of Yosef Yitzhak's death, and in the years immediately after, Schneerson referred to the deceased as still alive, and spoke of his status as the mashiach or as a prophet.[6] It is unclear from the available evidence whether Schneerson held these ideas with the same intensity in his later years, or whether they were the result of his intense grief at the time. Later in his reign Schneerson appears to have developed the idea that Yosef Yitzhak's leadership was manifest through his own,[7] and that his acts as leader were taken under Yosef Yitzhak's direction and instruction.

Schneerson may have intended his relationship with his Rebbe as a model for the future leadership of Habad; the successor would carry on the mission that he had inherited from Yosef Yitzhak. In his last years, Schneerson made reference to Yosef Yitzhak's status as mashiach,[8] and therefore may have viewed Yosef Yitzhak's leadership (spiritual or physical) as the solution to succession within the movement after his own death. The idea was most clearly expressed by Schneerson himself:

> Moshe rabeinu is the first and last *Moshiach*, hence it appears that the prince of the generation is also the righteous *Moshiach* of the generation. So when the *nasi* of the generation [Yosef Yitzhak] sends a representative (*shaliach*) and he fulfills his will with sacrifice and all his essence, then he becomes the essence of the sender, he becomes the *Moshiach*.[9]

Those who reject this idea or believe that Schneerson asserted his own messianic status over his predecessor's are left to explain why he changed his mind about Yosef Yitzhak's role as mashiach, and how Schneerson, as a zaddik, could have erred. Moreover, the messianists who assert that Schneerson is either not dead or will soon resurrect have not come to terms with the similarity of their claims to Schneerson's unrealized expectations for Yosef Yitzhak.

The singular behavior of Schneerson in declaring Yosef Yitzhak the true Rebbe despite his death has become a model for some Habad Hasidism who are trying to emulate and reenact Schneerson's response to Yosef Yitzhak's death upon the death of their own Rebbe. While this idea might facilitate the transfer of authority if a new Rebbe is elected, as it did with the transfer from Yosef Yitzhak to Schneerson, it is difficult to see how it might succeed as a leadership model without a new leader. The problem with the implementation of this transfer model in the Habad movement as presently constituted is the lack of a voice that could claim to speak for Schneerson. If more than one successor claimed to be fulfilling his intentions and acting under his direction, and attempted to assume power on that basis, it would doubtless either cause chaos in Habad or else create a situation where there are several rival Rebbes in the movement, each claiming to speak with the authority of the former Rebbe.

Schneerson's Transfer of Authority

During his life, Schneerson's authority extended to every facet of Habad life. Every success was ascribed to his visionary leadership, from the organizational structure of the movement to its outreach campaigns, publishing efforts, educational facilities, and the material prosperity of its followers, as well as much else besides. He gave infallible advice, exuded charisma, and brought success where there seemed little hope even of survival. He was, according to his followers, single-handedly responsible for the survival and dispersal of Hasidism throughout the world, and the survival and adaptation of Habad from an East European ghetto culture into a vibrant and influential component of the modern Jewish world.

Schneerson was an activist hands-on administrator during the early years of his leadership, but during the later years he slowed down and allowed for more independence and initiative on the part of his Hasidim. He moved from directly establishing organizations to providing the ideas for others to initiate projects and campaigns, supervising some projects directly and advising on others. As time passed, he left the development and implementation of most of these initiatives to his rather broadminded and enthusiastic devotees. Schneerson had a theoretical veto authority over the movement's activities but was not entirely cognizant of all of Habad's many initiatives, having delegated a great deal of authority, particularly at a local level, to his representatives and aides. These people were expected to carry out his instructions and suggestions without extensive supervision, and their autonomy was one of the strengths of Schneerson's leadership strategy, producing phenomenal expansion of the movement on all fronts.

Throughout Schneerson's reign, a mutual relationship of transferral between Hasid and Rebbe seems to have developed. That is, the more authority and responsibility Schneerson delegated to others, and the more they achieved under his broad instruction, the more they attributed their success to him, and hence the greater his leadership and authority became. As his leadership progressed, however, his role in Habad became increasingly spiritual, and less managerial. His public duties as Rebbe required him to speak to his followers on Shabbat and festivals, and it was through these discourses that he imparted his vision for the movement. As the dispenser of Habad's primary ideology and outreach vision, Schneerson came increasingly to be seen by his followers as the movement's figurehead, especially with the rise of messianism and the ideology of the redemption in his last decades.

Rather than communicating through the official bureaucracy and thus remaining aloof from the throngs of Hasidim, Schneerson chose to employ more direct methods of contact. This ensured his authority over and connection with the many individual Hasidim within Habad, maintaining a separate line of connection with the mass of his followers outside the movement's official bureaucracy.

As time passed and Schneerson grew older, the *yehidut* meetings that were the main basis of this personal connection became more restricted in number, duration, and frequency, Schneerson maintained contact with the common Hasid by his regular public appearances. He regularly distributed dollars, cakes, and drinks to the Hasidim, and also continued a voluminous correspondence to ensure that he remained in touch with more than the movement's leadership. In this way, he avoided becoming dependent on the movement's bureaucratic hierarchy for information and contact with the majority of Habad's followers.

Throughout his reign, Schneerson maintained a high level of independence from Habad's official bureaucracy and administrative hierarchy, at least until his first debil-itating stroke in 1992. After this event, the absence of any family or other close rela-tions necessitated greater reliance on the movement's hierarchy, and particularly on his aides, to allow him to communicate or have any contact with the Habad masses. From this point, any form of communication involving Schneerson, whether to him or from him, was carried out through his aides, who therefore became ever more important in Habad's internal power structure. The occurrence of Schneerson's strokes in the early 1990s therefore marks a significant change in the movement, and raises important points regarding the issue of transfer of authority. From this point, it seems, there was a necessary transfer of authority by Schneerson to others in the movement, which has implications for the question of succession.

It is certain that Schneerson, throughout his life delegated authority, at least in a temporal sense, to many of his Hasidim. This might be seen, in retrospect, as a form of leadership transferral, especially under the fiefdom model of succession that will be examined below. It must nevertheless be recognized that the primary signs of Schneerson's transferral of power, and the major importance of this for the question of succession, only became fully evident after his first stroke, when dependence on others became imperative to his own continuing leadership. Indications of transfer, or at least the assumption of power by others, became even more pronounced after his second stroke, which rendered Schneerson largely unable to communicate. When he was effectively silenced by his illness, others were able to use their connection (and access) to him to advance their own agendas, and even to fulfill their own leadership aspirations.[10]

Whatever its immediate impact and ideological significance, Schneerson's stroke was a significant moment for the transferral of authority and succession in Habad. It permitted Schneerson's aides and other close associates to use their own authority in his name, and presumably with his approval. The Habad bureaucracy, for the most part, did not attempt to justify their actions in any way, other than maintaining that they were enacting the explicit will of Schneerson. With access to him available only to those in authority over the movement, it was impossible for the average Hasid to verify that directives and instructions were actually from Schneerson, so leadership was effectively transferred to his aides.

One might argue that while Schneerson was alive, there was no source of Habad authority outside of his directives or desires, and this is certainly the case, but after his stroke those desires were more open than ever before to interpretation by his aides and staff. The growth in the power of the administrative hierarchy of the movement, and the increased independence of the various Habad institutions and emissaries from this time, need not be seen as an expression of real succession or transfer of essential power. Rather, it is possible to consider the greater influence of certain individuals as an intentional delegation of authority and responsibility to them by Schneerson. This need not detract from the sense that Schneerson was truly leading the movement, or from the perception of his complete authority, but represented an intensification of a process that had always formed a significant part of his leadership style.

The fact that some Hasidim may have used their closeness to Schneerson during this period to increase their own authority is not without precedent in the history of the movement, or even in the consolidation of Schneerson's leadership. Schneerson succeeded Yosef Yitzhak as the Habad Rebbe not by claiming individual authority, but by unilaterally declaring that he was loyally representing the will of his predecessor, and this is a stance he maintained throughout his life. Schneerson succeeded to the leadership in a passive, nonconfrontational manner by virtue of his claim to be speaking with Yosef Yitzhak's voice, and his continued authority and inspiration arose through ongoing communication with the deceased Rebbe. Some Hasidim today are claiming to have authority in much the same manner, which may prove to be an effective mechanism for real succession.

Most Hasidim today, however, reject the possibility of any form of succession, as Schneerson did forty-five years earlier, claiming that the deceased Rebbe is still in control of the movement. They continue to refer to his written instructions, directives, and mission statements, and have even elaborated a mystical system of "communication" with him through omens and oracles of various kinds, most significantly the *iggerot kodesh*. For these Hasidim, Schneerson is still the head of the movement, and therefore the appointment of a new Rebbe, the transfer of power to a new leader, or the official transfer of authority to the institutions is a pointless exercise. The fact that Schneerson regarded his predecessor as retaining power over Habad after his death did not preclude his own assumption of office, although he insisted that he was not a worthy replacement for his predecessor. Given this, it does not necessarily follow that the belief in Schneerson's continued leadership of Habad will prevent the appointment of a successor.

The claim that Schneerson is still in control of Habad after his death has at least temporarily ensured continuity in the movement. While the divine and unqualifiable nature of the zaddik's authority has been preserved in death, Schneerson's status as leader has remained unaffected by the political and administrative disruption arising from his passing, especially as caused by the maneuvering for authority by his aides. During the last years of Schneerson's life, his influence in the daily business of the movement was gradually divested to the institutions and activists, leaving him as a shadow figure of supreme authority and spiritual supremacy, but without ability to exercise real power. Schneerson, whether he lived or died, had become a remote and idealized figurehead for the movement. His real opinions on issues, his health, or even the fact of his death, while a source of concern for the individual Hasid, was immaterial to the institutional structure that had succeeded in preserving his authority in eternal stasis as an ideological construct.

The death of Schneerson was certainly shocking for the movement, and caused disruption to both the individual and institutional lives of Habad followers worldwide, but the gradual assumption of power by the institutions and the aides during his ill-

ness eased the transition. The need for continuity prevailed within the movement, and
the real power of the Rebbe remained in the hands of those who had assumed it: the
caretaker-institutional apparatus. Official succession could not have occurred so long
as Schneerson was projected as the senior authority in Habad, even if his authority
had no more than symbolic significance. After his stroke, he led the movement
through passive nods of approval to suggestions put to him and letters read aloud by
his aides, and since his death, mystical rites carried out at his gravesite have had much
the same effect. Continuity has prevailed in the institutions, at least for the time
being, but other means of succession and continuity are still possible, as will be
shown below.

Cultivation of Independent Leadership

Throughout his reign, Schneerson certainly appeared to encourage leadership traits
in his Hasidim. He saw them as soldiers or officers in his army, fighting a war for the
survival of Judaism, and he even developed a military-style leadership hierarchy in
the Zivot Hashem youth movement. Schneerson encouraged the mass ordination of
rabbis at the youngest possible age to provide large numbers of trained "troops" on
the battlefield,[11] even at the expense of their studies and the resultant loss in status of
rabbis in the community.[12] He delegated substantial authority to his emissaries, leaving them to run their local communities with often only the vaguest of instructions or
directions, and without direct interference in daily operations. Schneerson also
encouraged a diversity of leadership styles, and avoided adjudicating disputes to the
detriment of one authority over another.[13] In speeches, letters, and documents, he
extended authority to his Hasidim, to specific individuals, and to institutions.[14]

However, throughout his leadership there was a clear distinction between practical
authority, as over the institutions of Habad, and spiritual authority as Rebbe, which
he alone exercised. Schneerson did, however, delegate some spiritual authority to his
Hasidim during his lifetime, charging them with the responsibility for the coming of
mashiach:

> . . . what more can I do to motivate the entire Jewish people to clamor and cry
> out, and thus actually bring about the coming of the *Moshiach*? All that has been
> done until now has been to no avail. For we are still in exile; moreover, we are
> in an inner exile in regard our service to God. All that I can possibly do is to give
> the matter over to you. Now, do everything you can to bring *Moshiach*, here and
> now, immediately.[15]

He stated that he could do no more to bring mashiach (which he believed was the
primary goal of his leadership), and therefore was charging not only his Hasidim but
every Jew with the completion of the mission. This transfer of spiritual responsibility was consistent with Schneerson's policy of mass ordination, communal leadership,

posting of emissaries, and delegation of temporal authority. It did not necessarily imply a complete transfer of the authority inherent in the role of Rebbe, but certainly established a precedent for the idea of spiritual authority being delegated along with temporal responsibility.

The statement quoted above charges the Hasidim with spiritual duties once reserved to Schneerson alone, and until that time the responsibility and burden of one individual Rebbe. This transfer may be an indication of Schneerson's intentions for the continuation of authority in Habad after his passing, when the spiritual authority he had delegated could be expected to fill the vacuum left by his absence. Such an interpretation certainly falls within the operation of the mission model of succession that will be discussed in Chapter 21.

This, of course, would require the individual Hasid to accept the burden of leadership and responsibility for the future of Habad and its outreach and other activities, not out of desire for power or authority, but as an act of self-nullification. The needs of the Jewish people as a whole are greater than those of the individual Hasid, just as the needs of the Habad community were greater than those of Schneerson himself when he assumed the office of Rebbe. This scenario may give some idea of Schneerson's intentions toward the continuing leadership of the movement after his death.

The Aides

Schneerson's aides played an important role in the administration of the movement, especially by conveying information or instruction to the lower leadership, the institutional authorities, and the general Habad population. His aides, however, were not seen as holding authority in their own right. Their power and influence came from their function as the representatives of Schneerson, and they were not doted on by the Hasidic faithful, nor were they a source of intrigue or interest. In carrying out their duties, they were required to be extremely discreet, and by tradition did not share their inside information about the internal workings of the movement or of Schneerson's personal life.

As Schneerson grew older, the authority and influence of the aides began to increase, for they were responsible for determining his appointments and controlling access to the Rebbe. It was not until Schneerson suffered his first stroke, however, that he became almost completely reliant on his staff for any continuing connection with his Hasidim. Even the spiritual element of the Hasid-Rebbe relationship was dependent on their facilitation. Even before his stroke, the aides brought Schneerson mail and communiqués and informed him of events within the movement, but after his stroke they gained more power by interpreting his answers to questions put to him through a reading of his greatly restricted bodily movements. A nod or a gesture were the most explicit actions possible by Schneerson, and interpretation of these took on near-mystical dimensions. The interpretations were often preceded by manipulations of the way questions were worded and the selection of issue to be emphasized, in order to gain the desired response, which was then recorded explicitly. Even if Schneerson gave a response, the aides could decide whether to release it to the public, and thus they were able to affect the movement's public policy and operations. This put significant authority in their hands.

This process described above did not necessarily endow the aides with more institutional influence than they already wielded; the institutions of Habad were largely autonomous, especially after Schneerson's stroke, and they did not petition him for direction on a regular basis. The task of interpreting Schneerson's responses served the aides mainly by increasing their public prominence; the masses of individual Hasidim were the most dependent on these responses, especially as many of their requests were of a highly personal nature. The ability to speak for the Rebbe therefore greatly enhanced the status of the aides in the eyes of the Hasidim, whose only connection with Schneerson was through them.[16] Significantly, after Schneerson's first stroke more people received replies to letters of inquiry, and at a faster rate, than at any other time before in Schneerson's leadership career. One explanation for this may be the eagerness of the aides to obtain Schneerson's replies, to please the constituency and garner support for themselves, and attract Hasidim to their "court" and their "services," with the expectation of Schneerson's eventual death. It certainly indicates the competitive spirit that was emerging between the aides as to who might be the most suitable candidate to replace Schneerson.

Despite attempts to garner support for themselves, or at least attract attention to their own activities, the aides were sometimes appreciated for their assistance in facilitating communication with the Rebbe; more often, however, they were simply tolerated, and sometimes they were accused of interfering in Schneerson's direct rule of Habad.[17] At least in the last years of his reign, a tension existed between the hierarchical mechanism of the movement and Schneerson's own authority. The latter was adored by the Hasidim, whereas the former was deemed a necessary inconvenience. The aides also largely controlled Schneerson's infrequent public appearances, when he was rolled out in a wheelchair and received with massive public euphoria and excitement. He would even attempt to invigorate his followers, as he had always done, with physical gestures, but these were severely limited by his infirmity. Some no doubt felt that these appearances should be more frequent, and that the aides were restricting even this level of access to the Rebbe.

The attempt to control access to Schneerson was a point of contention in the movement and between the aides, for the perception of proximity to Schneerson endowed the respective aides with authority and prestige that were no longer counterbalanced by Schneerson's personal and direct relationship with the individual Hasid. There was less political posturing and playing of power games by Schneerson's aides than one might expect, but more than commonly believed by the Hasidim. Posturing for the appearance of closeness to the Rebbe during the last years of his life determined which aides would emerge as the primary players in the succession after his passing. Some of the aides did not participate in this posturing, including Rabbis Nissim,

Mindel, and Kline, but others did. Through the appearance of greater closeness to Schneerson, Rabbis Leibl Groner and Yehuda Krinsky were able to gain support for their respective primacy over the movement, as their closeness to him conveyed the impression that Schneerson had secretly entrusted them with his vision for the destiny of the movement.

Differences over Scheerson's medical treatment were an intense point of contention between the aides, and one of the areas where power politics had an influence. The question of Schneerson's medical treatment included discussions of whether his biology was the same as that of other people or different because of his status as zaddik or mashiach. Most important to the question of transfer of leadership was whether Schneerson's own opinion, as expressed through gestures, should be regarded in his treatment, particularly as he was believed by many to be divinely inspired. Such issues eventually hinged on the question of his messianic status, and the opinions of his aides on this issue determined their positions about medical matters. Krinsky held the more rational view, arguing for the latest and most suitable medical treatment available, which antagonized the many messianist Hasidim, led by Groner. They thought that outside interference in the Rebbe's medical situation might be just as dangerous as inaction. They saw his illness as an element in the messianic revelation; interference with Schneerson's physical state might therefore affect the redemptive process, which should instead be permitted to run its natural course.

Despite these arguments and the operation of internal politics, there were remarkably few attempts to override Schneerson's principle authority, or to argue his legitimacy or supremacy as leader of Habad. Nor were there any overt attempts to replace him or his authority in any way, except by controlling access and the interpretation of his desires.[18] Until his death, the authority of the movement's administrative hierarchy and of Schneerson's aides was solely derived from their proximity to him, and was not in any way due to a perception of their own independent eminence.

In the years between Schneerson's stroke and his death, a large degree of ambiguity entered the ideological and practical questions of continuation of Habad as an organization and way of life. The debate was mostly concerned with interpretation and speculation regarding the ambiguous directions provided by Schneerson, not only for the future of the movement but for its present activities. There was an attempt to understand why illness should have befallen a saintly and almost semi-divine being, and what this happening signified for the movement and its role in bringing the messianic redemption.[19] On this and other issues, especially those surrounding the question of messianism, the propagators of the various ideas fought for ideological supremacy in the public relations arena of the international Habad community on the basis of their interpretation of Schneerson's teachings. Schneerson's aides and their supporters opened a sequence of open hostilities, pent up until that time, that still divide the movement years after Schneerson's death.

In this period, a series of independent activists initiated projects based on their own perceptions of Schneerson's will. For example, the messianic faction launched a massive and unprecedented media campaign to propagate the messianic claim in favor of

Schneerson. There were also preparations and advertisements for a soon-to-be coronation of Schneerson as the official mashiach.[20] These and other such events caused a critical response from the more pragmatic institutional arm of the movement, led by Yehuda Krinsky. With the power struggle at the top of the movement, individual Hasidim and activists took the liberty of interpreting Schneerson's teachings for themselves, and personal as well as group initiatives were undertaken that advertised and expressed extreme messianic fervor. Every group, without exception, claimed to speak in the name of Schneerson.

To declare Schneerson's leadership and influence at an end because of his illness and inability to communicate was intolerable, and certainly did not find popular support within Habad. There was also little deliberation about the possibility of Schneerson's death, and subsequently no discussion about the future of the movement, at least in public. Krinsky attempted to discuss the logistics of Schneerson's funeral with other aides before Schneerson's death, and became the target of messianist attacks for his lack of faith in the Rebbe and his mission. During this period, the movement was united in its ambivalent yet desperate faith that Schneerson would miraculously recover from his stroke, and would reveal himself as the mashiach. Schneerson, for his part, remained incapacitated and largely incommunicative.

Had Schneerson died suddenly, rather than undergoing a long and gradual decline, the power positioning among his staff and the development of so many contradictory claims would not have had time to become entrenched and consolidated. As the need for succession was not immediate, factions had the opportunity to develop and gather support, and to ideologically justify their positions. The battle for power was permitted time to develop, however, during the years before Schneerson's death, and is a significant part of the current succession debate.

Legal Transfer

That Schneerson himself gave consideration to the future of the movement in the event of his death is evident from the fact that he wrote and signed at least one will, and possibly two, during the last decade of his life. These legal documents indicate the role of his aides in the succession of leadership, and possibly Schneerson's own intentions for the future guidance of the movement. The legality of these documents, and even their genuineness, is very much a subject of dispute in the post-Schneerson Habad movement, and so the solution to the question of succession that they provide has not been accepted by some segments of the Habad community and administration. The wills, and the claims made in them will form the focus of the next chapter. It is sufficient here to observe that Schneerson's writing of even one will, whatever its content, shows that he recognized the need for institutional continuity after his death, and thus can be taken as a sign that he acknowledged his own mortality. If one accepts this, the position of the messianist faction is greatly weakened, and thus the messianists do not accept the wills as a true indication of Schneerson's intentions.

The Beit Din

Habad tradition, in common with the broader Jewish tradition, has always respected the legal authority of the community Beit Din, and Schneerson often made complimentary remarks about that institution and its spiritual importance. Shortly before his wife's funeral in 1988, Schneerson gave a public talk stipulating how the movement would make decisions in the advent of his death.[21] He suggested that answers to questions both legal and spiritual could best be established after his death through the authority of the Beit Din, as has traditionally been the case throughout Jewish history. The Batei Din, he said, should ideally be made up of Hasidic rabbis, and located in every country and city throughout the Jewish world. He explained that the Shekhinah, or holy presence, dwells in such a forum, and that the Beit Din is therefore suited to guide the people. On other occasions, Schneerson made positive references to the institution of the Beit Din as a "noble institution." This may have been his way of indicating his desire for the future course of the international Habad communities, and for the movement as a whole, to be guided by its local authorities.

Schneerson always gave deference in halakhic decisions to the Beit Din of Crown Heights, and especially to Rabbi Zalman Shimon Dvorkin, its head. Dvorkin also headed the Va'ad Rabanei Lubavitch (Union of Lubavitch Rabbis), whose membership consisted of many important Habad rabbis and scholars. Schneerson's personal deference to Dvorkin in legal matters and his support of the Beit Din seem to indicate his preference for legal, scholarly management of the affairs of Habad after his passing, rather than the political chaos that loomed from his aides and a struggle for succession.

While the idea of rule by the Beit Din seems to cater to the needs of Habad Hasidim as individuals, it does not necessarily provide a solution to the dilemma of institutional continuity or the perpetuation of the mission of the movement. Schneerson's conception of the role of the Beit Din in the future organization of Habad seemed to acknowledge only the spiritual authority of the institution, and to see its control of temporal affairs as limited to local matters. He rejected the establishment of an international body of Habad rabbis,[22] discounted the appointment of a head rabbi for Habad,[23] and seems to have supported the autonomy of each community to decide legal and halakhic questions for itself. Thus, rabbis and Batei Din in each local community would ensure the continuation of the community. The international operations of Habad would continue under the administration established by Schneerson, which would not adjudicate on local matters, but instead would defer to the Beit Din.

Several problems with the post-Schneerson operation of the Crown Heights Beit Din have arisen, however, which might prove disruptive and divisive to the use of the Beit Din to resolve future disputes in Habad. A prominent Hasid, Yoel Kahn, wrote to the head of the rabbinic organization, Rabbi Hillel Pozner, to complain about the ineffectiveness of the Beit Din and its one-sided stance in the adjudication of several disputes.[24] Kahn also complained about the Beit Din's support for the so-called

Groner camp, named for the aide who heads the messianists. This support extended to the defense of small "terror groups" that have threatened individuals making anti-Groner remarks in the community. The letter objected to the involvement of the Beit Din in issues that were not its concern, such as the question of succession and internal authority in Habad, and to its neglect of crucial matters under its direct purview. In short, the letter called attention to the weaknesses of the Beit Din, the growing disillusionment with its authority and questions about its impartiality, and its overall ineffectiveness as a body able to provide leadership for Habad. Thus, despite its moral legitimacy as a spiritual body, the Beit Din had proven itself ill-equipped to meet the challenges of succession and leadership. However, as a traditional source of authority, it still has legitimacy, and may yet play a significant role in the discussion of succession and leadership within Habad.

[1] Consider, for example, the succession debates after the deaths of Shmuel, the fourth Rebbe, and Shalom Dov Ber, the fifth Rebbe. See Avrum Ehrlich, *Leadership in the HaBaD Movement*, pp. 236–257, for more details.

[2] See the debate surrounding the wills in the next chapter.

[3] This would emerge in the fiefdom model, to be discussed in the next chapter.

[4] Shemarhayu Gourary's only son, Shalom Dov Ber (known as Barry), would have been a prime candidate for Rebbe after the death of Yosef Yitzhak if not for his youth (he was only twenty when the Rebbe died). He was prominent in the movement, but there were perceived, if not actual, irregularities in his behavior that precluded his succession. He had shaved his beard at a young age and had a reputation for publicly desecrating halakhah. He also involved himself in the fight for his father's right to succeed, publicly slandering Schneerson. Such behavior effectively ended any possibility that he himself might succeed Yosef Yitzhak, and possibly ended his father's chances too. The reaction to his public behavior served only to estrange him from the movement, especially with the ascendancy of Schneerson. Barry eventually left the community and ceased to be religiously observant. As we have already discussed, he and his mother took Habad to civil court to fight for possession of Yosef Yitzhak's library. See Ehrlich, *Leadership in the HaBaD Movement*, pp. 339–342, for more details.

[5] He said that Yosef Yitzhak was still guiding the movement, and that this was possible because Eliyahu sent letters from his place on high. See *sichah* of 12 Tammuz 5710 (1950); *Torat Menahem*, p. 130.

[6] Schneerson also mentioned in his *sichot* the possibility of resurrection for individuals before the general resurrection. See *sichah* of 13 Shvat 5710 (1950), published in *Likutei Sichot*, vol. 2, p. 517. From this, today's messianists believe Schneerson is capable of individual resurrection.

[7] This idea appears in the *Zohar, Ra'ya Mehemna*, where it says that the souls of mashiach ben Yosef and mashiach ben David are connected with Moses, and will be revealed in the final generation. See Gershom Scholem, *The Messianic Idea in Judaism*, p. 53.

[8] Parshat Shoftim, 5751; Simchat Torah, 5742; Beit Rabeinu Bavel, 5751.

[9] From a *sichah* on Simchat Torah, 5745. Author's own free translation from the Hebrew. Although this passage can be interpreted as a message to the *shluhim* around the world, it also has implications for Schneerson's messianic status. Another instance when he associated him-

self with his father-in-law was when he said cryptically, "*onbek ontach*," a meaningless phrase in Hebrew, but when inverted as "*chatno kebno*," it takes on the meaning "the son-in-law is like the son."

[10] This has parallels with Schneerson's similar use of Yosef Yitzhak; he claimed that he ruled in his predecessor's place, and under his ongoing instruction, a claim that the deceased Yosef Yitzhak was not able to contradict.

[11] Jonathan Sacks, "The Man Who Turned Judaism Outward."

[12] When everyone is a rabbi, the qualification ceases to have any real meaning in the community.

[13] Schneerson tended to avoid adjudicating conflicts. On several occasions when people or organizations were infringing on one other's activities or authority, he is known to have either remained aloof or blessed both parties to the conflict.

[14] See, for example, the question of his wills.

[15] Excerpt from *sichah* of April 11, 1991.

[16] As this appears to have been the way Schneerson himself rose to power, this authority was not insignificant.

[17] Krinsky especially was criticized by Hasidim for impeding the Rebbe's will, and was strongly opposed by the messianists in the movement.

[18] Even the issue of preparing for Schneerson's funeral was not discussed. Krinsky was criticized by some Hasidim for raising the question, because the Rebbe's death was not something they believed could happen or wished to think about.

[19] Parallels were drawn, for example, to the famous suffering servant idea in Isaiah.

[20] This event was to have taken place in January 1993.

[21] *Sichah* of 2 Adar 5748 (February 20, 1988), given in his home.

[22] See the letters in *Yalkut Inyana Shel Agudat Chasidei Chabad*, p. 12.

[23] Ibid., p. 14.

[24] See the letter from Yoel Kahn to Rabbi Hillel Pozner, 24 Iyar 5754 (May 5, 1994).

Chapter 20
Institutional Authority

The Collective Leadership Model

While Schneerson seemingly left clear instructions about how disputes within Habad were to be resolved after his death, mainly by the Beit Din of each local community, this advice has largely been ignored by the leadership of the institutions of Habad. The power struggle among his closest aides, not only political but ideological, has caused severe disruption to the community, not least over who has the right to administer the institutions of Habad and their financial resources.

The idea of collective management of Habad came from Schneerson himself.[1] As mentioned, shortly after his wife died he gave an important speech in which he referred each community to the Beit Din to resolve problems of an individual, legal, and even spiritual nature. This instruction was subsequently reiterated on several occasions , which would seem to express Schneerson's desire for it to be taken seriously.[2] The collective leadership of Habad refers personal matters to the Beit Din, but the executive, educational, and outreach arms of the movement continue to be controlled by the institutions already administering these activities, namely AGUCH, Merkaz L'Inyanei Chinuch, and Mahane Yisrael. Immediately after his wife's death, Schneerson undertook to reorganize these institutions, and began a process of redrafting their constitutions that seems to have never been completed.[3] This instruction was further stipulated in a will composed in August 1988, in which Schneerson nominated three people to have authority on arbitrational and legislative matters within the movement. There is some controversy surrounding this document and its legality. Some parties (mainly Krinsky) maintain that it is not a valid legal document and was declared void by Schneerson. Whatever the legal aspects of this issue, it is certain that at least in 1988, Schneerson intended the leadership of Habad after his passing to be carried out on the basis of collective administration.

The First Will

The first will, signed and dated February 14, 1988, simply transfers all power over Schneerson's property, including books, manuscripts, *objets d'art,* and other items intended for Schneerson's personal use to Agudat Chassidei Chabad, or AGUCH, and

246

names Krinsky as executor of his estate. It was registered with the State of New York on this date, and there is no question as to its genuine nature. The only contention in relation to this will is whether it was superseded by a second will, of which only an unsigned and unregistered copy has been found. This will is the basis on which Krinsky has maneuvered for *de facto* leadership of the movement, through AGUCH, and he was the main party disputing the legality of the second and later will, which, as we will see, relegates him to a minor supporting role in Habad's administration.

The Second Will

On August 30, 1988,[4] Schneerson sat with Rabbis Hodakov, Pikarski, and Mindel and prepared a second will, the final draft of which was prepared later. This will has been the focus of a great deal of debate in the community since Schneerson's death, mainly because of the controversy surrounding its legality. Only an unsigned version of this second will has been discovered, causing some to doubt its authenticity. To complicate matters, Krinsky has been accused of interfering with the application of the second will, in which his powers are greatly reduced in comparison to those outlined in the official and registered first will.

The contents of the second will clearly indicate how Schneerson wanted Habad to be run after his death. He nominates three men as executors whom he, and his predecessor Yosef Yitzhak, considered trustworthy: Rabbis Hodokov, considered to be Schneerson's chief of staff, Mindel, the movement's main editor and publisher, and Pikarski, the head of the Central Lubavitch Yeshiva. These men had been associated with Habad from the time of Yosef Yitzhak and had his trust. They had also proved themselves under Schneerson, and so he effectively handed control of the movement to them.

Schneerson further instructed that the institutions established by Yosef Yitzhak when he came to United States, namely Merkaz and Mahane Yisrael, were to continue their operations as currently. These institutions, given him to administer in embryonic form by Yosef Yitzhak, had become the pillars of education throughout the Habad movement, and through them Habad had been able to accomplish an unprecedented degree of outreach and education. All other activities were run as part of these two movements, alongside AGUCH, which Schneerson had reactivated in 1985 after four decades of relative inactivity.[5] In all of these institutions, he specified, the organization and administration were to remain as they were at the time of the composition of the will, including the retention of the same senior staff. Merkaz was to be run by Rabbis Chodokov, Mindel, and Simpson; Mahane Yisrael by Chodokov, Mindel, and Krinsky; and AGUCH by Hodakov, Zalman Gourary, and Riskin. These three institutions were to be given an equal share of the *ma'amad*, money donated to the Rebbe personally, in order to function.

As a final action, the will gave power of attorney to Hodakov, Mindel, and Pikarski to decide matters where there might be doubt about how to proceed.

. . . the intention here is not to create doubt. If there arises doubt as to what to do, I give Power of Attorney to Hodakov, Mindel and Pikarski to decide, to *paskin* in doubt. This is how it should happen.[6]

Only an unsigned version of this will currently exists; after the will was prepared, Schneerson said he would look it over before signing it, and that is apparently the last that was seen of it. Some Habad members believe that Schneerson never signed this will, and that the draft version therefore does not have legal authority. Others believe that even if the will was not signed, it is nevertheless indicative of his general view of the issue of continuation, and therefore has validity as an expression of his intentions for the movement after his death. There are still others who believe that a signed copy of the will exists, but was stolen from Schneerson's drawer and hidden by an interested party who hopes to gain by its destruction.

The person who stood to gain most from the elimination of the second will was the executor named in the first will, Yehuda Krinsky. He has come under a great deal of suspicion for his possible role in either blocking the execution of the will or of hiding the signed copy. His involvement in the affair is further complicated by some events immediately preceding Schneerson's stroke that Krinsky has also been accused of causing. On the day before Schneerson's first stroke, that is, on March 1, 1992, Schneerson allegedly told Yehuda Krinsky to telephone Pikarski and tell him that the second will was to be cancelled. Krinsky canceled the will that very day, and Schneerson, due to the incapacitating effects of his stroke, was unable to confirm or deny later accusations of fraud on the part of Krinsky, who may have been vying for more authority in the event of Schneerson's death. Suspicion has been further aroused by Krinsky's refusal to testify before the Beit Din on the issue of the will, and he has therefore been accused of ignoring the express instructions of Schneerson,[7] who stated before his death that all disputes were to be arbitrated by the Beit Din.

The legal validity of the second will is a point of debate among the factions of Habad. Few, however, deny that it was composed. The disagreement pertains to whether Schneerson ordered that it be disregarded. They point to the fact that the will was unsigned to support this; if Schneerson had desired it to be recognized, and intended it as anything more than a draft, he would have approved it with his signature. However, for many, the fact that the will detailed how the movement should be run, who should remain as the heads of its central institutions, and who should be turned to for arbitration and guidance indicates unequivocally Schneerson's more sober intentions for the movement after his death.

The Institutions

Despite the controversy surrounding his involvement in the matter of the wills, Yehuda Krinsky, the head of the AGUCH organization, appears to be emerging as the chief administrator of the Habad movement in the post-Schneerson period, though not as his replacement as Rebbe. It seems unlikely that Krinsky will ever succeed Schneerson as Rebbe, not only because of the controversy surrounding the execution of the wills, but also because of the intense dislike for him by many of the leading messianist campaigners. Even so, Krinsky is probably the most powerful individual in the contemporary Habad movement. He has used to advantage the fact that he was named as executor of Schneerson's personal estate in Schneerson's only clear will, securing greater power and influence for himself, and ensuring continuity of activity within Habad after Schneerson's passing. The executorship was not over the institutions of the movement but over Schneerson's personal property, but as this included his library and other symbols of power and transfer, Krinsky has been able to place himself in a position of great influence. Following instructions Schneerson gave in 1985, Krinsky has reactivated AGUCH into an institution of great authority that is now at the center of the power struggle.

The existence of AGUCH, as we have seen, predated the physical presence of a Habad Rebbe in the United States, and the organization was instrumental in bringing Yosef Yitzhak, his household, and eventually his book collection out of Eastern Europe in the 1940s. It provided housing for Yosef Yitzhak and his family in the United States, and most importantly for the future of the movement, also set up the Habad infrastructure. AGUCH was the primary administrative body in Habad until the succession of Schneerson, and after the new Rebbe was appointed, the movement continued to be the chief executive body of Habad. Its role was somewhat downgraded, however, and many of its more important functions were carried out by Schneerson's own institutions, Merkaz L'Inyanei Chinuch and Mahane Yisrael.

From about 1952, AGUCH effectively ceased active operation, except in taking on a maintenance role over the Hevra Kadisha, a council responsible for Hasidic burial practices. Its other activities were passive, but despite this relegation to a position of lesser eminence, AGUCH continued to hold crucial power within Habad. Most important, AGUCH was the legal owner of the headquarters of Habad in Crown Heights, at 770 Eastern Parkway, a location that housed the Rebbe's residence and the administrative hub of Habad's activities. It also controlled one of the most important symbols of power in Habad, the massive book and manuscript collection that had belonged to Yosef Yitzhak.

In 1985, when a court case was opened on the issue of who owned this library, an important opportunity was provided to revive the power and influence of AGUCH as a central part of the Habad infrastructure. The institution, led by Krinsky, was at the time relatively unimportant, but it headed the case against Barry Gourary, who was suing for possession of the invaluable collection. After a lengthy case, the possession of the library was awarded to AGUCH, largely because of the difficulty resulting from the inseparability of the Rebbe and the infrastructure of Habad. The court decided that the Rebbe, whoever he might be, was the *de facto* owner of the collection, by virtue of his control of Habad's organizations, and Schneerson was declared to be the "trustee over the manuscripts."[8] As the central administrative body for Habad, the organization responsible for the collection's presence in the United States, and especially as the owner of the building in which the movement was headquartered, the collection was to be administered by AGUCH.

Largely because of the court decision, AGUCH was revitalized and reactivated, and from this time Krinsky began to play a more significant role in the public face of the movement. The power and influence of the institution was increased after the death of Schneerson's wife in 1988. At that time, Schneerson instructed that all of her property was to be given to AGUCH. As we have seen, he also wrote a will indicating that his own property was to be given to AGUCH in the event of his death, and nominating Yehuda Krinsky as the sole executer of his personal effects. This first will placed Krinsky in strong position, for a great deal of the symbolic power of Schneerson and the office of Rebbe was being transferred to AGUCH and its director. However, the second will, the will Krinsky has been accused of interfering with, places AGUCH in an inferior position and relegates Krinsky to minor role. If this second will is valid, it would represent a demotion for Krinsky, who wishes to see AGUCH become the umbrella organization of the Habad movement as originally conceived, a point he has made on a number of occasions.

Krinsky therefore held strongly to the validity of the original will, which transferred effective control over the movement to AGUCH, and by extension to him. As chief administrator of AGUCH, he has, with interpretive licence and marketing skill, managed to put forward a strong claim to succession, at least as far as the movement's management is concerned. His claims to authority have been resisted by several different forces, particularly the messianists who support the validity of the second will, if not as a legal document, then at least as an indication of Schneerson's desires for Habad. The major division within the movement immediately after Schneerson's death was between the conservatives led by Krinsky and the messianists represented by Groner.[9]

From the time of Schneerson's death, the AGUCH organization under Krinsky has tried to establish its control over the movement, and seemed to be succeeding, at least over some of the major organizations. Immediately after the death, it sent letters to communities and individuals worldwide, offering instruction on the appropriate forms of mourning and guidance on the future of Habad. This mainly took the form of an offer to give instruction to those who requested it.[10] AGUCH has since sent letters informing Habad followers that they are prohibited from using the Rebbe's name or the name of Lubavitch in any unauthorized venture, for these terms are effectively owned by AGUCH as executor of his estate.[11] The institution has therefore become the *de facto* central administration for Habad, and has tried to establish itself as the sole official voice for the movement. Neither of these efforts has been completely effective; they are ignored primarily by the messianist opposition.

Three days after Schneerson's death, AGUCH issued a statement about the future organization of Habad.[12] The statement establishes that Scheerson's *sichot* are the only source of authority for the future of Habad, the "eternal words" that would continue to guide the movement even after his death. The letter directs communities to refer questions of halakhah to their rabbis—that is, to the local Beit Din—and stipulates administrative procedures to be followed. Administration is to be carried out as before Schneerson's death, with local organizations continuing to be run by those in office before the Rebbe's passing. Anything that might influence the well-being of the movement as a whole is to be referred to the head of AGUCH, and policy statements on specific issues are to be "formulated and issued only after consultation with, and permission from, Agudas Chassidei Chabad." Similar permission is required to establish new institutions or funds bearing the name of the Rebbe. Personal questions should be referred to a Beit Din of three Habad rabbis, and objective advisers or friends should be consulted on other, less important matters. Finally, questions of a medical nature should be referred to a doctor, this last point possibly an oblique reference to the controversy surrounding the medical care of Schneerson during his illness.

Through official statements of this kind, AGUCH tried to establish itself as an umbrella organization for the institutions, the Batei Din, and all the other subsidiaries of Habad. By approaching communities so soon after the death of Schneerson, AGUCH was perceived to be the official voice of the movement, and was able to assume at least a semblance of centralized authority.

Thanks to the dispute over the legitimacy of the second will, the other organizations Schneerson led have become somewhat ineffectual. Merkaz L'Inyanei Chinuch was the main organization under Schneerson, effectively replacing AGUCH in further activism and as the major property holder.[13] Since it had been placed in Schneerson's charge by Yosef Yitzhak, he was concerned about its success, and his vision for the organization saw it develop into an educational dynamo.[14] If the second will is accepted as valid, it would seem that Schneerson wanted Merkaz to be the center of the movement after his death, an event which has not taken place.

Even if the second will is recognized as legitimate, control over Merkaz L'Inyanei Chinuch would still be a problematic issue. Schneerson stipulated in the second will that Mindel, Pikarski, and Hodakov were to head it, but only Mindel is still alive, and he is of greatly advanced years. While he was one of the foremost spokesmen for the movement under Schneerson, and published widely on Hasidic matters under the Rebbe's direction, he has always never been involved in the internal politics of Habad leadership. As a result, Merkaz has been transformed into a subsidiary of AGUCH, thus increasing Krinsky's power over the movement.

The administrative functions of Habad were managed through a process of collective leadership, with Krinsky the most prominent individual in the movement. Effectively, each institution is autonomous, with local communities running their own affairs, and many treat the self-proclaimed umbrella leadership with moderate distrust, suspecting the management of trying to obtain total control of the movement by centralizing everything under AGUCH. Others have embraced Schneerson's instructions to turn to the Beit Din for adjudication of disputes, and advertisements endorsed by the Beit Din have appeared. Important political issues in Habad have also been taken to the Beit Din for adjudication, including the matter of the second will. As noted, Krinsky refused to appear before the Beit Din, which only highlights the leadership tension between the two styles of collective management.

The practice of collective management is likely to create difficulties in the selection of one dominant figure as leader of Habad, especially because of the institutional infighting. Any candidate for the office of Rebbe would run the danger of being perceived as intimately connected to the institution he manages, and as prominence in the broader Habad community can only be attained through the successful administration of an institution, it is difficult to see how anyone could ever emerge supreme. As mentioned, Schneerson's spiritual and charismatic leadership played against the administration of the institutions and the bureaucracy. His charisma was attractive to his followers, and they tolerated the bureaucracy around him as a necessary annoyance. In the leader's absence, the bureaucracy may become more aggravating to the populace, and thus being a member of the movement's administration may prove counterproductive in the bid for leadership.

In the short term, collective management has helped to maintain the status quo, and as such might yet play a role in the emergence of leadership on the mission or fiefdom model, to be discussed in the next chapter. The activities of the movement as a whole have continued, and in some instances increased, despite the death of Schneerson, due to the autonomy permitted by the collective leadership style he established.

---

[1] Rabbi Moshe Kotlarsky, director of missionaries around the world, has noted the sentiment that "in the years before his death . . . Schneerson made provisions for the movement to continue without him." He did not believe that a true successor would ever be appointed, but the movement would continue. See "Lubavitch Rebbe Can't Be Replaced."

[2] See *sichot* of 2 Adar 5748 (February 20, 1988) and 15 Shvat 5748 (February 3, 1988), and in *yehidut* with AGUCH on 9 Heshvan 5749 (October 20, 1988). These outline procedures to be followed by *shluhim* and institutions in the event of his death.

[3] Throughout this period, there is mention of reorganization in Habad, the changing of organizational constitutions and their management by Schneerson's directives, and the drawing up of several wills, only one of which appears to have been finalized. For a description of the stages and occurrences in the writing of the wills and the reorganization, see the findings of the Central Committee of Habad Lubavitch Rabbis in the United States and Canada, in *Birur Dvarim Beinyan . . . Reshimat Dvarim Veshtar Tzava'ah*.

[4] In the Hebrew calendar, 17 Elul 5748.

[5] See "Protocols": Yehuda Krinsky testimony, pp. 718–719, and Chaim Halberstam testimony, p. 2616, where the inactivity of AGUCH is discussed. Schneerson revived AGUCH primarily in order to fight the legal battle over the ownership of Yosef Yitzhak's library. It was felt that AGUCH, as the institution responsible for bringing the collection to the United States in the first place and legal owner of the movement's main administrative buildings, had the clearest right to their possession. See "Protocols."

[6] Excerpt from the second will.

[7] See the open letter by Rabbi Shneur Zalman Gourary to Yehuda Krinsky, accusing him of refusing to carry out Schneerson's will by refusing to go to a Beit Din for adjudication and using the institution's money for unapproved matters. Krinsky is also accused of forging documents, creating a puppet institution, and legitimizing his actions by pretending that he was carrying out directives by Schneerson.

[8] See "Protocols": Memorandum Decision and Order, p. 24. See also Immanuel Schochet testimony, pp. 2553–2554.

[9] See Kahn to Pozner, 24 Iyar 5754 (May 5, 1994). The letter was sent to Habad emissaries on 10 Sivan 5754 (May 20, 1994) without the writer's knowledge. Since it was not intended for public dissemination, it appears to present an honest and concerned interpretation of the situation in Crown Heights and the underlying political issues.

[10] Letter from *Agudas Chassidei Chabad Lubavitch*, 6 Tammuz 5754 (June 16, 1994).

[11] Letter from *Agudas Chassidei Chabad Lubavitch*, January 19, 1993.

[12] Letter from *Agudas Chassidei Chabad Lubavitch*, 6 Tamuz 5754. (June 16, 1994).

[13] See "Protocols": Yehuda Krinsky testimony, p. 717. It is noted how Merkaz expanded financially, purchased Schneerson's house at 1304 President Street, and began to accumulate the "Rebbe's Library" at 766 Eastern Parkway. Other properties were also purchased by the organization on behalf of Habad.

[14] See Lawrence H. Schiffman, "Rebbe's Legacy of Hope Transcends His Death."

Chapter 21
Other Models of Succession

Whatever the theory behind the need for succession or the ideology surrounding the question of replacing Schneerson as head of Habad, there are a range of practical considerations pertaining to the daily running of the movement. With the failure of a successor figure to emerge, and legal problems in the organizations that might have ensured continuity within Habad, other models of succession have developed, and some even seem to be occurring on a wide scale. Several models relevant to the way Habad may be run in future are presented here, and discussed for their relevance to the future of the movement in both the short and the long terms. Some of these models are based on previous Habad or Hasidic patterns of succession, on the assumption that the future leadership of the movement may be based on patterns already established throughout the movement's history. Other models of succession from outside the movement that provide a workable solution to the lack of a successor are also explored.

One of the factors to be kept in mind during the following discussion is the absence of clear distinctions between the various categories: some Habad followers may adopt elements of more than one model in their effort to find a workable solution. There is also a significant possibility that, over time, one model may be adopted and then phased out and replaced with another. Leadership of any organization is fluid, and segments of Habad will no doubt adopt different models of succession as their needs vary.

The No-Succession Model

There are several reasons why the movement might opt not to appoint a successor to Schneerson, some of which have already been examined. The no-succession model seems to be favored by those who believe that even though Schneerson is dead, there is nobody of the same stature and ability to replace him. Schneerson was so far superior to the rest of humanity that finding a successor is an impossibility. There is much to recommend itself in this approach, including a long history of Hasidim refusing to accept the official successor to *their* Rebbe, with whom they had a personal connection.[1] The no-succession model also allows for other styles of leadership and succession to be enacted that involve a continuation of the mission and activities of Habad but do not actually require the appointment of a replacement Rebbe. The movement might thus be administered by a quasi-government or manager, but with no possibility of a real successor.

Of more concern to the future of the movement under the no-succession model is the fact that the premise of not appointing a successor is intimately linked with the messianic element of the movement, which falls into two basic categories:[2] those who acknowledge that Schneerson died but think he will soon resurrect as the mashiach, and those who claim that he has not died but is in hiding. Almost a decade after the death of Schneerson, both of these elements are still to be found within Habad, and are part of the vocal minority involved in the struggle for leadership of the movement.

The two groups share some fundamental tenets.

We believe in full faith that the Rebbe, *melech hamoshiach,* [king and mashiach], continues to exist exactly as before *gimmel tammuz* [the Hebrew date of Schneerson's death], and that nothing has changed. The Rebbe continues to be the *memutza hamechaber* ["joining intermediary"] between God and the Jewish people, and all godly influences and *brachos* ["blessings"] come solely from and through him.

We believe in full faith that the Rebbe, *melech hamoshiach* is the head of the body of Israel. Each and every Jew, the limbs of that body, can approach the Rebbe directly and ask for his help and blessing. Each and every Jew can receive clear and unequivocal answers to the problems that beset him.

We believe in full faith that everything the Rebbe said is true, and that everything he ever predicted has come about, is coming about and will come about— without exception. Most particularly this includes all of the Rebbe's statements concerning *moshiach:* that he already exists, he has already been revealed, and that *moshiach*'s actual effect on the physical world is starting to be felt, even with regard to *Eretz Yisrael.* The fact that we cannot always perceive it with the fleshly eye in no way detracts from the truth, or lessens our pure faith in the Rebbe's words.

We believe in full faith that the true and complete redemption will happen in our time, and that only a few minutes remain until the *geulah.* The Rebbe, *melech hamoshiach,* has already been revealed; all that is necessary is that we seek him out and make him welcome.[3]

On this basis, messianic groups find the idea of replacing the Rebbe not only distasteful but impossible. Their interpretation of Schneerson's teaching regarding the mashiach, and the effort of unraveling those teachings into an administrative doctrine, has proven difficult even in the messianist faction. Because of this, there are many subgroups within the messianic group, all with differing interpretations of what

Schneerson said and meant when he spoke of the mashiach. One point of agreement they all share, however, is the understanding that Schneerson will not and cannot ever be replaced as Rebbe.

Some of the messianists claim that because Schneerson indicated that he was the mashiach while he was alive, it would be disobedient and disrespectful to elect a successor, even if one accepts that Schneerson is dead. Other messianists, generally dubbed the resurrectionists, are waiting for him to return from the dead and fulfill his promise of redemption.[4] Still others deny that he is dead at all, but insist that he is merely in hiding, and they await his reappearance.

It is tempting to believe that all this messianism arose only to protect the sentimental from disappointment at their loss and to ensure the perseverance of the gullible. The piety, scholarship, and dedication to Schneerson among the messianists is usually of a high order, though, and they have been able to make and support their position through recourse to standard halakhic authorities accepted throughout Judaism.[5] Further, their messianic beliefs tend to lead them into greater commitment to Jewish law and increased dedication to Schneerson's teachings, and so they cannot be accused of lapsing from Jewish observance on the basis of practice.[6] Indeed, the opposite appears to be true, as lapses in observance seem to be more prominent among the non-messianist supporters of Habad. The messianist element, therefore, cannot be dismissed, and as has been seen throughout history, messianic expectations do not always die with the passage of time. Christianity, Shi'a Islam, Sabbateanism, and other messianic movements all provide a glimpse of one possible future for Habad.

It may well be that the resurrectionist doctrine, while acceptable and attractive to a few, might simply not be attractive to the Jewish or Habad populations at large, leading to the failure of the faction. While it is difficult to collect statistics based on a belief system, the resurrectionist doctrine seems to be increasing in popularity within Habad. At the very least, it is not diminishing, and the movement as a whole is threatened with division along the lines of verbal or symbolic allegiance or nonallegiance to the messianist ideology.[7]

Those opposed to messianism hope that the stigma associated with resurrection in Judaism might prove too great an obstacle for the idea to penetrate mainstream Habad ideology.[8] In time, if the return of Schneerson does not eventuate, it may well be that many messianists will become disillusioned with the faction and drift to other theological trends in Habad or mainstream Judaism. However, two thousand years of Christian expectation of the return of their mashiach from the dead indicates the resiliency of human hope, and the future of messianist Habad may well be a long one.

This future seems to be ensured by the level of social activism fostered by the messianist faction. Since Schneerson's death, their activities include the intensification of educational and outreach efforts to the non-Habad community, and in this they share common goals with the mission model, which will be discussed below. The messianists have taken on a number of new outreach campaigns. The first is to the non-

Jewish world, to spread Schneerson's message concerning the redemption of all humanity, and generally increase non-Habad awareness of Schneerson's life and vision.[9] The effect of this campaign on the rest of the world has been slight; of far more import to the future of Habad as a homogeneous movement is the massive and continuous outreach program the messianists have been conducting within the Habad community. The faction has been publishing booklets, a weekly journal (*Beis Moshiach*), and advertisements throughout the Habad community worldwide, in an attempt to convert its members to the messianist position. These methods have been extremely effective in garnering support for the faction, or at least of attracting attention to its fundamental ideals.

A campaign that commenced within the movement in March 1996, before Schneerson's death, has also assisted the messianist faction to garner support since his passing. Called *haderech hayasharah*, the program aims to teach the beliefs surrounding the coming of mashiach through Habad educational institutions across the globe. Its educational program began with a study of the mashiach in the Gemara, Midrash, and commentaries, demonstrating that the Habad community under Schneerson's direction accepted the traditional sources, and that its messianic ideology was not based on non-traditional texts or logic. Schneerson suggested that the mashiach would come because of programs of this kind, and as a result they have been encouraged by the messianists since his death to hasten his return.[10]

From our examination of messianism in Habad under Schneerson, it is evident that the ideology surrounding the mashiach is a central part of the modern Habad movement, with clear theological and practical support.[11] As a tool of consolidation, it served to elevate Schneerson from the position of zaddik and Rebbe to that of potential mashiach. The place of this ideology in the modern movement is still being explored, but it is certain that messianist ideology has already determined official Habad policy, and has been used to silence opponents of the resurrection movement.

The persistence of the messianist faction will likely have a number of effects in the transfer of authority after the death of Schneerson. By supporting the continuation of his leadership even after his death, and declaring that there is no need to replace him, the messianists will allow local leadership to evolve in individual communities all over the world. Widespread acceptance of the messianist ideology will result in the development of either the fiefdom model of leadership, where local authorities take control of their own segments of the movement, or the slow-succession model, where a new leader emerges over time from among the community. These models will be examined below.

The Fiefdom Model

Aside from the ideological minefield of the messianist position, there are a number of other motives for rejecting a succession. Many Hasidim, especially those in leadership positions across the world, are understandably tired of following after forty-five years of leadership by Schneerson. To these men, Schneerson was decidedly deserving of complete dedication, and while he was alive they did not question his leadership, but as they see it, appointing a successor just for the sake of appointing a successor is not necessarily a good idea. Many of Habad's community leaders are charismatic, educated, and in touch with the modern world. They have earned their leadership positions in their local communities through their own efforts, and indeed were often responsible for creating a Hasidic infrastructure where none was previously to be found. Even where there is no sizable Habad population, many Habad Hasidim have attained places of respect and dignity as responsible community rabbis. To expect such leaders to forgo their rights and privileges as independent leaders to another Hasid, a person just like themselves, is perhaps unreasonable, especially given the current situation where there is no clear successor. If Schneerson had produced children, or if it was obvious who ought to be chosen as successor, the case might be different, but no clear leader has thus far emerged.

Perhaps many of the community leaders, like the scholarly followers of Aharon of Staroselye who did not want to be *botel* ("nullified") to another leader after Shneur Zalman, are independent and do not need the social support and comfort offered by a Rebbe. This independence was given them by Schneerson, who might be seen as having weened his followers from dependence on him over the decades of his leadership. For these community leaders, the death of Schneerson was a tragedy that they would have prevented were it possible, but while some were to join the messianist ranks and deny the event of his death, most realized that Schneerson was gone, and that they were on their own. This realisation changed their perceptions of themselves and their role in the preservation of the community, a fact officially recognized by one Habad spokesman who said that the Hasidim should be Hasidim, not *Hasidelach*. In other words, the leaders should behave like leaders, as Schneerson had wanted, and not like children or naïve adults.

During Schneerson's lifetime, he made a concerted effort to instill a large degree of autonomy of operation and organization in his emissaries, and some commentators on the movement have interpreted this as a *de facto* delegation of authority.[12] Because of this delegation and autonomy, the international Habad community is composed of separate, autonomous units, operating originally from the missions Schneerson gave to Habad as a whole, but otherwise operationally independent of the central administration in Crown Heights, and funded largely by sources in their own communities. With this organizational apparatus, centralized leadership is not a crucial need for the movement's survival and expansion.

Keeping this organizational structure in mind, one of the most likely succession models (and there is strong evidence that it is already arising) is the division of the Habad movement into fiefdoms.[13] This model of leadership resembles the early days of Hasidism, when the Maggid of Mezritch gathered Hasidim around himself, and inspired scholars of distinction who later went back to the communities from which they came and themselves become leaders, zaddikim, and Rebbes. This theory is supported by the comparison of Schneerson's activities to the early days of Hasidism by Jonathan Sacks, England's Chief Rabbi and a disciple of Schneerson.[14] The fiefdom model of succession is even found in the history of the Habad movement, when the children of the Zemakh Zedek, Habad's third Rebbe, spread out to various localities to become Rebbes in their own right, although the town of Lubavitch maintained a special status in their eyes. They saw no problem in there being several Rebbes as a reflection of the diversity of people and territories that constituted the Habad movement. In light of these past models, it is not difficult to understand how Schneerson may have seen no need to prepare a successor, and was fully reconciled to the possibility that the movement might split into different spheres of influence.

As mentioned, this model of leadership has already begun to emerge in the international Habad community, indirectly fostered by the lack of a central authority. The movement is fracturing into local areas of authority, without coordination or concurrence by its ideological authorities. The broad division into messianist and non-messianist factions may be just the beginning. As each local authority becomes fully aware of his independence and of the lack of central control in Habad, each community may begin to examine and adopt otherwise unexplored theological territory.

We have already examined the difficulties involved in determining the "official" voice of the movement, and this lack of central direction is likely to continue indefinitely. The disintegration of Habad into fiefdoms may end up as the *de facto* organization, leaving many ideological and theological issues open for debate and for the emergence of several strong strands in the future. One way to avoid chaos as the movement fragments would be for Habad to issue an official policy on the matter. By issuing a definitive statement, the movement could avoid the ideological complications of false messianism, but the difficulty lies in the fact that the movement has already splintered and no single person or institution is likely to be accepted as authoritative by all factions. The question remains one of who speaks for the movement as a whole.

Shortly after Schneerson's death, there were attempts to appoint an executive as a temporary administrative replacement for him, and meetings were held to appoint a *mashpiah rashi*, a "head guide." One faction unsuccessfully suggested Rabbi Groner as a possible administrator for the movement. The agitation for a temporary leader was no doubt designed to ensure some measure of continuity and stability until a more permanent solution to the movement's leadership vacuum could be agreed upon. All such attempts have thus far been foiled, and the parties involved intimidated into withdrawing their initiatives and denying their desire for succession.

The Slow-Succession Model

One advantage of the fiefdom model of succession is that it allows talented individuals the opportunity to emerge within the movement, not leaping to attention but gradually assuming the leadership of a sizable following. This model is seen most graphically in the history of Habad itself, with the emergence of Shneur Zalman as the first Rebbe.

The emergence of a leader in Hasidism who was not stipulated by his predecessor is possible. In fact, the Rebbes rarely wrote wills or left instructions stipulating a clear succession. Where the Rebbe had children or an obvious successor to whom some authority had already been delegated, the situation was not particularly problematic. Shmuel, the fourth Habad Rebbe, wrote in his will that his children were to carry out certain functions of leadership, as did Shalom Dov Ber to Yosef Yitzhak. In this situation, leadership ability would be obvious, and the succession would follow a natural progression.

There is no instance in the annals of Habad of an incumbent Rebbe making a clear and unambiguous appointment of a successor. Outgoing Rebbes seem to have recognized the need for a subtle contest, a period of transition, or for Hasidim at large to decide on their next leader as parts of the succession process with which they were reluctant to interfere. Such a method of succession, however, takes time, before the new Rebbe can assume office.[15] Even Schneerson had to wait a year between the death of Yosef Yitzhak and his own assumption of office, and when he did, it was with none of the power and authority he later acquired. Chaim Potok has described the need for this period of transition in the post-Schneerson Habad movement:

> . . . the bereft hasidim will mourn deeply, will come to terms with reality, will rethink their theology, will heal in time. A new leader will arise. It will take a long time for him to attain, through deeds practical and mystical, a status and reputation even remotely approximating that of Rabbi Schneerson.[16]

A complete succession along the slow-succession model would be a slow and arduous process. Shneur Zalman did not achieve the status of zaddik immediately after the death of the Maggid, but took time to demonstrate his skill as an invaluable organizer and manager for another great teacher, Menachem Mendel of Vitebsk. Over a long time, and with the right political environment, external forces made Shneur Zalman invaluable to his mentor, who was then forced to endorse him as a zaddik.

The situation in the current Habad movement is quite different from the one faced by Shneur Zalman, and it may well prove impossible for a single figure to emerge and unite all of the diverse Habad communities worldwide. In many ways, the possibility becomes more remote the longer it takes. Every delay widens the gulf between messianists and non-messianists. Local authorities grow in power and influence, and natural dissonances are articulated over the few elements currently shared by the factions.

The successor under this model would need, above all, to demonstrate that he had a special relationship with Schneerson, just as Shneur Zalman had with the Maggid and Schneerson with Yosef Yitzhak.[17] A hereditary connection to the Schneerson lineage need not be an issue, for any relationship short of son would prove ineffectual as a claim. That is not to say, of course, that a family connection would not give additional prestige to a potential successor. More important would be the ability to unite the international community, to inspire the loyalty of powerful local leaders, and to defuse the issue of messianism, either by embracing it or discrediting it. One may confidently assert that such a succession over the entire movement is impossible, but candidates may yet emerge who could assume leadership over segments of the movement. Such figures will require immense skill and innovation, and above all the stamina to outshine any competitor, detractor, or ideology that might deter the faithful and convert the doubtful. They will also need skillful long-term planning and execution. The most significant factor in this successional model is longevity, both of life and of activity, as competitors either die or come to recognize the candidate as preferable to the movement losing all direction.

Some Habad leaders began to position themselves after Schneerson's death for a possible attempt in this direction. In public statements, Yehuda Krinsky, currently the nominal head of Habad, and Avraham Shemtov have both emphasized their close personal relationships with Schneerson, and have emphatically stated that Schneerson extended authority to them or told them his wishes regarding the leadership of Habad after his death. The technique of building power on the basis of the predecessor's instruction is a proven method of consolidating one's own authority, as Schneerson demonstrated so well. However, the traditional argument that every Hasid had a personal and equal connection to the Rebbe offsets any claim to enjoyment of a unique relationship with him. Whether any of the successional candidates has the skill to assume the ultimate leadership of Habad remains to be seen. All indications at present, however, suggest that the fiefdom and slow-succession models are the most likely means by which a new Rebbe may emerge, even if it is not for many years, or over a part of the movement and not the whole.

The Mission Model

The mission model is not really a model for succession but offers a solution to perpetuate the work of the movement while deferring a final decision about the succession. The policy is pragmatically sensible and ideologically compatible with the range of different theologies surrounding Schneerson, his death, the question of messianism, and the continuation of the movement, and all the other models of succession presented here. Its basic theme is to continue the work begun by Schneerson, which was Schneerson's own attitude toward the mission of Yosef Yitzhak, and it surely is the safest and least contentious way for the movement to continue today. The mission model insists that throughout his life, Schneerson unequivocally urged his followers to educate Jews in their religion, conduct outreach to spread Hasidism, and thus participate in and hasten the redemption. According to the mission model, this is what all Hasidim should do, now more than ever before, as this is the surest way to achieve the redemptive goal set down by Schneerson. While there is ideological confusion about messianism, succession, leadership, and perpetuation of the tradition in institutional form, at least the mission of Habad is still clear, and Habad activists are well trained and established to continue their education and outreach activities.

The mission model is, in effect, the closest thing to an official and universally accepted policy of how the movement should continue, largely for want of another strategy that might be agreed upon by all of Habad's elements and factions. Messianists and non-messianists are united by and economically dependent on the outreach and educational infrastructure of the movement. This model also appears to have the support of the institutions and of powerful figures like Yehuda Krinsky. Apart from being a good way to maintain stability and continuity in Habad, it is also an effective way for those implementing the policy to achieve leadership. Just as Schneerson acted as executor of Yosef Yitzhak's mission, and thereby was able to more effectively lead the movement and more easily replace him as Rebbe, some individuals in Schneerson's administrative hierarchy, particularly his aides, are supporting the implementation of the mission model. One may reasonably assume, given its success in the past, that the implementation of the mission strategy may eventually lead to the emergence of a new leader. After all, whoever succeeds in implementing outreach is implementing the essence of Schneerson's program. If any of Habad's administrators proves able to motivate the Hasidim to continue the hard work and achievements they produced under Schneerson, he might be perceived as the executor of Schneerson's will, and become his temporary, and possibly more permanent, replacement.

Whatever the motive for this model of leadership, it fills a number of ideological and practical needs. Work to spread the memory of Schneerson is important for the movement's image; increased effort in outreach utilized pent-up energy, is cathartic, and provides a sense of satisfaction for the Hasidim who thereby fill their time with useful and productive labor. Indeed, to continue the work of a deceased leader is a traditional rabbinic way to keep his memory alive. Many of the movement's emissaries responded to Schneerson's death by firmly resolving to rededicate themselves to the tasks set Habad by Schneerson, both as an indication of their dedication to his instructions, and as a means to preserve his memory.[18] One indication that the work of outreach and expansion has continued is the 1995 claim by Yehuda Krinsky that more than a hundred new Habad institutes were founded in the year after Schneerson's death.[19] Additionally, official programs that he has sponsored have brought younger Habad rabbis into many institutions for them to learn outreach techniques, and problem-solving committees have also been established.[20] One official estimate of the size of the movement at that time indicates that there were over two thousand Habad institutions worldwide,[21] and although reliable statistics are difficult to acquire, the number appears to have grown since.

One of the attractions of the mission model is its flexibility; it can accommodate either the appointment of a single individual as executor, group leadership by committee or institution, the fiefdom model of autonomous control, messianic models, or any other into which the mission of Schneerson can be incorporated. The stability it provides, through retaining Schneerson as the central figure and continuing his work, almost certainly will make it part of the succession debate for the future, and in the meantime provides continuity and activity for the activist, rather than intellectual, section of the Habad community. Only complete disillusionment with Schneerson and his mission can break this model, and in fact many people who have fallen out of the movement reject the mission model on grounds of opposition to its evangelical consensus. As this did not occur among the overwhelming majority at Schneerson's death, and has still not occurred at the time of writing, one may safely conclude that it is unlikely to occur without agitation. The only foreseeable and logical source of such agitation would be from a strongly resurrectionist group that makes unfulfilled predictions as to the date of Schneerson's return, and this would only succeed if the movement as a whole had adopted a resurrectionist ideology, which seems unlikely in the extreme. Only such a development could alter the fine balance established within the movement since Schneerson's passing.

The Ghost Model

The basic approach of the ghost model, as the name implies, is the belief that Schneerson, despite his death, is still in control and watching over his Hasidim. The model accepts the physical death of Schneerson, but maintains that he continues to communicate with his followers in some mystical way. This idea was basic to Schneerson's leadership succession after Yosef Yitzhak; as the new Rebbe, he claimed to be in contact with his predecessor and able to divine his will for the future direction of the movement. Schneerson also claimed that he received blessings from his predecessor, and that the former Rebbe intervened in human affairs.[22] It must be noted that such a connection between a living Rebbe and a dead one is not altogether uncommon to Hasidism, and certainly not unique to Habad. The events occurring today in some segments of the movement may therefore be seen as emulation of Schneerson's own behavior.

The ghost model is understandably popular with many of the messianist followers of Habad, who believe in the continued involvement of Schneerson in the movement, either through his yet-to-be-realized revelation as the mashiach or his hidden presence in the world. The model is a common element of many of the otherwise disunited factions because of its belief that communication with Schneerson is still possible, and that he is able to guide the movement despite his absence from the physical realm. The idea in itself does not automatically preclude the notion of a successor, because, as noted, this was a component in the succession of Schneerson. The main difference between the present phenomenon and what Schneerson did lies in the scale; today many thousands of Hasidim are seeking to emulate the actions of one person, Schneerson, in his behavior toward Yosef Yitzhak.

The ghost model relies for its success as a leadership model on the assumption and practice of continuing communication with the departed Schneerson. The primary mechanism for this is through consultation of the *iggerot kodesh*, the collected "holy letters" of Schneerson,[23] wherein are compiled many volumes of responsa—questions and answers, containing advice, blessings, and directions on a wide range of subjects. Theoretically, the method would work with any other holy book, but its application to other texts is much less common. The technique of divination has the perplexed inquirer write down or think a question or problem, then, usually with prayer or meditation, and sometimes after immersing in a mikvah (ritual bath), place it in a volume chosen at random or by inspiration.[24] Alternatively, a volume is opened at random after the question or inquiry is formulated. In either case, the pages between which the question are placed are read, and it is believed that somewhere on the two pages is Schneerson's response to the question, provided by a process of inspiration.

To the unbeliever, the success of the technique derives from the wide range of topics that Schneerson examined or touched upon in each of his letters, so that something of relevance to almost any question on any issue can be found. More important still is the fact that his letters can be interpreted allegorically, or in other ways, to elicit the (at least unconsciously) desired response. That the method works, at least for believers, is evident from the many stories of fortuitous answers and miraculous occurrences passed by word of mouth in the movement and published in messianist Habad journals.[25]

One of the main curiosities surrounding this method of communication pertains to its origin in the movement. While the phenomena of randomly consulting holy books for advice is common in the New Age movement, the practice seems to have little clear precedent in Jewish, Hasidic, or even Habad tradition, although those who employ it attempt to legitimize it by finding analogies in biblical and classic Jewish literature. It has been compared to the Urim and Tumim,[26] an oracular device used in the Temple. Another parallel for *iggerot kodesh* is found in the story of Mordechai in the biblical Book of Esther, who, according to the Midrash, is confused as to what course of action to take. He asks three randomly chosen children what they have learned in school. Each answers with a verse containing the words "do not fear," from which he is able to decide what to do. Other precedents with less authority are also cited to persuade the undecided to adopt the method of consultation.

There are many dangers to both the future of Habad and the faith and practice of individual Hasidim in the employment of *iggerot kodesh* as a means of obtaining guidance for the movement and for life decisions. As long as the inquirer is earnest and approaches the process with an awareness of halakhah and Jewish tradition, the dangers may be reduced, but there is significant potential for abuse. Messianist leaders have attempted to impose some guidelines to limit the potential exploitation and excesses of this system. One of the most explicit of these is Rabbi Ginsberg from Israel, who has advised that *iggerot kodesh* are not to be consulted when answers are forthcoming from other sources. For medical issues, for example, a doctor should be consulted, and a rabbi for questions of halakhah. In other words, the only issues for which the process of *iggerot kodesh* may be endorsed are those for which no normal solution is to be found.[27]

Gravesite Culture

Beside this "mystical" communication with the departed Schneerson, there are other, more traditional components to the ghost model of succession. The foremost of these is the constant vigil by Hasidim at the gravesite of Schneerson, which serves a number of purposes both for the movement and for the individuals involved. It enables the retention of contact with the remains of Schneerson, which is useful for the movement as a way of demonstrating its dedication to the deceased. Other, more spiritual purposes are also served by proximity to the gravesite. The *Tanya* explains that the benefit of the zaddik to the world is greatest after he dies, because his spirit is freed from his body and shared with all humanity.[28] The spirit, despite its freedom, is believed to reside closer to the body than anywhere else, and so proximity to the grave is considered meritorious and spiritually beneficial. There is also an element of messianist expectation at work here; the Hasidim keep the body company, and some await signs of its resurrection. Of course, those Hasidim who claim that Schneerson did not die refuse to visit his so-called gravesite, they believe it to be unoccupied.

The veneration of the gravesite of a deceased leader, especially a Rebbe and zaddik, has strong precedent in Habad and Hasidic history, including the tremendous respect with which Schneerson treated the grave of Yosef Yitzhak because it housed the disused receptacle for the departed Rebbe's soul. Throughout his life, Schneerson regularly visited the grave of his predecessor, often three or more times a week, and would stay in prayer for many hours. In emulation of this tradition, Schneerson's Hasidim now perform the same veneration at his grave. The *ohel* (gravesite) has become a place for prayer and contemplation for them, and is a place for communal bonding in a shared sense of sorrow and loss. The gravesite practices, however extreme they have become, are generally representative of the anti-messianist striving in Habad, because at the very least their observance acknowledges his death.

To allow Hasidim more easy access, a building was bought nearby to house guests and provide services for the Hasidim, particularly the scores that come to stay during festivals and Shabbat.[29] In addition to providing comfort and support to the visiting Hasidim, the building houses industrial-strength fax machines, which receive prayers for Schneerson and petitions for aid, literally around the clock. The volume of faxes sent from around the world indicates the immense reverence his followers had for their deceased Rebbe; in the first year after his death, it is estimated that sometimes as many as a thousand faxes were received each day. E-mail communication is also available, and messages are printed and left at the grave by diligent Hasidim.

Many Sephardim also come to visit the gravesite. There is a long Sephardi tradition of visiting graves, especially those of zaddikim and Rebbes, as a spiritual practice.[30] While the tradition is relatively new to Ashkenazim, it has long been observed in the history of Hasidism in general and especially in Habad; the town of Lubavitch housed the graves of several Rebbes, and visiting their graves was an important part of being in the hometown of the movement. The rising popularity of the site of

Schneerson's grave is hoped by some to indicate its emergence as a place of pilgrimage throughout the Jewish world, in the manner of the grave of Shimon bar Yochai in Meron, Israel.[31] This place attracts about half a million people on the anniversary of his death. Others have expressed a hope that the gravesite will become like the Western Wall in Jerusalem.[32]

The visits to the gravesite and the veneration of Schneerson's final resting-place are not deemed mystical or unusual by Habad, Jewish, or human standards, where remembrance of the dead is commonplace. Krinsky supported the focus on the grave, stating his belief that it is both therapeutic and cathartic for the sorrowful Hasidim to venerate and commemorate their Rebbe.[33] Heilman believes that the gravesite will remain an important part of a geographical and spiritual axis for Habad followers, shared with Crown Heights as a holy site, at least until a successor emerges (if ever).[34]

The ghost model of leadership is perhaps best understood as a communal effort to preserve the special connection that developed between Schneerson and his Hasidim. Despite his physical death, the Rebbe is still alive and pervades the Hasid's daily existence through the study of his works, the enhancement of his memory by means of stories, discussion, and prayer, and the fulfillment of his directives. More obviously, the physical presence of Schneerson is preserved through modern recording techniques, innumerable audio sources, videotapes, and recordings of satellite hookups. These are in addition to the standard and more traditional collections of books and pictures of Schneerson. At social gatherings throughout the movement since his death, the connection is sustained by the use of these media; tapes are played and replayed, to keep alive Schneerson's memory and give Hasidim an understanding of his continuing presence in the world. Alan Nadler has succinctly expressed this use of modern media by reminding us that Schneerson was the "first Rebbe in history that has a significant, VCR-accessible doctrine."[35]

The Normalization Model

The fundamental proposition behind the normalization model is, as the name implies, the return of Habad Hasidim to a "normal," that is, nonmessianist and nonresurrectionist, form of spirituality, and possibly their exit from Orthodox observance altogether. Rather than being part of a fringe movement of Hasidism, which is itself a fringe of Judaism, the normalization model posits the return of Schneerson's followers to nondivisive forms of spirituality as a result of either recognizing the failure of Schneerson's messianic promises or coming to terms with their inherent contradictions.

The normalization model assumes that the messianic fervor of the last years of Schneerson's life distanced his followers from the rest of Orthodox Judaism. During this period in the history of Habad, the morale of the movement was at an artificial high, bolstered and infused with emotional content by Schneerson's insistent demand for the coming of the mashiach, echoed most obviously in his song "We want *Moshiach* Now!"[36] While the demand for the coming of the mashiach is to be understood in light of Schneerson's attempt to end the exile immediately, as discussed in Chapter 9, it served to distance Habad from other strands of Judaism that reject calculations of, or heavy dependence on, the imminent coming of the messianic era. Spirits were high in the movement, but there had been ideological break with other schools of Hasidim and with Orthodoxy, not to mention with nonreligious Jews.

For those who rejected Habad's messianist ideology, other alternatives were available. The practice of outreach meant not only that Habad's followers had been exposed to modernity, but that many had established and maintained contacts with other groups within Orthodoxy. Some of the people who drop out of Habad end up, no doubt, in other branches of Judaism, some of which share elements of belief and practice with Habad. The integration of Habad Hasidim into other Jewish communities would fill the vacuum left by the death of Schneerson, but keep them active in a mission model, albeit reinterpreted in the changed circumstances. After a time, Habad followers who join other communities may be integrated completely into other forms of Jewish spirituality or practice, especially in the second and subsequent generations. These mechanisms would therefore serve as means for the normalization of Habad Hasidim into mainstream Judaism.

Integration into mainstream Judaism may very well take place for the community functionaries and rabbis who are active in non-Hasidic synagogues and communities. While they are central to Habad's outreach, and effectively form the voice of the movement to the normative Jewish world, they are also burdened with increasing pressure from mainstream Judaism to abandon the messianist doctrine that formed such an important part of Habad's ideology under Schneerson's leadership. While mainstream Judaism is vaguely tolerant of Hasidism, the antagonism to messianism has necessitated that community rabbis must often hide their true beliefs from their congregations; if they are open about their beliefs, they may suffer ridicule, ostracism, or loss of position and therefore livelihood. The only alternative is to adhere to the viewpoint of the community, send their children to normative Orthodox schools, and possibly risk the erosion of their Habad beliefs, slowly adopting mainstream attitudes. The adoption of mainstream ideas, even if only in public, while adhering to Habad doctrine in private, as many did during Schneerson's lifetime, will have a long-term effect on the movement. This happened once before in the history of Hasidism. Green describes how charismatic Hasidic Rebbes, early on, were tempted too far into marginal mysticism and speculation. As they made leadership inroads in the mainstream community, however, and even became the dominant local authority, they realized that they could not afford to indulge themselves in marginalism, and instead joined the mainstream.

The history of Hasidism bears witness to the fact that in this wedding of normative authority to the charismatic spokesman, it is chiefly the charismatic who is

transformed as he feels the mantle of tradition and the responsibility for its maintenance bear down weightily upon him. [37]

If something of the same sort happens to the Habad community rabbis and authorities, it would indicate their normalization and integration into the community at
large, and thus effectively end the separative existence of Habad as a distinctive force.
There is also a possibility that Habad followers will turn to other Hasidic Rebbes
for advice and blessings, and possibly join other Hasidic communities. While this is
not likely, it may conceivably take place, although it would not be easy for them to
transfer their allegiance from Schneerson to another Rebbe, especially given
Schneerson's superhuman image in the lives and thinking of Habad Hasidim. As
Habad antagonized many Hasidic groups with its messianism and fervent outreach,
it is also unlikely that Habad Hasidim would receive a warm reception should they
attempt to socialize to another Hasidic school. However appealing this option might
appear to an outsider, it is unlikely to occur. Apart from the fact that it would mean
breaking an emotional and spiritual connection with Schneerson, the act of leaving
Habad would be an admission of failure, which some might find difficult to accept.
There is also the social problem caused by the exposure of Habad Hasidim to the
modern world. To leave Habad and join the court of another Hasidic Rebbe, they
might well have to sever their connections with the outside world, because most (if
not all) Hasidic groups are much more restrictive in lifestyle than Schneerson encouraged his followers to be. For these reasons, there might be some movement from
Habad to other Hasidic courts, but it will probably be neither extensive nor completely satisfactory, and certainly does not provide a long-term solution to the question of succession in Habad.

Normalization will exact as its price the end of the vision of Habad Hasidism as the
primary force in bringing the messianic redemption. It would also mark the end of
the movement's active enterprise of building communities and schools beyond its
immediate internal needs. Normalization might even mean the end of Habad as a separate and distinctive stream of Hasidism, although admittedly this is very unlikely.
Even if such an event were to occur, there would undoubtedly remain a core of
diehard believers to continue Habad's messianist and resurrectionist causes, and these
elements might even radicalize their ideology in response to the normalization of the
rest of the movement.

Habad Fallout

Even during Schneerson's lifetime, some adherents of Habad began to grow weary
of the constant emphasis on messianism. Excessive exposure numbed them to aspects
of Habad spirituality connected with the notion of the messianic redemption. These
ideas became hollow words, part of an ideology that was no longer effective or realistic, exacerbated by the failure of Schneerson's messianic and redemptive promises.

It was one thing to be spiritual and idealistic, and even support an unpopular idea while there was a possibility that it might be actuated, but to assert a doctrine so clearly against empirical evidence was, for many, too much to expect. The messianist fervor is forcing those who merely tolerated religion in their lives to a decision, whether to tolerate blind dogma and archaic thinking or to reject the messianist ideology. Many pragmatist followers believed, while the Rebbe was alive, that the speculation concerning his messianic assertions might be justified, but see his death as signaling the end of such speculation. This, of course, pits them against those who believed more fervently in Schneerson's messianic status after his death, leading to the conclusion that the messianists see a challenge or threat in the normalization process.

One of the primary difficulties with monitoring the implementation of the normalization model is its lack of an organizational or collective ideology. There is no normalization movement or submovement, for it is a process. Normalization originates within individuals involved with the movement, and begins with an inclination to veer away from conventional Habad thinking. It occurs among those who desire to pursue new forms of social life or employment, and involves the cultivation of non-Habad friends and contacts, and possibly even a transfer to a non-Habad synagogue, and eventual cessation of direct involvement in Habad activities or the community. The number of such individuals is understandably difficult to monitor, let alone quantify. The situation is made more difficult by the fact that some Habad members are compelled for social reasons to remain in the community—because of marriage to a believer or to keep their employment in a Habad institution, for example—even though they feel little inclination toward its messianist ideas. Because they pay lip service to its belief system, it is impossible to judge the level of ideological fallout from the movement.

There is also a physical fallout from Habad in the post-Schneerson era. This is a natural consequence to be expected from a movement that once had a strong and idealistic leader but now lacks a cohesive function or focus. Some dropouts find the messianic domination of the movement intolerable. Unable to discern a middle path between messianist and standard Orthodox observance, they conclude that the traditions of Judaism, and often of religion in general, have no basis; they leave observance completely.

Exposure to non-Orthodox lifestyles, primarily through outreach activities, may tempt many Hasidim, inducing them to indulge in non-Hasidic or non-Orthodox behavior. In traditional non-Habad Hasidism in the East European shtetl (ghetto), where poverty and simplicity were commonplace, the Rebbe was a force for social cohesion and isolation, and there was a strong need for communal cohesion. The unity resulting from fear of the outside world kept Hasidic communities focused around their Rebbe, and for most schools of Hasidim eagerly instilled the ghetto mentality even in the New World. In the main, other Hasidic groups refused dialogue or interaction with anyone else,[38] a fact of which Habad was aware and against which it actively fought. While other Hasidic groups remained insulated from innovation and modernity, Habad actively sought to engage the modern world, and went into the community seeking dialogue, or at least a platform from which to preach its ideology. As part of the outreach mission of Schneerson, yeshiva students were sent to the business district of New York to talk religion to Jews in the workforce. Schneerson even involved himself in politics—local, national and international—and encouraged his followers to take an active interest in their local communities.[39] Across the country and the world, Habad Hasidim moved from Crown Heights into the streets and shopping malls, and they continue to do so even after Schneerson's death.

The almost unique status of Habad as a truly modern Hasidism has become something of which the movement is (perhaps justifiably) proud, but it has exposed its adherents to the many temptations offered by modernity. Without Schneerson as a guide, large numbers have succumbed to these pressures and left Habad, if not the religious life, entirely. Even if the present generation does not succumb, there is cause to fear for the future of the movement. Many younger Habad Hasidim are going to university, traveling, and working among the general population, increasing their exposure to outside life. These students are encouraged to concentrate on the movement's outreach activities, and many have been compelled to cut their yeshiva studies to accommodate the demand for outreach. If less concentration on studies is combined with more exposure to the modern world, there will be a greater chance of fallout from the movement, which could very well lose its religious force. If Habad's strong identity and ideology are not perpetuated at all levels, the movement will cease to have a strong effect on the upbringing and education of its children, and with each passing year, their normalization is increasingly likely.

The Habad Periphery:
Heretics, the Disenchanted, and Neo-Habadnikim[40]

There has always been fallout from religious groups and especially from Jewish observance. Many of the first Zionists were infamously slandered because they left the yeshiva, religious observance, and the shtetl to follow their dream of building a utopian community. It should come as no surprise that many are now leaving the Habad movement, but perhaps it is in some ways more surprising that so many people stayed for so long. Schneerson's charisma was probably the strongest factor inducing them to stay. The combination of a charismatic leader and an idealistic utopian mission encouraged many to remain in Habad. At one time, it was proudly observed in Habad circles that fallout to secularism took place in other Jewish religious groups but not in Habad. This was true, and throughout the reign of Schneerson, the influx to the movement was far larger than the fallout. Insiders attributed this to the power of Hasidic philosophy, and bore witness to the divine guidance of Schneerson's leadership. When the ideological bubble burst with his death, the trickle away from Habad grew into a flood, a phenomenon that has been the subject of media interest and sociological study.[41]

Over the years, many talented people had been attracted to the movement. With the death of Schneerson, some of them felt free to "find themselves." On returning to the world outside Habad, they have adopted many and varied vocations. Most are going to university, exposing themselves to the arts, or traveling and meeting people beyond the Habad community and even beyond the Jewish community. Some are following careers in business, but many are playing music, writing books and poetry, film scripts, and research dissertations, and some have even entered upon academic careers. Some who have left the movement have dabbled in New Age culture and spiritualism, which has many elements in common with Habad's mystical ideology and practice, though few, it seems, have entered another religious path. This is usually because their leaving Habad was brought about by a sense of being saturated with religion and charismatic groups, caused by years of the Rebbe's messianism. Smaller numbers who leave Habad join other Hasidic groups or modern Orthodox or national Zionist communities in Israel. Those who follow this path generally have an entirely different philosophical or political outlook from the ones mentioned above.

In consequence of these developments, the influence of Habad, or at least the expanding Habad periphery, is becoming increasingly diverse in a range of different areas. The full effect is not yet manifest, and will no doubt prove interesting to observe in future. The scope for immense creativity in these fallouts is great; many have skills developed through outreach, and if directed, their pent-up messianic frustration and disillusionment might produce some interesting results. Habad's people, work practices, and philosophy fuse effectively to influence many others, whether they recognize this influence or not.

Many of the former Hasidim who have left the movement still maintain, to some degree, Hasidic mannerisms or ideas, or a partiality to the Hasidic concepts so entrenched in their thinking, even if they are no longer religiously observant. Many were scholars, or at least deeply pious at one stage in their lives, and others were, through the necessities of outreach, very articulate in explaining the elaborate Habad philosophic system.

During the 1950s and 1960s a number of prominent Habad Hasidim left the movement and became prominent in new areas of endeavor. An example is Rabbi Zalman Shechter Aloni, who after leaving Habad dedicated himself to writing and teaching a fusion of Hasidism, Eastern religion and New Age ideas. Another example is the famous singing rabbi, Shlomo Carlebach, who was deeply influenced by Habad. He influenced an entire generation with his music, the lyrics of which blend Hasidic thinking and piety with, again, New Age themes. There are many other examples of influential ex-Habad Hasidim, but I think the point is demonstrated. The return of visionary people to the non-Habad world will no doubt spread the influence of Habad's ideas to a wider audience in the world at large.

The Habad periphery includes another group, people influenced by Habad teachings and activities but not fully associated with its doctrine or organization. Many Jewish soul-searchers (musicians, writers, poets, and film makers) have at one time or another found themselves in Habad Houses learning Hasidic philosophy. Perhaps they were friendly with a rabbi and picked up worldview-altering Hasidic concepts, or conversed with people who had. Certain Hasidic ideas are quite profound, and perhaps even life-changing, and it is not unexpected that some searchers will have been profoundly influenced by elements of Habad ideology. Some may even have been observant for a brief period before rejecting a fully devoted religious life. In this way, the influence of Habad may stretch beyond the beard and hat worn by identifiable Habad adherents, especially as many Hasidic ideas are so appealing to artisans, thinkers, and communicators.

An entirely different periphery to the Habad movement is found in the other Orthodox religious groups that have emulated Habad, either by copying its outreach methods or ideology directly or, in some instances, by adopting Habad techniques through osmosis. Students who once studied in Habad institutions but later moved on to other groups obviously embodied Habad methods of outreach, which they took with them and adapted to their new environment. Habad methods are now very popular with the Aish ha-Torah and Or Sameach outreach movements, as well as in the Sephardi renewal movement, Shas. Because they do not directly credit Habad with their methods, they are less identifiable as part of the Habad periphery, but the commonalities of methodology and emphasis are to be noted, and originated with Habad.

Alongside this emulation of Habad outreach and social activism comes the infiltration of certain ideologies that are specifically of Habad origin. The central Habad philosophical treatise, the *Tanya*, cannot be ignored for its influence outside Habad. The concepts, kabbalistic imagery, and metaphors have attracted outsiders to Jewish observance, and this influence has begun to be disseminated beyond the confines of the Habad movement.

---

[1] Including some of the Hasidim of Yosef Yitzhak, and indeed Schneerson himself.

[2] For more on succession and messianism in the post-Schneerson era, see David Berger, "The New Messianism." The articles by two leading messianists, Rabbis Shmuel Butman and Isser Weisberg, are polemic of the resurrection possibility and other issues in Habad today.

[3] Moshe Slonim, "*Emunah* in the Rebbe," p. 97.

[4] See Yosef Braun et al., *And He Will Redeem Us*; Shmuel Butman, *Countdown to Moshiach*; and countless *Beis Moshiach* articles.

[5] See Raquel Hasofer, "Messiah from the Living—Messiah from the Dead."

[6] Thus the failure of the Rabbinical Council of America's attempt to excommunicate Habad from Orthodox Judaism. See ibid., esp. pp. 30–42.

[7] In January 2002, a class in the Crown Heights Lubavitch High School yeshiva was torn apart by the divide, with a messianist class being established, at least temporarily, in opposition to the non-messianists. Messianist parents have taken their children out of the Habad class, where they represented approximately half of the students, and enrolled them in the new breakaway class. It will be interesting to see whether similar events take place in the future on a wider scale.

[8] One of Judaism's main arguments against Christianity is its insistence that the messiah must be alive at the coming of the redemption, and thus a dead person cannot be a messianic

candidate. See especially Berger, "New Messianism," pp. 35–42, 88; and *The Rebbe, the Messiah, and the Scandal of Orthodox Indifference*.

[9] This has even included advertising on buses, in subways, and in other public places; some Hasidim have even attached pictures of Schneerson to their vehicles, to serve as mobile billboards for the Rebbe.

[10] See *Beis Moshiach* 75 (February 16, 1996).

[11] See Chapter 9.

[12] Jonathan Sacks, "The Man Who Turned Judaism Outward" and "When Mysticism Saved the Jewish People."

[13] This was suggested in "Passing of a Tzadik."

[14] See Sachs, "Man Who Turned Judaism Outward."

[15] Laurie Goodstein, "Death of Lubavitcher Leader, Rabbi Schneerson, Stuns Followers." Goodstein quotes Heilman, professor of Jewish studies at Queens College, New York, as noting that if there is no designated successor at the death of a Rebbe, "then there is a period of transition in which a number of voices are heard and for a time nobody is dominant." This is indeed what has happened in Habad.

[16] Chaim Potok, "Rabbi Schneerson."

[17] Terrance Samuel, "Rabbi M. Schneerson, Lubavitch Leader, Dies in New York at 92."

[18] Chris Leppek, "The Lubavitcher Rebbe"; see also "Remembering a Great Jewish Leader."

[19] Ari L. Goldman, "The Late Rebbe Still Defines Chabad."

[20] David Gonzalez, "Lubavitchers Learn to Sustain Themselves Without the Rebbe."

[21] As claimed by Abraham Shemtov, chairman of AGUCH, in ibid.

[22] See *Torat Menachem*, Parshat Shlach, 12 Tammuz 5750, pp. 106 and 130.

[23] See *Beis Moshiach*. Every issue has a description of this process in the story section. See also "Yesh Haim le-Achar ha-Mavet" ("There Is Life After the Death"), *Yediot Aharonot* (March 6, 1995).

[24] The method usually involves using the volume to which one feels most strongly drawn at the time, rather than a favorite volume or some other method.

[25] See *Beis Moshiach* for weekly tales of *iggerot kodesh* miracles.

[26] See Numbers 28:21. No one is entirely certain what these devices were, or how they were used, but they are mentioned in connection with a breastplate. See also Leviticus 8:8.

[27] See "Yesh Haim le-Achar ha-Mavet."

[28] *Tanya*, pt. 4, chap. 27b (p. 568), in the name of the *Zohar*.

[29] The house was bought by the millionaire Hasid Joseph Gutnick and donated to the movement. Gutnick has given most generously to the movement over many years, and is one of its principal financial benefactors.

[30] See Issachar Ben-Ami, *Saint Veneration Among the Jews in Morocco*, esp. pp. 93–129.

[31] Shimon bar Yochai lived in the second century C.E. He is famous for assisting in the systematic classification of the halakhah and attempting to adduce a rational basis for it. He is also honored by kabbalists as the originator of the ideas codified in the *Zohar*, and the date of his death, Lag Ba'Omer, is a feast day throughout the Jewish world, traditionally observed by Habad with a street parade.

[32] Krinsky, quoted in Lynette Holloway, "Queens Holy Land."

[33] Ibid.

[34] Ibid.

[35] Alan Nadler, quoted in Pamela Druckerman, "Worldwide Outposts Called Key to Chabad Survival."

[36] "We want *Moshiach* now! We want *Moshiach* now! We want *Moshiach* now! We don't want to wait." Most of these songs have simple lyrics that are sung in repetitive cycles to heighten the mood and effect of the singing.

[37] Arthur Green, "Typologies of Leadership and the Hasidic Zaddiq," p. 152.

[38] Jerome R. Mintz, *Hasidic People*, pp. 29–31.

[39] See "Obituaries: Rabbi Menachem Schneerson."

[40] A term coined by Baruch Thaler.

[41] See Rebecca Segall, "Young Lubavitcher Hasidim in a Rebbe-less World." She discusses the ex-Lubavitch phenomenon, the use of drugs, New Age philosophy, pop culture and extreme secularism among former Hasidim.

Chapter 22
Factors of Influence on Succession: What's Next?

The Hasidic Groupings

Now that we have examined the current situation in the post-Schneerson Habad movement, the question remains, What next? While any answer to this question would be an exercise in pure speculation, it would be useful to discuss the possible influences that may come into play in this debate. Without considering the various models for succession presented above, there are a significant number of factors that will influence the future of Habad.

The movement that we find at the beginning of the twenty-first century is remarkably different from the one inherited by Schneerson in 1951, largely as a result of his leadership and influence. Differences in the composition of the movement are to be noted. At present, the vast majority of Habad followers are comparatively young, and were either raised in the movement or are Jews who came to religious observance after contact with Habad outreach in its various forms. The practice of outreach on a massive scale has altered the movement, making it more outward looking and in turn leading to the gradual admission of modern influences. Use of technology is a major factor in the movement, and has both positive and negative effects. While unifying a scattered population and enabling unprecedented opportunity for outreach, it has also brought exposure to non-Hasidic influences. The remote style of leadership adopted by Schneerson has also had an effect on the nature of the movement, as local communities have become independent of the parent body. This in turn has lessened contact with the physical seat of the Rebbe, so much a part of other schools of Hasidism.

Other factors pertaining to the growth of Habad have also changed over the last half-century. The impact of the Holocaust and Communist rule on the Jewish community, with increased migration and concern for future safety, has made many Jews rethink their connection to their traditional roots, and some have turned to traditional observance as a result. Increased secularization in the broader Jewish society, coupled with growing Hasidic insularity and Israeli nationalism, have led to deeper consideration of what it means to be Jewish in the modern world. Habad offered an articulate response to this issue, to the extent that it even became involved in the "who is a Jew?" controversy in Israel. Among other issues, this was concerned with establishing the Jewish status of communities such as the Falashas of Ethiopia, Reform Jews, converts of various types, and other peoples wishing to immigrate to Israel.

Within Habad, the role of the international community has been tilted in the balance of power as the movement has decentralized. The independence of the emissaries has led to decreased reliance on central authority, which some (most notably Krinsky) have tried to counteract, with some level of success. The elevation of youth raised in Habad to positions of power has also changed the nature of the movement. No longer are the respected leaders of communities venerable gray-bearded scholars, but increasingly Habad communities are led by "gung-ho," enthusiastic, energetic younger men. Many were raised with only one Rebbe, and a superhuman one at that; they had never lived through a power transfer at the death of a leader, and because Schneerson was so successful, they are far less likely to accept a successor. The position of scholarship and the intellectual style of Hasidim in Habad has also changed, being replaced with social activism, outreach, and fundraising as the main ladders to prominence in the movement. The growing presence of educated and business-aware leaders has also had an effect on the movement, with the rise of rationalism in some parts of the community, and an increase in mysticism in others. This is coupled with the incredible rise in messianist ideology, which now threatens to split the movement irrevocably. Amid all of this, the challenge for the next generation of Habad Hasidim will be to retain their distinctive identity and influence within the broader Jewish community, which is currently under threat from normalization and other factors.

The International Communities

The destruction of European Jewry in the Holocaust and under the rule of Communism in Eastern Europe depleted the natural prewar constituency of Habad Hasidim, and for the most part left only a few remnant refugee groups in countries such as Israel and the United States. Apart from those Hasidim trapped in the Soviet Union, the future of Habad seemed dependent on the presence of Yosef Yitzhak, and later of Schneerson, in the United States. As we have seen, through their efforts Habad grew from a refugee community to arguably the most influential single body on the contemporary Jewish scene in the United States.

The Crown Heights community, however, is not separated from the other Hasidic groups in New York, but is simply one of many enclaves in a large city. Some of the other dynasties, like the Satmar Hasidim, have been in New York as long as, if not longer than, Habad, and have a greater population. So, although the Crown Heights Habad community contains a sizable population of Hasidim, it is by no means the largest Hasidic community in the city. It does claim to be the most influential, however, or at least the most publicly recognized, largely because of the success of outreach and the massive publicity attracted by the movement.

The influence of Crown Heights on Habad is not as great today as it was in the early years of Schneerson's leadership, in large part because of the internationalization of the movement. Emissaries across the globe have established many large communities that rival the heartland of the movement in size and density of population, if not spiritual appeal. This is especially so in Israel and Europe. As we have noted in examining the fiefdom model of succession, the election of a Rebbe today does not depend necessarily on the Crown Heights constituency. Just as the children of the Zemakh Zedek became Rebbes in different communities outside the town of Lubavitch, so too the Hasidim of Schneerson may well become Rebbes in their own right. Although it is grossly incorrect to say that the Crown Heights constituency no longer has significance in the Habad movement, its influence is certainly less than what it once was. This change has not completely stripped Crown Heights of at least symbolic power, however. If a candidate was somehow chosen as Rebbe in an election conducted someplace other than Crown Heights, he would probably have less chance of achieving eminence in the movement as a whole than if that locality had endorsed his election. However, if such an election were held in the Crown Heights community, the international community would no longer feel obliged to accept the Crown Heights candidate. This is especially so with the oldest Habad community, the one located in Israel. The presence of Habad Hasidim in Israel extends back to the time of Shneur Zalman, and so the Israeli Habad community has a longer pedigree than the Crown Heights community. Because of their presence in the Holy Land, they could also theoretically garner the same degree of moral support as Crown Heights, and in the event of a proposed successor to Schneerson emerging from Crown Heights, the Israeli community might well select a candidate of its own. While this is decidedly speculative, and cannot be substantiated until an attempt at election of a new Rebbe is made (if ever), it is an important observation concerning the decentralization of Habad under Schneerson.

The significance of Crown Heights in the international Habad community has also lessened, especially after the death of Schneerson. While it must be acknowledged that the gravesites of former Rebbes in the Russian town of Lubavitch contributed to the survival and eminence of the Lubavitch dynasty as opposed to the other Habad dynasties, the same need not occur with the graves of Yosef Yitzhak and Schneerson in New York. The transformation of Habad from geographical dependence on the town of Lubavitch as the seat of the Rebbe to a "universal mission" through the outreach of Schneerson has reduced the dependency on Crown Heights for authority and guidance. For those Hasidim who wish to retain a physical connection to the sites of Schneerson's life or to visit his grave, modern technology allows frequent visits with relatively little inconvenience and only marginal involvement with the Crown Heights authorities. The communications facilities (especially fax and e-mail) established at the *ohel* have made it unnecessary to visit in person; messages can be communicated from across the globe, instantly, further lessening the geographical dependence on Crown Heights. Hasidim can live on the other side of the world and still maintain a personal relationship with the Rebbe. Scholars travel regularly, Habad manuscripts are in ample and varied supply, and the Rebbe is dead, so it might be argued that locality is no longer essential in sustaining the movement. In fact, the whole question of locality seems an anachronism, considering that Habad is now, more than ever before, an ideology rather than a homogeneous group resident in one area and seeking a new territorial leader.

It is also important to note that some of the messianists in Habad completely dismiss the significance of the gravesite to their spiritual service; interestingly, they too represent a universalization of the ideology of the movement, which is no longer dependent on a particular geographical location. Their claim that Schneerson is not dead, and therefore not buried in the gravesite venerated by others, makes the universal mission of the movement more apparent, placing the focus on the work, and not the locality of Schneerson or his remains. The dependence on a geographical locality for policy-making therefore becomes less significant, with the focus being directed to the words and teachings of the Rebbe to carry on the mission he set the Habad movement.

The Youth: A New Constituency

The crucial decisions in the Habad movement's policy were once made, or at least advised upon, by the elderly, and thus experienced, advisers and aides in the Rebbe's court, even down to the appointment of a new Rebbe. In the last few decades, the death of most of Yosef Yitzhak's followers through old age has led to the burgeoning power of younger Hasidim, raised in Habad under the leadership of Schneerson. As Schneerson outlived many of his own close associates, by the time of his death in 1996 there were no authoritative candidates who might be expected to take over the leadership of Habad. Schneerson had delegated responsibility to predominantly young men, who had the energy and zeal to pursue the outreach goals he had set. This drastically changed the power dynamics in the movement, giving much more power to younger and more inexperienced men, who were encouraged by Schneerson to take on positions of great importance in the movement, due to the growing demands of outreach and community work. Thousands of young students became rabbis and community leaders under Schneerson's leadership, and many of these men have since risen to positions of prominence in their local communities.

Schneerson encouraged every young man in Habad to study for rabbinical ordination before getting married, and consequently more men have been ordained into the rabbinate than at any previous time in Jewish history. One of the unfortunate results of this mass ordination was a lowering of the standards required of new rabbis; the system allowed men to be ordained who were not up to the usually high scholarly standards expected of rabbinic candidates, and were often, in addition, intellectually and emotionally immature. Ordination as a rabbi became a political and social action, and the criterion for ordination changed from high scholarly standards to such issues as piety and commitment to the Habad outreach principle. While once the rabbinate was restricted to only a few dedicated scholars, today many Habad youth have been elevated to rabbinic status, making them nominally indistinguishable from true scholars and holders of wisdom, and subsequently lowering the perception of learning that was traditionally associated with the role of rabbi.

Despite the preponderance of rabbis in Habad, the younger generation, who knew only Schneerson as Rebbe and have little sense of the Habad movement's history, are perhaps less suited to appoint a new Rebbe than the followers of previous Rebbes. Some of the oldest Hasidim at the time of Schneerson's appointment had witnessed the election of Shalom Dov Ber and Yosef Yitzhak before him, and therefore were able to recognize the undeniable need for continuity that must play a significant role in the appointment of a new Rebbe. Generally, these elder Hasidim had also been reluctant to accept a successor to *their* Rebbe, but had lived to see his passing, and realized at that time the cohesive role of the Rebbe for the health of the movement. The younger generation have not benefited from these experiences, and are therefore less likely to recognize a successor to Schneerson, a pattern which is to be found in the history of Habad.[1] Most of the older Hasidim favor the appointment of a successor to Schneerson, recognizing needs greater than their own.[2] One of the difficulties in the Habad movement at present is that these elder Hasidim play much less active roles in the movement than their younger counterparts, and hence their voices of moderation and preservation are not heard in the present debate. This is exacerbated by the use of technology in the modern Habad movement; as older Hasidim are more reluctant to use technological devices, their voice in the movement is even quieter, whereas the youth have embraced the developments of the modern world and use technology to disseminate their ideas.[3] The stabilizing factor inherent in the presence of an older generation therefore does not play a strong role in the successional foray, which is being waged between younger men.[4]

An additional difficulty for the succession debate, resulting from the youthfulness of the movement's decision-makers, is that many of them have built empires of their own as emissaries of Schneerson and Habad. They will no doubt be somewhat reluctant to defer to someone they regard as an equal, with whom they might have jostled for space in the court of the Rebbe or with whose children they may have played. This might be the case if another Hasid were appointed to the role of Rebbe. It is equally unlikely that these young leaders would accept a replacement for their beloved Rebbe, the only leader they have ever known and to whose mission they have dedicated their lives.[5] Another important obstacle is age; there are cases in Habad where twenty-three-year-old men have a great deal of influence as heads of communities, despite their youth. Because of this lack of maturity, it is unlikely that older men would accept the leadership of any such individual, no matter what his qualifications or credentials.

The young people raised in Habad, especially the second generation of Hasidim under Schneerson's leadership, were themselves leaders and activists, and not at all the archetype of subservience to the will of a Rebbe. Part of Schneerson's genius at leadership was in knowing how to harness the energy, enthusiasm, and idealism of these youth, training and directing them to eventually fill positions of leadership and eminence. However conducive the environment may have been for the emergence of a generation of trained outreach professionals, however, the Habad movement under Schneerson was not conducive to the emergence of a new Rebbe. Connection was made to the person of Schneerson rather than to the office of Rebbe, and in consequence the very idea of transfer has become difficult for some to contemplate. To such Habad followers, there will only ever be one Rebbe, Menachem Mendel Schneerson.

If there were descendants of Schneerson who might step into the role of Rebbe, or a clear candidate to lead the movement into the next generation, these young leaders might be able to accept another Rebbe. At least the idea of succession might be more tolerable to them. If they are expected to embrace a new leader solely for the sake of continuity and "the children," rather than through the gradual development of an emotional bond to an individual, the chances of finding a suitable candidate become increasingly unlikely. Should this be the case, it is quite probable that the movement will enter the next generation without a new Rebbe.

Even if we assume that a suitable replacement Rebbe might emerge as a dominant spiritual personality from among the many successful emissaries over a period of time, as the fiefdom model proposes, the issue of youth will doubtless require the candidate to live for many years, constantly proving his candidacy until he is accepted by his peers as their superior. If the present generation's leaders were older than they are, any rivals to the succession would either die out naturally or defer to a new Rebbe because of the need for continuity, and the younger generation would not dare refute the decisions of the elders. This is not the case, however, and the youthfulness of the generation contributes to Habad's successional difficulties.

The Ba'al Teshuvah Movement

It is appropriate to conclude on the subject of the ba'alteshuvah and his importance to the movement's continuity, for it was the return of Jews to Judaism that was uppermost in Schneerson's thinking. One significant effect of the comparative youthfulness of members of the Habad movement is the fact that, even to those born into observant Hasidic families, Schneerson is the only Rebbe they have ever known. This is an even more significant factor in the lives of most newly religious ba'alei teshuvah, who generally joined Habad because of an emotional connection to Schneerson. Many members of the movement are therefore unfamiliar with the issue of traditional Hasidic succession, and have been further encouraged to disregard the question of succession through decades of messianic indoctrination. Idealization of Schneerson has been a decisive factor in the avoidance of the succession issue in some quarters, most especially in the ranks of the newly religious, who seem to feel that their "guru" cannot be replaced.

One consequence of the large numbers of ba'alei teshuvah in the Habad movement is the lack of a deep-seated connection to the history and subtlety of Hasidic culture.

Those to whom religious life and thinking are commonplace because they were born into observant families tend not to adopt extreme positions. With their convert's zeal, the ba'alei teshuvah are often more radical and extremist in their observance and devotion to the traditions and customs of their new religious life than those who have grown up in the tradition, as is generally the case among converts to any tradition.

As a result, many of those who have joined Habad as adults appear to have taken more extreme positions, not only in terms of activism and outreach, but most important, regarding Schneerson's status as the mashiach. While it is difficult to quantify this, many members of the messianist faction of Habad are either ba'alei teshuvah or their children. Perhaps because of a lack of cultural and social perspective and life-long familiarity with the unwritten traditions of the Habad movement, many ba'alei teshuvah have come to regard Schneerson as the ultimate zaddik, akin to the guru figure in an Eastern religious tradition. As such, his words are to be treated as statements of fact. Thus, when he spoke about the mashiach, many of the ba'alei teshuvah (and they were by no means alone in this) interpreted it to mean that he himself was the long-awaited messianic redeemer.

Another factor affecting the influence of the ba'alei teshuvah on the question of succession and leadership in the movement is not only the determination with which they hold to their beliefs, but the fervor with which they proclaim them to the world. While initially the messianist factions in Habad were small and not very influential, the number of messianists has grown in the years since Schneerson's death, many of them ba'alei teshuvah, and their influence has greatly increased, such that many messianists now hold positions of authority in the movement. Most important for the future of Habad, messianist ba'alei teshuvah are found in large numbers throughout the educational and publication divisions of the movement, which naturally implies that the messianist ideology will be effectively disseminated to the next generation. Just as Schneerson expanded his influence over the movement through his educational efforts, the potential is there for the messianists to do the same. The influence of the ba'alei teshuvah therefore has great potential to affect the future course of Habad, possibly determining not only the continuation of the movement through outreach, but its ideology of the movement in future generations.

From Local Particularism to Universal Mission

The Habad movement is not the same at this successional juncture as it was when Schneerson ascended to its leadership. Over the last two generations Habad has changed, developing in many ways into a vibrant and up-to-date part of the religious landscape. While many of its members may be inclined to insularity and retreat from modernity without Schneerson impelling them to reach out and interact with Jews everywhere, another possibility for the movement is suggested by the sociologist Menachem Friedman. He has described the process by which the historical Habad movement was transformed from a group with local influence in the towns of Liadi and Lubavitch in Russia, to emerge as an ideology that claimed messianic importance beyond the scope of the movement or even the Jewish people. Under its messianic ideology, Habad aimed to bring world peace, with its mission expanding to include the gentile nations under the Laws of Noah. The messianic role of the movement was spoken of as representing a change in the physical and spiritual worlds. Despite these grandiose aspirations, however, the movement retained a local, particularistic element, located in the late twentieth century in the person of Menachem Mendel Schneerson, from whose world headquarters, a mock-Tudor building in a Brooklyn ghetto, the redemption of humankind was to commence.

The passing of Schneerson provides the perfect opportunity to erase the last remnants of local particularism from Habad, and for it to embrace the final transformation to universalism, wherein the notion of locality ceases to have importance in the messianic vision. It is even a possibility, however remote, that the physicality of a living mashiach might disappear from Habad ideology completely, either through the implementation of the ghost model of succession or through an ideological transformation wherein each Habad adherent internalizes the messianic redemption.

Schneerson proclaimed that the effects of the redemption are already being felt, and even with the death of the figure regarded by his followers as the mashiach, this idea might provide a breakthrough in Hasidic thinking. The messianic age is already upon us, and local identification is not an issue, for "Israel is the world, and the world is Israel." This is reminiscent of Scholem's idea of the Hasidic neutralization of messianism, where the concept of redemption was reformulated to occur within every individual. The Hasidim have to take on the job of bringing mashiach, and even the gentile world has a place in Schneerson's scheme of redemption.[6]

Arthur Green has been quoted as saying that the leadership void left by Schneerson cannot be filled, and thus that he was the end of the line of Habad Rebbes. Schneerson's passing, he continues, could mark a "real moment of transformation for the movement" in which Habad abandons the temptations of messianism and returns to its spiritual roots.[7] This statement recognizes the potential for transformation in Habad, largely a by-product of the universality of Schneerson's teachings. Ironically, this same ideology, with its mysticism, idealization of Schneerson and 770, and obsession with messianism and resurrection, is preventing large elements of the movement from becoming universal. Instead, the messianist ideology connects more strongly to the past, and to the deceased leader of Habad, becoming more firmly entrenched in local particularism, and preventing the hoped-for transformation.

It is perhaps fitting to conclude with the sentiments of Rosenzweig about the rising of false mashiachs in Judaism:

Belief in the advent of the messiah would be no more than an empty phrase if false messiahs did not constantly arise in whom this belief might assume reality and shape. The false messiah exists as long as does the genuine hope in the true messiah, and he divides every generation in which he appears into two camps:

those who have the power of faith to believe and hence to err, and those who have the power of hope not to err but rather continue to endure until the advent of the true redeemer. The former were perhaps the better Jews, the latter were the stronger Jews.[8]

Whatever the future of the Habad movement, and the outcome of the succession question, it cannot be denied that one of the most significant and influential leaders of Judaism in the latter half of the twentieth century was Rabbi Menachem Mendel Schneerson, the Rebbe, whose impact will no doubt be felt for decades, if not centuries, to come.

---

[1] Young Hasidim who had known the predecessor Rebbe often did not accept the incumbent. This was true even of some Rebbes. The Zemakh Zedek had been a Hasid of Shneur Zalman and at least for a time refused to accept the leadership of Dov Ber after his passing. Similarly, Yehuda Leib, the son of the Zemakh Zedek, would not accept his father as the new Rebbe, being himself a Hasid of Dov Ber. Part of the price of having a long-lived Rebbe is the absence of change in the movement and the inability of followers to cope with leadership crises.

[2] They recognize that even if the incumbent Rebbe will not be their own, he will be a *"Rebbe far de kinder,"* a Rebbe for the children. They too may be silenced for fear of loosing support; Chitrik, an elderly Hasid, for example, was known to be against messianism, but said nothing about this to his grandson.

[3] The ability of a small group to influence a greater number of people was made possible by modern technology, and the messianist element of the movement uses the latest tools as zealously as the movement itself did to work within Judaism.

[4] In discussions with some prominent elderly Hasidim in Crown Heights who knew both Yosef Yitzhak and Schneerson.

[5] One of the reasons for the acceptance of Schneerson as Rebbe in 1951 was the brief exposure of many of the American Hasidim to Yosef Yitzhak, who had been in the country for only a decade before his passing. This relatively brief time (especially compared to Schneerson's forty-five-year reign) was not long enough for deep and unchangeable commitment to develop.

[6] Schneerson encouraged non-Jews to follow the Noahide Laws. These laws, given to Noah in the Torah, apply to all humanity. They are seven in number, and include the establishment of law courts and prohibitions of blasphemy, idolatry, sexual immorality, bloodshed, theft, and eating a limb from a living animal. The campaign did not attract wide attention, although there are small communities of Noahides across the globe. See Yirmeyahu Bindman, *The Seven Colors of the Rainbow*; J. David Davis, *Finding the God of Noah*; and Chaim Clorfene and Yakov Rogalsky, *The Path of the Righteous Gentile.*

[7] Cited in Steve Feldman and Marilyn Silverstein, "Rebbe's Death Stirs Deep Feelings on Local Scene."

[8] Franz Rosenzweig, quoted in R. J. Zvi Werblowsky, "Messianism in Jewish History," pp. 45–46.

Glossary of Terms

Aguda Organization.

Agudat Ha-Rabonim (Organization of Rabbis) Umbrella body of American Orthodox rabbis in the 1940s.

Agudat Hasidei Habad (Organization of Habad Hasidim) (AGUCH) Habad organization, established in the 1930s, that became the "umbrella" organization for other Habad enterprises.

Agudat ha-Temimim Organization to help ex-Lubavitch yeshiva scholars integrate in the United States and provide them with social and religious support.

Agudat Yisrael Political organization founded in Germany in 1912 to oppose political Zionism; it spread to Israel and the United States. At present it represents ultra-Orthodoxy, involves itself with political Zionism, and has a strong Hasidic representation.

Ahi Temimim ("My Pure Brothers") Rabbi Yosef Yitzhak's "old-boys" organization of former students from the Lubavitch yeshiva system. Originally an East European organization, it was established in the United States in the 1930s.

Ari ("Lion") Appellation for Rabbi Yitzhak Luria of Safed, who among other things composed a siddur inspired by his mystical ideology. A group of synagogues were named after him and therefore indicate the usage of this prayer formula. They are generally associated with Habad Hasidism.

Ashkenazi, pl. **Ashkenazim** Jews of Franco-Germanic origins, now including most Central and East European Jews. The Hasidic movement is generally considered an Ashkenazi movement.

Ba'al Shem Tov ("Master of the Good Name") The leader of the Hasidic movement, Yisrael the son of Eliezer. Many ba'alei shem (masters of the Name) were believed to be practicing in Eastern Europe in that period. This name suggests that the "master" may manipulate and recite the "good name" of God in secret combinations, thus wielding mystical powers and able to perform wonders.

Ba'al Teshuvah, pl. **ba'alei teshuvah** A newly repentant Jew.

Bar Mitzvah ("Son of the Commandments") Ceremony celebrated when a boy reaches the age of thirteen and is thereafter obligated to keep the commandments. *Bat Mitzvah* is the female equivalent.

Beinoni ("Intermediate") A person who has committed both sinful and meritorious deeds in equal measure throughout his life. Habad Hasidut offers a novel interpretation (*Sefer Tanya*, chap. 1), describing such a person as pious in every respect, his only fault being the struggle he endures in achieving this perfection. He is contrasted with the zaddik, who does not even struggle to be perfect.

Beit Din Jewish Court of Justice.

Beit Rebbe ("House of the Rebbe") The physical and the spiritual house of the Rebbe, including his family and his offspring, and even the Hasidic faithful, if they feel sufficiently close to the Rebbe. This term is also the name of a Habad leadership chronology written by one of Shalom Dov Ber's Hasidim, Meir Hielman.

Beit Mashiach ("House of the Mashiach") Habad headquarters is referred to by this name, indicating faith in the Rebbe as the mashiach; the numerical value of this Hebrew term is equivalent to 770, which is the street number where the headquarters is situated. The numerical equivalent of the three terms *Hokhmah, Binah,* and *Da'at* (Habad) is also 770. Finally, *Beis Moshiach* is the name of a weekly journal published in Brooklyn which supports the messianist camp in the movement.

Bimah ("Stage") Podium in the synagogue from which the Torah is read.

Binah ("Understanding") Second of the ten sefirot; the second stage of the intellectual process developing the original concept of *hokhmah*.

Birur Nezuzot ("Sifting the Sparks") Lurianic kabbalistic concept describing the way goodness is sifted from evil, as sparks of godliness are trapped in the mundane world. This function is also the mission of the Jewish exile, which is to find these sparks and facilitate their return to their divine origins (through acts of piety), and thus bring about the redemption.

Bitul ("Nullification") Kabbalistic practice in meditation and general behavior that attempts to nullify one's ego, thereby ridding the soul of obstacles so that godly light can enter.

Bochur, pl. **Bochurim** Young adults, particularly yeshiva students.

Da'at ("Knowledge") The third sefirah of the intellectual faculty in Habad theosophy.

Diaspora The dispersion of the Jews to lands outside the ancient borders of Eretz Yisrael. This term is often used to describe the dispersion of a group from its cultural epicenter, such as Habad Hasidim exiled from Lubavitch.

Doresh Ha-Dor ("Preacher of the Generation") Term used in reference to the Rebbe.

Eretz ha-Kodesh The Holy Land.

Eretz Yisrael The Land of Israel.

Ethapkha ("Reversal") Hasidic term describing a high spiritual art whereby one's evil desires are turned around to the service of the divine. This stage is reached primarily by the zaddik.

Etkafia ("Repression") Hasidic term describing the spiritual art of repressing one's evil desires. This function is lower than *ethapkha*.

Farbrengen ("Gathering") Yiddish term for a Hasidic gathering. If the Rebbe is present, he gives a Hasidic discourse or talks on Hasidic issues. If the Rebbe is not present, songs are sung, stories are told about the Rebbe, and people commit themselves to greater piety and more devotion. Alcohol contributes to the intimate nature of these gatherings.

Frankists Messianic adherents of the cultic leader Jacob Frank. The movement was characterized by extreme antinomianism and ethical perversion by Frank's followers.

Galut Hebrew designation for the Diaspora, or Exile.

Gedolim ("Great Ones") Great rabbinic and spiritual leaders.

Gematria Method of reaching or supporting conclusions on the basis of the numerical equivalents of the letters of key words.

Gimmel Tammuz Hebrew date of the death of Menachem Mendel Schneerson.

Habad Acronym formed from the initial letters of the Hebrew words *hokhmah* ("wisdom"), *binah* ("understanding"), and *da'at* ("knowledge"), the first three of the ten sefirot. Habad is also the name of the intellectual school of Hasidism founded by Shneur Zalman of Liadi.

Habad House Home used for outreach purposes in modern Habad; by extension, any Habad home.

Hakriah Ve-Hakedushah ("The Calling and The Holiness") The Mahane Yisrael publication in the United States.

Halakhah Generic term for the entire body of Jewish law, religious as well as civil. This body of law is the source of Jewish-religious practice. Adjective: halakhic.

Hanukah Festival celebrating the rededication of the Temple by the Maccabees after its desecration by Greek invaders.

Hasid, pl. **Hasidim** ("pious") Followers of the Ba'al Shem Tov and other Hasidic masters.

Hasidishe amalek Hasidic Amalekite.

Hasidut Hasidic philosophy based on Kabbalah and its application in social wisdom.

Haskalah ("Enlightenment") Movement to assimilate Jews into modern European culture and promote secular education, during the eighteenth and nineteenth centuries.

Ha-Tamim Habad magazine under Yosef Yitzhak.

Heder Small study house for young children.

Hevra Kadisha ("Holy Friends") Elite society of pious people. Its main function is to facilitate burials.

Hitkashrut ("To connect"). Used in reference to the bond between Hasid and Rebbe.

Hitva'adut Hebrew term for *farbrengen.*

Hokhmah ("Wisdom") The first sefirah of the intellectual faculty in Habad theosophy.

Hokhmei Hador ("Wise ones of the Generation").

Hozrim ("Repeaters") Hasidim who would listen on Shabbat or a festival to the Rebbe's talk, remember it all by heart, and after Shabbat write it down word for word so that it could later be published. A very prestigious function.

Humash ("Five") The Five Books of Moses (Pentateuch), otherwise known as the Torah.

Iggerot kodesh ("Holy letters") Bound collection of Schneerson's letters, consulted by some as an oracle.

Kabbalah ("Tradition") Jewish mysticism, particularly that which emanated from thirteenth-century Spain.

Kashrut Dietary laws of kosher and unkosher.

Keter ("Crown") First sefirah of theosophic Kabbalah.

Kfar Habad Habad Hasidic village in Israel just outside of Tel Aviv.

Kiddush Hashem Glorification of God's name.

Knesset Israeli Parliament, established in 1949.

Lag Ba-Omer ("Thirty-third of the Omer") Day celebrated in Jewish tradition because it symbolically marked the end of an especially calamitous period in Jewish history.

Levi, pl. **Levi'im** The Levite clan.

Likkutei Torah ("Collection of Torah") A collection of discourses and *drashot* given by Shneur Zalman.

Lishkat Hashayin ("Secret Service") Department of the Mahane Yisrael organization which dealt with discreet issues, from politically sensitive matters to charity.

Ma'amad Money sent to the Rebbe for his upkeep.

Ma'amar Hasidic discourse.

Maggid Preacher.

Mahane Yisrael ("Camp of Israel") Social arm of the Habad movement in the United States, put under Menachem Mendel Schneerson's control in the 1940s.

Malakh, pl. **Malakhim** ("Angels") Breakaway group of Habad Hasidim who followed their Rebbe, Avraham Der Ailer Levine, the Malakh.

Maot ("Money") Fund established by Menachem Mendel of Vitebsk and Shneur Zalman for the benefit of Hasidim who emigrated to Eretz ha-Kodesh.

Mashiach Messiah.

Matzah Unleavened bread eaten during the festival of Pesach (Passover).

Melamed Teacher of children, whether as a private tutor or in a school.

Merkaz ("Center") Central headquarters and command center of Habad movement.

Merkaz L'Inyanei Hinukh ("Center for Educational Issues") Primary organization of Habad movement under Menachem Mendel Schneerson.

Mikvah Pool of water used for ritual immersion.

Minyan Quorum of ten male Jews with whom it is permissible to recite certain prayers.

Mitnaged, pl. **Mitnagdim** ("Opposition") Mainstream Orthodoxy opposed to Hasidic movement. Adjective: mitnagidc.

Mitzvah, pl. **mitzvot** Biblical commandments.

Mitzvah Mobile / Mitzvah Tank Vehicle used for Habad outreach.

Nasi Title of head of ancient Sanhedrin; now used as title of President of State of Israel. Strictly, a captain, important official, or prince. In Habad context, an ultimate authority.

Nissan Jewish month approximately corresponding with February.

Nusah Formula of prayer; can vary from country to country.

Ohel ("Tent") Hut built on a gravesite. In particular, designates gravesites of Rebbes.

Pesach Passover.

Pidyon Nefesh ("Redemption of the Soul") Note to the Rebbe asking him to intercede on writer's behalf; invariably accompanied by a sum of money.

Pilpul Method of halakhic study characterized by subtle dialectic and distinctions.

Posek Authoritative decision-maker and codifier on halakhic/legal/religious issues.

Purim Festival celebrating annulment of national death warrant in Persia, as described in Book of Esther.

Rabbi Jewish religious scholar and leader.

Rebbe Hasidic spiritual leader.

Rebbetzin Wife of a rabbi or Rebbe.

Responsa Replies by a *posek* to halakhic questions.

Rosh Ha-Shanah Jewish New Year.

Sabbatians Followers of sixteenth-century messianic aspirant Sabbetai Zevi.

Sanhedrin Assembly of seventy-one people which constituted the supreme legislative and judicial authority of Jews during Second Temple period and for some time thereafter.

Seder The highly ritualized meal on the first night of Pesach.

Sefer, pl. **Sefarim** ("books") Holy books.

Semichah Rabbinic ordination.

Sephardi, pl. **Sephardim** Jews of the Iberian Peninsula (Spanish), their descendants, and those who have adopted the Sephardi rite, especially in lands around Mediterranean.

Shabbat, pl. **Shabbatot** ("Sabbath") Saturday, the Jewish day of fast. It is both celebratory and characterized by strict legal restrictions on work and technology.

Shaliach ("To be sent") A representative, emissary, ambassador.

Shirayim ("Leftovers") Food ritually handed out by a Rebbe to his Hasidic followers.

Shivah ("Seven") The seven days of strict mourning after the death of a close relative.

Shlihut Work undertaken by an ambassador; a mission.

Shofar Ram's horn, the traditional instrument calling Jewish people to war, repentance, or other public requirement.

Shochet Ritual slaughterer of kosher meat.

Shvat Month corresponding to November.

Siddur Prayer book.

Sichah, pl. **Sichot** Informal, less structured monologue by Rebbe.

Semichah Rabbinic ordination.

Sefirah, pl. **Sefirot** ("Gradations") Ten divine emanations through which the infinite of God expresses itself.

Sukkah ("Booth") Hut built on the biblical festival of Sukkot.

Sukkah-mobile Mobile sukkah used for Habad outreach.

Talmud The Mishnah and its accompanying commentary, called Gemara. Adjective: talmudic.

Tamuz Hebrew month corresponding to July.

(Sefer) Tanya Major work of Shneur Zalman and today the primary Habad Hasidic text; also known as Sefer shel Beinoni and Likkutei Amarim.

Tefillin Phylacteries worn each weekday morning during prayers.

Tehilat Hashem Siddur used by Habad Hasidim, based on the Ari's formulation.

Tehillim Book of Psalms.

Temimim ("Pure Ones") Students in the Lubavitch yeshiva system.

Tevet Hebrew month corresponding to December.

Tish Hasidic meal eaten with the Rebbe.

Tishrei Hebrew month corresponding to October.

Tomhei Temimim ("Supporters of the Pure Ones") Name of the Lubavitch yeshivot.

Urim Ve-Tumim Ornaments of ritual, religious, and magical function worn by the biblical high priest.

Yehidut Hasidic practice of being alone with the Rebbe wherein a communion of souls is believed to occur. In Habad, this practice was originally used for the purpose of spiritual instruction.

Yeshiva, pl. **Yeshivot** Theological seminary.

Yom Kippur The Day of Atonement, marked by prayer and fasting.

Zaddik, pl. **Zaddikim** ("Righteous") Term used in reference to Hasidic Rebbes, believed to be perfect.

Zaddikei Hador ("Righteous of the Generation") Hasidic Rebbes.

Zohar ("Light") Major book of Kabbalah, traditionally attributed to the second-century scholar Shimon Bar Yochai. Academics maintain that it was written by Moshe DeLeon in thirteenth-century century Spain.

People, Abbreviations, and Acronyms

ACHACH (Agudat Chasidei Anshei Chabad; "Organization of Habad Hasidic People").

AGUCH (Agudat Chasidei Habad; "Organization of Habad Hasidim").

Aharon Ha-Levi Horowitz of Staroselye (1766–1828) Descendant of the Maharal of Prague, chief disciple of Shneur Zalman for over thirty years and candidate for succession.

Avraham Dov Ber Ha-Kohen, "the Malakh" Disciple of Shalom Dov Ber who left for the United States after an argument over the education of Yosef Yitzhak. Leader of Habad splinter group, the Malakhim

Avraham ha-Malakh (1740–1776) Son of the Maggid of Mezritch; study partner of Shneur Zalman.

Ben-Gurion, David (1886–1973) Labor Zionist pioneer, first Prime Minister of Israel.

Chaya Mousia (1901–1988) Second daughter of Yosef Yitzhak and wife of Menachem Mendel Schneerson.

Deutsch, Shaul Shimon. Rebbe of a modern, post-Schneerson Habad splinter group and independent Habad historian.

Dov Ber Shneur, Son of Shneur Zalman of Lubavitch (1773–1827) Competed with Aharon of Staroselye and considered to be the second Habad Rebbe; otherwise called *der mitler Rebbe* ("the middle Rebbe"). He allegedly died on his fifty-fourth birthday.

Eliyahu Elijah the Prophet.

Frank, Jacob (1726–1791) Leader of a messianic movement.

Gaon of Vilna (d. 1797) Elijah ben Solomon Zalman; otherwise called Ha-Gra. The esteemed leader of mitnagdic Jewry and strongest opponent of Hasidic movement.

Groner, Leible Secretary of Menachem Mendel Schneerson; unofficial leader of the messianist faction of Habad.

Gourary, Barry (b. 1923) Only grandson of Yosef Yitzhak.

Gourary, Hana. Eldest daughter of Yosef Yitzhak and wife of Shemaryahu Gourary.

Gourary, Shemaryahu Oldest son-in-law of Yosef Yitzhak and failed successional candidate.

Habad (Hokhmah, Binah, Da'at; "Wisdom, Understanding, Knowledge").

Hevra Kadisha Council responsible for Habad burial practices.

Hornshtein, Menachem Mendel Descendant of Shmuel and third son-in-law to Yosef Yitzhak by marriage to Sheina. Both were killed in Treblinka.

Kahn, Yoel Student in New York in 1950s; author of diary from this period; Hasid of Menachem Mendel Schneerson and significant personality in Habad leadership and politics.

Kehot (Karnei Hod Torah; "Rays of Torah Light") Habad publishing company.

Kline, Yaakov Secretary to Menachem Mendel Schneerson.

Krinsky, Yehuda Aide to Menachem Mendel Schneerson and official of Mahane Yisrael and AGUCH organizations. One of the primary administrators of the Habad movement today.

Levi Yitzhak (1878–1944) Father of Menachem Mendel Schneerson and third-generation descendent of the Zemakh Zedek through his eldest son, Barukh Shalom.

Levi Yitzhak of Berditchev (1740–1810) Esteemed disciple of Maggid of Mezritch and Ba'al Shem Tov, broadly considered a zaddik but did not have Hasidic followers. He firmly supported Shneur Zalman in favor of publishing mysticism.

Liberman, Haim Librarian for Yosef Yitzhak.

Luria, Yitzhak (d. 1572) Famed Safed kabbalist; otherwise called Ha-Ari.

Maggid of Mezritch (Dov Ber) (d. 1772) Foremost disciple of the Ba'al Shem Tov, succeeding him in 1761. He trained a class of Hasidic leaders and zaddikim and can be considered the true founder of Hasidism.

Mahane Yisrael Social service arm of Habad; controlled by Menachem Mendel Schneerson under the guidance of Yosef Yitzhak.

Menachem Mendel of Schachna (Zemakh Zedek) Third Habad Rebbe.

Menachem Mendel of Vitebsk (1730–1788) Disciple of Maggid of Mezritch and leader of Russian Hasidism until he emigrated to Eretz ha-Kodesh along with about three hundred Hasidim, leaving Shneur Zalman to succeed him as leader of Russian Hasidim.

Menachem Nahum (1789–?) Eldest son of Dov Ber of Lubavitch; was a candidate for Rebbe but deferred in favor of the Zemakh Zedek.

Merkaz Le-Inyanei Chinuch "Center for Educational Issues"; one of the organizations given to Menachem Mendel Schneerson by Yosef Yitzhak, in charge of Habad education.

Mindel, Nissan Aide to Yosef Yitzhak and Menachem Mendel Schneerson.

Moshe Moses.

Nahman of Breslav (1772–1810) Hasidic Rebbe descended from the Ba'al Shem Tov who entertained extreme mystical and messianic ideas. He has no successor as Rebbe, but his sect has continued without a leader.

Nathan Sternhartz of Nemirov (1780–1845) One of the most famous of Nahman of Breslav's disciples.

NKVD ("People's Commissariat of Internal Affairs") Communist police.

Sabbatai Zevi (1626–1676) Pseudo-messiah, led a widespread messianic movement that resulted in his conversion to Islam and the apostasy of some of his followers.

Sacks, Jonathan Chief Rabbi of the United Kingdom.

Schneerson, Menachem Mendel (1902–1994) Seventh Lubavitcher Rebbe; referred to by followers simply as "the Rebbe."

Schneerson, Shalom Dov Ber (1860–1920) Fifth Lubavitcher Rebbe.

Schneerson, Yosef Yitzhak (1880– 1950) Sixth Lubavitcher Rebbe; also known as the *Freirdicker* ("Former") Rebbe.

Scholem, Gershom Noted scholar of Kabbalah and Jewish mystical and messianic movements.

Shmuel (1834–1882) Fourth Lubavitcher Rebbe.

Shneur Zalman son of Barukh of Liadi (1745–1812) Founder of Habad ideology and movement.

Shneur Zalman Aharon (1859–1899) Eldest son of Shmuel and original candidate for succession after him.

Tzeirei Habad ("Habad Youth") Habad organization particularly active in Israel that runs youth activities, lobbies, and brings out publications.

Tzivot Hashem ("Armies of God") Habad youth movement.

Va'ad Rabanei Lubavitch Union of Lubavitch Rabbis

Yehuda Leib Brother of Shneur Zalman; close aide to him and Dov Ber of Lubavitch.

Zemakh Zedek (1789–1866) Posthumous name of Menachem Mendel Shachna (Schneerson), third Lubavitcher Rebbe.

Bibliography

Primary Classical and Rabbinic Sources

The Holy Scripture. var. eds.; English trans. (Philadelphia, 1917).

Hirsch, Samson Raphael. *The Pentateuch* (5 vols.). Trans. Isaac Levy (New York, 1971).

Humash Mikraot Gedolot. (5 vols.). (New York, n.d.).

Mishnah. var. eds.; English trans. H. Danby (Oxford, 1933).

Babylonian Talmud. Romm, Vilna, various dates; English trans. ed. I. Epstein (London, 1948–52).

Jerusalem Talmud. (Krotoschin, 1886).

Tosefta. ed. M. S. Zuckermandel (Pasewalk, 1881). (also printed in Talmud text).

Midrash Rabbah. Romm, Vilna, var. dates.

Zohar. (Zhitomir, 1862).

Caro, Joseph. *Beit Yosef* on *Tur Or HaHayim*.

———. *Kesef Mishneh* (printed as commentary to Maimonides' *Mishneh Torah*).

———. *Shulhan Arukh*, var. eds. (10 vols.). (New York, 1959).

Maimonides, Moses. *The Code of Maimonides, Book Fourteen: The Book of Judges*, trans. Avraham M. Hershman (New Haven, 1949).

———. *Commentary to the Mishnah,* var. eds. (printed in Talmud Bavli).

———. *Guide of the Perplexed*. Trans. S. Pines (Chicago, 1965).

———. *Mishneh Torah* (6 vols.). (New York, 1956).

———. *Sefer ha-Mitzvot*. (New York, 1955).

Malbim, Meir Leibush. *Mikra'ei Kodesh* (2 vols.). (Jerusalem, 1956).

Primary Hasidic Sources

Barnai, Y., ed. *Hasidic Letters from the Holy Land* (Hebrew). (Jerusalem, 1960).

Binyamin of Zelazitz. *Torei Zahav* (Mohilev, 1816).

Dov Ber of Mezritch (Maggid of Mezritch)). *Likkutei Amarim, Maggid Devarav le-Yakov* (Koretz, 1781); ed. Rivka Schatz-Uffenheimer (Jerusalem, 1976).

Efraim of Sudzilkov. *Degel Mahaneh Ephraim: Bereshit* (n.p., 1808; Jerusalem, 1963).

Elimelekh of Lizhensk. *Noam Elimelekh* (Lvov, 1788; New York, 1956; ed. G. Nigal, 2 vols., Jerusalem, 1978).

Ganzfried, Solomon. *Kitzur Shulhan Arukh* (Leipzig, 1933).

Gottlober, A. B., "Zikhronot mi-Yemei Ne'urai," *Ha-Boker Or*, collected in *Zikhronot u-Masa'ot*, ed. R. Goldberg (Jerusalem, 1976).

Gurkow, Meir. *Sefer ha-Zikhronot: Divrei ha-Yamim* (Brooklyn, 1977).

Ha-Tamim (periodical published in Warsaw in 1930s, collected vol. *Ha-Tamim*, Kfar Habad, 1971; Brooklyn, 1975).

Hielman, Haim Meir. *Beit Rebbe* (3 vols.). (Berdichev, n.d.; Jerusalem, 1930).

Hillel Halevi of Paritch. *Pelah ha-Rimon: Bereshit* (Vilna, 1847; Brooklyn, 1954).

Hillman, D. Z. *Iggerot Baal ha-Tanya u-Venei Doro* (Jerusalem, 1953).

Kahn, R. N. *Shmuot ve-Sippurim* (Kfar Habad, 1976).

Levi Yitzhak of Berditchev. *Kedushat Levi: Shoftim* (Slavuta, 1798; Zolkiev, 1806; Jerusalem, 1958).

Menahem Mendel (Zemakh Zedek). *Derekh Mizvotekha* (Poltava, 1911; Kfar Habad, 1976).

Menahem Mendel of Vitebsk. *Iggerot ha-Kodesh* (Zolkiev?, 1800?; Jerusalem, n.d.).

Mondschein, Y., ed. *Likkutei Reshimot u-Ma'asiyot* (Kfar Habad, 1969).

———, ed. *Migdal Oz* (Kfar Habad, 1980).

Nahman of Breslav. *Likkutei Muharan* (Ostraho, 1806; Zolkiev, 1809; Jerusalem, 1969).

Qalonius Qalman Halevi Epstein. *Maor va-Shemesh* (ed., Tel Aviv, 1964).

Rivkin, M. D. *Ashkavta de-Rebbe*.

Rodkinsohn, Mikhael Levi. *Toledot Amudei Habad* (only pts. 1 and 4 published). (Koenigsberg, 1876).

———. *Shivhei Ha-Rav* (Warsaw, 5680; Jerusalem, 1961).

Ruderman, Pesah. "Hashkafah Kelalit al ha-Zaddikim ve-al ha-Hasidim," *Ha-Shahar* (Vienna, 1875), pp. 86–104.

Schneerson, Levi Yitzhak. *Toledot Levi Yitzhak* (Brooklyn, n.d.).

Schneerson, Menahem Mendel. *B'suras Hageulah* (Brooklyn, 1993).

———. *Iggerot Kodesh* (11 vols.). (Brooklyn, 1987–89).

———. *Likkutei Sichot* (26 vols.). (Brooklyn, 1967–88). Trans. J. I. Schochet, *Likkutei Sichot* (Brooklyn, 1980–87); trans. Jonathan Sacks, *Torah Studies* (London, 1986).

———. *Sefer ha-Ma'amarim Bati le-Gani* (Brooklyn, 1977).

———. *Sefer ha-Ma'amarim (Hanahot)*. (ongoing series 1951–92).

———. *Sefer ha-Ma'amarim Melukat* (Brooklyn, 1986).

———. *Sichot Hanahot (Transcripts)*. (pamphlets and bound volumes, Brooklyn, 1951–52).

———. *Torat Menachem* (Israel, 1992).

———. (ed.). *Ha-Yom Yom* (Brooklyn, 1943). Trans. Y. M. Kagan, *Ha-Yom Yom: "From Day to Day"* (Brooklyn, 1988).

Schneerson, Yosef Yitzhak. *Ha-Zemakh Zedek u-Tenuat ha-Haskalah* (Brooklyn, 1946). Trans. Z. Posner, *The "Tzemach Tzedek" and the Haskala Movement* (Brooklyn, 1969).

————. *Iggerot Kodesh* (12 vols.). (Brooklyn, 1982–85).

————. *Kuntres Bikkur Shikago* (Brooklyn, 1944).

————. *Sefer ha-Zikhronot* (2 vols.). (Brooklyn, 1947–1965). Trans. N. Mindel, *Lubavitcher Rabbi's Memoirs* (Brooklyn, 1956).

————. ed. *Ha-Keriah ve-ha-Kedushah* (Brooklyn, 1941–45).

————. Articles in *Ha-Tamim* (periodical published in Warsaw in 1930s, collected as *Ha-Tamim* (Kfar Habad, 1971; Brooklyn, 1975).

Shalom Dov Ber. *Iggerot Kodesh* (5 vols.). (Brooklyn, 1982–87).

————. *Kol ha-Yoze le-Milhemet Beit David* (n.d.).

————. *Kuntres Ez ha-Hayyim* (Brooklyn, 1946).

————. *Kuntres ha-Avodah* (Brooklyn, 1946).

————. *Kuntres Hanokh la-Na'ar* (Brooklyn, 1943).

————. *Kuntres ha-Tefilah* (Vilna, 1924).

————. *Kuntres Hehalzu* (Brooklyn, 1949). Trans. U. Kaploun, *Heichaltzu: On Ahavas Yisrael* (Brooklyn, 1988).

————. *Kuntres u-Ma'ayan mi-Beit Hashem* (Brooklyn, 1943). Trans. Z. Posner, *Kuntres Uma'ayan* (Brooklyn, 1969).

————. *Kuntres: Kol ha-Yozeh le-Milhemet Beit David* (Crown Heights, 1995).

————. *Sefer ha-Ma'amarim* (1882–1919). (20 vols.). (Brooklyn, 1974–86).

————. *Torat Shalom: Sefer ha-Sichot* (Brooklyn, 1946).

Shlomoh Zalman of Kopys, *Magen Avot* (2 vols.). (Berditchev, 1902).

Shneuri, Dov Ber of Lubavitch, *Bad Kodesh* (Warsaw, 1871; Brooklyn, 1963).

————. *Inyan ha-Hishtathut* (Shklov, after 1813; mimeographed Kfar Habad?, 1965).

————. *Kuntres ha-Hitpa'alut* (Koenigsberg, 1831?). Trans. L. Jacobs, *Tract on Ecstasy* (London, 1963).

Shneur Zalman of Liadi (RaSHaZ), *Iggeret ha-Kodesh* (Shklov, 1814).

————. *Likkutei Amarim-Tanya* (*Tanya*). (Slavuta, 1796; Vilna, 1900). Bilingual ed., trans. N. Mindel, N. Mangel, Z. Posner, and J. I. Schochet (London, 1973).

————. *Ma'amarei Admur ha-Zaken*: (5). 562 [1801–2] (Brooklyn, 1964).

————. *Ma'amarei Admur ha-Zaken*: (5). 562 [1801–2] pt.2 (Brooklyn, 1981).

————. *Ma'amarei Admur ha-Zaken*: (5). 563 [1802–3] pts. 1 and 2 (Brooklyn, 1981–2).

————. *Ma'amarei Admur ha-Zaken*: (5). 564 [1803–4] (Brooklyn, 1980).

————. *Ma'amarei Admur ha-Zaken*: (5). 565 [1804–5] pts. 1 and 2 (Brooklyn, 1980–81).

————. *Ma'amarei Admur ha-Zaken*: (5). 566 [1805–6] (Brooklyn, 1979).

————. *Ma'amarei Admur ha-Zaken*: (5). 567 [1806–7] (Brooklyn, 1979).

————. *Ma'amarei Admur ha-Zaken*: (5). 568 [1807–8] (Brooklyn, 1971).

————. *Ma'amarei Admur ha-Zaken*: (5). 568 [1807–8] pt. 2 (Brooklyn, 1982).

————. *Ma'amarei Admur ha-Zaken*: (5). 569 [1808–9] (Brooklyn, 1981).

————. *Ma'amarei Admur ha-Zaken*: (5). 570 [1809–10] (Brooklyn, 1981).

————. *Ma'amarei Admur ha-Zaken: Al Ma'amarei Razal (Shas, Zohar u-Tefilah)* (Brooklyn, 1984).

————. *Ma'amarei Admur ha-Zaken: Al Parshiot ha-Torah ve-ha-Moadim*, pts. 1 and 2 (Brooklyn, 1982–83).

————. *Ma'amarei Admur ha-Zaken: Ethalekh Loznya* (Brooklyn, 1957).

————. *Ma'amarei Admur ha-Zaken ha-Kezarim* (Brooklyn, 1981).

————. *Ma'amarei Admur ha-Zaken: Hanahot ha-R. P[inhas]* (Brooklyn, 1957).

————. *Ma'amarei Admur ha-Zaken: Inyanim* (Brooklyn, 1983).

————. *Ma'amarei Admur ha-Zaken: Ketuvim*, pts. 1 and 2 (Brooklyn, 1985).

————. *Ma'amarei Admur ha-Zaken: Nevi'im* (Brooklyn, 1984).

————. *Shulhan Arukh* (Kopys, and Shkolv, 1814; Kfar Habad, 1968).

————. *Torah Or* (Kopys, 1837; Brooklyn, 1972).

Vital, Hayyim. *Ez Hayyim* (Tel Aviv, 1960).

————. *Sefer Hisyonot* (Book of Visions). Ed. A. Z. Aescoly (Jerusalem, 1954).

Yakov Cadaner. *Sippurim Noraim* (Lemberg, 1875; Jerusalem, 1957).

Yakov Yosef ha-Kohen of Polonnoye. *Ben Porat Yosef* (Koretz, 1781; New York, 1954, photog. reprint of Piotrikov, 1884).

————. *Toledot Yakov Yosef* (Jerusalem, 1966, photog. reprint of Koretz, 1780).

Yitzhak Aizak Halevi Epstein of Homel. *Hanah Ariel* (Berdichev, 1912).

Zevin, S. Y. *Sippurei Hasidim, "Torah"* (Tel Aviv, 1955).

Academic and Miscellaneous Works

Abramsky, Ch. "The Crisis of Authority Within European Jewry in the Eighteenth Century," in *Studies in Jewish Religious and Intellectual History Presented to Alexander Altmann* (Tuscaloosa, Ala., 1979).

Aescoly, A. Z. "Ha-Hasidut be-Polin," in I. Halpern, ed., *Beit Yisrael be-Polin,* vol. 2 (Jerusalem, 1953).

Ahad ha-Am. *See* Ginzberg, Asher.

Altschuler, M. *The Yevsektsiya in the Soviet Union* (Hebrew). (Tel Aviv, 1980).

Alfasi, Y. *Hasidism and the Return to Zion* (Hebrew). (Tel Aviv, 1986).

Alon, Menahem. *Jewish Law* (3 vols.). (Philadelphia/Jerusalem 1994).

Amikam, Yair. *Yamah va-Kedmah* (Rishon le-Zion, 1980).

Aviad, J. *Return to Judaism: Religious Revival in Israel* (Chicago, 1984).

Baily, F. G. *Humbuggery and Manipulation: The Art of Leadership* (Ithaca, N.Y., 1988).

Bar, M. "Banav shel Moshe be-Agadat Hazal," in *Bar-Ilan Annual, Studies in Judaica and the Humanities,* vol. 13.

Baron, Salo W. *The Jewish Community* (Philadelphia, 1945).

————. "Messianic and Sectarian Movements," in M. Saperstein, ed., *Essential Papers on Messianic Movements and Personalities in Jewish History* (New York, 1992).

————. "Reappearance of Pseudo-Messiahs," in M. Saperstein, ed., *Essential Papers on Messianic Movements and Personalities in Jewish History* (New York, 1992).

————. *A Social and Religious History of the Jews* (12 vols.). (New York, 1952–67).

Bartal, Israel. "True Knowledge and Wisdom; On Orthodox Historiography," *Studies in Contemporary Jewry* 10 (1994), pp 178–192.

Beis Moshiach (weekly magazine). (Crown Heights, 1994–present).

Belfour, Ella. (ed.). *Manhigut Ruhanit be-Yisrael* (Ramat Gan, 1982).

Ben-Ami, Issachar. *Saint Veneration Among the Jews in Morocco* (Detroit, 1998).

Ben-Sasson, Haim Hillel. *A History of the Jewish People* (Cambridge, Mass., 1976).

————. *Atah Yadati* (Hebrew) (Betar Illit, 1999).

————. *Perakim be-Toledot ha-Yehudim bi-Yemei ha-Beynayim* (Tel Aviv, 1969).

Berger, A. "The Messianic Self-Consciousness of Abraham Abulafia: A Tentative Evaluation," in J. L. Blau et al., *Essays on Jewish Life and Thought Presented in Honor of Salo Wittmayer Baron* (New York, 1959), pp. 55–61.

Berger, David. "Is the Rebbe Becoming God?" *Ha'aretz*, January 11, 1998, p. 19.

————. "The New Messianism: Passing Phenomenon or Turning Point in the History of Judaism?" *Jewish Action* (Fall 1995), pp. 35–42, 88.

————. *The Rebbe, the Messiah, and the Scandal of Orthodox Indifference* (Oxford, 2001).

Berger, L. Peter. "The Sociological Study of Sectarianism," *Social Research* 21 (1954), pp. 467–485.

Berger, Rhonda Edna. "An Exploration into the Lubavitcher Hasidic Leadership Alliance Network," in *Yivo Institute for Jewish Research* (New York, 1977).

Berger, Milton. (ed.). *Roads to Jewish Survival* (New York, 1967).

Bindman, Yirmeyahu. *The Seven Colors of the Rainbow* (San Jose, Calif., 1995).

Boteach, Shmuel. *Dating Secrets of the Ten Commandments* (London, 1999).

————. *The Jewish Guide to Adultery* (London, 1995).

————. *Kosher Sex* (London, 1998).

Branover, Herman. *Be'en ha-Lev: Al ha-Rabi mi-Lubavits* (Ramat Gan, 1989).

Braun, Yosef, et al. (eds.). *And He Will Redeem Us: Moshiach in Our Time* (Translation of *V'Hu Yigaleinu*, with additional materials). (New York, 1994).

Braver, A. J. *Galizia vi-Yehudeha* (Jerusalem, 1956).

————. "On the Quarrel Between R. Shneur Zalman of Liadi and R. Abraham of Kalisk" (Hebrew). *Kiryat Sefer* 1 (1924).

Briggs, Charles. *Messianic Prophecy* (New York, 1987).

Bryman, Alan. *Leadership and Organizations* (London, 1986).

Buber, Martin. *Hasidism and Modern Man* (New York, 1958).

————. *Moses, the Revelation and the Covenant* (New York, 1958).

————. *The Origins and Meanings of Hasidism*, ed. and trans. Maurice Friedman (New York, 1960).

————. *The Tales of the Hasidim* (New York, 1947).

Butman, Shmuel. *Countdown to Moshiach: International Campaign to Bring Moshiach* (New York, 1995).

————. and I. Weisberg. "Response to David Berger," *Jewish Action* (New York, 1995).

Campbell, Joseph, with Bill Moyers. *The Power of Myth*, ed. B. S. Flowers (Princeton, N. J. 1974).

Chavel, Charles. "Shneur Zalman of Liadi," in *Understanding Rabbinic Judaism* (New York, 1974).

Clorfene, Chaim, and Rogalsky, Yakov. *The Path of the Righteous Gentile* (Southfield, Mich., 1987).

Cohen, Gershon D. "Messianic Postures of Ashkenazim and Sephardim," in M. Saperstein (ed.), *Essential Papers on Messianic Movements and Personalities in Jewish History* (New York, 1992).

Cohen, Stuart A. *The Three Crowns: Structures of Communal Politics in Early Rabbinic Jewry* (Cambridge, 1990).

Cohn-Sherbok, D. (ed.). *Divine Intervention and Miracles in Jewish Theology* (New York, 1996).

Court Protocols. U.S. District Court, Eastern District of New York, *Agudas Hasidei Chabad of U.S. against Barry S. Gourary and Hanna Gourary* (1985–86). (cited as "Protocols").

Crown, Alan D. "Jewish Roots of Christian Liturgy," *Australian Journal of Jewish Studies* 9:1–2 (1995).

Dan, Joseph. "The Contemporary Hasidic Zaddik: Charisma, Heredity, Magic and Miracle," in Dan Cohn-Sherbok, ed., *Divine Intervention and Miracles in Jewish Theology* (New York, 1996), pp. 195–214.

———. *Gershom Scholem and the Mystical Dimension of Jewish History* (New York, 1987).

———. *The Hasidic Story: Its History and Development* (Hebrew). (Jerusalem, 1975).

Danzger, M. Herbert. *Returning to Tradition: The Contemporary Revival of Orthodox Judaism* (New Haven, 1989).

Davidman, Lynn. "Accommodation and Resistance to Modernity: A Comparison of Two Contemporary Orthodox Jewish Groups," *Sociological Analysis* 51:1 (1990), pp 35–51.

Davis, J. David. *Finding the God of Noah* (Hoboken, N.J., 1996).

Dein, S. "Letters to the Rebbe; Millennium, Messianism and Medicine Among the Lubavitch Hasidim of Stamford Hill, London," *International Journal of Social Psychiatry* 38 (1992). 262–272.

Deutsch, Shaul S. *Larger Than Life: The Life and Times of the Lubavitcher Rebbe Rabbi Menachem Mendel Schneerson*, vol. 1 (New York, 1995).

———. *Larger Than Life: The Life and Times of the Lubavitcher Rebbe Rabbi Menachem Mendel Schneerson*, vol. 2 (New York, 1997).

De Vaux, Roland. *Ancient Israel: Its Life and Institutions* (2nd ed., London, 1965).

Dinur (Dinabourg), Benzion. "The Beginning of Hasidism and Its Social and Messianic Elements" (Hebrew), *Zion* 8–10; reprinted in *Be-Mifneh ha-Dorot* (Jerusalem, 1955).

———. "The Messianic-Prophetic Role of the Baal Shem Tov," in M. Saperstein, ed., *Essential Papers on Messianic Movements and Personalities in Jewish History* (New York, 1992).

———. "The Origins of Hasidism and Its Social and Messianic Foundations," in G. D. Hundert, ed., *Essential Papers on Hasidism* (New York, 1991), pp. 86–208.

Dresner, Samuel H. *The Zaddik: The Doctrine of the Zaddik According to the Writings of Rabbi Yaakov Yosef of Polnoy* (New York, 1960).

Douglas, Mary. *How Institutions Think* (New York, 1986).

Downton, James V. *Rebel Leadership: Commitment and Charisma in the Revolutionary Process* (New York, 1973).

Dubnow, Simon. "The Beginnings: The Baal Shem Tov (Besht) and the Center in Podolia," in G. D. Hundert, ed., *Essential Papers on Hasidism* (New York, 1991), pp. 25–57.

———. *History of Hasidism* (Hebrew). (4th ed., Tel Aviv, 1975).

———. *History of the Jews in Russia and Poland* (3 vols.). (Philadelphia, 1916).

———. "The Maggid of Miedzyrezecz, His Associates, and the Center in Volhynia (1760–1772).," in G. D. Hundert, ed., *Essential Papers on Hasidism* (New York, 1991), pp. 58–85.

Durkheim, Emile. *The Division of Labor in Society* (Glencoe, Ill., 1947).

———. *Elementary Forms of the Religious Life* (New York, 1965).

———. *Primitive Classification* (Chicago, 1963).

Ehrlich, Avrum M. "Arab Christian Views on Judaism and the State of Israel," paper presented at the Eighth Conference on Arab Christianity at the University of Sydney, Australia, July 2000.

———. *Leadership in the HaBaD Movement: A Critical Evaluation of HaBaD Leadership, History and Succession* (Northvale, N.J., 2000).

——— . "Sabbatean Messianism as Proto-Secularism: Examples in Modern Turkey and Zionism," in *Mehmet Tutuncu* (ed.), Turkish–Jewish Encounters (Haarlem, 2001).

Ehrmann, Naftali Hertz. *The Rav* (Jerusalem, 1977).

Elazar, D. (ed.). *Authority, Power and Leadership in the Jewish Polity* (Lanham, Md., 1991).

Elior, Rachel. "The Anthropocentric Position in Habad Thought" (Hebrew), *Da'at* 12 (1984).

———. "The Controversy over the Leadership of the Habad Movement," *Tarbiz* 49 (1980).

———. "The Dialectics of Perfection and Revelation" (Hebrew), *Da'at* 9 (1982).

———. "Dov Ber Schneersohn's Kuntres ha-Hitpa'alut" (Hebrew), *Kiryat Sefer* 54 (1979).

———. "Habad: The Contemplative Ascent to God," in *Jewish Spirituality*, ed. A. Green (New York, 1985), pp. 157–205. Expanded Hebrew version: "Iyunim be-Machshevet Habad," *Da'at* 16 (1986).

————. "The Minsk Debate" (Hebrew), *Jerusalem Studies in Jewish Thought* 4 (1982).

————. "The Theory of Divinity and Worship of God in the Second Generation of Hasidut Habad" (Hebrew), doctoral diss., Hebrew University (Jerusalem, 1976).

————. *Torat Ha-Elohut be-Dor ha-Sheni Shel ha-Hasidut Habad*, (Jerusalem 1982/5742).

Encyclopaedia Judaica (16 vols.). (Jerusalem, 1972).

Encyclopedia Talmudit (Jerusalem, 1947–).

Enlow, Hyman G. "Kavvanah: The Struggle for Inwardness in Judaism," in *Studies in Jewish Literature in Honor of Kaufmann Kohler* (Berlin, 1913).

Epstein, Joseph. (ed.). *Masters: Portraits of Great Teachers* (New York, 1981).

Etkes, Israel. "Hasidism as a Movement: The First Stage," in B. Safran, ed., *Hasidism: Continuity or Innovation* (Cambridge, Mass., 1988).

————. "R. Shneur Zalman of Liadi as a Hasidic Leader" (Hebrew), Jubilee Vol. of *Zion* 50 (1986).

————. "R. Shneur Zalman of Liadi's Rise to Leadership" (Hebrew), *Tarbiz* 54 (1985).

————. "Shitato u-fo'alo shel R. Haim mi-Volozhin ki-Teguvat ha-Hevrah ha- 'mit-nagdit' la-Hasidut," (Hebrew), *Proceedings of the American Academy for Jewish Research* 38–39 (New York, 1972).

Ettinger, S. "Ha-Hanhagah ha-Hasidit be-Izuvah," *Dat ve-Hevra be-Toledot Yisrael u-ve-Toledot he-Amim* (Jerusalem, 1965). English version: "The Hasidic Movement: Reality and Ideals," *Journal of World History* 2 (1968).

————. "The Hasidic Movement," in G. D. Hundert ed., *Essential Papers on Hasidism* (New York, 1991).

Faber, Salamon. "The Lubavitch Library" *Jewish Book Annual* 46 (1988), pp. 177–183.

Feingold, Henry C. *Zion in America* (New York, 1974).

Finkel, Avraham Y. *Contemporary Sages: The Great Chasidic Masters of the Twentieth Century* (Northvale, N.J., 1994).

Fishbane, Michael. *The Kiss of God: Spiritual and Mystical Death in Judaism* (Seattle, 1994).

Fishman, David E. "Preserving Tradition in the Land of Revolution: The Religious Leadership of Soviet Jewry, 1917–1930," in *The Uses of Tradition* (1992), pp. 85–118.

Foxbruner, Roman A. "Habad: the Ethical Thought of R. Shneur Zalman of Lyadi," doctoral diss., Harvard University (1984).

————. *The Hasidism of Rabbi Shneur Zalman of Lyadi* (Tuscaloosa, Ala., 1994).

Friedlaender, Israel. "Shiitic Influences in Jewish Sectarianism," in M. Saperstein, ed., *Essential Papers on Messianic Movements and Personalities in Jewish History* (New York, 1992).

Friedman, M. "Haredim Confront the Modern City," *Studies in Contemporary Judaism* (Bloomington, 1986).

————. "Habad as Messianic Fundamentalism: From Local Particularism to Universal Mission," *The Fundamentalism Project* (vol. 4), (Chicago, 1994), pp. 328–357.

————. "Religious Fundamentalism and Religious Jews: The Case of the Haredim," in *Fundamentalism Observed* (1991).

Freeman, Jenny A. "Soviet Jews, Orthodox Judaism and the Lubavitcher Hasidim," *Eastern European Jewish Affairs* 23:1 (1993), pp. 57–77.

Gansburg, Y. *Sefer ha-Maftehot le-Sifrei Admur ha-Emzai* (Brooklyn, 1982).

Garvin, P., and Cohen, A. *A People Apart: Hasidism in America* (New York, 1970).

Gershoni, A. A. *Judaism in Soviet Russia* (Hebrew). (Jerusalem, 1961).

Gilbert, M. *The Jews of Russia* (London, 1976).

Ginzberg, Asher. (Ahad ha-Am). *Kol Kitve Ahad ha-Am* (Tel Aviv, 1947).

Ginzberg, Levi I. *Mashiah Akhshav* (Kfar Habad, 5753).

Gitelman, Z. *Jewish Nationality and Soviet Politics* (Princeton, N.J., 1972).

Glitzenstein, A. H. *Sefer ha-Toledot* (10 vols.). (Brooklyn, Kfar Habad, 1960–74).

————. *Tomkhei Temimim* (Brooklyn, 1969).

Glitzenstein, Sh. *Ha-Admur ha-Emzai* (1950).

Goldberg D. "Chasidus and History," *Di Yiddishe Heim* (Autumn 1976).

Gottschalk, Alfred. *To Learn and to Teach: Your Life as a Rabbi* (New York, 1988).

Graff, G. *Separation of Church and State, Dina de-Malkhuta Dina in Jewish Law*, 1750–1848 (Tuscaloosa, Ala., 1985).

Green, Arthur. *Devotion and Commandment: The Faith of Abraham in the Hasidic Imagination* (New York, 1989).

————. *Jewish Spirituality* (ed.). (New York, 1987).

————. "Nahman of Braslav's Messianic Strivings," in M. Saperstein, ed., *Essential Papers on Messianic Movements and Personalities in Jewish History* (New York, 1992).

————. Rabbi Nahman of Bratslav: A Critical Biography, doctoral diss., Brandeis University (1975).

————. *Tormented Master: A Life of Rabbi Nahman of Braslav* (Tuscaloosa, Ala., 1979).

————. "Typologies of Leadership and the Hasidic Zaddiq," in *Jewish Spirituality* (New York, 1987).

————. "The Zaddiq as Axis Mundi in Later Judaism," *Journal of the American Academy of Religion* 45 (1977).

Greenberg, L. *The Jews in Russia* (New Haven, 1965).

Greenberg, Gershon. "Assimilation as Churban According to Wartime American Orthodoxy (Chabad Chasidim)," in *Jewish Assimilation, Acculturation and Accommodation: Past Traditions, Current Issues and Future Prospects* (New York, 1989).

———— ."Mahane Israel—Lubavitch 1940–1945: Actively Responding to Khurban," in *Bearing Witness to the Holocaust* 1934–1989, ed. Alan L. Berger (1991), pp. 141–163.

——. "Redemption after the Holocaust According to Mahane Israel—Lubavitch 1940–1945," *Modern Judaism* 12:1 (1992), pp. 62–84.

Gries, Z. "Mi-Mitos la-Etos—Kavim li-Demuto shel R. Avraham mi-Kalisk," *Umah ve-Toledoteha* (Jerusalem, 1984).

Gross, Eli. Unpublished diary, New York, 1950–53.

Grynberg, Yosef Yitzhak (ed.). *Yemei Be-Reishis* (Historical Biography 1950–51). (Brooklyn, 1993).

Gurary, E. E. *Toledot . . . R. 'Yishak Aizak ha-Levi Epstein* (Kfar Habad, 1980).

Ha-Keriah ve-ha-Kedushah (HaBaD journal). (Brooklyn, 1941–45).

Hallamish, Moshe. "A Commentary to the Tanya" (Hebrew), *Da'at* 13 (1984).

——. *Netiv la-Tanya* (Tel Aviv, 1987).

——. "Rabbi Shneur Zalman of Liadi and his Conception of Charity" (Hebrew), *Da'at* 1 (1978).

——. "R. Shneur Zalman of Lyady in the Land of Israel" (Hebrew), *Hebrew Union College Annual* 61 (1990).

——. "The Theoretical System of Rabbi Shneur Zalman of Liady (Its Sources in Kabbalah and Hasidism)" (Hebrew), doctoral diss., Hebrew University (Jerusalem, 1976).

——. "Yahasei Zaddik ve-Edah be-Mishnat R. Shneur Zalman mi-Liadi," *Hevrah ve-Historiyah* (Jerusalem, 1980), pp. 79–92.

Halpern, I. *Ha-Aliyot ha-Rishonot shel ha-Yehudim le-Erez Yisrael* (Jerusalem, 1946).

——. "Hevrot le-Torah u-le-Mizvot u-Tenuat ha-Hasidut be-Hitpashtutah," *Zion* 23 (1957), also in *Eastern European Jewry* (Hebrew). (Jerusalem, 1968).

——. (ed.). *Beit Yisrael be-Polin* (Jerusalem, 1948).

——. (ed.). *Iggerot Hasidim me-Eretz Yisrael* (Jerusalem, 1980).

Ha-Maraha le-Hazalat ha-Rabbanut by Va'ad le-Hazalat ha-Rabanut (Jerusalem, 1973).

Hanoch, Reviv. *The Elders in Ancient Israel* (Jerusalem, 1989).

Ha-Rabbanut ha-Rashit le-Yisrael, Israeli Education Ministry (Tel Aviv, 991).

Harris, Lis. *Holy Days: The World of a Hasidic Family* (New York, 1985).

Hasofer, Raquel. "Messiah from the Living—Messiah from the Dead: Issues in Contemporary Judaism," B.A. (Hons.) thesis, Department of Semitic Studies, University of Sydney, 1999.

Ha-Tam (periodical published in Warsaw in 1930s, collected vol. *Ha-Tamim*, Kfar Habad, 1971; Brooklyn, 1975).

Heilman, Samuel C. *Jewish Unity and Diversity: A Survey of American Rabbis and Rabbinical Students* (New York, 1991).

Herring, Basil. (ed.). *The Rabbinate as a Calling and Vocation: Models of Rabbinic Leadership* (Northvale, N.J.,1991).

Heschel, Abraham Joshua. *The Circle of the Baal Shem Tov: Studies in Hasidism* (Chicago, 1985).

——. *The Prophets* (Philadelphia, 1962).

Hill, B. S. "Hebrew Printing in Russia," *British Library Journal* (Autumn 1995).

Hodgkinson, Christopher. *The Philosophy of Leadership* (Oxford, 1983).

Hoffman, Edward. *Despite All Odds: The Story of Lubavitch* (New York, 1991).

Horodecky, Samuel. "Le-Korot ha-Hasidim," *Ha-Shiloah* (1902).

———. *Ha-Hasidut ve-ha-Hasidim* (Tel Aviv, 1928).

Horowitz, Yishayahu. *Kizur Shtei Luhot ha-Brit*, ed. Yehiel Mikhal Epstein (Zolkiev, 1795

Hugo, Mantel. *Studies in the History of the Sanhedrin* (Cambridge, Mass., 1961).

Hutton, Rodney R. *Charisma and Authority in Israelite Society* (Minneapolis, 1994).

Idel, Moshe. *Hasidism Between Ecstasy and Magic* (New York, 1995).

———. *Kabbalah: New Perspectives* (New Haven, 1988).

———. *Religious Experience in the Thought of Abraham Abulafia* (New York, 1988).

Isaacs, Stephen. "Hasidim of Brooklyn," in *A Coat of Many Colors* (London, 1977).

Jacobs, Louis. "The Doctrine of the Divine Spark in Man in Jewish Sources," in *Studies in Rationalism, Judaism and Universalism, in Memory of Leon Roth* (London, 1966).

———. *Hasidic Prayer* (London, 1972).

———. *Hasidic Thought* (New York, 1976).

———. *The Jewish Mystics* (London, 1990).

———. *Seeker of Unity: The Life and Works of Aaron of Starosselje* (London, 1966).

———. *Theology in the Responsa* (London, 1975).

———. trans., Dobh Baer of Lubavitch, Tract on Ecstasy (London, 1963).

Jacobson, Simon (ed.). *Toward a Meaningful Life: The Wisdom of the Rebbe* (New York, 1995).

Jacobson, Y. "R. Shneur Zalman of Lyady's Doctrine of Creation" (Hebrew), *Eshel Be'er Sheva* (1976), pp. 306–368.

Johnson, Benton. (ed.). *Conversion, Charisma and Institutionalization* (Seattle, 1992).

Jospe, Raphael, and Wagner, S. (eds.). *Great Schisms in Jewish History* (New York, 1981).

Jung, Leo. (ed.). *Jewish Leaders* (New York, 1953).

Kahn, Benjamin. *Leadership and the Jewish Community* (n.p., n.d.).

Kahn, Yoel. Unpublished diary (New York, 1950–53).

———. Sefer Erkhim (Brooklyn, n.d.).

Katchen, Martin H. "Who Wants Moshiach Now? Pre-Millennialism and Post-Millennialism in Judaism," *Australian Journal of Jewish Studies* 5:1 (1991). pp. 59–76.

Katz, J. *Halachah and Kabbalah: Studies in the History of the Jewish Religion* (Hebrew) (Jerusalem, 1984).

———. "Israel and the Messiah," in M. Saperstein ed., *Essential Papers on Messianic Movements and Personalities in Jewish History* (New York, 1992).

Katz, S. "Iggerot Maskilim bi-Genutam shel Hasidim," *Moznayim* 10 (1940).

Kellner, Menachem. "Messianic Postures in Israel Today," in M. Saperstein, ed., *Essential Papers on Messianic Movements and Personalities in Jewish History* (New York, 1992).

Ketzad Mesalfim (booklet, Satmar Hasidim). (Bnei Brak, 1989).

Kfar Habad (weekly magazine). (Kfar Habad, 1980–present).

Klapman, Laura Alter. "Sectarian Strategies for Stability and Solidarity: A Theory for the Remarkable Durability of the Lubavitch Movement," doctoral diss., Northwestern University (Evanston, Ill., 1991).

Klapholz, Y. Y. *Tales of the Baal Shem Tov.* <please provide publication facts; cited in chap. 1>

Klausner, Israel. *Vilna bi-Tekufat ha-Gaon* (Jerusalem, 1942).

Klorman, Bat-Zion Eraqui. "The Messiah Shukr Kuhayl II (1868–75) and His Tithe (Ma'aser): Ideology and Practice as a Means to Hasten Redemption," in M. Saperstein, ed., *Essential Papers on Messianic Movements and Personalities in Jewish History* (New York, 1992).

Koskoff, Ellen. "The Sound of a Woman's Voice: Gender and Music in a New York Hasidic Community," in *Women and Music in Cross-Cultural Perspective* (1989). pp. 213–223.

Kovacs, Malcolm Louis. "The Dynamics of Commitment: The Process of Resocialization of Baalei Teshuva, Jewish Students in Pursuit of Their Identity at the Rabbinical College of America (Lubavitch)," doctoral diss., Union Graduate School (1977).

Kranzler, Gershon. *Rabbi Shneur Zalman of Liadi* (New York, 1967).

Krassen, Miles A. "Agents of the Divine Display: New Studies in Early Hasidism," *Religious Studies Review* 20:4 (1994). pp. 293–301.

Kupfer, E. "New Documents Concerning the Polemic Between R. Shneur Zalman of Liady, R. Abraham ha-Kohen of Kalisk and R. Barukh of Medzibezh" (Hebrew), Tarbiz 47 (1978).

Laufer, Mordechai Menasheh. *Yemei Melech* (3 vols.). (Brooklyn, 1989).

Lavender, D. Abraham. *A Coat of Many Colors: Jewish Sub-communities in the U.S.* (Westport, Conn., 1979).

Leavy, Brian. *Strategy and Leadership* (London, 1994).

Lenowitz, Harris. *The Jewish Messiahs: From the Galilee to Crown Heights* (New York, 1998).

Leibowitz, Yishayahu. *Ha-Olam u-Melo'o* (Tel Aviv).

———. *Yehadut Am Yehudi u-Medinat Yisrael* (Tel Aviv, 1979).

Levine, S. B. *History of Chabad in the Holy Land, 1777–1950* (Hebrew). (Brooklyn, 1988).

———. *History of Chabad in the U.S.A., 1900–1950* (Hebrew). (Brooklyn, 1988).

———. *History of Chabad in the U.S.S.R., 1917–1950* (Hebrew). (Brooklyn, 1989).

———. "Note on R. Elior's Dov Ber Schneersohn's Kuntres ha-Hitpa'alut" (Hebrew), *Kiryat Sefer* 44 (1979).

——. *Sefer Sifriot Lubavitch* (Brooklyn, 1988).

Levinger, J. B*ein Philosoph le-Posek* (Jerusalem, 1989).

Levitats, I. *The Jewish Community in Russia, 1772–1844* (New York, 1943).

Levy, Sydelle Brooks. "Ethnic Boundedness and the Institutionalization of Charisma: A Study of the Lubavitcher Hassidim.," doctoral diss., City University of New York (1973).

Liebes, Y. "The Messiah of the Zohar," in *The Messianic Idea in Israel* (Hebrew). (Jerusalem, 1982).

Lipson, Juliene G. *Jews for Jesus: An Anthropological Study* (New York, 1990)

Loewenthal, Kate Miriam. "Patterns of Religious Development and Experience in Habad-Hasidic Women," *Journal of Psychology and Judaism* 12 (1988), pp. 4–20.

Loewenthal, Naftali. "The Apotheosis of Action in Early Habad," *Da'at* 18 (1986).

——. *Communicating the Infinite: The Emergence of the Habad School* (Chicago, 1990).

——. "The Concept of Mesirat Nefesh ('Self Sacrifice') in the Teachings of R. Dov Ber of Lubavitch (1773–1827)," doctoral diss., University of London (1981).

——. "Contemporary Habad and the Paradox of Redemption," in *Studies in Mysticism and Religion in Memory of A. Altmann*, ed. Ailvry E. Wolfson (forthcoming).

——. "Early Habad Publications in Their Setting," *Hebrew Studies Colloquium* (1991). pp. 94–104.

——. "Early Hasidic Teachings: Esoteric Mysticism, or a Medium of Communal Leadership?" *Journal of Jewish Studies* 37 (1986).

——. "Habad Approaches to Contemplative Prayer, 1790–1920," *Polin* (in press).

——. Hebrew and the Habad Communication Ethos," Hebrew in *Ashkenaz* (1993). pp. 167–192.

——. "The Neutralization of Messianism and the Apocalypse," in *Studies in Mysticism and Religion in Memory of A. Altmann*, ed., Ailvry E. Wolfson (forthcoming).

——. "The Paradox of Habad," *Jewish Studies* 34 (1994). 65–73.

——. " 'Reason' and 'Beyond Reason' in Habad Hasidim," *Alei Sefer* (1990). pp. 109–126.

——. "Self-Sacrifice of the Zaddik in the Teachings of R. Dov Ber, the Mitteler Rebbe," in *Jewish History, Essays in Honor of Chimen Abramsky* (London, 1988).

Lubavitch in the News. Compiled by Lubavitch News Service (Washington, D.C., June 1995).

Mahler, R. *Hasidism and the Jewish Enlightenment* (Philadelphia, 1985).

Maman, P. *Torato Shel Mashiah* (Brooklyn, 1993).

Maimon, L. J. *Hiddush ha-Sanhedrin be-Medinatenu ha-Mehudeshet* (Jerusalem, 1967).

Ha-Maraha le-Hazalat ha-Rabbanut by Va'ad le-Hazalat ha-Rabanut (Jerusalem, 1973).

Marcus, Jacob R., and Peck, Abraham J. (eds.). *The American Rabbinate: A Century of Continuity and Change*, 1883–1983 (Hoboken, N.J., 1985).

Medding, P. Y. *From Assimilation to Group Survival: A Political and Sociological Study of an Australian Jewish Community* (Melbourne, 1968).

Meizlish, Shaul (ed.). *Ha-Rabbanut be-Sa'arat ha-Yamim* (Tel Aviv, 1991).

Mesibos Shabbos: Program and Guide (Brooklyn, 1960).

Mindel, Nissan. *The Philosophy of Chabad* (Brooklyn, 1974).

——. *Rabbi Schneur Zalman of Liadi. Vol. 1: Biography* (New York, 1969).

——. trans. *Liqqutei Amarim* (Tanya). (Brooklyn, 1962).

Mintz, Jerome R. *Hasidic People: A Place in the New World* (Cambridge, 1992).

——. *Legends of the Hasidim: An Introduction to Hasidic Culture and Oral Tradition in the New World* (Chicago, 1968).

Mirsky, S. K. (ed.). *Mosdot Torah be-Eropa be-Binyanam ve-be-Hurbanam* (New York, 1956), p. 233 and pp. 314–316.

Mondschein, Y. "Dorshei Yihudekha: Mikhtavei ha-Rav ha-Kadosh R. Aaron ha-Levi mi-Staroselya el kevod kedushat Admur ha-Emzai," *Kerem Habad* 1 (1986).

——. "Ha-Sefarim Mazref ha-Avodah u-Vikuha Rabah," *Alei Sefer* 5 (1978).

Morgenstern, A. "Messianic Concepts and the Settlement of Israel," in M. Saperstein, ed., *Essential Papers on Messianic Movements and Personalities in Jewish History* (New York, 1992).

Morris, Bonnie J. "The Children's Crusade: The Tzivos Hashem Youth Movement as an Aspect of Hasidic Identity," *Judaism* 40:3 (1991), pp. 333–343.

Moshkovitz, Mordechai. *Kuntres ha-Emet al Tnuat Habad be-Shnot ha-80* (Israel, 1988), found at Bar-Ilan Library: serial no. A672 Mosh 5748—82111.

Neusner, Jacob (ed.). *Judaisms and Their Messiahs at the Turn of the Christian Era* (New York, 1987).

——. *Messiah in Context* (Philadelphia, 1984).

Nigal, G. *Manhig va-Edah* (Jerusalem, 1962).

Oro Shel Mashiah (Kfar Habad, 1991).

Page, Edward C. *Political Authority and Bureaucratic Power* (New York, 1992).

Pastner, Stephen, and Berger-Sofer, Rhonda. " 'Rebbe' and 'Pir': Ideology, Action and Personhood in Hasidism and Sufism," *Studies in Islamic and Judaic Traditions*, 11 (1989), pp. 113–139.

Patai, Raphael. *The Messiah Texts* (Detroit, 1979).

Pegishot Im ha-Rabi (Kfar Habad). no known author.

Piekarz, Mendel. *The Beginning of Hasidism* (Hebrew). (Jerusalem, 1978).

——. " 'The Inner Point' of the Admorim of Gur and Alexander as a Reflection of Their Ability to Adjust to Changing Times," in *Studies in Jewish Mysticism, Philosophy, and Ethical Literature Presented to Isaiah Tishby* (Jerusalem, 1986).

Potok, Chaim. The Gift of Asher Lev (New York, 1990).

——. *My Name Is Asher Lev* (London, 1972).

——. *The Promise* (London, 1970).

Pozner, Avraham B. *Al ha-Zaddikim* (Kfar Habad, 5751).

Rabinowicz, Harry. Hasidism and the State of Israel (Rutherford, N.J., 1982).

———. *The World of Hasidism* (London, 1970).

Rapoport-Albert, A. "God and the Zaddik," *History of Religion* 18:4 (Chicago, 1979).

———. "Hagiography with Footnotes: Edifying Tales and the Writing of History in Hasidism," in *Studies in Jewish Historiography in Memory of Arnoldo Momigliano*, supplement to *History and Theory* (1988).

———. "The Hasidic Movement After 1772: Continuity or Change?" *Zion* (in press).

———. "The Problem of Succession in the Hasidic Leadership, with Special Reference to the Circle of R. Nahman of Braslav," doctoral diss., University of London (1974).

Ravitzky, Aviezer. "The Contemporary Lubavitch Hasidic Movement: Between Conservatism and Messianism," *Fundamentalism Project*, vols. 2/3, chap. 12 (Chicago, 1994).

Rav Rashi be-Emet (Jerusalem, 1993). By friends of Rabbi SharYeshuv Ha-Kohen.

The Rebbe: Changing the Tide of Education (New York, 1982). Uncited author.

Redekop, Calvin, and Shaffir, William. "Communal Organization and Secular Education: Hutterite and Hasidic Comparisons," *Communal Life* (1987), pp 342–357.

Redman, Barbara J. "Strange Bedfellows: Lubavitch Hasidim and Conservative Christians," *Journal of Church and State* 34:3 (1992), pp. 531–548.

Reinharz, J., and Swetschinski, D. (eds.). *Mystics, Philosophers and Politicians* (Durham, N.C., 1982).

Ronn, Micheol. "Chabad-Lubavitch Literature as a Genealogical Source," Avotaynu 8:3 (1992), pp. 40–44.

Rosenbloom, J. *Conversion to Judaism from the Biblical Period to the Present* (Cincinnati, 1978).

Rosman, M. *Founder of Hasidism: A Quest for the Historical Ba'al Shem Tov* (Berkeley, 1996).

———. "Miedzyboz and Rabbi Israel Baal Shem Tov (Besht)," *Zion* 52 (1987). Reprinted in G. D. Hundert, (ed.), *Essential Papers on Hasidism* (New York, 1987), pp. 209–225.

Rubin, Israel. "Chassidic Community Behavior," in *A Coat of Many Colors* (London, 1977).

Safran, Bezalel (ed.). *Hasidism: Continuity or Innovation* (Cambridge, Mass, 1988).

Salinger, Peter Shmuel. "Publishing Developments of Habad Teachings, 1794–1989," *Hebrew Studies Colloquium* (1991), pp. 105–110.

Sapperstein, Marc (ed.). Essential Papers on Messianic Movements and Personalities in Jewish History (New York, 1992).

Schachter, Zalman M. "The Dynamics of the Yehidut Transaction," *Journal of Psychology and Judaism* 3:1 (1978).

Schatz-Uffenheimer, Rivka. "Anti-Spiritualism ba-Hasidut," *Molad* 17 (1962), pp. 1–72.

———. "Ha-Yesod ha-Meshihi be-Mahashevet ha-Hasidut," *Molad* 24 (1967).

———. "Le-Mahuto shel ha-Zaddik ba-Hasidut," *Molad,* 144–45 (1960).

———. *Quietistic Elements in Eighteenth Century Hasidic Thought* (Hebrew). (Jerusalem, 1968).

Schechter, Solomon. "Safed in the Sixteenth Century: A City of Legalists and Mystics," *Studies in Judaism,* 2nd series (1908), pp. 202–306.

Schiffman, Lawrence H. "Confessionalism and the Study of the Dead Sea Scrolls" *Jewish Studies* 31 (1991).

Schochet, Jacob Immanuel. *Chassidic Dimensions: Themes in Chassidic Thought and Practice,* vol. 3, *The Mystical Dimension* (New York, 1990).

———. *The Mystical Tradition: Insights into the Nature of the Mystical Tradition in Judaism* (Brooklyn, 1990).

Scholem, Gershom G. "Demuto ha-Historit shel R. Yisrael Baal Shem Tov," *Molad* 144–45 (1960).

———. "Devekut, or Communion with God," *Review of Religion* 14 (1949–50), collected in The Messianic Idea.

———. *Major Trends in Jewish Mysticism* (reprint of 3rd ed., New York, 1961).

———. *The Messianic Idea in Judaism* (New York, 1971).

———. "The Neutralization of the Messianic Element in Early Hasidism," *Journal of Jewish Studies* 20 (1969), collected in The Messianic Idea.

———. *Sabbetai Sevi: The Mystical Messiah* (1626–1676). (Princeton, N.J., 1973).

Schwarzfuchs, Simon. *A Concise History of the Rabbinate* (Cambridge, Mass., 1993).

Schweid, Eliezer. "Jewish Messianism: Metamorphoses of an Idea," in M. Saperstein, ed., *Essential Papers on Messianic Movements and Personalities in Jewish History* (New York, 1992).

Sefer ha-Ken: Kovetz Ma'amarim al Admur ha-Zaken R. Shneur Zalman mi-Liadi (Jerusalem, 1969).

Sefer ha-Likkutim (encyclopedia of Habad concepts, based on the writings of Zemakh Zedek, including a general index to Habad teachings; 27 vols.). (Brooklyn, 1977–84).

Sefer ha-Zeazaim: Admur ha-Zaken (Jerusalem, 5741).

Sha'arei ha-Geulah (Kfar Habad, 1992).

Shaffir, William. "Jewish Messianism Lubavitch Style: An Interim Report," *Jewish Journal of Sociology* 35:2 (1993), pp. 115–128.

———. "Interpreting Diversity: Dynamics of Commitment in a Messianic Redemption Campaign," *Jewish Journal of Sociology* 36:1 (1994), pp. 43–53.

———. "When Prophecy Is Not Validated: Explaining the Unexpected in a Messianic Campaign," *Jewish Journal of Sociology* 37: 2 (1995), pp. 119–136.

———. and Redekop, Calvin. "Communal Organization and Secular Education: Hutterite and Hasidic Comparisons," in *Communal Life* (1987), pp 342–357.

Sharp, Helen. "The Lubavitch Chassidim of Melbourne: Jewish Activists Against Secularism," *American Jewish Historical Society Inc.* 11:3 (1991), pp. 491–505.

Shteinman, A. *Ber ha-Hasidut* (2 vols). (Tel Aviv, 1944, 5704).

Sicker, M. *The Judaic State: A Study in Rabbinic Political Theory* (New York, 1988).

Singer, Isaac Bashevis. *The Collected Short Stories of Isaac Bashevis Singer* (London, 1982).

———. *A Day of Pleasure: Stories of a Boy Growing Up in Warsaw* (New York, 1969).

Sobel, B. "The M'lochim: A Study of a Religious Community," M.A. thesis, New School for Social Research, 1956.

Sokol, M. (ed.). *Rabbinic Authority and Personal Autonomy* (Northvale, N.J.,1992).

Soloveitchik, Joseph B. *Divrei Hagut ve-Ha'araha* (Jerusalem, 1982).

———. *Halakhic Man* (Philadelphia, 1983).

Steinsaltz, Adin. "Maamarei Admur ha-Zaken," in *Sefer ha-Ken: Kovez Ma'amarim al Admur ha-Zaken R. Shneur Zalman mi-Liadi* (Jerusalem, 1969).

Smith, Peter B. *Leadership, Organization and Culture* (London, 1988).

Smith, Morton. "Robbers, Jurists, Prophets and Magicians," in M. Saperstein, ed., *Essential Papers on Messianic Movements and Personalities in Jewish History* (New York, 1992).

Strauss, Leo. *Persecution and the Art of Writing* (New Haven, 1973).

Stevens, Elliot. (ed.). *Rabbinic Authority* (New York, 1982).

Sugiot be-Geulah (booklet). (Crown Heights, 5756, 1996).

Szmeruk, Ch. "The Social Significance of the Hasidic Shechitah" (Hebrew), *Zion* 20 (1955).

Tal, Uriel. "Foundations of a Political Messianic Trend in Israel," in M. Saperstein, ed., *Essential Papers on Messianic Movements and Personalities in Jewish History* (New York, 1992).

Ha-Tam (periodical published in Warsaw in 1930s, collected vol. *Ha-Tamim*, Kfar Habad, 1971; Brooklyn, 1975).

Tauber, Yanki. *Once Upon a Chassid* (Brooklyn, 1994).

Taubes, J. "The Price of Messianism," in M. Saperstein, ed., *Essential Papers on Messianic Movements and Personalities in Jewish History* (New York, 1992).

Tauger, Eliyahu, and Tauger, Malka. *To Know and to Care: Contemporary Chassidic Stories About the Lubavitcher Rebbe Shlita*, Rabbi Menachem M. Schneerson, Sichos in English (New York, 1993).

Teitelbaum, M. *Ha-Rav mi-Liadi u-Mifleget Habad* (2 vols.). (Warsaw, 1920, 1913).

Tishby, Isaiah. "Acute Apocalyptic Messianism," in M. Saperstein, ed., *Essential Papers on Messianic Movements and Personalities in Jewish History* (New York/London, 1992).

———. "The Messianic Idea and Messianic Trends in the Growth of Hasidism" (Hebrew), *Zion* 32 (1967).

Trachtenberg, Joshua. *Jewish Magic and Superstition* (New York, 1970).

Ukreitz, Stanislavovitch. *Istorichesky Vestnik* (Moscow, 1905). (Lenin Library).

Urbach, Ephraim. E. *The Sages, Their Concepts and Beliefs* (Jerusalem, 1979).

———. "The Traditions about Merkavah Mysticism in the Tannaitic Period" (Hebrew), in *Studies in Mysticism and Religion Presented to Gershom G. Scholem* (Jerusalem, 1967).

———. *The World of the Sages* (Hebrew). (Jerusalem, 1988).

Vaksberg, Arkady. *Stalin Against the Jews* (New York, 1994).

Volpa, Shalom D. *Yechi ha-Melech ha-Mashiach* (Hebrew) (Kiryat Gat, 1993).

Wallis, Ron (ed.). *Millennialism and Charisma* (Belfast, 1982).

Weber, Max. *Ancient Judaism* (New York, 1952).

———. Economy and Society (2 vols.). (California, 1925, 1978).

———. "The Pure Types of Legitimate Authority," in Max Weber, *On Charisma and Institute Building,* ed. S. N. Eisenstadt, (*The Heritage of Sociology* series, ed. Morris Janowitz). (Chicago, 1968).

———. *The Protestant Ethic and the Spirit of Capitalism* (New York, 1976).

———. "The Sociology of Charismatic Authority," in Max Weber, *On Charisma and Institute Building,* ed. S. N. Eisenstadt, (*The Heritage of Sociology* series, ed. Morris Janowitz). (Chicago, 1968).

———. *The Sociology of Religion* (Boston, 1922, 1964).

Weiner, Aharon. *The Prophet Elija in the Development of Judaism* (London, 1978).

Weiner, Herbert. *9½ Mystics: The Kabbala Today* (New York, 1969).

Weiss, Yitzhak I. ben Avraham. *Toledot Yitzhak* (2 vols). (Munkatch, 1904).

Weiss, G. Joseph. "The Beginnings of Hasidism" (Hebrew), *Zion* 15 (1951), collected in *Rubinstein's Studies in Hasidism* (q.v.).

———. "A Circle of Pneumatics in Pre-Hasidism," *Journal of Jewish Studies* 8 (1957), collected in Studies in Eastern European Jewish Mysticism.

———. "R. Abraham Kalisker's Concept of Communion with G-d and Men," *Journal of Jewish Studies* 6 (1955), collected in Studies in Eastern European Jewish Mysticism.

———. *Studies in Braslav Hasidism* (Hebrew). (Jerusalem, 1974).

———. *Studies in Eastern European Jewish Mysticism*, ed. D. Goldstein (Oxford, 1985).

Weissbrem, I. *Hai Aggurot, A Novel by Israel Weissbrem* (Tcherikover, 1983). Also published in *The World of Israel Weissbrem,* trans. Alan D. Crown (Buffalo, 1993).

Weissman-Joselit, Jenna. *New York's Jewish Jews: The Orthodox Community in the Interwar Years* (Bloomington, Ind., 1990).

Werblowsky, R. J. Zwi. *Joseph Karo, Lawyer and Mystic* (London, 1962).

———. "Messianism in Jewish History," in M. Saperstein, ed., *Essential Papers on Messianic Movements and Personalities in Jewish History* (New York, 1992), pp. 35–52.

Wertheimer, Jack. (ed). *The Uses of Tradition: Jewish Continuity in the Modern Era* (New York, 1992).

Wiesel, Elie. *Four Hasidic Masters and Their Struggle Against Melancholy* (Notre Dame, Ind., 1978).

————. *Souls on Fire and Somewhere a Master* (London, 1984). (*Souls on Fire*, originally published London, 1972).

Wildavsky, Aaron B. *The Nursing Father: Moses as a Political Leader* (Birmingham, Ala., 1984).

Wilensky, M. *Hasidim and Mitnagdim: A Study of the Controversy Between Them in the Years 1772–1815* (Hebrew). (Jerusalem, 1970).

————. "Ha-Yishuv ha-Hasidi be-Tiveriah be-Sof ha-Meah ha-18," *Proceedings of the American Academy of Jewish Research* 48 (1981).

———— (ed). *Ha-Yishuv ha-Hasidi be-Teveriah* (Jerusalem, 1988).

Willner, Ann R. *The Spellbinders: Charismatic Political Leadership* (New Haven, 1984).

Wilson, Bryan. "An Analysis of Sect Development," *American Sociological Review* 24 (1959).

————. *Sects and Society* (Berkeley, Calif., 1961).

Wolfson, I. Z. "Megilat Vitebsk," in *The Book of Vitebsk* (Hebrew) (Tel Aviv, 1957).

Wonders and Miracles: Stories of the Lubavitcher Rebbe (booklet) (Kfar Habad, 1982).

Yaari, A. *Shluhei Erez Yisrael* (Jerusalem, 1951).

Yagdil Torah (magazine). (Brooklyn, 1975–?).

Yedid, Yosef Mordechai. *Pesak be-Inyan Hasarat Rav Rashi me-Misrato* (Jerusalem, 1993).

Di Yiddishe Heim (Yiddish magazine) (published in 1950s).

Yinger, Milton J. *Religion, Society, and the Individual* (New York, 1957).

Zimmels, H. J. *Magicians, Theologians and Doctors* (London, 1952).

Zipperstein, S. J. *The Jews of Odessa: A Cultural History, 1794–1881* (Stanford, Calif., 1985).

Zivot Hashem Handbook, Marching as One (Crown Heights, 1991).

Zivotovsky, Ari Z. "The Leadership Qualities of Moses," *Judaism* 43:3 (Summer 1994).

Newspaper and Magazine Articles

Bearden, Michelle. "Lubavitchers Mourn and Ponder Future," *Tampa Tribune* (June 18, 1994) (in *Lubavitch in the News*, p. 54).

Birnbaum, Susan, and Druckerman, Pamela. "Thousands Mourn Lubavitcher Rebbe," *Jewish Exponent* (June 17, 1994) (in *Lubavitch in the News*, p. 34).

Boteach, Shmuel. "The Colossus and Me: In Tribute to the Rebbe," *L'Chaim Society Weekly Essays* (Oxford University, June 16, 1994).

Brin, Herb. "Through the Night: Discourse with the Rebbe," in *San Diego Jewish Press* (n.d.) (in *Lubavitch in the News*, p. 27).

Druckerman, Pamela. "Worldwide Outposts Called Key to Chabad Survival," *Wisconsin Jewish Chronicle* (September 2, 1994) (in *Lubavitch in the News*, p. 82).

Dunn, Ashley. "Delayed Ceremony for Grown Men," *New York Times* (March 4, 1995) (in *Lubavitch in the News*, p. 101).

"Editorial," *The Journal* (June 24, 1994) (in *Lubavitch in the News*, p. 9).

Feldman, Steve, and Silverstein, Marilyn. "Rebbe's Death Stirs Deep Feelings on Local Scene," *Jewish Exponent* (June 17, 1994) (in *Lubavitch in the News*, p. 73).

"The Fountains Have Been Disseminated" (no author), *Beis Moshiach* 42 (June 16, 1995), p. 60.

Friedlin, Jennifer. "The Thais That Bind," *Jewish Week* (April 21,1995) (in *Lubavitch in the News*, p. 105).

Gambardello, Joseph, and Liff, Bob. "A Potent Figure in Judaism," *New York Newsday* (June 13, 1994) (in *Lubavitch in the News*, p. 36).

Goldman, Ari L. "The Late Rebbe Still Defines Chabad," *Baltimore Jewish Times* (n.d.) (in *Lubavitch in the News*, p. 79).

———. "The Nation," *New York Times* (June 20, 1994) (in *Lubavitch in the News*, p. 16).

———. "Rabbi Schneerson Led a Small Hasidic Sect to World Prominence," *New York Times* (June 13, 1994) (in *Lubavitch in the News*, p. 29).

Goldman, Zev. "Geulah Insights on Torah," *Beis Moshiach* (February 9, 1996), pp. 87–89.

Gonzalez, David. "Lubavitchers Learn to Sustain Themselves Without the Rebbe," *New York Times* (November 8, 1994) (in *Lubavitch in the News*, p. 80).

Goodstein, Laurie. "Death of Lubavitcher Leader, Rabbi Schneerson, Stuns Followers," *Washington Post* (n.d.) (in *Lubavitch in the News*, p. 28).

Gorenberg, Gershom. "Get a Job," *Jerusalem Report* (August 22,1996).

Gothard, Judy Noah. "The Wait Is Over," *Atlanta Jewish Times* (July 10, 1994) (in *Lubavitch in the News*, p. 22).

Gross, Netty. "Tradition Can Wait," *Jerusalem Report* (August 8, 1996).

Halevi, Yossi Klein. "Can Chabad Outlive the Rebbe?" *Jerusalem Report* (April 7, 1994), pp. 18–23.

Handelman, Susan. "Chicago Native Reflects on Her Experience with the Rebbe," *JUF News* (August 1994) (in *Lubavitch in the News*, p. 17).

Holloway, Lynette. "Queens Holy Land: Paying Homage at Rebbe's Grave," *New York Times* (March 11, 1995) (in *Lubavitch in the News*, pp. 78–79).

Jerusalem Post International Edition, no. 1836 (January 13, 1996). See advertisement section on Joseph Gutnick.

Jolkovsky, Binyamin L. "The 'Messiah Wars' Heat Up: Online Gets Out-of-Line," *Jewish World Review* (February 19, 1990).

Kupfermann, Jeanette. "How I Nearly Succumbed to the Charm of the Rebbe," *Daily Telegraph,* London (June 17,1994) (in *Lubavitch in the News*, p. 14).

Landau, David. "His Influence," *Jewish Exponent*, (June 17, 1994) (in *Lubavitch in the News*, p. 40).

Leppek, Chris. "Levels of Sadness: The Passing of the Lubavitcher Rebbe," *Intermountain Jewish News* (June 17, 1994) (in *Lubavitch in the News*, p. 6).

————. "The Lubavitcher Rebbe: His Outreach," *Intermountain Jewish News* (June 17, 1994) (in *Lubavitch in the News*, p. 41).

Lifton, Kimberly. "Judaism's Foot Soldiers" (n.d.) (in *Lubavitch in the News*, pp. 89–91).

Lipsky, Sam. "Interview with Gutnik," *Australian Jewish News* (February 10th 1995).

"Lubavitch Rebbe Can't Be Replaced," *Ottawa Citizen* (July 9, 1994) (in *Lubavitch in the News*, p. 67).

Mark, Jonathan. "A Kingdom of Faith," *Jewish Week* (March 18–24, 1994) (in *Lubavitch in the News*, pp. 33–34).

————. "A Man of Letters," *Jewish Week* (July 8–14, 1994) (in *Lubavitch in the News*, p. 39).

————. "The Last Dance," *Jewish Week*, (June 17th– 23, 1994) (in *Lubavitch in the News*, p. 28).

"Menachem Mendel Schneerson" (no source) (in *Lubavitch in the News*, p. 9).

"Obituaries: Rabbi Menachem Schneerson," *Daily Telegraph*, London (June 13, 1994) (in *Lubavitch in the News*, p. 30).

"Obituary: Rabbi Menachem Schneerson," *The Times*, London, (June 13, 1994) (in *Lubavitch in the News*, p. 32).

O'Sullivan, Arieh. "Jewish Leaders Praise Departed Rabbi," *Akron Beacon Journal* (June 13, 1994) (in *Lubavitch in the News*, p. 34).

"Passing of a Tzadik," *Baltimore Jewish Times* (June 14, 1994) (in *Lubavitch in the News*, p. 8).

Pearl, Lesley. "Cyber-matza?" *Jewish Exponent* (April 14, 1995) (in *Lubavitch in the News*, p. 104).

Potok, Chaim. "Rabbi Schneerson: One of a Kind," *Philadelphia Inquirer* (June 16, 1994) (in *Lubavitch in the News*, p. 23).

Poupko, Yehiel. "Of G-d and Man: Some Thoughts on the Rebbe," *JUF News* (in *Lubavitch in the News*, p. 13).

"Rabbinical Ruling," *Jewish Tribune* (December 10, 1998), p. 33.

"Rabbi Power at the Polls," *U.S. News and World Report* (November 14, 1988).

"The Rebbe," Jewish Chronicle (June 17, 1994) (in *Lubavitch in the News*, p. 10).

"The Rebbe's Empire," *National Jewish Post and Opinion*, Indianapolis (June 15, 1994) (in *Lubavitch in the News*, p. 7).

"Remembering a Great Jewish Leader," *Jewish Horizon* (June 16, 1994) (in *Lubavitch in the News*, p. 63).

Rohde, Marie. "Steadfast Amid Change: Small Lubavitch Group Here Is Influential," *Milwaukee Journal* (June 17, 1994) (in *Lubavitch in the News*, p. 67).

Rosenblatt, Gary. "The Sounds of Lubavitch," *Jewish Week*, June 17–23 1994 (in *Lubavitch in the News*, p. 12).

Sacks, Jonathan. "The Man Who Turned Judaism Outward," *Jewish Chronicle* (n. d.) (in *Lubavitch in the News*, p. 27).

————. "When Mysticism Saved the Jewish People: A Memorial Tribute to the Lubavitcher Rebbe," *Le'ela: A Journal of Judaism Today* (n.d.). Edited transcript of address at Logan Hall, London (September 11, 1994) (in *Lubavitch in the News*, pp. 19–21).

Samuel, Terrence. "Rabbi M. Schneerson, Lubavitch Leader, Dies in New York at 92," *Philadelphia Inquirer* (June 13, 1994) (in *Lubavitch in the News*, p. 37).

Sandman, Joshua. "Rebbe Played Profound Role in Judaism," *New Haven Register* (June 21, 1994) (in *Lubavitch in the News*, p. 24).

Schiffman, Lawrence H. "Rebbe's Legacy of Hope Transcends His Death," *Long Island Jewish World* (n.d.) (in *Lubavitch in the News*, p. 26).

Segall, Rebecca. "Young Lubavitcher Hasidim in a Rebbe-Less World," *New York Jewish Week* (n.d.).

Sheler, Jeffery L. "A Movement Goes On Without Its Leader," *U.S. News & World Report* (December 26, 1994–January 2, 1995) (in *Lubavitch in the News*, p. 81).

Slonim, Moshe. "Emunah in the Rebbe," *Beis Moshiach* (February 2, 1996). p. 97.

Swados, Harvey. "He Could Melt a Blizzard," in Zivot Hashem Handbook, *Marching as One* (1990), in honor of its tenth birthday, pp. 49–53.

Weiner, Herbert. "Farewell, My Rebbe: Thoughts on Leadership," *Upfront* (June 2, 1994) (in *Lubavitch in the News*, p. 11).

Wilson, Marc. "The Rebbe's Counsel," *Charlotte Observer*, (June 27, 1994) (in *Lubavitch in the News*, p. 15).

"Worldwide Seders Set by Chabad," (n.d.) (in *Lubavitch in the News*, p. 104).

"Yesh Haim le-Achar ha-Mavet" (Hebrew) ("There Is Life After the Death"), *Yediot Aharonot* (March 6, 1995)

"You Felt Like the Space Around Him Was Holy," *The Sun* (San Bernardino, Calif.), (June 12, 1994) (in *Lubavitch in the News*, p. 35).

Letters

Kahn, Yoel, to Hillel Pozner, Iyar 24, 5754.

Gerarie, Zalman, to Chabad Hasidim.

"Open Letter to Habad Hasidim," 6 Tamuz 5754 by International Vaad of AGUCH.

Yalkut Inyana Shel Agudat Chasidei Chabad, collected by *Iggud Tmimim ve-Avrechim* (a collection of letters).

Lectures

Rabbi Lau, public lecture, Sydney, July 27, 1995.

Sacks, Jonathan. "When Mysticism Saved the Jewish People," talk given at Logan Hall, London, Sept. 11, 1994.

Booklets and Pamphlets

ZaCH (Zeirei Chabad). Prophecies Fulfilled

Zivot Hashem Handbook, *Marching as One* (1990), in honor of its tenth birthday.

Index